THE TOTEM POLE

Writing a poem is like trying to describe a totemic column
which passes right through and beyond the world.
We see it, but its existence is elsewhere.

—Stanley Diamond, *Totems*

THE TOTEM POLE

AN INTERCULTURAL HISTORY

ALDONA JONAITIS

AARON GLASS

University of Washington Press

Seattle/London

Douglas & McIntyre

D&M PUBLISHERS INC.

Vancouver/Toronto

This publication was made possible in part by a grant from the Naomi B. Pascal Editor's Endowment, supported through the generosity of Janet and John Creighton, Patti Knowles, and Mary McLellan Williams and other donors; and by a grant from the Joan Paterson Kerr Fund.

Printed in China

Design by Ashley Saleeba

18 17 16 15 14 13 12 11 10   10 9 8 7 6 5 4 3 2 1

UNIVERSITY OF WASHINGTON PRESS

P.O. Box 50096 Seattle, WA 98145 U.S.A.

www.washington.edu/uwpress

Library of Congress Cataloging-in-Publication Data

Jonaitis, Aldona, 1948–

The totem pole : an intercultural history /

Aldona Jonaitis and Aaron Glass.

p. cm.

Includes bibliographical references and index.

ISBN 978-0-295-98962-4 (cloth : alk. paper)

1. Totem poles—History. 2. Indians of North America—Northwest coast of North America—Social life and customs. 3. Northwest coast of North America—Social life and customs. I. Glass, Aaron. II. Title.

E98.T65J66 2009   79.5004'97—dc22   2009053809

Published simultaneously in Canada by

DOUGLAS & MCINTYRE

An imprint of D&M Publishers Inc.

2323 Quebec Street, Suite 201

Vancouver BC Canada V5T 4S7

www.douglas-mcintyre.com

Library and Archives Canada Cataloguing in Publication

Jonaitis, Aldona, 1948–

The totem pole : an intercultural history /

Aldona Jonaitis and Aaron Glass.

Includes bibliographical references and index.

ISBN 978-1-55365-421-6

I. Glass, Aaron II. Title.

E98T65J66 2010   C813'.6   C2009-906843-5

Jacket front: Miniature model totem pole. Photograph by Thomas Eykemans, 2010. *Spine*: Yuquot (Nuu-chah-nulth) Captain Jack Pole, 1939. Photograph by Frank Nowell. University of British Columbia Archives, 27.1/18-1. *Back*: Howkan (Kagani Haida), 1897. Photograph by Winter and Pond. Alaska State Library, 7-0050. *Flap*: Advertisement for Chevrolet Bel Air in *Saturday Evening Post*, 16 March 1957.

Jacket photo: Christian Heeb/Aurora Photo

The paper used in this publication meets the minimum requirements of American National Standard for Information Sciences—Permanence of Paper for Printed Library Materials, ANSI Z39.48–1984.

CONTENTS

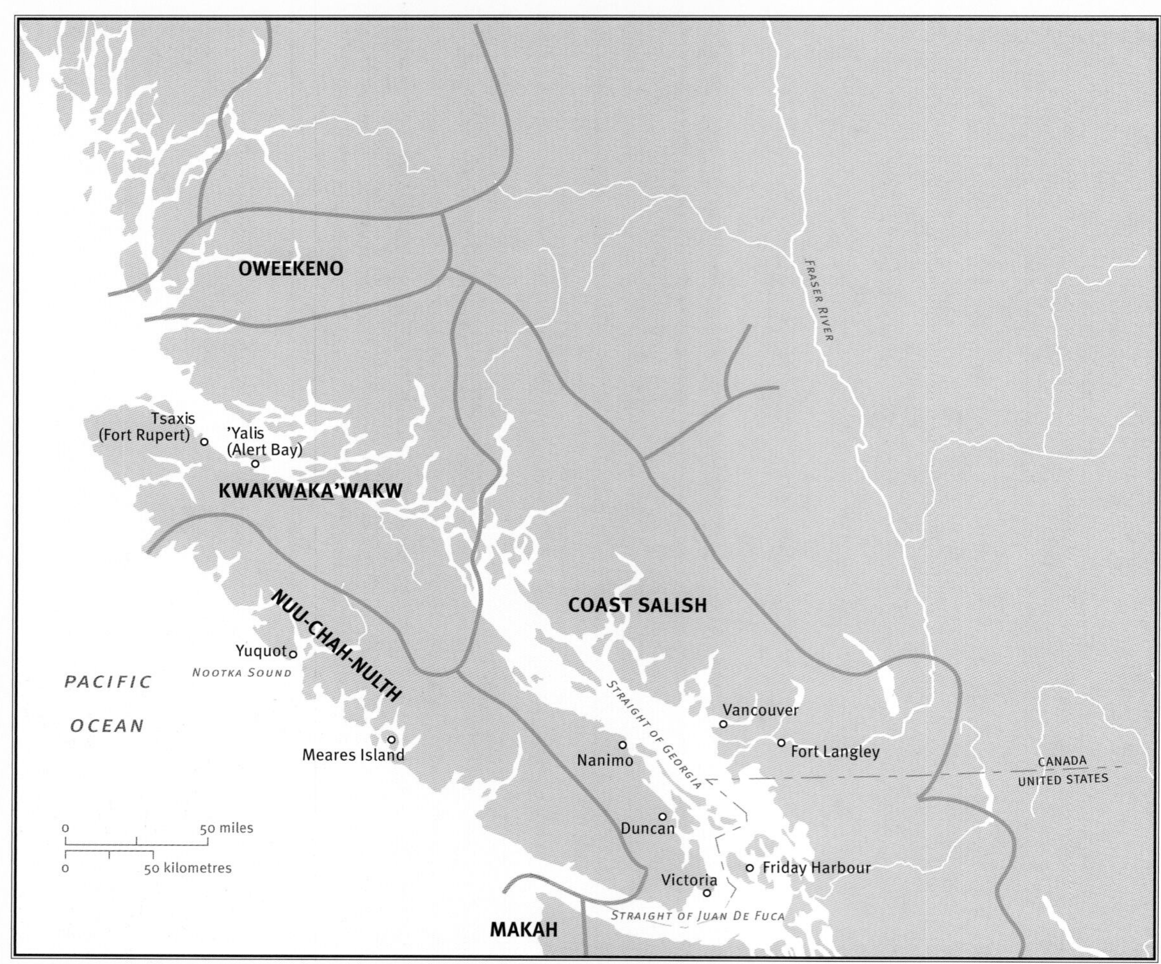

The Southern Region of the Northwest Coast

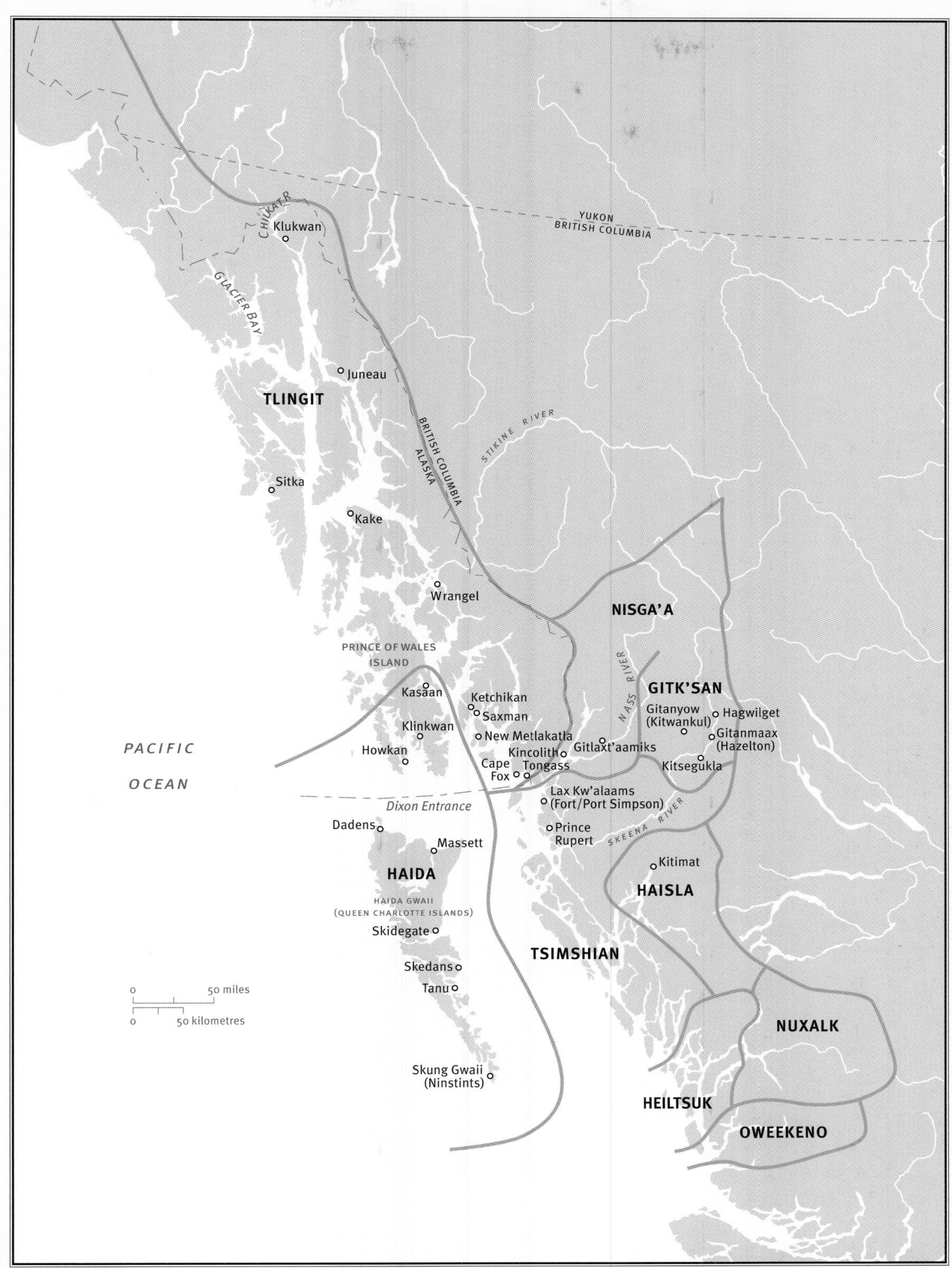

The Northern Region of the Northwest Coast

PREFACE

Writing a book sometimes feels like watching a tree grow, knowing that the eventual product—be it a totem pole, a table, or a ream of paper—is years off. This book was a long time in gestation and represents the accumulation of many years of personal interest, scholarly research, and collaborative relationship on the part of both authors. We begin with our own narratives.

AARON GLASS

Some of my first memories trace back to an Alaskan cruise I took with my parents the summer I turned three. The ship was named *Arcadia*. I remember climbing a ladder on deck with my father's reassuring assistance when the ship's whistle blew, terrifying me and dislodging my grip. I remember the strangely saturated orange light of the ship's interior (which years later I discovered was largely an artifact of the decaying Ektachrome slides that for over two decades mediated my personal memory of the ship). And I remember standing under the towering totems that seemed to beckon at every port of call and fuel my emerging imagination. For years afterwards, I had two souvenirs from this trip proudly displayed in my room: a miniature life preserver with the ship's name emblazoned upon it, and a miniature, hand-carved, and garishly painted winged wooden totem pole.

On occasion during my formative educational years, I would return figuratively to Alaska to write papers on Native Americans and their art. Then there were the eagerly anticipated visits to natural history museums. But it was not until I attended college in the Pacific Northwest that I again saw firsthand, in situ, the dramatic masks, abstracted flat designs, monumental totem poles of the Northwest Coast Native peoples. Studying art and anthropology, I increasingly came to focus on the coastal groups and their remarkable visual culture. At this time—perhaps like most students at this particular psychosocial juncture—I was largely interested in the symbolic and transformatory potential of Native art forms. Yet I became increasingly uneasy with the theoretical and (a)historical terms of my engagement with indigenous societies. This troubled sense was focused for me during a semester spent living in Germany, where I casually attended an English class on American short stories only to find the students discussing a Jewish tale with the same mixture of exotic fascination and removed, if earnest, curiosity with which I studied Native Americans. I resolved that day to seek opportunities to spend time in a Native community, to see for myself a contemporary Native life in order to balance the frozen ethnographic portraits I was exposed to in museums and photographs and texts.

The following summer I traveled up the coasts of Washington State and British Columbia, speaking with people in Native cultural centers and carving sheds, in metropolitan museums and roadside tourist attractions. Two fortuitous events of this trip would help shape my life. Through a series of intermediaries, I made contact with the U'mista Cultural Centre in Alert Bay, British Columbia, and coordinated a summer of volunteer work for the following year. They told me they had no money to pay me, nor could they find me lodging; I said "fine." They asked, probingly, if I was willing to work bingo every week; I said, in slightly bewildered ignorance, "sure." This halting conversation initiated what has become a decade-long relationship with this Kwakwa̱ka̱'wakw community. And in Victoria I saw a traveling exhibit called Chiefly Feasts: The Enduring Kwakiutl Potlatch, curated by Aldona Jonaitis. A few months later, Aldona came to speak in Portland and I skipped class to hear her describe her experience collaborating with Kwakwa̱ka̱'wakw people to mount this important exhibit. The following summer, while working in Alert Bay, I had the privilege of attending a potlatch with Aldona, who had come through town on her way to her new post in Alaska. I was also hired to do some research in "The Bay" for Judith Ostrowitz, a graduate student of Aldona's. My senior year, Aldona was generous enough to read a copy of my thesis chapter on Kwakwa̱ka̱'wakw art, and—with Judith's reference—the following year she hired me as her research assistant on a book on the history of totem poles.

I moved to Vancouver to begin research on the Canadian history of totem polery while working as a docent at the University of British Columbia's Museum of Anthropology. Over the next few years of intensive research for this book, I had the opportunity to travel up the coast many times, visiting First Nations communities as well as civic museums and archives. I got a very direct and personal sense of both the role of museums, art historians, and anthropologists in the history of the totem, and the role of the totem in contemporary Native cultural and political life. I've come to a renewed appreciation for the dynamism of First Nations art—historically as well as currently—and a reinvigorated dedication to intercultural communication and cooperation. I owe a good measure of gratitude to Aldona for making me her traveling companion on this exciting project, and to the numerous Native individuals and communities as well as scholarly institutions that have contributed to the research and to my personal understanding. I'd also like to thank Esteban Gutierrez and Laura Friesan for their patience on long road trips as I insisted upon stopping to photograph every roadside totem pole.

All of these experiences—from my first visit to Alaska to my return twenty-five years later—inform my interest and investment in the intercultural history of the totem pole: the transformations wrought on Native art through tourism and commerce; the mediation of personal and cultural memory through technological representations; the distortions resulting from scholarly knowledge to the exclusion of direct experience; the unexpected nature of cross-cultural identifications; the value of interdisciplinary research; the role of museums as cultural brokers in the collection and presentation of Native material; and the personal investment in current indigenous empowerment that comes from extended relationships with individuals and communities.

As we will show, the history of the totem pole is a history of cultural exchange and transformation, of adherence to tradition and remarkable creativity, of negotiations and collaborations between indigenous people and the newcomers to their lands. By adding our small voices to this complex dialogue, I hope that we can continue the conversations about and appreciation for the monumental wooden legacies with which the First Nations of the Northwest Coast mark their territories, stake their claims, and celebrate their rich personal and community histories.

ALDONA JONAITIS

My parents would often take my sisters and me to the American Museum of Natural History on rainy Saturdays. It was so exciting driving from Queens into Manhattan (“the city”) across what we named the “dragon bridge” (the 59th Street Bridge) and entering the huge spaces of that esteemed institution. I loved everything there, but felt drawn by the cylindrical carvings that lined the North Pacific Hall. That darkened hall, full of intricate carvings that seemed magical to a young girl, would be with me forever. Since that time Northwest Coast art has become part of who I am.

After choosing art history as a major in college, I attended Columbia University for graduate study. The question we all had to answer, preferably very early on in our tenure there, was, “What area will you specialize in?” Most of my fellow graduate students concentrated upon Western art, such as northern Baroque or French Postimpressionism. I started Columbia in the early ’70s, which could be considered part of the ’60s, and wanted none of the art made by the ruling class. What was then called “primitive art” proved attractive, both because I liked the art but also because studying this subject was a way to share with the public the wonderful creations of colonized and marginalized peoples, thus (in my youthful idealism) contributing to tolerance and cultural understanding. I was lucky enough to work with Douglas Fraser, a charismatic Africanist, who approved my proposal to study the Northwest Coast art that had impressed me years earlier. Dissertation research got me to the Northwest Coast for the first time in my life, and I fell in love with the rocky shorelines and fragrant cedar trees.

Tlingit art appealed to me most, in large measure because it presented an interesting problem in that some of it was made for the elite and some for shamans. I wanted to compare these two types of art to identify their relationship from the then-fashionable structuralist perspective. The paradigm under which I—and my fellow graduate students—operated was that of “salvage ethnography,” that is, using data such as art and written documents to identify and then analyze the precontact nature of Native culture. We all recognized that trade and settlement had greatly influenced our subjects of study and wanted to extract from these materials the “pure” vestiges of Native cultures prior to being “polluted” by Westerners. As a result, my dissertation, which became my first book, *Art of the Northern Tlingit* (1986), completely ignored any item, such as beadwork, button blankets, or decorated spruce root baskets, that either used non-Native materials, such as beads or were made for sale to tourists, such as the baskets. Since I focused completely on nineteenth-century art, my work also ignored the contemporary Tlingit people. I’d never do that again.

The most dramatic influence on my scholarship was collaborating with the Kwakwa̱ka̱’wakw when curating the exhibit Chiefly Feasts: The Enduring Kwakiutl Potlatch, which opened in 1991 at the American Museum of Natural History. Instead of writing to a small group of theoretically oriented scholars, it became clear that I had to take into account the ideas, feelings, and contributions of the people whose artworks I was analyzing. The experience of witnessing many community members and, most significantly, cocurator Gloria Cranmer Webster contributing information and perspectives on Kwakwa̱ka̱’wakw art and culture taught me an important lesson. As an outsider, I can never hope to understand with clarity and depth the “true meaning” of a Native artwork. And I don’t even have the right to try—that information is for the community to choose to share, if they wish.

I had always been fascinated by how fascinating totem poles are for non-Native people. So I began to think about a book on the cultural biography of the totem pole as it developed among indigenous Northwest Coast villages, then spread as a result of Euroamerican contact and became appropriated in a bewildering variety of ways by non-Natives. It was at that point that I began collecting what is now a broad representation of totem pole kitsch. It was my intention that the book be not a "reading" of a lot of poles but instead a presentation to the public of what I hope will be a new perspective on a very familiar Native American icon.

My responsibilities as the director of the University of Alaska Museum of the North kept me busy, and I knew I could not manage to do the research for this book. I had known Aaron Glass from his excellent work with Judith Ostrowitz, and I hired him to work on totem poles. He began sending me vast amounts of information, meticulously researched, well organized and exceptionally useful. He also, however, sent along absolutely brilliant comments about the material at hand. It became clear to me that Aaron should not just be a researcher; he had to be a full partner in this endeavor. Thus we became coauthors. It has been a delight working with Aaron, and I have learned so much from this young anthropologist.

Aaron and I wanted to include other voices in this book—and not just as quotes. We wanted to ensure that some Native artists who carve totem poles were heard. Thus we requested "sidebars" from a range of Native and non-Native individuals. These men and women very graciously agreed to contribute short essays, which we believe enhance this book immensely. We appreciate the works the contributing artists and their colleagues have made over the years, and continue to make, as well as the distinguished group of scholars who have written pieces.

ACKNOWLEDGMENTS

The artists and scholars who graciously agreed to write sidebars enhanced this book immensely. We are both so grateful for their contributions. We also wish to thank our colleagues who read and commented on this manuscript: Janet Berlo, Steve Brown, Bill Holm, Molly Lee, Judith Ostrowitz, Ruth Phillips, Charlotte Townsend-Gault, and Robin Wright.

Once we began researching this book, and told people of our interest in totem poles, many friends began sending us images and information on poles, much of it highly humorous. We thank them all: David Blackard, Alan Borass, Anne Cassidy, Wanda Chin, Carlo Krieger, Ken Deroux, Kate Duncan, Christian Feest, Nora Foster, Karen Franklin, Joyce Herold, Jonathan Holstein, Carol Ivory, Barbara Kampfer, Carol Kastner, Tom Kizzia, Thomas Larson, Steve Loring, Phyllis Morrow, Jim Movius, Gail Parsons, Patricia Partnow, Zena Pearlstone, Dorothy Jean Ray, Gregory Reinhardt, Anne-Lillian Schell, Judy Scherer, Megan Smetzer, Glen and Melissa Simpson, John and Judith Glass, and Nik Tongas.

During our research, we had very useful conversations with a variety of people, and we thank them as well. They include David Boxley, Peter Corey, Doug Cranmer, Robert Davidson, Jane Wallen Demmert, Nathan Jackson, Stephen Jackson, Lee Heinmiller, Steve Henrikson, Marjorie Halpin, Calvin Hunt, Richard Hunt, John Livingston, Victoria Lord, Michael Kew, Peter Macnair, Phil Nuytten, Tim Paul, Wayne Price, Ida Smit, Wayne Suttles, Sharon Svenson, Donald Varnell, Andy Wilbur, and Joe Wilson. Very special thanks go to Dawn Biddison, who did a wonderful job obtaining the photographs as well as permission to publish them.

We appreciate the contributions of the illustrations of Robin Heller at Creative Productions; Jessie Caryl at Catriona Jeffries Gallery, Vancouver; Karen Dosen at White Spot Limited; Don Lecca; Vanessa Flores at Tournament of Roses Archive; Debra Steel, *Ha-Shilth-Sa*; Lawrence Migdale at Lawrence Midgdale/PIX; and Julie Heath at Warner Bros. Entertainment.

Much of the research upon which this book is based was conducted at and illustrations were acquired from various libraries, museums, and universities. We thank the following individuals for their assistance: Lynn Maranda at Vancouver Museum; Michael Ames, Elizabeth Johnson, Jennifer Webb, and Anne Stevenson at the University of British Columbia Museum of Anthropology; Dan Savard, Susan Hasbury, Kelly-Ann Turkington, and Frederike Verspoor at the Royal British Columbia Museum; staff at the British Columbia Provincial Archives and Records Service; Jeannie Hounslow at the Vancouver City Archives; Leslie Field at the University Archive at the University of British Columbia; Nicolette Bromber at the University of Washington Libraries; Risa Carlson, Richard H. Van Cleave, and Sheri Wylie at the Totem Heritage Center in Ketchikan; Angela Linn at the University of Alaska Museum of the North; Theresa Thibault and Tracy Churchill at the Wrangell Museum; Orriene First Denslow at the Sitka Historical Society; Sue Thorsen at the Sitka National Historical Park; Donna Baron and Sorrel Goodwin at the Alaska State Museum in Juneau; Sarah Johnson at the Alaska State Library; Mary Linscome at the University of Northern Colorado; and

Norman Vorano and Huguette Desmarais-Foisy at the Canadian Museum of Civilization; Kelly Anderson at the American Museum of Natural History; Kathy Hertel-Baker at the Anchorage Museum; Jonathan Lathigee at the Art Gallery of Greater Vancouver; Susan Snyder at the Bancroft Library, University of California, Berkeley; Rina Luzius at the Burke Museum; Bryan McDaniel at the Chicago History Museum; Cory Pallister at the City of Victoria Archives; Eric Enno Tarn at Ecotrust Canada; Brenda Duncan at Na Na Kila Institute; Laurel Lauren at 'Ksan; Janine Butler and Linda Morita at the McMichael Canadian Art Collection; Ellen Thomasson at the Missouri Historical Society; Anne Murray at the Museum of Ethnography, Stockholm; Timothy McCarthy at MoMA Art Resources; Howard Giske at the Museum of History and Industry, Seattle; Merrideth Miller at *The New Yorker*; Kristin Standaert at the Paul V. Galvin Library; Christina Michelini at the Peabody Essex Museum; Julie Brown at the Peabody Museum, Harvard; Amanda Lee at the Pilchuck Glass School; Tammy L. Peters at the Smithsonian Institution Archives; and Danielle Currie at the Vancouver Art Gallery.

As always, the University of Washington Press staff did a brilliant job at editing and producing this book.

PROLOGUE

THE WIDE WORLD OF TOTEM POLES

Wherever you go, it sometimes seems, you are likely to encounter a totem pole in some form or another.

On November 25, 1997, Canadian Prime Minister Jacques Chrétien welcomed the heads of eighteen Pacific Rim nations to the ministerial meeting of APEC, the Asia Pacific Economic Community. This conference took place in the Great Hall of the Museum of Anthropology (MOA), an outstanding space on the University of British Columbia campus in Vancouver. Ruth Phillips, then director of MOA, described the scene during the press briefing:

> In a perfectly synchronized sequence reminiscent of an Olympic Games opening ceremony four Royal Canadian Mounted Police in full dress uniform rode up and stood to attention on the berm outside the floor-to-ceiling glass windows of the Hall. . . . the leaders of Australia, China, the United States and the other fifteen countries appeared seated against a backdrop of totem poles, Mounties, and the distant vista of snow-capped mountains and sea. This pageant-like spectacle aligned all the symbols most commonly employed to construct a Canadian identity distinct from that of the United States (R. Phillips 2002, 182).

During his opening remarks, Prime Minister Chrétien pointed to the monumental carvings standing in the cathedral-like space and commented on how appropriate it was for APEC to be meeting there, for the First Nations, whose culture the museum celebrated, had been the first Pacific Rim international merchants when they crossed the Bering Strait on their way from Siberia to the Americas. In one short phrase, Chrétien conflated

I.1. Trading post at Jackson, Wyoming, 1994. Postcard.

Native art and the 12,000-year history of human habitation in the Western hemisphere with a capitalist free-trade alliance.

Another conflation of commerce and culture, admittedly more trivial, occurs when a tourist exploring Jackson, Wyoming, comes upon a large log cabin with the words "Indian Trader" emblazoned in red on a bright yellow banner (fig. I.1). In front, twenty-four "cigar-store" statues depict, in varying heights, Indians wearing the large feather bonnets characteristic of Plains tribes (such scenes are typical of roadside attractions across North America). To the right, a crude carving proudly claims the pole to be "Wyoming's *Largest* Totem Pole." The shopkeeper describes how the pole's head carver, a full-blooded Mandan (a Plains group, who were not indigenous totem pole carvers) "learned from his father—this is all he does." Other male members of his family join him to carve poles, which the women then paint (Glass 1994). With the feather bonnets and the totem pole, only a teepee is missing from the trinity of Indian icons. This classic grouping—likely dating to the nineteenth century—appears, for instance, on a cigar box dated ca. 1910–1920 and entitled "Totem" (fig. 1.2). A pole stands near a bundle of eagle feathers positioned on a bow and arrow, and across a pond from a canoe and three teepees, indiscriminately juxtaposing Indian creations from the eastern woodlands, plains, and Northwest Coast with no regard for the significant cultural differences of Native people living thousands of miles apart.

Long used to market consumer products, in 1991 the totem pole entered the realm of high fashion. In April of that year, the New York fall couture collections premiered to a lukewarm reception that criticized the lack of innovation on the part of American designers. But one dress, designed by Isaac Mizrahi, wowed the critics. This "show-stopper dress" a strapless full-length sheath, was decorated, quite incongruously, with a beaded totem pole design (fig. 1.3; Donovan 1991, 48). The brows of an unidentifiable being neatly accentuate the model's breasts while its hands point to her groin, decorated with the nose of another creature. So striking and appealing (and obviously eroticized) was this dress that it appeared in the daily *Times* as well as in a Sunday *Times* feature. The totem pole, sexualized and translated into high fashion, transformed its wearer into a strangely feminine yet vaguely hermaphroditic being.[1]

Though intrinsically visual and material, totem poles have even inspired musical compositions. *The Alaskan, An Original Comic Opera*, written by Joseph Blethen and Harry Girard in 1907, features a rousing song—along the lines of Gilbert and Sullivan—entitled "The Totem Pole" (fig. 1.4).[2] In the first stanza, a Native man sings about the "wonders of my pedigree" and cites his ancestors:

My father's father an eagle was;
My mother's mother a duck;
My uncle Jack was a raven black;
And that's what brings me luck.

1.2. Cigar box, ca. 1910–20. Courtesy of Zena Pearlstone.

I.3. Isaac Mizrahi, "Totem Pole Dress," 1991. Photograph by Dan Lecca. Courtesy of *New York Times*.

The lineage elucidation continues in this vein, mentioning faunal relatives that include salmon, crow, polar bear, frog, fox, and seal. The second stanza parallels the first, but in the voice of a sourdough (gold miner) whose own pole stands before his tent:

My father's father a Mason was;
My mother's mother a dear;
My uncle Tripp was a knight of gripp;
And hence my taste for beer.
My father's uncle a Hoo-hoo was;
My mother's an Eastern star;
My uncle Lee was a Maccabee
And king of the Pullman car.

I.4. Cover, *The Alaskan, An Original Comic Opera*, 1907. Courtesy of Zena Pearlstone.

In this song, the totem pole transforms a white person's simple ancestry, through reference to various tribes and secret fraternities, into a burlesque of Native culture.

Like many other (mis)representations of indigenous North Americans, images of totem poles in film saturate popular consciousness—and have for decades. The operetta *Rose Marie*, although best known in its classic 1936 movie version with Jeanette MacDonald and Nelson Eddy, first appeared on stage in 1924, with music by Rudolf Friml and Herbert Stothart, and a libretto by Otto Harbach and Oscar Hammerstein. For the number in the play, a chorus line of women wearing totem pole dresses—not unlike the Mizrahi version illustrated above—perform a number entitled "Totem Tom-Tom" (Traubner 2003, 380; Green 1984, 36). For this same song in the MacDonald-Eddy film version, women wearing Plains-style fringed buckskin dresses surround a man in a fringed loincloth and feather head-

I.5. Scene from *Rose Marie*, 1954. *Rose* Marie © Turner Entertainment Co. A Warner Bros. Entertainment Company. All rights reserved. Courtesy of Warner Bros.

dress who sports large "wings" attached to his arms. He stands before a totem pole, his outstretched wings mimicking those of the Thunderbird. For the "Totem Tom-Tom" scene of the 1954 film version of *Rose Marie*, a woman wearing a fringed buckskin two-piece outfit stands, legs wide, face raised up in an ecstatic expression, her arms held by kneeling, admiring Indians—all in front of a totem pole (fig. 1.5).

The totem pole has been further co-opted by multiple forms of mass media, which capitalize on its ubiquity and symbolic resonance. In a full-color advertisement published in the *Saturday Evening Post* (1957), a tall pole stands next to a new, blue '57 Chevrolet Bel-Air two-door sedan (fig. 1.6). The owners' young son sits happily on the protruding beak of a raven, while mom snaps a photo. According to the text, this car is "full of spunk . . . but beautifully behaved." Though thoroughly safe and modern, "it's still a stickler for tradition, and in the grand Chevrolet manner it's known to be as trouble-free as that totem pole in our picture." Although it is evident to all what a trouble-free car should be, whatever elements make a totem pole "trouble-free" are obscure to us. Apparently, this geographically unmoored totem pole is meant to suggest the freedom and cultural rewards of automobile travel. Tradition and modernity, religion and kinship, commerce and culture: the totem pole comes to stand for them all in various—and often conflicting—guises. It is even the victim of an erroneous interpretation of the positions of individuals on a pole, namely the cliché "low man on the totem pole." In truth, there is no hierarchy implied in an image's position on a pole.[3]

These few examples, as well as the cartoons in the following photo-essay, give some sense of how thoroughly the totem pole has been incorporated into popular visual culture.[4] Any encounter that most people might have with actual totem poles from the Northwest Coast of North America will be mediated in part by the accumulated representational baggage from two centuries of such misappropriations. As we argue in this book, the history of the totem pole can only be told through narratives of complex interaction between the indigenous residents of the region and its endless waves of explorers, settlers, governments, and tourists.[5]

We had two interconnected goals for this book. First, we wanted to tell a great story about how a monument of Native culture transmuted into the forms we've just described, as well as myriad others you will discover in these pages. Second, we wanted to contribute to the scholarly art historical and anthropological literature that interprets these and other transmutations. The first chapter, in particular, presents the intellectual foundations of this book. Throughout, endnotes provide supplementary information both on the contents of the chapters and on the theoretical concepts that informed our analyses. We hope that the casual reader might reflect on the more academic side of the story, and that the serious scholar might enjoy the story we tell. And that everyone will find the illustrations and their interpretations interesting, compelling, surprising, and, at times, amusing.

I.6. Advertisement for Chevrolet Bel Air in *Saturday Evening Post*, 16 March 1957.

TOTEM POLES IN CARTOONS AND COMICS

Robin Heller, Mukluk & Honisukle, 1995. Courtesy of Creative Productions.

"... I'm making a pencil, that's what! ..."

Robert Bierman, "Mungo Martin Totem Carving," likely from the Victoria Times Colonist, early 1960s.

"When I was a child, my mother's mother told me it was for scaring dust out of the tepee."

From Cartoonbank.com.

Robert J. Day. From Cartoonbank.com.
The New Yorker Collection, 1939.

"You might have known who the high man was going to be."

"I hope it doesn't make you nervous to have me watch you."

Richard Taylor. From Cartoonbank.com.
The New Yorker Collection, 1939.

Leo Cullum. From Cartoonbank.com.
The New Yorker Collection, 1939.

"You're in luck. We have an opening for low man on the totem pole."

SIDEBARS

PHOTO ESSAYS

THE TOTEM POLE

1

EXCURSIONS

TOWARD AN INTERCULTURAL BIOGRAPHY OF THE TOTEM POLE

The totem pole is not all things to all people.

A tourist visiting a totem pole park, such as Saxman in Ketchikan, Alaska, or Thunderbird Park next to the Royal British Columbia Museum in Victoria, B.C., may observe how well cared for and preserved the monuments are. Once he or she has learned the identities of all the figures on a specific pole by reading the available literature or labels, the typical tourist will probably be satisfied that he or she now understands the pole and will go on to the next one. In 1995, Aaron Glass interviewed forty visitors to the totem poles in Stanley Park and the Museum of Anthropology in Vancouver to gain an idea of what typical tourists think of poles. When asked what poles are used for, seven related them to family concerns, six said they told stories (as in folklore), and thirteen stated that they were worshiped or used to defend houses from malevolent supernatural forces. In response to queries about their age, four answered that the poles were twenty years old or less, five said between 20 and 100 years, nine said 100 years, eight said 200 to 500 years, and six said that they were ancient (i.e., before white settlement; Glass 1995). This admittedly unscientific survey indicates the many popular misunderstandings about totem poles. Yet most respondents did not seem especially interested in learning more; they wanted to take photographs and return to the bus. In mainstream visual culture, totem poles are typically assumed to be the object of indigenous reverence or spiritual regard, and are generally approached as monumental ethnic artworks, perhaps worthy of appreciation at some aesthetic or cultural level.

In contrast, for the Native chief who erected a pole originally, the totem pole is a material record of the privilege that his extended family has to depict certain images, and of the lavish potlatch—a feast at which valuables are distributed by the hosts to the guests—that celebrated the pole's raising and enhanced the host's standing in his community. Following the potlatch, the pole might be used as a mnemonic device to recall the family's claims or the event itself, but the pole would also be left to the elements, which decided its ultimate fate. Although aesthetic sophistication may confer additional prestige on a pole's carver or owner, totem poles were and are not typically objects of artistic contemplation, much less worship, for the communities from which they come.

TOTEM POLES: MYTHS, IMAGES, AND REALITIES

The Native people who invented the totem pole still live today on the shores and islands between the Pacific Ocean and the coastal mountain range of Alaska, British Columbia, and Washington State in an ethnographic zone long known as the Northwest Coast.[1] They are usually classified into three clusters that share significant social and artistic features: the northern group, composed of the Tlingit, Haida, Tsimshian, Nisga'a, and Gitk'san, who have strictly matrilineal rules on marriage and inheritance and who developed the two-dimensional "formline" style of graphic design; the central group, including the Salishan-speaking Nuxalk and the Wakashan-speaking Heiltsuk, Kwakwa̱ka̱'wakw, and Nuu-chah-nulth (with the Haisla and Makah being transitional groups to the north and south, respectively), who have more flexible marriage rules and a more flamboyant sculptural style; and the southernmost Coast Salish groups, who share flexible marriage rules and have a more minimalist art.

The inhabitants of the Northwest Coast developed cultures quite distinct from those of aboriginal people elsewhere in North America. So abundant were the region's marine resources that between 500 BCE and 500 CE these inhabitants settled into permanent villages to "farm the sea." Their forests, made lush by a mild, rainy climate, provided towering cedar trees from which they constructed large plank houses and crafted a wide array of carvings, including totem poles. Within villages, hierarchies developed, and families and individuals were ranked (or classed) from commoners to chiefs. Two primary factors determined relative status: one's inherited position and wealth (material and immaterial), and the potlatches that validated that position. One might be the eldest of an esteemed and elite lineage, but without hosting potlatches on various occasions—including funerals, marriages, initiations, investitures of new chiefs, births, and the completion of large plank houses—one would not be considered a proper chief. Within villages, extended lineages were organized into clans that identified themselves publicly through hereditary, heraldic crest images. It was among these hierarchical societies blessed with abundant, easily carved cedar that the totem pole developed to memorialize chiefs, to publicly display family crests, and to establish and maintain stratified positions.

As the following chapters will describe, totem poles were not evenly distributed on the coast. They likely originated in one particular region, around Haida Gwaii (the Queen Charlotte Islands) or possibly in neighboring Tsimshian territory, spreading over time to both northern and southern groups. Nor are they a unitary phenomena, as the widespread application of the term "totem poles" implies. There were and are variants of carved columns of the coast (most with distinguishing terms in the local, indigenous languages in which specific types are found): "house posts" are interior structural features that hold up the roof beams of large cedar plank houses; "house frontal poles," "portal poles," or "entry poles" are attached to the exterior façade of the house and occasionally include a carved out passage that can act as a door; "memorial poles" are freestanding posts, often erected in front of houses or in burial grounds, which memorialize individuals; and "mortuary poles" contained the remains of the memorialized individual, often interred in a box attached to the pole itself. Furthermore, there were types of carvings in narrower distribution, such as "speaker figures" used to depict host chiefs or their orators, "welcome posts" placed at the entry points of villages, and "shame poles" or "ridicule poles" erected to humiliate or challenge rival chiefs (see H. Stewart 1993; Malin 1986). All of these carved posts have been subsumed under the generic term "totem pole," the ideal-typical version of which is a freestanding, painted, multifigured pole, often with outstretched wings. Wherever they stand—regardless of the number of carved images or the presence or absence of painted designs—poles generally depict heraldic crests representing beings that, in the past, had interacted with an ancestor and given him or her the privilege to portray their identifying image on artworks. Appearing together on a pole, the crests signify episodes in a family's history or legendary narratives, including the specific potlatch event that celebrated the monument's erection. And, since a potlatch is the mechanism by which rank is validated, the pole acts as a marker of and monument to its owner's social standing.

However, in the contemporary popular imagination, represented by the anecdotes and images in the prologue, such complex, socially oriented indigenous meanings have vanished. Instead, totem poles have become signifiers of a great nation, inspirations for poetry and song, symbols of generalized indigeneity, exoticisms appropriated for fashion, strange elements in advertisements, and props for the most unlikely of film scenes.

Although originally placed within or before plank houses that were lined up in coastal Native villages, today totem poles show up in locations as varied as museums, parks, city squares, private homes, university campuses, theme parks, cruise ships, and gift shops around the world. Many misconceptions have followed these poles on their travels away from Native villages and into the public domain. For example, poles do not tell narrative stories that can be "read" from top to bottom or bottom to top like a comic strip or hieroglyph. Instead, poles are to be seen more as a cast of characters from lineage narratives and family tree branches. In general, positions of figures on the pole have little bearing on their significance, despite the cliché "low man on the totem pole": in fact, some groups put the most important family crest on the bottom, at eye level. Neither are poles suffused with spirituality, despite repeated attempts to portray them as such.[2] For example, on a 1909 card produced by Seattle's Ye Olde Curiosity Shop is their "History of Totem Poles": "Totemism embraces forms of Deity, Demon, Myths, Charms, Evil Spirits, Legend and Witchcraft. These Totemism symbols are regarded with superstitious, almost sacred, reverence. . . . Many are gaudily painted, elaborately carved, tracing the geneology [sic] of a once semi-savage, barbarous people" (Duncan 2000, 169). Other such misinterpretations assert that poles were worshiped as idols, that humans worshiped their crest animals, and that poles protected villages by scaring away evil spirits. As will be explained in this book, none of that is true. Neither is the popular and often unquestioned assumption that totem poles represent a form of Northwest Coast art that existed in static abundance for centuries before the arrival of Europeans.

Even the name "totem pole" is based upon a misunderstanding. *Dodem*, an Algonkian word (Ojibwa/Anishinaabe *ototeman*; Cree *ototema*) meaning "his clan name or clan animal" (J. Long 1891, cited in Tylor 1898, 139–40), was introduced into the English language in the late eighteenth century. During the nineteenth century, as anthropologists began classifying elements of culture according to universal categories, they defined the totem as a particular lineage group's protective animal that cannot be slain or eaten and from which they were said to have descended. However, animal images on Northwest Coast poles represent family crests or narrative characters that are neither protective nor subject to culinary taboo. Thus, according to the social scientific definition, they are not "totems." Moreover, prior to the late nineteenth century, "totem" was not the word of choice used by outsiders to describe the carvings found along the coast. Among the variety of terms for these monuments were "heraldic columns" (MacKenzie 1801, traveling in the early 1800s); "posts" and "carved columns" (Deans 1899, traveling in the 1860s); "pillars" (G. Dawson 1880; Chittenden 1884); and the German *Wappenpfahlen* (lit., "crest posts"; Jacobsen 1977, traveling in the early 1880s).[3]

Historian James McCabe was among the first to use the word "totem" when in 1876 he discussed "totem posts" in his history of the Philadelphia Centennial Exposition. According to the racialist ideologies embraced by late-nineteenth-century Europeans and North Americans, Native societies around the globe stood at low levels of social evolution. Totemism became generally accepted as the "religion" of one developmental class of primitive people, the "savage." This designation coincided with the popularization of the idea among the Victorians, in part inspired by James Frazer's widely read *Totemism* (1887) and *The Golden Bough: A Study in Comparative Religion* (1890). Emile Durkheim's *Elementary Forms of Religious Life* (1912) investigated Australian Aboriginal totemism for a sociological perspective on the origins of all religious expression. Even Sigmund Freud investigated this concept, publishing four essays in 1912 and 1913 on primal psychological patterns, English translations of which could be read in *Totem and Taboo* (1918). Considering the Victorian fascination with a phenomenon so closely linked with the "primitive," it is not surprising that "totem" became the adjective of choice for Northwest Coast monumental carving, modifying "posts," "columns," and "poles." As a result, Northwest Coast carved columns have merged so fully with a popular, primitivist concept, that today one often hears them being referred to simply as "totems."

The totem pole, as the most popular and well-known example of Northwest Coast art, has been the subject of numerous publications (see appendix A for an annotated list of books on totem poles). Although we refer to specific poles and, in some cases, offer explanations for their imagery, our intention is not to describe or interpret individual carvings, nor to duplicate the few excellent publications that do so. Neither shall we elucidate in any detail the stylistic variations between carvings of different artists or tribes, as many publications offer formal analyses of Northwest Coast art. Instead, we offer new ways of looking at the intercultural history of the totem pole—both as a material object and as a category of colonial and contemporary visual culture.

ART HISTORY AND WORLDS OF OBJECTS AND IMAGES

Each of us comes to the totem pole from different disciplines—Jonaitis from art history, Glass from anthropology—both of which have changed considerably over the last several decades. In the past, the art historian tended to understand culture solely through its visual manifestations, while the anthropologist attempted to understand art through its broad social and cultural contexts or functions. Art historians were more interested in the stylistic relations between objects, while anthropologists focused on the social relations between people. Today, art historians and anthropologists are no longer such purists, for art history increasingly investigates social, cultural, economic, and political influences on art, while material culture-oriented anthropology places visual objects and images more centrally in its conception of cultural practice. Applied to the totem pole, our different perspectives complement each other and encourage a broader comprehension of the complex topic of totem pole history and meaning. In addition, both of us have spent much time in each other's realm. Glass has training in studio art and art history, while Jonaitis has often approached Northwest Coast art from a more anthropological than art historical position. Moreover, we have each based much of our scholarly research on extended experience among and collaboration with the First Nations on the coast (see preface).

As is now appropriate and commonplace, we use the term "art" for totem poles and "artist" for those who carve them. This has not always been accepted terminology for Native carvings and paintings.[4] For generations, art history was largely founded upon connoisseurship, which judged those paintings, sculptures, and similar works falling comfortably into the category of "fine art" as the sole objects worthy of study. Bracketed as mere "artifact" and relegated to anthropology or archaeology, Native creations simply did not qualify as "art." The major exception to this rule was in those situations where major Western artists—such as Picasso or some surrealists—directly cited so-called primitive art in their own works. During the early to mid-twentieth century, there was a robust celebration of primitivism (in part an avant-garde rejection of conservative taste, and in part a more general critique of modernity) that garnered specific attention from certain art historians and critics.[5] Along with other social and artistic forces, such valedictory discourses helped revalue Native creations in the minds of scholars and the public alike, and helped expand the boundaries of art history. In this book, we demonstrate how acceptance of Native carvings transformed them from "artifact" to "art" during the twentieth century, and we analyze them from the perspective of the "new art historians," who embrace artworks that exist well beyond the former limits of the Western canon.[6] In addition, instead of addressing only the visual, as did many scholars in the past, contemporary art history incorporates aspects of social history and cultural insights derived from anthropology, as we ourselves shall do.

In keeping with this more open-ended approach to art, we join those who challenge the notion that art describes an immutable, static, material object that inexplicably draws in admirers. In fact, poles, like other objects, have "cultural biographies," life narratives that track their changing contexts, meanings, functions, and values.[7] To understand the biographies of specific totem poles, we ask where they came from; who made them and under what circumstances; where and why they have traveled; how their use and their status changed; what they communicate about both the cultures in which they are produced and the cultures in which they are appreciated and appropriated; how viewers look at, utilize, understand, and make meaning of them; and how images circulate around the world, between and among different social arenas and cultures. Moreover, through many such exemplars, we also offer a historicized biography of the totem pole not as a specific object but as a transient stereotype and symbol, idea and icon.

As such, our work is situated comfortably within the transdisciplinary field of visual culture studies. In addition to expanding art historical notions of what constitutes a possible focus of study, visual culture focuses on the unprecedented and dominant role that visual media play in the present age, as advertisements, photographs, television, videos, movies, and computers influence our attitudes, lifestyles, and perspectives on the world.[8] Visual studies greatly expand the scope of material worthy of serious investigation to encompass not only those items classified as "fine arts" but other categories previously judged inferior, such as "craft," "popular art," and "kitsch." We suggest that valuable insights can be gleaned from addressing not only the finely carved, full-size totem poles carved by master Northwest Coast artists (which have long been the focus of study and connoisseurship) but also a broad range of other visual images, including souvenir models and depictions of poles in photographs, print advertising, Web sites and other media. These representations of actual poles, as well as countless other objects and images and over two hundred years of written texts, have contributed to the formation of a highly complex and multifaceted concept in the popular imagination—"the totem pole."

ANTHROPOLOGY AND WORLDS OF PEOPLE

Anthropology, like art history, has changed considerably in recent decades. In the past, its mission, often presented in tones of considerable urgency, was to salvage the "disappearing" aboriginal cultures being overwhelmed by the more powerful forces of colonization. Franz Boas, the most influential anthropologist to have studied the Northwest Coast, engaged in such salvage ethnography. While curator at the American Museum of Natural History from 1895 to 1905, he orchestrated a major collecting effort in British Columbia: the Jesup North Pacific Expedition (1897–1901). Boas urged his field collectors to acquire the most "traditional" objects—i.e., those that appeared to be unacculturated—and to disregard culturally hybridized objects such as souvenirs made for tourists and button blankets made with trade items.[8] This limited notion of authenticity would characterize much of anthropology during a large part of the twentieth century.

The concept that "pure" Indian cultures once existed but became irredeemably polluted as a result of contact with non-Native peoples adheres to this now-discarded paradigm of authenticity being equated with the past. Now anthropology has a different perspective on authenticity, in part because Native people have survived and not disappeared as predicted, in part because indigenous people today criticize, with good cause, their past representations. Contemporary Northwest Coast Native people today are just as "authentic" as those who lived during the seventeenth century. Instead of bemoaning the changes resulting from the colonial encounter, most current students of culture acknowledge and endeavor to understand Native people's endurance and ability to adjust creatively to new conditions. Thus, anthropology no longer seeks the oldest, least acculturated form of culture but—recognizing the mutability and constantly evolving nature of culture—concentrates on the dynamics of Native/non-Native interchanges from initial encounters to the present.[9] Consequently, the totem pole, like other examples of material culture, transcends its apparently static materiality and becomes part of the history of intercultural understanding and mutual respect, as well as misunderstanding and ambivalence. This dynamic process underlies the fundamental colonial paradox regarding indigenous arts: the tension between trends toward appreciation and appropriation. That is, the process of learning to appreciate Native material culture as fine art is usually accompanied by the practices of collecting it for museums, commodifying it for local and international markets, and claiming it as an—perhaps *the*—essential component of national heritage.[11]

Because the effects of colonization and settlement were so drastic, and the actions of some involved in those processes so cruel, it is easy to dismiss those actions as completely destructive and all those players as simply malevolent. In reality, colonial encounters were not strictly dualistic phenomena with Euroamericans oppressing and Native peoples succumbing. Sometimes colonized people maintained elements of control over their destinies, infusing their changing cultural practices with altered, yet identifiable, elements of tradition or distinction from their colonizers.[12] Instead of becoming passive recipients of an imposed and alien order, losing their identity and becoming subsumed by the dominant society (if they survived at all), Native people often became active participants who, over several hundred years, engaged, responded to, and negotiated with their colonizers.[13] The sites and processes of such constructive as well as destructive interchange between indigenous people and settlers have become fascinating arenas for anthropological investigation, and we locate our historical study of totem poles at many of these points of exchange.

How we look at totem poles today reflects the large-scale reevaluation of modernism's celebration of the new and simultaneous dismissal of the old. A great deal of the literature on Native Americans accepted the dichotomy of the traditional and the modern. Even if some works expressed "imperialist nostalgia" (Rosaldo 1989) for what was being lost, few actually endorsed a return to the "old ways." Since the 1960s however, decolonization and international movements of liberation have inspired some to challenge modernist assumptions and to seek alternate, revisionist versions of history. Andreas Huyssen (2001, 52) identifies "the emergence of memory as a key concern in Western societies, a turning toward the past that stands in stark contrast to the privileging of the future so characteristic of earlier decades of twentieth-century modernity." Visual culture plays a significant role in this process. As Huyssen suggests, memory, be it private or public, is inseparable from the media representations (such as films, videos, the Internet, museums, television shows, and photographs) that turn it into a commodity and a spectacle. (We return to this notion in the final chapter). For these reasons, we pay specific attention to the various visual cultures of the totem pole as they express shifting colonial relations between indigenous and settler societies, between notions of the traditional and the modern, between approaches to artifact and art.

Mary Louise Pratt (1992), in a book on the literature of imperialism that draws inspiration from Cuban sociologist Fernando Ortiz, argues that the term "acculturation" misrepresents the process by which societies interact, as it implies a process whereby engagement with a new culture leads to destruction of the old one. Pratt substitutes the concept of "transculturation," a process that results in a new form of culture related to, but also different from, the cultures of both the colonizer and colonized. Pratt identifies as "contact zones" those places where this productive interaction occurs.[14] Likewise, the notion of the "intercultural" suggests the negotiated nature of colonial encounter and the variegated quality of its results (see Hay 1999). There are dual senses in which we use the term "intercultural" in this book: it suggests both the dynamic *process* of cultural contact, exchange, and relation; and a particular *quality* of the material and visual products that result from the shifting relations. Our use of "intercultural" and "transcultural" builds on these critical insights and implies a more active process and a more interconnected social network than does the more neutral term "cross-cultural," which tends to reify the distinctions supposedly being bridged.

REPRESENTING INDIGENOUS CULTURES AND COLONIAL CONTEXTS

In the past, most anthropological literature devoted to studying tribal people ignored the involvements of their colonizers in the ongoing processes of culture formation, whereas much historical literature neglected the influence of indigenous populations on colonial cultures. In more recent years, both history and anthropology have begun addressing these interconnections. In their book on colonialism in New Guinea, Chris Gosden and Chantal Knowles acknowledge the involvement of both participants in the colonial encounter:

> Chemists make a distinction between a mixture and a reaction. A mixture is a solution in which different chemicals combine, but retain their original form, whereas a reaction creates something new out of its original constituent parts. Colonial New Guinea was a reaction to which all parties contributed, so that there can be no question that all had influence and agency. Anthropologists have tried to undo or ignore the reaction and focus upon one part, New Guineans, creating a partial and static picture in the process (Gosden and Knowles 2001, xix).

As we shall demonstrate, the totem pole represents just such a "reaction." Non-Natives—from their first contact with Northwest Coast people in the late eighteenth century to the present—have been integral to totem pole history. Including the involvement of Euroamericans is not intended to diminish the centrality of Native people to this story, nor to further appropriate the totem pole as a simple product of colonial culture, but to demonstrate instead that "the totem pole"—as an idea—actually emerged and continues to change as a negotiation and involvement with, as well as reaction to, intruders into indigenous territories. The totem pole is a flexible technology that continues to express shifting identities in a world consisting, for better or worse, of Native and non-Native peoples.

The most central participants in this transformative process are, naturally, Native people themselves. But others have contributed considerably to this history as well—fur traders, missionaries, government officials, artists, tourists, journalists, settlers, academics, art critics, museum professionals, and photographers. Many of these outsiders found totem poles the most fascinating of Native artworks, subjecting them to varied judgments, interpretations, appropriations, or celebrations, and in the process imposed on the artworks meanings that their Native creators could never have imagined. These reactions have integrated themselves into the concept of the totem pole itself. The multiple meanings that adhere to totem poles comprise both indigenous realities and nonindigenous misconceptions (be they simple factual errors or wild, romantic imaginings). Thus the history of "the totem pole" is also a history of colonial relations, for it emerged over a lengthy period of time and in the context of transactions between the original inhabitants of and the newcomers to the Northwest Coast. Whatever totem poles were and are to Native people themselves, they also embody a history of intercultural contact, conflict, and exchange.

This book addresses varied interactions between those Native peoples from whose cultures totem poles emerged and those non-Natives whose responses over the years have ranged from fascination to repulsion, from appropriation to appreciation. The terms by which non-Native people represent indigenous cultures in museum exhibits, publications, and paintings are neither homogenous nor value-free. They can be seen to fall into several different categories—ranging from obliteration to idealization—all of which consciously or unconsciously support the various (and often conflicting) values of colonialism.[15] For instance, "obliteration" figuratively or even literally erases the "beingness" of aboriginal people. "Debasement" is the conscious and public dismissal of Native peoples as distinctly inferior. "Calibration" entails mapping, measuring, naming, identifying, and describing an alien culture to assume control over it and ensure order. "Aestheticization" promotes appealing elements of aboriginality—art, spiritualism, connection to the earth—to hide the attempts at obliteration and debasement. And "idealization" positions the indigenous—or rather, idealized images of it—as superior to the modern or even as utopian. These are some of the terms of and preconditions for the kinds of ambivalence that we document in this study as they have been expressed through or projected onto totem poles.

Since first contacts, those who encountered Northwest Coast cultures in general and totem poles in particular reacted in many, often contradictory, ways. The first explorers to the Northwest Coast and later anthropologists, working in the Enlightenment mode, scientifically described and measured poles as components of alien worlds. Missionaries tried to obliterate poles by encouraging their physical destruction as well as the eradication of the cultural basis for their creation. Nineteenth-century colonial agents and settlers to the Northwest Coast needed to debase Indians and their cultures if they were to seize their land and claim moral authority over them. Those more sympathetic to Native people aestheticized poles as signifiers of deep spirituality, thus adhering to the stereotype of Indian-as-shaman. Sometimes non-Natives appropriated poles as territorial advertisements or as honored symbols of Alaska, British Columbia, or Canada. Others, who admired and romanticized the "noble savage," idealized poles and their Native creators and lamented their disappearing cultures, many of which (at least in their ancient form) were held to be a superior alternative to the modern, industrial West. It is important to note, however, that values and reactions do not map neatly onto the categories of colonial experience. Attitudes of settlers and travelers toward totem poles and indigenous peoples—as well as attitudes of Native peoples toward their colonizers—have more often been characterized by outright ambivalence, conceptual conflict, and ethical negotiation.

HISTORICIZING THE TOTEM POLE

This book is organized both thematically and chronologically, with each chapter focusing on a different facet of the pole's complex, intercultural biography. Part one addresses the development of "the totem pole" as a category within the colonial imagination. Chapters 2 through 6 investigate the creation of the totem pole (as an idea) on the Northwest Coast proper. We begin with the mutual attempts by Natives and non-Natives to understand each other and to ensure mutual advantage in emerging colonial trade relations. Within the context of the fur trade era, from first contact in the late eighteenth century to the mid-nineteenth century, totem poles began to flourish as indigenous social and cultural statements, particularly within newly amalgamated villages. With the replacement of the fur trade enterprise by settler colonialism during the second half of the nineteenth century, outsiders—especially government agents, social scientists, and visual artists—began to impose new meanings on poles not necessarily connected to their aboriginal significances. This transformation of the totem pole (as a type of object) occurred in the context of these shifting and complex social environments, and amidst colonial relations that included missionization, settlement, disease, and, in British Columbia, prohibition of the potlatch ceremony.

Beginning in the late nineteenth century, destination tourism to the Northwest Coast—especially to Alaska—began to play a significant role in the transformation of poles into generalized regional emblems of the Northwest. Further transformations of the pole into a stereotyped icon resulted from developments in tourism marketing, which included major pole restoration projects, the creation of new totem pole categories designed to attract visitors (such as "the world's tallest pole"), and the growth of the souvenir industry that replicated thousands of model poles, ranging from valuable works of art to the most trivial of mass-produced kitsch.

Part two traces the global circulation of totem poles and the spread of their visual popularity. Chapters 7 through 9 shift the focus from poles experienced on the Northwest Coast to those removed from the region. Collectors purchased poles from their owners and took others from seemingly abandoned villages, transporting them to relatively close destinations such as Vancouver and Seattle, and to world's fairs and museums in the more remote cities of North America and Europe. Responses to these transported totem poles changed over the decades, reflecting the changing popular attitudes toward colonized people and their art from the late nineteenth to mid-twentieth century. After Northwest Coast Native people became minorities in their own lands and attitudes toward their artwork became increasingly positive, efforts began to salvage deteriorating poles that still stood in villages. Motivations for these projects included scientific preservation, economic development, national and regional commemoration, and tourist marketing. One individual, Wilson Duff, who worked at the two principal

British Columbia museums, promoted several of these restoration projects, personally balancing anthropological perspectives with an approach to poles as fine art. These efforts enhanced the values attached to poles, changed the way they became displayed, influenced non-Native attitudes toward poles, and resonated with Native political mobilization. Over the course of the book, other individuals—such as Franz Boas, Marius Barbeau, Mungo Martin, Bill Holm, and Bill Reid—will appear as major culture brokers who helped to manage the shifting attitudes toward indigenous peoples and their artistic creations.

Part three, which includes chapters 10 to 12, brings the story of the totem pole into the present. After 1960, beginning with the era of reempowerment of ethnic minorities, totem pole carving once again flourished, as both Natives and non-Natives negotiated new terms of relations, and "ethnic art" became increasingly valued in the international art world. Concurrent with those processes, reinvigorated production among Northwest Coast people and increasingly popular cultural tourism began to promote totem poles as authentic and vital components of living Native cultures. Soon totem poles were appearing at theme parks, in the digital media, as aspects of Native-run tourist ventures, and as subjects of contemporary souvenirs. The dynamics of tourism, art, place, indigeneity, appropriation, and appreciation have become increasingly entwined with and inflected by current political concerns, such as land claims and treaty negotiations. In recent decades, totem poles have regained their primary aboriginal function as markers of identity and place, but in national and global as well as local contexts. Today, their expressive range has been extended from kinship identification to tribal sovereignty or aboriginality in general.

Totem poles are and have been many things to many people. Given the complicated nature of colonial relations and the visual promiscuity of totem poles, we have adopted intertextual and multivocal perspectives for analyzing them.[16] As we have stated, this book asserts that the history of totem poles—a story of cultural contact, political conflict, and creative exchange—is best told through multiple voices and visions. Toward this end, we have paid particular attention to aspects of both the indigenous creation of poles and the non-indigenous reception of them, and to the multiple and complicated processes and relations that bridge these two sites of cultural production. Most importantly, we have invited First Nations artists and intellectuals as well as non-Native scholars to provide portraits of specific totem poles of their own choosing. The sidebars scattered throughout the book provide specific case studies of many of the general topics we discuss, directly illustrating the various kinds of relationships that people today maintain with totem poles. The chapter endnotes, admittedly eclectic, supplement the main text with additional citations, theoretical comments, and historical material. Appendices at the back compile useful source data for those wishing to pursue specific aspects of totem pole history. This book also includes a number of photo essays that represent widely ranging but visually recurring uses of poles. We hope that all of these features encourage a nuanced and layered reading of this intercultural history of totem poles.[17]

WHAT DO TOTEM POLES WANT?

According to visual culture theorist W. J. T. Mitchell, objects with a certain vitality have

> lives of their own, [and] cannot be explained simply as rhetorical, communicative instruments or epistemological windows onto reality. . . . Vision is never a one-way street, but a multiple intersection teeming with dialectical images. . . . The questions to ask about images are not just "what do they mean?" or "what do they do?" but . . . "what do they want?" (W. J. T. Mitchell 2002, 297).

In a book that addresses these questions, Mitchell (2005) asserts that people have a "double consciousness" toward images manifested by varied reactions to them, from critical objectivity to a belief in the power of images to influence, seduce, and wield magic (see also Freedberg 1991 and Gell 1998). He points out that this is true for everyone, not only non-Western people.

Regarding totem poles, the answer to "What do

they mean?" is at first fairly straightforward: totem poles are monuments erected by families to communicate their histories and status; for a Northwest Coast family, the totem pole is an index of the family's worth. Yet the specific meanings for individual poles are often restricted, even within Native communities. Without specialized knowledge, a viewer can neither understand a pole's imagery (beyond identifying broad categories of crest beings) nor fully comprehend its reification of social status. What they "do" is considerably more complicated, and changes over time and across intercultural space. Considering the vast, popular appeal of the totem pole, it is notoriously hard to capture visually. Their height defies photographs; if one wants the entire carving in the frame, the pole becomes too thin and distant to be easily read, while if one wants a detail of its imagery, the resultant close-up denies the whole. So tall and heavy is the pole that, despite the considerable number in museums around the world, to actually obtain one is a major undertaking done with far less frequency than collecting more portable artifacts.[18]

What totem poles "want," how they influence and affect people, might be the most elusive question. Despite the many transformations, representations, and misrepresentations that totem poles have experienced over two centuries, they remain compelling, intriguing, and fascinating to people of all ethnicities and backgrounds. Despite—or, perhaps, because of—its enigmatic and ephemeral qualities, the totem pole has imprinted itself indelibly onto the aesthetic imagination of Natives and non-Natives alike, becoming in the process an even more complex, even more meaningful icon.

PART ONE

TOTEM POLES IN THE COLONIAL IMAGINATION

ON COMMERCE AND CULTURES

EXPLORERS AND MERCHANTS ENCOUNTER CARVED COLUMNS

There is something picturesque in the whole appearance of this large village: it is particularly remarkable for the monstrous and colossal figures which decorate the houses of the principal inhabitants, and the wide gaping mouths of which serve as a door.

—CAMILLE DE ROQUEFEUIL, ON SEEING THE HAIDA VILLAGE OF MASSETT IN 1818

In 1745 the British Parliament offered a reward of £20,000 to find the Northwest Passage. This dreamed-of sea route between Hudson Strait to the east and the Pacific Ocean to the west would enable the British to sail quickly from England to the Far East, avoiding the Spanish territories in South and Middle America. Captain James Cook, a man who had already taken two voyages around the world, pursued this prize on his third trip in 1778. While he would never find the nonexistent Northwest Passage, he would have the privilege of becoming the first non-Native to record a Northwest Coast carved column.

Cook sailed the *Resolution* from England to the Cape of Good Hope and across the Pacific to Vancouver Island. In March 1778 he brought his ship into a calm harbor that he named Friendly Cove. Maquinna, chief of Yuquot—a town of 1,500 Mowachaht, the local band of Nuu-chah-nulth—welcomed the foreigners and invited them into his home, which stood along a cobbled beach facing the cove. Cook needed to repair his ship, so he and his crew spent several weeks at Yuquot. Although he was not the first European who traveled to the Northwest Coast—the Spanish could boast that accomplishment with Juan Perez Hernandez's 1774 trip to Vancouver Island and Haida Gwaii, and Juan Francisco de la Bodega y Quadra's 1775 voyage as far north as southeast Alaska—Cook became the first European to interact extensively with an indigenous group on the coast.

In keeping with the scientific approach to new cultures characteristic of the Enlightenment, Cook carefully detailed the appearance of Yuquot, using quantitative measurements for accuracy:

> Their houses or dwellings are situated close to the shore. They consist in a long range of buildings, some of which are one hundred and fifty feet in length, twenty four or thirty broad and seven or eight high from the floor to roof, which in them is all flat and covered with loose boards. The walls are also built up of boards and the framing consists of large trees or logs. . . . Many of these boards are thirty feet in length and from three to five broad, and are all procured by splitting large trees (Beaglehole 1967, 317).

No totem poles stood before these houses, but inside the spacious structures were carved house posts that depicted anthropomorphic beings (fig. 2.1). John Webber, an artist who accompanied Cook on this voyage, drew Maquinna's house interior with walls of split cedar planks, a central hearth, peripheral platforms

2.1. Interior of Chief Maquinna's house, Yuquot (Nuu-chah-nulth), 1778. Drawing by John Webber. © Peabody Museum, Harvard University, N1-72-10/499.

upon which people sat, and the posts. This drawing represents the first visual record of what would become a source of endless fascination for many.

It took the Europeans some time to learn what these posts signified. Cook called them *klumma,* presumably after a Native term, and commented on how the Mowachaht spoke of them in a puzzling fashion. He suggested that they might be idols or figures of ancestors. Acknowledging his ignorance, Cook goes on, "But all this is mere conjecture as may well be supposed, for we never saw any kind of homage paid them and we could gain nothing from information, as we had learnt little more of their language, than to ask the names of things and the two simple words yes and no" (quoted in Walker 1982, 234).

In April, Cook left the region of Nootka Sound and sailed farther north, exploring other parts of coastal Alaska as far north as Anchorage today, then west along the Aleutians. Although Cook himself was killed in what we now call Hawaii, his ship returned to England with both disappointing and enticing news. The Northwest Passage remained undiscovered, but the coastal regions abounded with sea otters. Their luxurious pelts, admired by the Chinese nobility, who paid large amounts of money for them, would soon motivate traders from Europe and the United States to sail thousands of miles in order to reap the lucrative profits of the Northwest Coast maritime fur trade. Between 1774 and the second decade of the nineteenth century, the abundance of this marine mammal, whose fur was called "soft gold," attracted hundreds of ships to the Northwest Coast. In turn, the indigenous residents who sold the outsiders pelts would profit as well.

Prior to settlement in the Northwest Coast region and the implementation of overt imperial tendencies (beyond fur extraction), the visiting merchants displayed considerable ambivalence toward the indigenous inhabitants and their artistic creations. These attitudes are indexed by their attempts to describe in words and depict in images the carved columns that they encountered (parallel Native attempts to depict their European trading partners will be surveyed in chapter 4). Furthermore, the seasoned sailors compared the coastal people with others they had met on their global travels in an attempt to reflect on the more fundamental relationship between Europeans and the world's indigenous populations. In these early decades of the fur trade, indigenous people benefited from contact through an influx of trade wealth, new technologies and materials for tool making, and, among some chiefs and villages at least, the consolidation of regional power. These developments also encouraged certain transformations of Native social structures, village organizations, and displays of art and other forms of cultural property.

THE MARITIME FUR TRADE

Today, most people who sail up the Inside Passage, as well as those who simply read travel books, know what the totem pole looks like—a tall, elaborately carved column of wood. If pressed, the knowledgeable traveler might say that the pole ranges from Puget Sound to southeast Alaska, and is the most emblematic artwork of the Northwest Coast peoples. In fact, poles probably originated during precontact times in a rather small area in northern British Columbia, and spread north and south after the arrival of the Europeans. The earliest accounts from sailors were silent on the presence of large, freestanding, exterior poles, either because none existed or because voyagers bypassed communities with such monuments. It was only in 1791 that a European drew a Haida totem pole conforming to today's standards. In the spirit of the age, Europeans and Americans wrote accounts of their travels, made drawings, and collected artifacts, thereby providing valuable data about Northwest Coast cultures at the earliest stages of contact with non-Native people. We quote traveler's comments extensively in the following pages, for their specific words often reveal difficulties in describing and explaining sights and events largely alien to their European or American experiences (see appendix B for a chronological list of these voyages, observers, destinations, and pole sightings).

Temporary Spanish settlements at Neah Bay and Yuquot and one small Russian fort near what is now Sitka were the only early attempts to establish European villages on the Northwest Coast. In 1789, the Spanish built a small fort in Yuquot—the same place Cook had stayed on the west coast of Vancouver Island—but remained there for only three years. During this failed attempt to establish the northernmost Spanish settlement in North America, Chief Maquinna's entire community removed themselves from those interlopers and settled in an older site north of Yuquot. Once the Spanish left, the Mowachaht returned to their homes. The Spanish also established another settlement at Neah Bay, on the northwest Olympic Peninsula.

In 1799, Alexander Baranof, director of the Russian-American Company that worked out of Kodiak, founded Redoubt St. Michael near the place now known as Sitka. The relationship between these newcomers and the Tlingit was consistently tense. It worsened in 1802, when 600 Tlingit destroyed the Russian American fort and killed nearly all its colonists. In 1804, Baranof retook Sitka Sound. In order to ensure control of this region and its aggressive Native people, he moved the capital of Russian America from Kodiak to this site. But even so, there were never more than a few hundred Russians in the region at one time.

Most Europeans and Americans were content to travel seasonally to the Northwest Coast to trade. The early years of the fur trade were highly profitable for the Europeans, who could purchase large numbers of pelts from the local people for insignificant amounts of goods. However, Northwest Coast people had been skilled tradesmen prior to contact, and soon demonstrated shrewd bargaining by demanding very high prices. The influx of wealth from these exchanges began affecting some aspects of Northwest Coast life. Certain chiefs, such as Maquinna of Yuquot, assumed monopolistic control of the fur trade in their territory and insisted that traders deal with them exclusively. As a result, these individuals became particularly wealthy and powerful. Throughout the region, more wealth meant more opportunities to publicly exhibit status in the form of monumental art.

HOUSE POSTS AND PAINTED FAÇADES

Captain Cook had wondered what the interior carvings in Chief Maquinna's house signified. Later visitors, similarly perplexed, struggled to describe these unusual art works, lacking the appropriate vocabulary for the visual punning, the abundance of faces and eye images, and the transformational elements so characteristic of Northwest Coast art. In 1785, Alexander Walker of the East India Company visited another Nuu-chah-nulth village in the Ahousaht area, where he saw eight *klumma*:

> These are monstrous wooden representations of fictitious beings about twice the size of a stout Man. They are made after different forms, but the principal parts generally consist of the human figure. Some, that we saw here, had two faces on one body, others had two sets of Eyes. There were some even more unnatural than these; as in the place of Noses they had the snouts of foxes, or the beaks of Eagles. In some upon the Body of a Beast was but the hand of a Man, with two pair of Eyes in the forehead (Walker 1982, 47).

During the maritime fur trade years, various travelers to the west coast of Vancouver Island also noted the presence of house posts and attempted to both understand and describe them. However, Europeans did not recognize the Northwest Coast style, and thus most were unable to identify the animals portrayed.

In 1792, the botanist Jose Mariano Moziño, who traveled on Spanish voyages to record natural history, visited Yuquot and finally helped to clarify the significance of Nuu-chah-nulth *klumma*: "The first travelers assumed that these figures were objects of superstitious worship, and I also suspected the same until informed otherwise by the Indians themselves. I learned that they were nothing more than a simple decoration, and if by chance a figure had some significance, it was purely that given to it by the man whose labor had brought the [sculpture] tree to the place in which it was found" (Moziño 1970, 18).[1] Moziño was in error stating that these were "nothing more than simple decoration," for although not sacred, this art, like most from the region, had social importance, signifying the status of the family that owned it. Most Northwest Coast art objects—and almost all totem poles—depict the crests of families, usually animal images but sometimes plants, geological formations, or celestial events, which represent ancestral or supernatural beings. To the lineage that claims a particular image, crest display constitutes an account of its origin story, a validation of its social standing, and an expression of filial pride.

In 1792, the North West Company headquartered in Montreal sent Alexander Mackenzie on an expedition to the Northwest Coast by land. He traveled along the Bella Coola River to the sea, where he visited Nuxalk communities, reporting the presence of interior house posts:

> The ground-plot of it was fifty feet by forty-five; each end is formed by four stout posts, fixed perpendicularly in the ground. The corner ones are plain and support a beam of the whole length, having three intermediate props on each side, but of a larger size, and eight or nine feet in height. The two centre posts, at each end, are two feet and a half in diameter, and carved into human figures, supporting two ridge poles on their heads, at twelve feet from the ground. The figures at the upper part of this square represent two persons with their hands upon their knees, as if they supported the weight with pain and difficulty; the others opposite to them stand at their ease, with their hands resting on their hips. . . . The posts, poles, and figures were painted red and black; but the sculpture of these people is superior to their painting (quoted in Keithahn 1963, 41).

This last comment should not be taken at face value, as it says more about European artistic tastes of the time than about Native artistic quality. Northwest Coast three-dimensional work tended toward a naturalism that would have appealed to a European, while the more abstract two-dimensional work could easily have been dismissed by that same would-be connoisseur.

Interior house posts depicted family crests, as most likely did the images on house façades. John Meares, also of the East India Company, traveled to Clayoquot during his 1788 voyage and wrote:

> Three enormous trees, rudely carved and painted, formed the rafters, which were supported at the ends and in the middle by gigantic images, carved out of huge blocks of timber. . . . The door by which we entered this extraordinary fabric was the mouth of one of these huge images, which, as it may be supposed, was not disproportioned to the other features of this monstrous visage. We ascended by a few steps on the outside, and after passing this extraordinary kind of portal, descended down the chin. . . . In most of their houses they have, as has already been observed, certain huge idols or images, to whom we never saw them pay any mark of common respect, much less worship or adoration. These misshapen figures occupied, as it appeared, somewhat of a distinguished and appropriate place, wherever we saw them; but they seemed to have no exclusive privilege whatever, and shared the common filth of those who lived beneath the same roof with them (quoted in Barbeau 1950, 803).

This quote represents the first record of a sculpted face whose mouth serves as an entry, in this case the home of another great Nuu-chah-nulth, Chief Wickaninnish. The following year, American trader Robert Haswell visited Clayoquot Sound and, like Meares, found Wickaninnish's house extraordinary, with "Clumas or carved pillars . . . more numerous and better executed [than those at Yuquot]" (Howay 1941, 69).

Although no traveler to the Nuu-chah-nulth mentioned anything resembling a freestanding totem pole, it is evident that interior house posts and exterior façade images served the same indigenous function as public presentations of crests. In 1792, Bostonian John Boit wrote an account of structures in Clayoquot Sound: "This village was about half a mile in diameter, and contained upwards of 200 houses, generally well built for Indians; every door that you'd enter was in resemblance of a human and beast's head, the passage being through the mouth, besides which there was much more rude carved work about the dwellings, some of which were by no means inelegant" (quoted in Gunther 1972, 74). In 1794, Haswell re-visited Clayoquot Sound and commented on those same house façades:

> Some of these are so large that the Mouth serves as doarway into their houses some of their ridgepoals which are of incredible length and bulk are neatly Fluted others are painted in resemblance of various sorts of beasts and birds we met with resemblances of the Sun both painted and carved the rays shoot from every side of the orb which like our Country Sign painters they picture with eyes nose and mouth and a round plump face (quoted in Drucker 1948, 391).

To the east of the Nuu-chah-nulth live the Kwakwa̱ka̱'wakw, who also painted their houses' façades. In 1792, artist John Sykes of the Vancouver Expedition (which conducted a detailed survey of the region) illustrated Cheslakee's Village in Johnstone's Strait, a Kwakwa̱ka̱'wakw town of four tiers of structures rising from the beach, some with decorated fronts (fig. 2.2). Sykes's schematic circles, dots, lines, and arcs demonstrate his difficulty replicating the two-dimensional style. Also in 1792, Spanish artist Jose Cardero drew the village of Chief Maguaa near the Nimpkish River, a long line of houses facing the water, some of which were decorated.

Some Salish also presented images on the exteriors of their houses. In 1808, fur trader and explorer Simon Fraser described the entrance to a Salish Halkomelem house somewhere above New Westminster (inland from the current city of Vancouver): "the posts or pillars are nearly three feet [in diameter] at the base, and diminish gradually to the top. In one of these posts is an oval opening answering the purpose of a door. . . . Above, on the outside, are carved a human figure large as life, and there are other figures in imitation of beasts and birds" (Lamb 1960, 103–4). Closer to Kwakwa̱ka̱'wakw territory, the Salish painted their house façades as well. John Sykes, artist on the Vancouver expedition, drew an image of the Salish village at Point Mudge, which the surgeon and naturalist on that expedition, Archibald Menzies, described as "a village . . . of about twelve houses or Huts plankd over with large boards

2.2. *Cheslakee's Village in Johnstone Strait* (Kwakwa̱ka̱'wakw), 1792. Drawing by John Sykes. University of Washington Libraries, Special Collections, NA3987.

some of which were ornamented with rude paintings particularly those on the fronts of the houses" (Henry 1984, 114). Even though few multifigured poles were described by these early explorers, crest display on houses was fully elaborated throughout the region.

MORTUARIES

On the Northwest Coast, where rank or status is typically vested in the possession of hereditary wealth (both material and immaterial, in the form of crests, names, and ceremonial prerogatives), death and mourning are times at which the lineage identity of the deceased chief is publicly displayed (often on carved or painted posts) and validated (through potlatches or feasts). Travelers to Tlingit territory observed and described different types of monumental sculptures, most associated with mortuaries. In 1786 at Portlock's Harbour, a bay on the west side of Chichagof Island in southeast Alaska, British seaman Joseph Woodcock drew an elevated platform that held the remains of Tlingit elite. A box painted with anthropomorphic imagery containing the remains of a notable Tlingit rested upon a rough-hewn platform twelve to fifteen feet above the ground and supported by posts: "This edifice was composed of four posts, each about twenty feet long . . . in a quadrangular form. About twelve or fifteen feet from the ground there was a rough boarded floor . . . in the middle an Indian chest was deposited, which most likely contained the remains of some person of consequence; and on that side . . . to the Westward . . . there was painted the resemblance of a human face" (Henry 1984, 88). The poles that supported the platform and its box were themselves not said to be carved or painted; only the box, presumably a bentwood container depicting formline-style images, was adorned.

The Spanish also ventured to Tlingit territory. In Jose Cardero's 1791 drawing of the "Grave Monuments of the family of the current chief of Port Mulgrave" from the

Yakutat area, a large-headed being sits on its haunches, bent forepaws resting on a carved box. On either side is a decorated box raised high above the ground on four posts, similar to those seen and drawn in 1786 by Woodcock. Pedro Colson, scribe of the Malaspina voyage, wrote:

> We do not know whether the colossal monster which occupies the foreground is an idol or merely a frightful record of the destructive nature of death, but the fact that in its vicinity are various pyres on which bodies have been cremated inclines us to the first idea. In a casket which lay beneath its claws or hands was a bowl-shaped basket, a European hat, an otter skin and a piece of board. The height of the monster was no less than ten and half feet. The whole was of pine wood and the ornaments on the casket were of shells embedded in the same wood. The colouring was of red ochre with the exception of the teeth, the claws and the upper part of the head which were painted black and white. In the upper chambers of the two sepulchral deposits were two baskets . . . the lower chamber . . . contained a basket with some calcined bones (Henry 1984, 162).

Travelers to the Salish region described carvings which later ethnographic information identified as funerary monuments associated with cemeteries. In 1792, on the Vancouver expedition through Puget Sound, Lieutenant Peter Puget wrote in his journal: "We have passed Several deserted Villages in all were wooden Images crudely carved, each I think contained one large & others of Smaller Dimensions the former was a very rough Imitation of the Countenance but the features by no Means in proportion, it bore more the Appearance of an horrid distorted Face & whether this Image was a Representation of Deity or an Ornamental piece of Furniture is at present impossible to determine as either may prove fallacious" (Puget 1939, 215–16). In 1808 Fraser saw raised grave houses in the Spuzzum region at the boundary of the Coast and Interior Salish territories, writing, "Upon the boards and posts are carved beasts and birds, in a curious but rude manner, yet pretty and proportioned" (Lamb 1960, 98). According to later ethnographic evidence, some Salish grave figures represented ancestors, which may be the subjects of these eighteenth-century carvings as well. Like the presence of abundant crest displays on house fronts, the use of decorated mortuary monuments is well documented along the entire coast.

TOTEM POLES AMONG THE HAIDA

None of the accounts cited thus far mentions the tall, cylindrical, freestanding carved monument we think of as the totem pole. It was on Haida Gwaii (the Queen Charlotte Islands) that the first iconic totem poles—as opposed to house posts, house façade images, or carved mortuaries—were described. In 1789, Captain John Meares described the first such poles, and in 1791, John Bartlett, a seaman on the ship *Gustavus III*, drew the earliest known depiction of a multifigured totem pole (fig. 2.3), a forty-foot carving in the Haida village of Dadens that stood against the façade of the house: "The Dore of it is made like a man head the Passage in to the House is Between his teeth and was Boult be fore thay nkowd the youse of Iron" (Henry 1984, 191).[2] Dadens actually had two poles, one attached and another that may or may not have been freestanding (Wright 2001, 50). American trader and explorer Joseph Ingraham commented on both poles:

> [There were] two pillars which were situated in the front of the village about a quarter of a mile distant from our vessel on the north shore. They were about forty feet in height, carved in a very curious manner indeed, representing men, toads, etc., the whole of which I thought did great credit to the natural genius of these people. In one of the houses of this village the door was through the mouth of one of the before mentioned images. In another was a large square pit with seats all around it (Wright 2001, 46).

In 1791, Frenchman Etienne Marchand offered his own description of a Dadens totem pole:

> The door, the threshold of which is raised about a foot and a half above the ground, is of an elliptical figure; the

2.3. Pole at Dadens (Haida), 1791. Drawing by John Bartlett. Photograph courtesy of Peabody Essex Museum, A4956.

> great diameter, which is given by the height of the opening, is not more than three feet, and the small diameter, or the breadth, is not more than two. . . . This opening is made in the thickness of a large trunk of a tree which rises perpendicularly . . . it imitates the form of a gaping human mouth. . . . Over the door is seen the figure of man carved, in the attitude of a child in the womb, and remarkable for the extreme smallness of the parts which characterize his sex; and above this figure, rises a gigantic statue of a man erect, which terminates the sculpture and the decoration of the portal. The head of this statue is dressed with a cap in the form of a sugar-loaf, the height of which is almost equal to that of the figure itself. On the parts of the surface which are not occupied by the capital subjects, are interspersed carved figures of frogs or toads, lizards, and other animals, and arms, legs, thighs and other parts of the human body; a stranger might imagine that he saw the ex voto suspended to the door-case of the niche of a Madonna (Wright 2001, 55).

Marchand tried hard to describe a kind of monument Europeans had never seen and would have had difficulty imagining. The same year, American John Hoskins described similar Haida structures, but with the negative terms so characteristic of those who encountered art which diverged from European canons: "In front is a large post reaching above the roof neatly carved but with the most distorted figures at the bottom is an oval or round hole which is either the mouth or belly of some deformed object this serves for a door way" (Duff 1964a, 91).

Some newcomers actually became involved with totem pole raisings. Traders sometimes had to accommodate the unusual demands of those whose furs they wished to buy, and, as trading partners, the Haida presented special challenges. In 1794, the Kiusta chief Cunneah asked Captain Josiah Roberts to help carve and raise a pole (Howay 1941, 89). In the log of the *Jefferson*, Bernard Magee described the process of what was undoubtedly an extremely early, if not the earliest, totem pole worked on and raised by non-Native people:

> 17 June
> . . . In the afternoon the Capt. with the Carpenters & some hands in the pinnace went to the village at the request of Cunneah to plane and smooth a monumental pillar of wood previous to its erection on the morrow. . . .
>
> 18 June
> . . . In the morning I went in the pinnace with the Carpenters & 2 hands to the village took along with us 2 spars top masts for sheers & sufficient tackling to set up the pillar . . . , which in the afternoon got in its place . . . after finishing the necessary requisites for its intended purpose of sepulture of a daughter of Cunneahs . . .
>
> 19 June
> . . . About noon Cunneah with his wife & son came on board to request the Captains atendance at the village with the officers . . . Cunneah adressed his Chiefs & peoples on the occeasion of this our visite, & urging the properity of thine making such acknowledgements to Roberts for his service & assistance in setting up the monument as the[y] saw fit . . . the[y] were conducted into the house & each of them presented with a skin . . . [they] expressd a desire that he would cause the pillar to be painted . . . which signified to them would be done the first fair weather.

> Several weeks later, 8 July, 1794
> In the afternoon I went to the village with some hands at the desire of Cunneh in the morning to raise an image on the monument lately set up. which the[y] cut & carved with a great deal of art being the representation of some wild anemile unknown to us. some what the Resemblance of a tode (quoted in Wright 2001, 70–72).

On both June 19 and July 9, Roberts and his officers were treated to ceremonial gifts and speech making, in keeping with the proper traditions of formal payment for services rendered. Those gifts included furs.

In 1799, Boston fur trader Samuel Burling visited Kiusta and described the pole Roberts and his men had helped erect five years earlier:

> In the morning I was early to examine the Village and take a sketch of it before I went on board. The Village consisted of eight houses of which Cunneaw's [Cunneah] was the largest being about fifty feet long, thirty broad, and fifteen to the rise of the roof—to the peak of it I suppose it was about twenty two or three feet. At the right hand of the village as you go to it were a number of wooden structures raised I suppose over the bodies of their dead chiefs. Some were exactly like a gallows, some a solid square piece of timber about fifteen feet high on which were carved figures of men and children. But the only thing that I saw which had any idea of proportion was a pillar by the side of Cunneaw's house on the top of which was a figure intended to represent a bear; the figure and pillar were both painted with red ochre. The teeth, eyes, nostrils, and the inside of the ears (which were stuck forward) of the animal were made of the mother of pearl shell; which gave it a very beautiful appearance in comparison to what Northwest sculpture generally has (quoted in Wright 2001, 84).

By the late eighteenth century, travelers to Haida Gwaii had documented three types of poles: in Kiusta, the freestanding mortuary and the memorial pole; and in Dadens, the attached frontal or façade pole. These were to proliferate on these islands over the next half century, resulting in communities such as Skidegate and Massett that literally bristled with poles.

THE LAND-BASED FUR TRADE, AMALGAMATED VILLAGES, AND THE FLOURISHING OF CREST ART

So profitable was the maritime trade that those chiefs who controlled access to the furs, such as Maquinna of Yuquot, became immensely wealthy and powerful. But by the first decade of the nineteenth century, the rapacious sea otter harvest caused near extinction of these aquatic fur bearers. As a result, communities that had prospered began to experience significant losses of income and status. After the precipitous decline of the maritime fur trade, the Mowachaht economy never recovered, and this once-eminent group never reinstated their earlier prominence and wealth (Marshall 1993). But then other communities with access to coastal and interior fur bearers experienced breathtaking ascent to power and riches.

Starting in the early nineteenth century, the Hudson's Bay Company consolidated a presence in the Northwest, establishing forts in interior British Columbia at Fort Nelson in 1805 and Fort St. James in 1806. Two decades later, the company reached the coast to found Fort Langley on the lower Fraser River and Fort Vancouver on the Columbia River in 1827, Fort Simpson in northern British Columbia at the mouth of the Nass River in 1831, and Fort McLaughlin on Milbanke Sound in 1833. In 1840, they also arranged with the Russians to use Fort Stikine in Alaska. Fort Victoria on southern Vancouver Island opened for trade in 1843, and became a popular destination for northern Native groups who canoed down the coast on annual trading expeditions.

The coastal people, talented traders for centuries who honed their skills during the maritime fur trade years, remained formidable exchange partners and successfully negotiated what were considered high prices for the terrestrial pelts. Even though the Hudson's Bay Company expected the kind of monopoly they enjoyed with other Canadian First Nations, they never successfully imposed one among the Northwest Coast people.

TWO INTERESTING NUUCHAANULTH POLES

BY ḴI-ḴE-IN, HUUPACHESAT-H HISTORIAN AND ARTIST[3]

Nuuchaanulth poles represent crest figures of the families that own the poles. The poles refer to the traditions, possessions, rights, and privileges of the families, which own them. As well, Nuuchaanulth poles illustrate a larger political reality, confederation. Our people know and express our connections with each other constantly in many ways. In our way, the two most important questions that one can ask a person are: Who are you? (meaning: What is your name?) and Where are you from? (meaning: Who are your mother, father, grandparents; who are your relatives?). We trace our family trees backward for each other with the hope that we will get to a place where we reach a common root, a family connection, a blood tie. Then we can say "Uuwaatsasa," "We are relatives." This is the basis for a deeper, respectful relationship. These are powerful questions. Who are you? Where are you from? Nuuchaanulth poles speak powerfully to these questions.

We do not know when the earliest Nuuchaanulth poles were carved, however, when the Maatmalthnii first came ashore at Yuukwaat [Yuquot], in 1778, the artist John Webber drew house poles inside a Muu-ach'at-h chief's house. In the late 1700s, Meares wrote rather flamboyant descriptions of Wikananish's house-entrance pole at Huupitsat. Meares entered the bighouse through the monstrous mouth of the bottom figure on the house post. Aahuusat-h, Chiiktlisat-h, Kaa'yuukw'at-h, Muu-ach'at-h, and Yuulthuu-ilthat-h house posts show up in historic photographs, too. Pre-World War I photographs of freestanding nonarchitectural poles at half a dozen other Nuuchaanulth villages also exist.

There was a woman of royal standing called Chamaatuk, known at the time of her death, around 1916, as Hakumaatkw. She was the eldest sister of Mukwina [Maquinna] the Fifth, and a member of the Yaalthuu-ashtakamlthat-h Clan of Iihatisat-ht. She had a lot of relatives at Huukh, but no offspring. When Queen Hakumaatkw died, the Iihatisat-h branches of her Mukwina family hosted

2.4. Yuquot (Nuu-chah-nulth) Captain Jack Pole, 1939. Photograph by Frank Nowell. University of British Columbia Archives, 27.1/18-1.

a *thlaakt'uultha* ("end of mourning ceremony") and erected a memorial pole to honor her.

Typically one's descendants host a *thlaakt'uultha* to publicly announce they have completed their official mourning period. This feast or potlatch is usually put up one, two, four, eight, or twelve years after the death of a loved one. As the event approaches, the host family ask relatives, friends, and neighbours to render certain services: "We'd like you to cook," "We'd like you to dance," "We'd like you to attend and witness our business." They are free to make such requests, but, if someone is *ehak* ("in mourning") and hasn't hosted a *thaakt'uultha* yet, then it is unthinkable to ask them to participate in public affairs. That would be rude and insensitive. Hakumaatkw had no descendants to *thaakt'uultha* for her, so the Iihatisat-h people decided to erect a pole in her memory.

The *atsiqnuk* ("gifted-hands people") at Huukh decided to cooperate and erect this pole. The pole was designed and carved by six men without an overarching boss. They cooperated, with each of the six carvers producing one crest figure on the pole. The crests belonged to the family of Hakumaatkw. It was a collective project, which reflects the Nuuchaanulth value of working together. It wasn't a clan matter alone; everyone in that village agreed that this great old *hakum*, this queen, should be shown respect for who she was. Their way of doing this was to raise this memorial pole.

This spectacular pole at Huukh was taken down in the 1980s and replicated at the Provincial Museum in Victoria. Immediately after the replica was put up, it was struck by lightning and badly damaged. The old timers commiserated and said that the original pole should have been left standing, and if it fell it should have been left alone. Taking the old pole down in the first place was wrong. Interestingly, the Iihatisat-h took the damaged replica pole down and had it burned.

The other interesting pole I want to talk about is called the Captain Jack pole. It was commissioned and erected by Chief Kwaayatsapalth, at Yukwaat, circa 1920. In 1928, to mark the maiden voyage of the *SS Nora*, a freight ship serving the West Coast, this pole was given to Lord Willingdon, Governor General of Canada, who accepted the pole on behalf of the dominion. Later, a bronze plaque was put on the pole acknowledging the generosity of Kwaayatsapalth, a.k.a. Captain Jack. The governor general asked local people about protocol: "What does one do when a chief gives one a totem pole—do you cut it down and take it away?" He was told, "You always answer the gift from a chief with a return gift; that is the proper thing to do." An intermediary told Willingdon that Kwaayatsapalth wanted a power saw. Thus, on the next freight day at Yukwaat, a drag saw for Chief Kwaayatsapalth came. Willingdon left the pole at Yuukwaat. It fell recently, during a particularly nasty West Coast storm.

The same six carvers who created the pole at Huukh also carved the pole at Yuukwaat. Three of those carvers were: Mituunii Jim and Queen's Cove John (both Iihatisat-h), and Tushkaayilthim "Giant Cod Fish in the Sky" (the famous Muu-ach'at-h master carver). Another of the carvers was a Nuuchaalthat-h. It is interesting that the Huukh pole in Iihatisat-h territory and the Yuukwaat pole in Muu-ach'at-h country were both joint projects produced through the cooperation of six *atsiqnuk*. In two different tribes' territories, the same six men from at least three different tribes (I am not certain where the remaining three carvers were from) got together and cooperated on these poles.

The Nuuchaanulth practice of cooperation among tribes on the West Coast, as the creation of these two poles illustrates, reflects the complexity of our social and political relations, which are in turn based on marriage and blood ties. Often heard at our feasts and potlatches is the expression "Histakshitl tsawaatkwii" ("We come from one root," "We are one").

In 1977, Chief Buukwiila and his family raised the first Nuuchaanulth pole in our lifetime at Balaatsad on Nitinat Lake. Tsaxwasap of the Niitiinaa-at-h, Kakawinchiilth of the Tla-o-kway-aht, and Ḳi-ḳe-in of the Huupachesat-h worked cooperatively on it. The three of us from different tribes are closely related, and this formed the basis of our work.

2.5. Fort Simpson (Tsimshian), 1867. Painting by E. A. Porcher. Courtesy of Yale Collection of Western Americana, Beinecke Rare Book and Manuscript Library, DL1021842.

If Russians or Americans offered better terms for these furs, the Hudson's Bay Company lost out. By happily encouraging competition among traders of different nationalities, the Northwest Coast people continued to occupy a position of strength in a mutually beneficial relationship, some even monopolizing trade as Maquinna had done previously. For example, the Stikine Tlingit Shakes dynasty established a monopoly over interior Athabascan trappers, denying anyone else direct access to their furs and becoming as a result wealthy and powerful.

Permanent trading forts attracted residents from traditional villages who moved closer to the new sources of income. Before European arrival, ten Coast Tsimshian villages lined the lower Skeena River, Prince Rupert Harbor, and the islands of Metlakatla Pass. In 1831, the Hudson's Bay Company founded Fort Simpson on the mouth of the Nass River at a eulachon-fishing campsite. Nine groups of Tsimshian from the region (the tenth had already become extinct due to epidemics) moved their winter houses to be near the fort, thus establishing a new, very large permanent village that by 1858 had a population of approximately 2,560 people living in 140 houses (Robert Boyd 1999, 215).

This type of amalgamation created problems among these clan-based and status-conscious people. Within individual communities, hierarchies had been established over time, but in this new, variegated village, the relative ranking of chiefs from different villages was sometimes less certain. To work out these rankings, potlatches became intensely competitive and often outright hostile as chiefs attempted to outdo each other, producing more lavish ceremonies, displaying larger numbers of artwork, and distributing more and more goods. Prior to their move to Fort Simpson, the Tsimshian had had three "classes"—chiefs, commoners, and slaves—but now added a fourth, wealthy elite, which outranked the existing nobility.

To determine royalty, competitions sometimes became personal, as happened between two high-ranking Fort Simpson chiefs, Tsibasa and Legaic. At one point, Tsibasa installed a moveable staircase at the entrance to his house; when his arch rival Legaic arrived for a feast at Tsibasa's house, the staircase moved, flinging the unsuspecting chief onto the floor. This immense disgrace required that Legaic host a face-saving potlatch (Guedon 1984, 152). Legaic, for his part, indulged in dramatic stagecraft for effect: he dressed a slave up like himself and had the man publicly killed so that the community would think that the chief had died. After the slave-double had been cremated, Legaic emerged from the box containing his ashes, demonstrating phenomenal supernatural power, which enhanced his already significant social standing (Halpin 1984, 286). In keeping with the age-old practice of forming alliances through marriage, Legaic strategically married his daughter to a Hudson's Bay Company physician, and he established a monopoly on all trade with the Gitk'san who lived on the upper Skeena River.

Displays of increasingly large and more numerous monumental artwork contributed to these rivalries. The Tsimshian themselves claimed that "house front paintings were the most important; they were the real crest boards. The poles . . . were merely commemorative" (Barbeau 1929, 15). Nonetheless, many totem poles arose in Fort Simpson. In 1867 E. A. Porcher, commander of the British ship *Sparrowhawk*, painted a watercolor of the fort itself, with Hudson's Bay Company houses, stores, and trading facilities behind a twenty-foot-high stockade, and Tsimshian houses erected on both sides (fig.2.5). Porcher wrote that the houses "as regards structure, external and internal decoration are the most superior we have seen on this coast . . . the doorways and pillars are most elaborately carved with a great variety of the representations of animals [and] inanimate objects . . . of most artistic finish" (Porcher 2000, 53, 96–97). As an expression of his superior rank in the village, Legaic's totem pole was the tallest.

The most abundant stands of poles existed in Haida Gwaii, where, by 1870, as many as 500 poles stood in various villages (MacDonald 1983a). Different events spurred the development of amalgamated villages there. The Haida lived originally in numerous different villages, most of which were devastated during an especially fierce smallpox epidemic in 1862. Survivors abandoned their traditional communities and moved either to Massett in the north or to Skidegate in the middle of the archipelago. As a result, Skidegate and Massett became the two most impressive nineteenth-century totem pole villages as, in addition to existing structures and monumental carvings, houses were built and poles erected by the newcomers. These poles, which functioned as memorials to the dead, receptacles for ashes, and entryways into houses, visually communicated the status of the family near whose house they stood. As among the Tsimshian, the most eminent chiefs displayed the largest poles. One of the most striking examples of this is the Monster House of Chief Wiah in Massett (fig. 2.7). This immense structure, twenty-one meters wide and situated in the most prestigious part of the village—the center—is said to have been constructed by two thousand Haida between 1840 and 1850. To supplement its conspicuous display of grandness, the house faced a boardwalk that provided a dry and elegant path from the shore, had a towering carving for the entryway, and boasted eight other poles, more than any other house in Massett (Blackman 1981, 116–20).

Among the Kwakwa̲ka̲'wakw on Vancouver Island, Fort Rupert became the major amalgamated community during the fur trade era. In 1849, the Hudson's Bay Company established Fort Rupert at Beaver Harbour not long after coal had been found in the area. As at Fort Simpson, the presence of the Hudson's Bay Company stimulated the establishment of a new town where only summer subsistence camps had previously been. Four closely related tribes, together named the Kwakiutl by later ethnographers, had winter villages on islands north of Johnstone Strait, but possessed the land on Vancouver Island bordering Queen Charlotte Strait—which includes Beaver Harbour. In 1849, all four

2.7. Monster House of Chief Wiah, Massett (Haida), 1879. Photograph by O. C. Hastings. AMNH 334106. Courtesy the Library, American Museum of Natural History.

moved to the village of Tsaxis, adjacent to Fort Rupert, to be in closer proximity to the trading post. In the 1879 painting made by Helen Kate Woods (fig.2.8), the fort itself is on the left, the Native houses on the right. Fort Rupert became a major community that would assume great importance in the ethnographic and art history of the region. It became an early site for the escalation in potlatch rivalries, due again in part to the influx of wealth the fort provided (see Codere 1950; Drucker and Heizer 1967). However, interestingly—and as we shall point out, significantly—Fort Rupert and the nearby community of Alert Bay had few carved totem poles until the end of the nineteenth century.

2.8. Fort Rupert, 1879. Painting by Helen Kate Woods. Courtesy of Royal British Columbia Museum, BC Archives, PDP01660.

THE THUNDERBIRD POLE OF CHIEF WIXHA

BY MARJORIE HALPIN, ANTHROPOLOGIST

In 1958 Chief Wixha, Chief Gunoo, and Chief Gamalyelt of the village of Gitanyow (then called Kitwancool) on the upper Skeena River, agreed to permit the salvage of five old totem poles for preservation in museums. In return they asked that the history, territories, laws, and stories of the poles be published and taught, specifically, to future generations of students at the University of British Columbia (Duff 1957). They also asked that replicas of the poles be returned to the villages (which they were).

The Thunderbird pole of Chief Wixha—now in the Great Hall of the UBC Museum of Anthropology—is one of these old totem poles. The carver, Haesemhliyawn of the Frog-Raven clan, is known only through his work, some seven poles carved between about 1840 and 1888. Anthropologists and art historians have long considered the Thunderbird pole his finest known piece. In the subtle modeling of the facial features, the alternation of large and small figures, and the expressive posturings of the two rows of little people, the pole has been declared definitive of the carving style of the Nass and Skeena River people.

What are the little figures doing? In the 1958 *adaawk* (written family history), Chief Wixha said only that they were house carvings. Most people have thought they were "dancing." But in 1995, Greg Brass, a First Nations (Saulteaux-Ojibway) intern in the Museum, offered a new interpretation. He said that as he looked at them, "a memory flowed out of my mind," and he recalled seeing a game on a Blackfoot reservation in Montana a couple of summers before. It is a game known locally as *slahal* or *lahal*, which is widely played throughout aboriginal North America. In it, players engage in a series of stylized movements (similar to those seen on this pole), designed to trick their opponents into losing the match. Other First Nations bone-game players with whom we have shared Brass' interpretation agree with him.

Objects in museums continue to take on meanings in their new contexts. What do you think? Is it appropriate for museums to include new meanings in their labels?

Reprinted with permission from Webb 2000, 17

2.6. Thunderbird pole of Chief Wixha (Kitwancool, Gitk'san), mid- to late nineteenth century. University of British Columbia Museum of Anthropology, A50019.

NINETEENTH-CENTURY DISTRIBUTION OF TOTEM POLES

During the middle decades of the nineteenth century, totem poles increased in numbers, but only in certain places. In the late seventeenth and early eighteenth centuries, groups of Haida moved north from Graham Island, forcing out the resident Tlingit and establishing the villages of Kaigani, Koianglas, Howkan, Sukkwan, Kasaan, and Klinkwan on Prince of Wales, Dall, Sukkwan, and Long islands. By the mid-nineteenth century, these towns boasted large, well-carved, and abundant poles, similar to those of their Haida Gwaii kin.[4] Tlingit communities near these Haida towns, such as Tongass and Tuxecan, also carved and erected poles, perhaps inspired by their neighbors. Wrangell, somewhat farther to the north, also displayed a number of poles, such as those that stood before the houses of the Shakes dynasty. In the 1850s, another member of the Wrangell elite, Chief Kadashan of the Kasqaguedi clan, received a carved staff from the Massett Haida Chief Edenshaw, perhaps because some of Kadashan's ancestors had come from the Queen Charlottes before they migrated to the Stikine River area. Not long after that, Kadashan commissioned two full-size poles (one modeled on that staff), perhaps from a Haida artist (Wright 2001, 148, 151).

But the farther north one traveled, the fewer free-standing poles appeared, probably in part because the red cedar from which large poles were carved did not grow north of Wrangell.[5] Instead, house posts, such as those that stood in the celebrated Whale House of Klukwan (fig. 2.9), remained a favored means of presenting crests. The Russians made no mention of large carvings, although Captain Urey Lisiansky in 1805 did describe mortuary poles, not unlike those recorded by late-eighteenth-century travelers to the region. By 1825, when Russian explorer Otto von Kotzebue came to Sitka, the cremated dead were placed not in mortuary poles but in small grave houses (Keithahn 1963, 42). A drawing of Sitka in the 1840s by Ilia Gavrilovich Voznesenskii illustrates in the left background the pitched-roof grave houses, but any kind of carved poles are absent. Only one tall, thin mast or flagpole-like pillar alludes in any way to the prevalence of totem poles farther south. German geographers Aurel and Arthur Krause, who visited the northern Tlingit in 1881–1882, and United States Navy Lt. George Thornton Emmons, who was stationed in Alaska in the 1880s and 1890s, commented on the relative rarity of poles in contrast with the Haida and Tsimshian (Krause 1956, 89; de Laguna 1991, 194). The residents of Klukwan, one of the most conservative Tlingit communities, considered poles foreign, and thus limited their heraldic carvings to shorter posts located within houses.[6] It was only in the late nineteenth century that an eighteen-to-twenty-foot pole stood in the northern Tlingit village of Angoon.

Directly across from Haida Gwaii on the British Columbia mainland, some Tsimshian seem to have had numerous poles around the same time (or a bit later) than the Haida did. Like the northern Tlingit, however, the people to the south of Tsimshian lands also had relatively few totem poles throughout much of the nineteenth century, perhaps because the Nuxalk, Kwakwa̱ka̱'wakw, and some Nuu-chah-nulth maintained a preference for painted façades. Among the Nuxalk, house-front paintings served the same function as poles, as long as they were properly validated (McIlwraith 1942, 252); an example is the village of Komkotes, which in 1873 had several painted house façades but no poles. Although most Coast Salish did have figural mortuary sculpture and carved interior house posts (fig. 2.10), the only communities that had exterior poles were the most northerly Comox, Klahuse, and Sliammon, presumably influenced by the Kwakwa̱ka̱'wakw (Barnett 1942).[7]

ENCOUNTERS AND EVALUATIONS

Eighteenth-century travelers who described Northwest Coast art often resorted to concrete measurements, reflecting the scientific approach of the Enlightenment era. At the same time, they struggled with the aesthetic quality of those works that deviated from the familiar European canons. As we have seen, Nuu-chah-nulth

2.9. Interior of Whale House, Klukwan (Tlingit), 1895. Photograph by Winter and Pond. Alaska State Library, PCA 87-0013.

2.10. Interior house posts lined up outside house, Nanaimo (Salish), 1903. Photograph by Arthur Church. Courtesy of Royal British Columbia Museum, BC Archives, PN1479.

carving was for Alexander Walker "monstrous" and "unnatural," and to Robert Haswell "distorted," "rudely carved," and "monstrous." John Hoskins considered Haida sculpture "distorted" and "deformed." Nonetheless, several early observers took note of the artistry of Northwest Coast Native people—some were even positive in tone. For John Boit, the house façade painting at Clayoquot Sound was "by no means inelegant." Haida art in particular received praise. Joseph Ingraham found the Dadens pole "very curious," but "the whole of which . . . did great credit to the natural genius of these people." Cunneah's pole was singled out; for Bernard Magee it was "carved with a great deal of art," and for Samuel Burling, its details of mother of pearl "gave it a very beautiful appearance in comparison to what Northwest sculpture generally has."

In attempts to describe an art fully unknown by their readers, writers sometimes compared it with more familiar art. Etienne Marchand associated the various carvings populating a pole with "the ex voto suspended to the door case of the niche of a Madonna," and Robert Haswell likened the Clayoquot image of the sun to "our Country sign painters."[8] During the eighteenth and early ninteenth centuries, when Europeans and Americans engaged with different cultures, many reacted simultaneously positively and negatively toward those alien groups, an ambivalence that frequently characterized colonial encounters. This range of evaluations of material culture parallels the debates, during this period, between those for whom aboriginal people were "civilized" and those for whom they were not.[9] The category and terms of "art"—since the Renaissance, at least, a definitive component of "culture" or "civilization"—were frequently appealed to in these debates.

The first non-Native people to visit the Northwest Coast encountered a population distinctive in its artistry, skilled in commerce, and highly self-confident. The Euroamericans reacted with ambivalence to the carvings and paintings of these sophisticated groups. Unlike the situation in later years, when non-Natives claimed Northwest Coast art as their own (as in the various examples presented throughout this book), early visitors neither assimilated nor appropriated what they saw; instead, they tried, with limited success, to represent unusual forms and motifs in their written and illustrated accounts. The "primitive people" of the globe—who, in the spirit of discovery and scientific inquiry, were being described by explorers—stimulated the popular imagination of the reading public back East and across the Atlantic. At this time, totem poles were such rare items that they came to signal the exoticism of the Northwest Coast and the presumably savage artistry of its inhabitants.

During the late eighteenth century, European and American reactions toward Northwest Coast art—although sometimes confused, occasionally critical, and often replete with misunderstandings—were for the most part respectful.[10] Even the negative assessments of artistry were often accompanied by a sense of wonderment at the overall impressiveness of Northwest Coast art and architecture. As will become evident in subsequent chapters, these representations differ significantly from the deprecating comments that would be made one hundred years later by those who judged Indians as fully inferior beings incapable of any artistic sensibility. While engaging in the fur trade, European and American merchants had to respect their powerful trading partners, who assumed commercial positions of equality or even superiority. Moreover, having no interest in settling the land, these non-Natives could afford politically to appreciate the cultures they encountered, for they planned to leave when their business was finished. When settlers moved in, the attitudes of permanent colonists to Native people on the West Coast would change drastically, as we shall see in the next chapter.

Although it is often assumed that as soon as Native and non-Native people encountered each other, indigenous groups began suffering from the abuses of their visitors, this was not entirely the case on the Northwest Coast (R. Fisher 1977).[10] That is, of course, excepting the population decline caused by epidemics, which we will discuss later. On balance, until the mid-nineteenth century, Northwest Coast people gained more than they lost from their interactions with Euroamericans. The relationships between the inhabitants and outsiders were relatively peaceful, for maritime fur traders came and went, and the land-based traders settled in small numbers. Even in Alaska, where Orthodox priests worked to convert Alaskan Native people to Orthodoxy, early Russians did little to significantly alter Tlingit culture (Kan 1999). The most positive consequence was the influx of wealth that enhanced the position of certain families, transformed social structures, encouraged potlatch ceremonialism, and nurtured art production in the service of exaggerated displays of wealth and power. Chiefs like Maquinna of Yuquot, Shakes of Wrangell, and Legaic of Fort Simpson achieved unparalleled heights of power. With more refined tools, Northwest Coast art increased in scale and quantity, and great attention was paid by artists to the quality of its design. Depending on the area, monumental art flourished, providing visual and material documents of some positive results from early contact. Painted house fronts, boxes, and interior screens presented lavish two-dimensional images of crests. Intricately carved interior posts welcomed visitors into clan houses. And freestanding totem poles became larger, more complex, and more abundant.

But as the century progressed, some communities ceased erecting poles while others commenced doing so. An inventory of totem poles in 1875 would reveal their abundance among the Haida Gwaii and Kaigani Haida; a substantial number among the coast Tsimshian, Gitk'san, Nisga'a, and southern Tlingit; and some among central British Columbia groups. Ten years later, some of these communities stopped erecting poles altogether, while, in contrast, the Kwakwa̲ka̲'wakw—who had relatively few poles throughout the nineteenth century—began erecting impressive stands of poles. While the Nuu-chah-nulth never raised the number of poles that their Kwakwa̲ka̲'wakw neighbors did, in 1915 Yuquot raised its first totem pole, erected by Captain George, and, a few years later, its second, Captain Jack's (Marshall 2000, 121–22). Why did this happen? Why did poles proliferate in some areas and decrease in others? The answer once again lies in part with the ongoing colonial history of the Northwest Coast, which we explore later.

By the 1870s, newcomers had begun moving into both British Columbia and Alaska, bringing with them new ideas about how Native people should be treated. Ambivalence gave way to appropriation. Settlers took the lands and wealth of the indigenous inhabitants. Government officials endeavored to assimilate them into the mainstream by both persuasion and force. Missionaries worked hard to convert them. And, instead of respect, many of these new non-Natives treated the ancient residents of these lands with disdain, discrimination, and overt racism. In some communities, this led to a decline in pole production. In others, families erected poles in active opposition to these intruders. The history of the totem pole after the 1870s demonstrates the effects of settlement on the coast as well as the changing relationships of Native and non-Native people in British Columbia and Alaska. The next chapter will elucidate some of the shifting colonial dynamics that set the stage for these various transformations.

THE RISE AND FALL OF TOTEM POLES

THE DYNAMICS OF SETTLER COLONIALISM AND THE EMERGENCE OF ANTHROPOLOGY

Our fathers in previous years have taught us their beliefs in our superstitions, witchcraft, burning our dead, and the erection of our totem poles. In accepting this new way of life everything will be contrary to what we have been taught. Needless to say, it will not be an easy task and will require a great deal of self-discipline and what we have been taught in the Christian religion as faith in God.

—CHARLES GUNNOCK, TLINGIT MAYOR OF KAKE, ALASKA, 1912

After Mayor Charles Gunnock made this speech about his community's transition into modernity, he symbolically placed "our witchcraft, superstitions and other dark things" into a box nailed shut by a silver spike, "signifying our complete change of beliefs." Following this enthusiastic declaration of religious beliefs, residents of Kake cut down and burned their poles. For several decades, the unremitting immigration of non-Native settlers to the region had exerted considerable pressures on the local residents, some of whom may have internalized the stereotypes applied to them by the outsiders. Those pressures came from miners and fishermen who exploited resources, the government that appropriated Native land, and missionaries who insisted that converts abandon the crest system and renounce the potlatch. Those newcomers who intended to stay on the Northwest Coast treated the indigenous people in ways strikingly different from the more benevolent fur traders. In the early decades of settlement, when the newcomers were minorities in this lush land, many felt nothing but fear of and disdain for the indigenous people. This attitude, tragically, continues up to this day among certain elements of the non-Native population. However, once the settlers dominated—or, more accurately, believed they dominated—the Native residents, "the Indian" changed from a dangerous savage to an interesting remnant of a rapidly disappearing past. That is, once no longer perceived as a threat to the settlers' lives and economy, the First Nations of the Northwest Coast were amenable to aesthetic appreciation and nostalgic longing for the "vanishing primitive."

Native responses to Northwest Coast colonization varied from group to group and from the mid-nineteenth century, when settlers began moving first into British Columbia and then into coastal southeast Alaska, until the early decades of the twentieth, when non-Natives could enjoy a comfortable majority status. For some, like the community of Kake, accepting new values entailed destroying clan paraphernalia and embracing the misguided evangelical dictate that totem poles were connected with ancestor worship, witchcraft, and general heathenism. In other communities, such as Massett and Skidegate on Haida Gwaii, totem pole carving gradually ceased in response to population decline and what the Haida considered new opportunities for prosperity by accepting white ways. Others, including the Kwakwa̲ka̲'wakw, actually increased their totem pole production during these years, in part as a reaction to their own resettlement and in part as a challenge to colonial authority.

By the last decades of the nineteenth century, it appeared, from the outside, that most Northwest Coast cultures were disappearing. More and more families lived in single-family homes instead of communal houses (sometimes forced by government agents to do so). Virtually everyone wore clothes of store-bought materials and much art production decreased—indicators that Natives had succumbed to the forces of "civilization." Some sympathetic non-Natives became increasingly interested in salvaging whatever elements of Northwest Coast culture they could in order to preserve for future generations information about aboriginal peoples before the advent of Europeans. Partly in response to this desire, on the coast and in the whole colonial world, the discipline of anthropology developed in the late nineteenth century to systematically acquire and scientifically analyze information on aboriginal people. It would take generations before anthropologists as well as the public realized something that the Northwest Coast Native people knew all along: their cultures had not disappeared. Instead, they had transformed to accommodate their new circumstances.

The Northwest Coast offered a fertile region for anthropological investigation. The lavish late-nineteenth-century potlatches and masked dances of the Kwakwa̲ka̲'wakw, the regional focus on wealth and status, and, of course, the enigmatic totem pole presented fascinating problems to the scientist of culture. Now, instead of simply describing, sometimes with awe, the tall monuments, as earlier traders had done, anthropologists and natural historians attempted to document and reconstruct their history, asking where totem poles came from, how they evolved, and what they meant.

BRITISH COLUMBIA

Settlement, like the fur trade, greatly affected totem pole history. The lives of British Columbia's Native people began to change rapidly, and for the worse, after 1849, when the British Crown granted the Hudson's Bay Company a royal charter for the colony of Vancouver Island. Until then, interest in British Columbia had been purely economic, but the mercantile government wanted to encourage settlement and so in 1851 appointed James Douglas, chief factor of the company, as governor of Vancouver Island. The next year, discovery of gold brought non-Natives to Haida Gwaii. Ever-increasing numbers of newcomers began moving onto both Vancouver Island and the mainland. By 1858, the mainland was chartered as the colony of British Columbia, and Douglas became its governor as well.

A longtime resident of the region during the fur trade years, Douglas was more sympathetic to its Native residents than most colonists and attempted to treat them fairly, especially in response to settlers' demand for Native lands. Thus Douglas negotiated a few limited treaties with some Salish and Kwakwa̲ka̲'wakw groups, in which village sites and other land became Native reserves while the balance of land became property of the Crown in perpetuity. But these were the only treaties signed by coastal people, and in the two colonies of Vancouver Island and British Columbia, official policy held that Native title to land simply did not exist, in contrast to long-held Canadian and U. S. policies. Except for Douglas and his supporters, the settlers of this region believed it unnecessary to sign treaties with the region's First Nations. This lack of legally binding agreements would become extremely important in later years.[1]

In 1881, British Columbia's First Nations population was approximately 26,000, and that of the settlers (most of whom lived on lower Vancouver Island and the southern mainland) 24,000. In 1891, the indigenous population was slightly less than the previous decade, but the number of settlers had increased to 70,000. By 1901, British Columbia had a total population of 178,657, of which only 24,000 were Native people (R. Fisher 1977, 202). Settler attitudes to the locals were almost from the start suffused with a racism we find appalling today. Fort Victoria, founded in 1843, became a town of newcomers, frightened by the local Salish as well as the northern groups such as the Haida and Tsimshian who canoed from the north annually to trade or to raid other Native villages. These settlers began to clamor for more protection from, if not expulsion of, the "savages" from their "civilized" community. A letter to the *British Colonist* in 1859 stridently asked, "How much longer are we to be inflicted with the intolerable nuisance of having hundreds of hideous, half-naked, drunken savages in our midst . . . teeming. . . . reeling about and shouting" (R. Fisher 1977, 114). In addition to the treatment of First Nations as inferior cultures, in the 1870s commercial fishing and canneries began appropriating aboriginal fishing territories, thus depriving residents of their traditional means of subsistence.

Government officials who succeeded Douglas were both ignorant of Native culture and at best condescending toward Native people. They worked on behalf of the settlers who detested the indigenous people, and of the missionaries who believed submission to Christianity and rejection of traditional ways would improve these "savages" and transform them into responsible, productive people. When British Columbia and Vancouver Island (the two united into a single colony in 1866) joined the Confederation of Canada in 1871, official responsibility for Native people shifted from local authorities to Ottawa. A contentious issue between Ottawa and British Columbia, which would remain problematic for years, was the proper amount of land to be allocated Native families for reserves. Official Canadian policy prescribed 160 acres per family, but Ottawa was willing to allocate reserves of 80 acres for British Columbian Native people. Provincial officials thought 20 acres per family sufficient. This anomalous policy would not be resolved for decades and, like the general lack of treaties on the coast, would have repercussions until the present.

While specific issues of the British Columbia First Nations were being deliberated, national policy was being formulated. Shortly after 1867, when the British parliament created the nation of Canada, the new legislature in Ottawa passed the Act to Encourage the Gradual Civilization of Indian Tribes in this Province, and to Amend the Laws Relating to Indians, which established the dominion government's rights over indigenous peoples and their lives, initiating the formal policy of assimilation. Merchants and missionaries petitioned the federal government to intervene in the rampant ceremonialism in British Columbia. As traditional activities were considered heathen impediments to progress, the 1884 Indian Advancement Act outlawed potlatches and related ceremonies. It included the following clause: "Every Indian or other person who engages in or assists in celebrating the Indian festival known as the 'Potlatch' or the Indian dance known as the 'Tamanawas' is guilty of a misdemeanor and shall be liable to imprisonment." In other words, in addition to taking their lands, reducing their ability to maintain a subsistence economy, and endorsing racist attitudes, the newcomers outlawed the ceremonies central to Native social, political, and cultural organization. And since totem poles were inseparable from the potlatches that validated them, poles became less and less frequently erected in most communities.

The main exceptions to this rule were the Kwakwa̱ka̱'wakw, who soon gained a reputation among missionaries and Indian agents as uncooperative with assimilationist endeavors, and whom Canadian officials designated "the Incorrigible Kwakiutl." Until 1870, small Cormorant Island on the northeast of Vancouver Island had been uninhabited but in the control of the 'Na̱mgis band. When some entrepreneurs opened up a salmon saltery there, the 'Na̱mgis moved from their traditional site to the new village of Alert Bay, constructing large plank houses that faced the curving shoreline. At first, no carved poles stood there; in 1873, the only vertical element was a flagpole with a flag and upside-down "copper," a distinctively shaped ceremonial shield of pounded copper, that rose from the gable of a house façade painted with a whale and Thunderbird.[2] In 1881, one house was surmounted by a flock of wooden birds on posts, and one of the flagpole-like posts had a figure on top (fig. 3.1). In 1898, the handful of flagpoles and bird-mounted poles paled near the

(opposite, upper)

3.1. Alert Bay (Kwakwa̱ka̱'wakw), 1881. National Anthropological Archives, Smithsonian Institution, 38582D.

(opposite, lower)

3.2. Alert Bay (Kwakwa̱ka̱'wakw), 1898. Photograph by Harlan Smith. Courtesy the Library, American Museum of Natural History, 411790.

INDIAN VILLAGE, ALERT BAY.

3.3. Alert Bay (Kwakwa̲ka̲'wakw), 1910. Courtesy of Royal British Columbia Museum, BC Archives, E-04633 47366.

highly ornate Wakas (or Wakius) pole, which featured a large raven through whose open beak one could enter the house (fig. 3.2). By the early twentieth century, Alert Bay, now boasting a boardwalk, was a celebration of brightly painted and dynamic poles, many with projecting elements like bird beaks and extended wings (fig. 3.3). As the town became a center of colonial governance (home to a customs office, courthouse, Royal Canadian Mounted Police outpost, hospital, and residential school), it displaced Fort Rupert—the site of earlier fur trade activity—as a hub for Kwakwa̲ka̲'wakw cultural fluorescence. This flamboyant proliferation of poles among the Kwakwa̲ka̲'wakw stands in stark contrast to their drastic rejection by other communities. Instead of acquiescing to white laws, the Kwakwa̲ka̲'wakw stubbornly maintained many traditions, challenging officials with speeches stating "a strict law bids us dance," and hosting more and more lavish potlatches, replete with increasingly complex, dramatic, and dynamic art (see Jonaitis 1991). Images of potlatches at Alert Bay, with piles of blankets outside houses waiting to be distributed, suggest that the presence of totem poles in these early twentieth-century communities stood as statements of cultural survival and territorial sovereignty.

ALASKA

Although the Russians located their colonial capital at St. Michael near Sitka, it would be wrong to think that they truly settled in Alaska, for at any one time, probably no more than 500 Russians and 1200 Creoles (of mixed Russian-Native descent) resided in the entire territory. Before and after the transfer of Alaska from the Russians to the Americans, Orthodox missionaries treated Alaskan Native cultures largely with respect, sometimes even incorporating into their Catholic rituals elements of Native ceremonies (see Kan 1999).

On October 18, 1867, the Russian flag was lowered and the American one raised, transforming the Tlingit (and all other Alaska Native people) into wards of the

THE WAKAS POLE

BY ANDREA LAFORET, ANTHROPOLOGIST

In the early 1890s Wakas, a high-ranking person of Awik'inuxw and 'Namgis descent, commissioned a pole to be carved for the entrance to his house in Alert Bay. Modeled on a speaker's staff that had been in Wakas's family for generations, the figures on the pole recalled the journey of three brothers to the home of Baxbaxwalanuxsiwae, Man-Eater-at-the-North-End-of-the-World, a journey that restored their sister to her family, brought lost relatives back to the village, saw Baxbaxwalanuxsiwae lured to his death, and brought the treasures of the winter dance to Wakas's ancestors.

During its life the Wakas pole has stood in three different communities and has undergone several transformations. A combination of oral and recorded histories as well as photographic evidence allows us to reconstruct this process to some degree.

When the Ma'amtagila carver Yuxwayu first carved the pole, the mouth of the bottom figure, Baxbaxwalanuxsiwae, formed the entrance to the house. Wakas's house was a large multi-family dwelling constructed of thick, hand-split planks, but the pole stood in the centre of a newly made white house front of narrow milled boards. By the late 1890s another carver, Dick Price, had made a beak with a complex painting for the bottom figure. Although the beak opened, a second door was cut into the house front beside the pole. By September 1900, the painted wings and tail feathers of a raven stretched across the house front, complementing the beak and completing the lower figure of the pole in an entirely new way. With the body of the raven now on the house front, the beak was painted a dark colour, with a single face on the underside. In the legendary house of Baxbaxwalanuxsiwae the body of the raven was painted on the front of the house of Raven-at-the-North-End-of-the-World.

Wakas's pole stood in Alert Bay until the 1920s, when it was sold, transported to Vancouver, and re-erected in Stanley Park to be part of an assemblage of totem poles from different villages. In 1966, at the request of the Vancouver Parks Board, Wakas's great-nephew, Doug Cranmer, repainted the pole and carved a new thunderbird for the top figure, a new beak for the *huxwhukw* [a supernatural bird], and a new beak for the raven figure at the bottom. Twenty years later, the pole was again in need of repair. In 1986, the Vancouver Parks Board and the Canadian Museum of Civilization agreed to an exchange that brought a new-generation Wakas pole to Stanley Park and took Wakas's original pole to the museum for restoration and display. Doug Cranmer carved the new-generation pole, recreating the figures of the old pole, but with the original complex painting reinterpreted by the artist and restored to the lower beak. The original pole, refurbished again by Doug Cranmer and Bruce Alfred, with a new head for the thunderbird and a new beak, now stands in front of a facsimile of the Wakas house in the museum's Grand Hall.

3.4. Wakas house with frontal pole, Alert Bay (Kwakwaka'wakw), 1910. Courtesy the Library, American Museum of Natural History, 46014.

federal government, as was the United States' policy. In the early years of American control, life for settlers was difficult; barely 100 settlers lived in Sitka in the mid-1870s, and even by the 1880s, less than 500 non-Native people lived in the region. At first, the American occupation was managed by the army and then the navy, resulting in a chaotic and intermittent imposition of law and order as well as a plummeting economy. During the Russian days, it had been illegal to sell spirits to Native people, but now the Tlingit learned how to construct stills and distill alcohol, and moonshine became part of Tlingit culture.

According to the 1867 Treaty of Cession, "The uncivilized tribes will be subject to such laws and regulations as the United States may, from time to time, adopt in regard to the aboriginal tribes in that country" (Hinckley 1996, 88). The Tlingit had a reputation for being aggressive and confrontational, and General Jefferson Davis, military commander for the District of Alaska, received orders to "exercise the most careful vigilance as these Natives are known to be both warlike and treacherous" (Hinckley 1996, 69). The military certainly took those warnings to heart. In 1868, after some residents of Kake killed two white men in retaliation for an earlier killing of a Kake resident by the army, the navy sailed up to Kuiu Island and burned down virtually all the Tlingit homes. Then, in 1882, the navy destroyed Angoon in retaliation for Tlingit demands for payment following the death of an important Tlingit killed when a harpoon gun exploded.

Whatever peace and stability existed in the newly purchased region further deteriorated when in 1880, Joe Juneau and Richard Harris found gold in Auk territory, precipitating the first Alaska gold rush and the booming of Juneau. Soon entrepreneurs founded salmon canneries and salteries in various locations to take advantage of the abundant fish runs. In this virtually lawless territory, Native land was overrun and subsistence activities became increasingly difficult. Into this chaos came a Presbyterian missionary, Sheldon Jackson, an intensely focused man devoted to the conversion and welfare of Alaska Native people. Jackson found the situation in Alaska intolerable, especially for the indigenous residents, and petitioned Congress to impose civil rather than military authority. Finally, in 1884, the U.S. government passed the Organic Act that made Alaska subject to the laws of Oregon (the closest state at that time), with a governor, district judge, attorney, four deputy marshals, and four U.S. commissioners. The act also addressed indigenous Alaskans who were not placed upon reservations, as occurred elsewhere in the country; instead, the act stipulated that "Indians or other persons in said district were not to be disturbed in the possession of any lands actually in their use of occupation or now claimed by them" (quoted in Hinckley 1996, 195). Unfortunately for the Tlingit, the interpretation of "lands actually in their use" was quite narrow, and the act left vast tracts of Native land open for exploitation by salmon processors and timber companies. Miners in particular found this interpretation most useful when claiming title to lands they desired. English-only policies were imposed in schools in the 1880s and, as was the case in Canada, assimilation became formal policy. Unlike their neighbor to the south, Alaska never formally criminalized the potlatch, but non-Natives encouraged ad hoc potlatch bans.

Like so many other Native groups, the Tlingit figured out ways to apparently accommodate the newcomers while still maintaining important traditions. Like the wealthier white people, some elite Tlingit constructed large houses that facilitated new ways of communicating noble rank. For example, around 1880, Chief Kadashan tore down his plank house in Wrangell and replaced it with a two-story Queen Anne–style house with lumber he received from the founder of the local sawmill in exchange for some land (figs. 3.5 and 3.6).[3] In 1887, Governor A. P. Swineford commented, "As fast as they can accumulate the means they tear down their old houses and build new ones of more modern style . . . [Chief Kadashan's house] was the finest and most pretentious private residence . . . in the Territory" (Hinckley 1996, 256). Kadashan's old poles now stood before this new house, a comfortable, intercultural juxtaposition of two quite different expressions of status—his carved pole had been inspired by a Haida carving,

3.5. Chief Kadashan house, Wrangell (Tlingit), 1868. Photograph by Muybridge. University of California, Berkeley. Bancroft Library,1971.055:484.

3.6. Chief Kadashan house, Wrangell (Tlingit), 1895. Photograph by Winter and Pond. Alaska State Library, P87-0120.

his home inspired by white settlers. Chief Kadashan apparently had no problem with borrowing concepts that worked within the Tlingit system.

DISEASE AND THE TRANSFORMATION OF NORTHWEST COAST CULTURES

Before Canadians and Americans began to seize Native land and attempt to control their lives—indeed, even before many physical encounters with non-Natives—Northwest Coast people had experienced the single most devastating consequence of the colonial encounter: disease. The demographic history of the Northwest Coast tells a tragic story in which wave after wave of diseases penetrated the region, killing large numbers of Native people. In the 1770s, before many on the Northwest Coast had actually met their first non-Native, a smallpox epidemic from the south claimed 60,000 lives up and down the coast. Venereal diseases and tuberculosis were introduced early in the encounter and remained problematic throughout the nineteenth century. Another major smallpox epidemic began among the Tlingit in 1835 and continued in various coastal locales until 1838. A serious epidemic of measles affected all groups in 1847 and 1848. Precipitous population decline was followed by periods of relative stability; only by the 1870s did declines became more gradual (Robert Boyd 1999).

In late winter 1862, an infected passenger on a ship from San Francisco landed in Victoria, bringing into the Northwest Coast region its most disastrous smallpox epidemic yet. The close quarters of the "Northerner's Encampment," where Tlingit, Haida, Tsimshian, Heiltsuk and Kwakwa̱ka̱'wakw traders stayed when in Victoria, facilitated the disease's spread throughout the Native population. Large numbers of people began to die. Local non-Native residents, already hostile to the masses of northern coastal Natives who descended annually upon their city, took quick advantage of this opportunity. City officials argued that to protect Victoria, those traders had to be evacuated immediately. When they moved to encampments considered insufficiently distant from Victoria, officials sent British gunboats in a show of force. Canoes full of smallpox-infected Native peoples paddled north, leaving their dead and dying on beaches, infecting each community with which they came in contact. This appalling expulsion was aggravated by the existence of a smallpox vaccine that was administered only to some individuals, often by missionaries.

An estimated 184,000 people lived along the coast from Yakutat Bay to northern California in the years immediately preceding contact, making this among the most densely populated nonagricultural regions in the world. By 1880, 37,000 Native peoples remained. Every community experienced considerable mortality over the years of disease outbreaks, yet some fared worse than others. The Tlingit, for example, experienced a 76 percent decline from approximately 48,000 to 11,000, and the Tsimshian a 74 percent decline, from 15,000 to 4,000. From a precontact population estimate of 13,000, the Kwakwa̱ka̱'wakw numbered only 2,000 by the turn of the century (Robert Boyd 1999, 309–21).

The loss of life was especially staggering among the Haida, whose precontact population estimate was 14,200, while a postepidemic census numbered only 1,598, a loss of 83 percent. As was mentioned in the previous chapter, after the 1862 smallpox epidemic, entire villages became ghost towns, as the few remaining survivors moved to the two largest communities on Haida Gwaii, Massett, and Skidegate. Demographer Robert Boyd has suggested that these epidemics contributed to the nineteenth-century proliferation of totem poles, for as individuals died, their families erected mortuaries and memorials. Boyd (1999, 222) proposes that "if a meaningful sample of North Coast totems could be accurately dated, it seems likely that their times of construction would cluster in two periods, 1836–46 and 1862–72," the two periods of the most devastating epidemics. For a few decades, the numbers of totem poles grew, and the two towns became celebrated for their monuments, many of which might well have been erected for the massive numbers of recently dead. This compounded the effect, mentioned in chapter 2, of amalgamating previously disparate systems of status display.

One chapter in the totem pole story ends with this rapid and complete decline of Haida monuments. But appearances can be deceptive, because some traditions continued among the Haida, albeit in considerably altered form. In response to missionary pressure, the Haida modified their funerary rites to be more compatible with the newcomers' values. Instead of carving and erecting memorial and mortuary poles, the Haida ritually paid their moiety opposites to carve crests onto tombstones and to perform Christian funeral rituals.[4] The same thing occurred on other parts of the coast as well. Northwest Coast societies would simply not be destroyed—they adapted and thus survived.

PHOTOGRAPHS: MAKING THE INVISIBLE VISIBLE (AND VICE VERSA)

The quintessential representational technology of modernity is the photograph. Once photography was invented, colonized lands and people became popular subjects for its technological gaze. Colonizers frequently used photographs to portray, with supposed unmediated truth and scientific objectivity, the lands and peoples under their control. These photos supplemented the record-keeping visual depictions that were made on eighteenth- and nineteenth-century voyages of exploration, which together constitute valuable records of where poles stood in the first century of contact. In fact, much of what we know about nineteenth- and early twentieth-century totem poles is based on photographs (see appendix C for a list of early images of poles as well as major photographic expeditions).

Around the turn of the twentieth century, photographs of Native people served various purposes: for the colonial government they were records of dominions; for anthropologists they represented scientific records of distinct cultures; for tourists they became post-trip memory enhancers; and for romantics they served as time-effacing indicators of archaism. Although there is sometimes an unexamined faith that photographs are indexical reproductions of reality, in fact they filter, modify, and sometimes even alter historic truth. As the camera shapes the image it captures, framing the subject, highlighting what is thought to matter, hiding that which does not, or eliminating that which may interfere with the intended message, each image invokes a new reality. Ethnographic photographs represented the colonial's gaze upon the colonized in that they expressed the attitudes of settlers and scientists toward the aboriginal inhabitants of the land. Thus they rendered visible what people thought about the subjects—albeit in a frequently subtle and usually unconscious fashion.[5]

Some photographs reinforced the power of colonial authority by recording official expeditions. Soon after British Columbia became a province, government agents, accompanied by professional photographers, began conducting "inspection tours" of villages. Israel Wood Powell, British Columbia's first Indian commissioner and regional history aficionado—a man who knew little about the province's Native people before being appointed commissioner, and never learned much during his tenure—toured coastal villages throughout the 1870s and 1880s. Reinforcing the history that ultimately led to settlement of the Northwest Coast, Powell retraced whenever possible the great navigational voyages of the late eighteenth and early nineteenth century, and sometimes even ordered photographs of the same views sketched by artists on those voyages (A. Thomas 1981–82, 69). He also instructed his photographers to show him standing among those he considered his Native wards.

In one striking shot taken by O. C. Hastings in 1879 (see fig. 2.7), Powell stands before a house in Massett. A broad central walkway brings one's eye to the group of Haida and non-Native people standing and sitting before this immense house with its enormous entrance pole. Close to the center—the position of high rank among the Haida—stands the Indian commissioner himself, the colonial official surrounded by the colonized. It was perhaps not by accident that Powell chose this particular house for his portrait, as the Monster House, by far the largest in the village, was erected by a chief who utilized architecture and art to communicate his great power and prestige (see chapter 2). By positioning himself before such a structure, Powell seems

CLAQ°UNS: THE PEACE OFFERING

BY LYLE WILSON, HAISLA ARTIST

Totem poles are remarkable, but their background is also important. The essence of the Claq°uns totem poles' story concerns three young Haida men who threw a supernatural frog into a fire. As a result they were cursed to die in succession, and their village and people to perish by fire with only a small girl to tell the tale. A Haida rescuer adapted and passed down this account until it became a much-valued possession. The transmission of the Haida Claq°uns story, rights, and privileges to the Haisla people adds depth to its legacy.

In that early era, the Haisla village was not situated on the saltwater channel, but rather a mile up the Kitimat River and off to one side on a tributary slough's banks. At that time the relationship between the Haida and the Haisla was violent and bloody.

The raiding warfare of that era has been romanticized and glorified by some people. The reality was that those raids were a brutal and dirty business. The favored tactic was a dawn sneak attack while people slept deeply. Men, women, and children were killed, maimed, or taken as slaves. Food and ceremonial regalia were stolen, and canoes and bighouses damaged and destroyed. Anyone lucky enough to survive faced further hardship due to the northern weather and isolation. Such "warfare" deserves neither romanticism nor glory but rather acknowledgement of that era's cowardly brutality.

Five or six Haida raids forced the Haisla people to take defensive measures. Although the first attack was devastating—many Haisla were killed—successive raids became more costly for the raiders. In one instance, while the Haisla and Haida were fighting, a young Haisla boy—about ten years old—heard tapping noises from a bighouse. Peering through a knothole he could see a raider tapping a wooden staff on the floorboards and listening intently. The Haida raider was trying to find eulachon oil buried beneath the floorboards. Picking up a fallen bow and arrow, the lad shot the arrow through the knothole. The arrow struck the man, and when he fell, the arrow was driven through his body, killing him. When the raiders realized that he was dead, they broke off the fighting and retreated with the man's body, singing a dirge, "Ha jah dee, Ha jah dee!"

The boy had killed a Haida chief and later took that raider's name as a war trophy.

The culmination of the Haisla defensive measures involved lookouts and ropes. The lookouts were posted on a hill where they could see the river's entrance. In one account, the rope was put across the swiftly flowing river. The raiders' canoes hit the rope, capsized, and were swept under a log jam in the river. A second account has the forewarned Haisla defenders stretching ropes across and sinking them in the slough. The defenders hid on both sides of the bank. As the Haida canoes passed over the ropes, they were pulled upwards, to capsize the canoes. The raiders floundered in the water and, with one exception, the Haida were mercilessly killed. To deter future raids, the lone man spared was given a canoe and allowed to go home to relay a warning—presumably the ancient Haisla law of retribution: Blood for blood, twice over!

As a result, a Skidegate Haida chief named Gitx°wun sent two braves, Ginayan and Doemeech—to make a peace offer to the Haisla people. Among many things, his name Gitx°wun, the name and the story of the Claq°uns, and a carved totem pole were offered to and accepted by the Haisla Eagle chief, Son.axed. This transfer of rights and privileges symbolized the peace pact.

Long afterwards, approximately in the mid-1800s, the successor of the original Son.axed had another Claq°uns pole carved. Keeping that date in mind, the peace pact between the Haida and Haisla people would have taken place in the later 1700s to early 1800s.

Whether the Haisla who carved the second Claq°uns pole followed the Haida carving style is doubtful, but presumably the original format was followed by Noah, who carved the frog; Laadac, who carved the halibut; and Gups Nugwilk, who carved the little man on top. Although both totem poles no longer exist, their history is known and a photograph of the last pole was found, and that led to another version being carved by Robert Steward in the late 1960s. This Claq°uns totem pole still stands outside the village gymnasium—ironically the site of modern basketball "wars."

3.7. Claqᵒuns totem pole, Kitamaat (Haisla), ca. 1910. Courtesy of Royal British Columbia Museum, BC Archives, PN2492.

to be appropriating a Native expression of dominance to express his own governmental authority.

Both official photographers and entrepreneurs traveled to Northwest Coast communities to record totem poles. Skidegate and Massett in particular became favorite subjects of photographers who traveled the region. George Mercer Dawson took an image of Skidegate (fig. 3.8) when he visited the Queen Charlottes in 1878 on a Canadian Geological Survey expedition, whose main purpose was to identify potential mineral resources. This, the earliest image of that village, has become perhaps the single most-well-known photograph of nineteenth-century totem poles and cedar plank houses. Exquisitely carved poles of varying heights stand attached to, as well as before and behind, a long, gracefully curving line of houses. Canoes line the beach, facing the water, suggesting a vibrant community intimately connected to the sea. It is a monumental image, dignified and timeless, an image that has been reproduced over and over again, becoming in the process one of the iconic images of "the Village with Totem Poles"—the proverbial "forest of poles"—standing in not only for the Haida at this time but for the whole Northwest Coast, for all time.

3.8. Skidegate (Haida), 1878. Photograph by George Mercer Dawson. Canadian Museum of Civilization, 253.

Ironically, considering how deeply impressive this and other contemporaneous photographs are, Dawson's image depicts a moment right before totem pole carving ceased entirely among the Haida. By the century's end they had abandoned their monuments, in part because they embraced a Christianity that discouraged, and even sometimes forbade, traditional practices. For example, Aurel Krause, who visited the Northwest Coast in 1881–1882, commented about Haida Gwaii that "at present a new pole is very rarely erected, and the numerous fallen and rotten columns in abandoned or utterly deserted villages are mute evidence of the rapid downfall of a noteworthy and remarkable culture" (Krause 1956, 208–9).

Thus these images represent selective truths, denying the epidemics that forced the Haida to emigrate into these amalgamated villages, ignoring the attitudes of the missionaries toward these monuments, and overlooking the laws that made ceremonies associated with pole raising illegal. The realities of death, disease, discrimination, and social ills have no place in the absolute perfection of these images. They put their viewers back in time, stilling for eternity one moment, bringing the past fully into the present, and obliterating any history that occurred before or after the image was taken. The frequent reproduction of the most striking images of Massett and Skidegate can lead

CONVERSATION ON THE TOTEM POLE BURIAL GROUND

BY VICKIE JENSEN, AUTHOR AND PHOTOGRAPHER, WITH NORMAN TAIT, NISGA'A ARTIST

3.9. Vickie Jensen and Norman Tait 2000. Photograph courtesy of Vicki Jensen.

For nearly two decades I've shot hundreds, if not thousands, of photographs of Norman Tait and his crews. I've also tape-recorded hours of their commentary about carving totem poles. Much of this documentary work became the heart of *Where the People Gather: Carving a Totem Pole* (later reissued in paperback as *Totem Pole Carving*).

Some of our conversations didn't go into the book, but they certainly etched themselves in my mind. I particularly remember Norman saying that the Nisga'a did not allow totem poles to fall down—rather, that when they became too old to prop up anymore, the poles were hauled away to a kind of totem pole burial ground.

I've thought about that statement often because in all the years I've worked with carvers from other places, I've never heard of anything similar. Recently, I asked Norman if he would tell me more. This is our conversation.

Vickie: Norman, I've never heard of any group doing this, taking totem poles down before they rotted and then taking them to a totem pole graveyard.

Norman: Me either. But then, we give a totem pole a name when it's raised. I don't know of others who do that.

V: You've said before that totem poles are storytellers, they're the teachers.

N: Yes. And according to our tradition, when the pole is getting old, maybe 75 to 100 years, you don't let it fall down. You prop it up. And when you can't do that anymore, you bring it down. It's an old man or an old woman. It has a name.

In earlier times, when the last chief responsible for the totem pole was gone and the pole was old, it was time to take it down. Honored guests would take the pole down. They gave a feast, and there would be the same ceremony as when it had gone up. Then they would walk it to the Nass River, and a canoe would take it. When they got to a certain spot, they would carry it again or drag it up as far as they could and leave it there. Then the pole was covered with lots of cedar branches. By the time those branches rotted and turned to mush, you couldn't recognize the totem pole anymore. No one was supposed to go back up there.

V: How is it different when you take a pole down?

N: Well, you're not giving it a name. You're calling out a name. And you're calling out the nephews' names. It's the same today when someone dies. The nephews are the ones responsible for burying their uncle. That's how it was with the totem pole.

V: Where did they take the poles?

N: There was a whole graveyard between Greenville and Kincolith. My grandfather Rufus Watts brought me there once. I was only twenty-five, maybe twenty-seven, at the time. I was commercial fishing, not carving yet.

V: That would have been almost thirty years ago?

N: Yeah. I had gone to Kincolith to visit my aunties. My grandfather was eager to show me this place. But he didn't want me to tell them what we were doing. They were Wolf; he was Eagle. My grandfather said to tell them we were just going fishing. He wanted me to see it.

V: What did that place look like?

N: All moss, all moss. Just long lumps of moss. It was eerie. The place was very guarded, like a graveyard. It felt like you were reaching back 500 years. I asked my grandfather if he was sure he wanted me to go there. He said, "The pole is your grandparent."

V: Could you recognize anything on the totem poles?

N: The cedar is already very old; there's not much left once the moss grows on it. My grandfather told me, "If you peel back the moss, put it back. It's like opening a coffin. You close it again." He only took me to his heritage poles. Some of the other poles were taken and hidden near their uncles' places. We couldn't go to those. That wouldn't be right.

V: Did you look under the moss?

N: I told him I wanted to see one of the poles. He took me to one I could look at. He wouldn't let me look at any others. I did peel back the moss. There's not much to see. The moss grows into the cedar, so when you pull it back, about half an inch of the rotting wood comes off. Most people wouldn't recognize anything. You'd have to know what you're looking for.

V: Any other comments about the Nisga'a taking their old poles down?

N: The totem pole goes back to the forest, back to the land. Just like us. We are born of the land. We believe it was the trees that sustained us, so when people died, they were put into a box and it was raised up into the trees. The cycle was complete. The same was true of our totem poles.

My grandfather wanted me to see all this. But he said, "Keep it quiet." Seeing that place is what sparked me to carve.

the unsuspecting viewer to believe that many villages throughout the coast, not just those two amalgamated Haida communities, looked like this.

ALONG CAME THE ANTHROPOLOGISTS: RECONSTRUCTIONS OF TOTEM POLE HISTORY

For the casual observer, the totem pole is a sculpture—maybe exotic, certainly impressive, absolutely worth a photograph. But for the anthropologist, the totem pole poses questions fundamental to the discipline. From its very beginning, academic anthropology has struggled with the puzzling questions inevitably raised during eras of exploration and colonization: Why are cultures so different and what do these differences suggest about human history? Students of the Northwest Coast speculated on some of the more striking aspects of the region—potlatches, social hierarchy, shamanism, and, of course, totem poles. Though each of the scholars surveyed below agreed about the need to reconstruct specific, historical processes among particular cultures, their theories on totem poles were also inflected by their own unique intellectual and political proclivities.

Franz Boas, a German-Jewish immigrant often called the "father of American anthropology," was the first to investigate systematically the origin, development, and diffusion of totem poles as part of his larger reconstruction of Northwest Coast cultural history. A passionate, left-leaning progressive, Boas devoted much of his life to promoting the equality of races, a battle that encountered formidable resistance in the climate of Victorian evolutionary ethnology. Trained as a physicist, he became interested in ethnography when he spent 1883–1884 on Baffin Island among the Inuit researching adaptation to the environment. This experience made him realize that Native people were not the "inferior savages" of popular imagination but were as intelligent and capable as any other group; the main difference between the Inuit and Euroamericans was the whole range of values, beliefs, and customs shared by each group—in other words, their culture. This was, at the time, a remarkable and paradigm-shifting perspective.[6]

Prior to Boas's academic intervention, cultural differences were usually explained as manifestations of differential physical and mental development, with dark-skinned people standing lower on the evolutionary ladder than the presumably more advanced light-skinned people. It was assumed that the rungs of that ladder determined the group's culture, that everyone at the same stage of cultural development would share similar technologies, myths, social organization, kinship systems, art, etc. To contravene this racialist theory, Boas explained the presence of cultural elements among groups as consequences of historical processes: at some point, certain groups invented elements of culture that then diffused over time and space to other groups, who accepted some elements (adapting them to local systems) while rejecting others.

Although Boas's first field experience was with the Inuit, he became smitten by the Northwest Coast when, in 1885, he helped Adolf Bastian catalogue a shipment of material from British Columbia and the Arctic at Berlin's Royal Ethnology Museum. The next year, he met a troupe of Nuxalk brought to Europe during 1886 by Adrian and Fillip Jacobsen to perform ceremonial dances with masks, decorated garments, and musical instruments. The splendid Northwest Coast material culture at the museum and the fascinating ceremonies of the Nuxalk inspired in Boas a lifelong commitment to Northwest Coast studies. He hoped to use the rich cultural life of the groups to reconstruct the region's developmental history by tracking similar occurrences of myths, songs, dances, and decorated objects across geographic and linguistic zones.

When Boas finally visited coastal British Columbia in 1886, he found many of the Native groups highly acculturated and thus uninteresting for his purposes.[7] However, the Kwakwa̲ka̲'wakw had by then garnered a reputation for serious resistance to colonialist intrusions, and Boas quickly directed much of his professional activity toward them. While curator at the American Museum of Natural History in New York City from 1895 to 1905, Boas obtained data and artifacts with the help of George Hunt, a half-Tlingit, half-Eurocanadian raised at Fort Rupert as a Kwakwa̲ka̲'wakw. During his almost half-century study of Kwakwa̲ka̲'wakw culture, Boas produced thousands of pages of ethnographic documentation, orchestrated the collection of Northwest Coast artifacts, and formed a lasting relationship with Hunt (see Jonaitis 1988; Jacknis 2002).

It is perhaps inevitable that anthropologists devoted to a particular culture credit it with great importance and originality, as was the case when Boas began to speculate on the history of totem poles. In 1888, shortly after his first visit to Vancouver Island, Boas stated:

> I am inclined to believe that another custom of the North West Americans besides their dances originated among the Kwakiutl. I mean the use of heraldic columns. This view may seem unjustified, considering the fact that such columns are made nowhere with greater care than in the northern regions, among the Tsimshian and Haida, and farther north and south they are less frequent and less elaborately carved. The Haida, however, frequently took up foreign ideas with great energy, and developed them independently. . . . It appears that the tribe has a remarkable faculty of adaptation (Boas 1888, 195).

Boas ascribed to the Kwakwa̲ka̲'wakw, a group that still clung tenaciously to its traditions in the late nineteenth century, the honor of inventing the totem pole, and suggested that the Haida, who by that time were quite acculturated, had simply adopted the idea and elaborated upon it to create the large numbers of poles seen in Massett and Skidegate. Later, as a result of a far more careful historical reconstruction of the region, Boas reversed his position. In *Primitive Art* (1927), he ascribed to the northern groups the development of the formal crest style that then diffused north and south, and credited the Haida with originality and creativity; in fact, Boas came to see the Kwakwa̲ka̲'wakw as the great synthesizers of the region (Boas 1955, 281). Despite Boas's early reading of history, his premise that one group invented poles, which then spread to other groups, signaled a new historical consciousness that would pervade subsequent studies of the totem pole.

Yet Boas's personal brand of historical consciousness, founded on the principle that only precontact cultural elements had scientific worth, virtually ignored a century of Native interactions with non-Native people. For Boas and many others, indigenous societies appeared on the verge of being overwhelmed by modernity; at the very least, they became diluted as they encountered Europeans and Americans. As anthropology's task at that time was to record for posterity some imagined golden age of cultural purity, Boas and his colleagues omitted from their analyses any external influences that resulted in cultural transformations (other than utter destruction, that is). The idea that the proliferation and spread of totem poles could have been in part a reaction to the colonial encounter would simply not have occurred to him and others of his generation.

One subsequent anthropologist did incorporate influences from non-Native people in his totem pole history—an idea almost universally rejected at that time. This was Marius Barbeau, a French Canadian who became the second man employed as a professional anthropologist in Canada.[8] Passionate about positioning Canada as a nation distinct from both its English progenitor and its American neighbor, Barbeau fought a lifelong battle to celebrate national cultures, both indigenous and settler. In addition to promoting Québécois folklore, Barbeau studied Northwest Coast groups, especially the Nisga'a on the Nass River and the Gitk'san on the Skeena River. The Gitk'san were as conservative and antagonistic to the anti-potlatch law as the Kwakwaka'wakw, and they, too, maintained a tradition of potlatching through the prohibition period (Dawn 1981).

Barbeau was smitten by totem poles, especially those of the Nisga'a, which in 1927 he judged "the very best in existence" (Nowry 1995, 236; fig. 3.10). He also conducted extensive research on Gitk'san poles, which—while lacking, in Barbeau's estimation—were more abundant; indeed, along the Skeena River stood the largest numbers of totem poles still erect in the 1920s (fig. 3.11). Barbeau's major work, a two-volume publication entitled *Totem Poles* (1950), was unfortunately more ambitious than he could manage, and suffered from abundant factual errors and misleading illustrations. One reason Barbeau expended such energy publishing this and other texts on totem poles and other types of Northwest Coast art was to salvage whatever remained of (what he perceived to be) dying traditions. Barbeau shared the views of Boas and

3.10. Minesqu house (Nisga'a), Gitlaxdamiks, British Columbia, 1903. Courtesy of Royal British Columbia Museum, BC Archives, PN4110.

3.11. Kitwancool (Gitk'san), 1910. Photograph by George Emmons. University of Washington Libraries, Special Collections, NA3498. (Detail of pole at left in fig. 2.6.)

others in his statement, "This art now belongs to the past. Ancient customs and racial stamina are on the wane everywhere. . . . Totem poles are no longer made" (Barbeau 1929, 1).

Barbeau carefully read the accounts of eighteenth-century travelers, and noted the absence of references to freestanding monumental carvings. This inspired his controversial viewpoint that totem poles were the consequence of Native people's contact with whites:

> The art of carving poles is not really as ancient as is generally believed. Its growth to the present proportions is largely confined to the nineteenth century, that is, after the traders had introduced European tools, the steel ax, the adze, and the curved knife, in large numbers among the Natives. The lack of suitable tools, wealth, and leisure in earlier times precluded the existence of elaborate structures. The benefits that accrued from the fur trade, besides, stimulated ambitions and rivalries between leading families. Their only desire was to outdo the others in wealth, and the display of prestige. The totem pole became, after 1830, the fashionable way of showing one's power and crests, while commemorating the dead or decorating the houses. The size of the pole and the beauty of its imagery published abroad the fame of those it represented (Barbeau 1929, 12).

For Barbeau the fur trade stimulated the proliferation of totem poles. Whereas Boas ignored colonialism, bracketing its influence out of his ethnohistorical reconstructions, Barbeau gave it complete agency in the totem pole story.[9]

Sometimes academic disputes become heated, which certainly happened with the refutations of Barbeau's theory. Phillip Drucker (1948), an opinionated and sometimes aggressive anthropologist with the Bureau of American Ethnology, vigorously argued the aboriginality of the totem pole. He denied that Euroamerican technology was necessary for carving poles, both because the Northwest Coast people had some metal prior to contact, probably as a result of elaborate trade routes that extended into northwestern Asia, and because some postcontact carvers employed stone tools in making monumental totem poles. Drucker then asserted that mortuary poles represented a localized version of the widespread and ancient funerary monument complex found from northwestern Asia around the Pacific Rim to the Northwest Coast. Finally, he explained that the earliest travelers failed to mention totem poles not because they did not exist, but because the sailors arrived during the summer, when Native people lived in smaller, temporary villages. Had they visited the large permanent winter villages, they certainly would have found totem poles. Drucker was determined to prove poles to be authentically Native and thus in no way influenced by outsiders.

Aside from colonial influences, Barbeau desired to identify the group that had originated the pole. Boas had at first given that honor to the Kwakwa̱ka̱'wakw, but later modified his position and cited the Haida as inventors of significant crest art. Barbeau, as might be expected from a man who spent a great deal of time among the Tsimshian groups, argued that it was the

Nisga'a, successful traders and long-distance travelers, who created the earliest poles, with the Gitk'san and Haida later copying and then elaborating upon them (Barbeau 1929). This prompted another rebuttal, this time by W. A. Newcombe (1931), a Victoria-based collector who had spent considerable time among the Haida. Newcombe claimed that, because there existed no firsthand written accounts by whites who actually visited Nisga'a villages, "we have to depend entirely on Indian tradition as to whether they had totem poles at this period" (Newcombe 1931, 239). In other words, Newcombe assumed that histories could not be accurate unless written down, a myopic dismissal of Native oral traditions that would be repeated throughout the century, not only in publications but in law courts. A supporter of the Haida origin of poles, Newcombe cites abundant documents written by whites recording Haida totem poles, concluding that poles were a "common practice [among the Haida] many years before 1830" (Newcombe 1931, 239).

Another anthropologist entered the fray in 1964. Wilson Duff began his academic career as an empirically oriented scientist, but in later life produced subjective and often poetic interpretations of Northwest Coast art. Utterly devoted to the cultures, histories, and social conditions of Native people, Duff played a major role in the revitalization of totem pole carving in British Columbia (see chapter 9). Duff was the first critic to clarify that Barbeau did not argue that *all* totem poles were postcontact—only that the freestanding memorial poles were. Indeed, Barbeau identified precontact house posts and frontal poles as well as the grave monuments that Drucker noted were circumpolar in distribution. Duff's point was that many academic arguments could be reduced in intensity, or even dispelled, if all parties read the works they attack more carefully.

However, Duff did identify a destructive and erroneous bias underlying Barbeau's work: the assumption that Native people lacked the ability to create the kind of elaborate art for which they are so justly famed. Duff used as an example of this premise of aboriginal inferiority a 1940 quotation by Barbeau: "Advanced stylization [of art] can be the result only of intense cultural development, such as never happened on the North Pacific coast in prehistoric times." Duff disagreed, claiming, "The two old Haida houses at Dadens with their large frontal poles had required essentially as highly developed a technology, social system and art style to bring them into existence as anything that came later. Their very presence at the opening of the historical period carries with it the proof of intensive cultural development in prehistoric times" (Duff 1964b, 93). Duff challenged the concept that the impressive Northwest Coast traditions required external colonial stimuli and instead stated that totem poles should be "credited to the American Indians as an indigenous and aboriginal accomplishment" (Duff 1964b, 94). His position celebrating the agency of aboriginal people resonated with the values becoming increasingly prevalent at the time. This was the 1960s, when a host of activist movements, including those organized by Native Americans, challenged sexism and racism and foregrounded the accomplishments of those who suffered prejudice and discrimination. Duff's assertion that Native people needed no inspiration from non-Natives was in part a political statement of aboriginal pride consonant with his own values and those of the period during which he wrote.

After Duff, no serious scholar proposed that the totem pole was a purely postcontact invention, even though most agree that the abundance and size of poles was the result of encounters with non-Native people, as we have argued. Today it is generally accepted that the tradition of carved poles diffused from the north coast, though we may never locate its absolute origin. Bill Holm (1983, 38) suggests one way this might have occurred: in the late nineteenth century, northern Native wives of Hudson's Bay Company traders on Vancouver Island might have introduced the fully carved poles to that region, which then began appearing among the Kwakwa̲ka̲'wakw to replace the uncarved poles that sometimes supported coppers or single figures. Then, according to Drucker (1951, 76), the Nuu-chah-nulth copied those multifigured poles from Kwakwa̲ka̲'wakw. In *Totem Poles of the Pacific*

Northwest Coast (1986), Edward Malin illustrates maps showing the distribution of various types of carved monuments: interior posts ranged from Alaska to Puget Sound; memorial and frontal poles from Alaska to the Kwakwa̱ka̱'wakw; freestanding heraldic poles from Alaska to the Kwakwa̱ka̱'wakw, with late-nineteenth- and early-twentieth-century introduction among the Nuu-chah-nulth; and mortuary poles among some Tlingit, Haida, and Tsimshian (Malin 1986, 22–24). In Malin's reconstruction, the Haida invented the concept and developed frontal, memorial, and mortuary poles, some of which inspired envy among their neighbors, who began to imitate them. Thus, totem pole carving diffused from Haida Gwaii, first reaching the Coast Tsimshian, who in turn influenced the Nass and Skeena River people. The Coast Tsimshian stimulated the production of poles among the northern Wakashan speakers, while the Kaigani Haida influenced the southern Tlingit as well. Later in the nineteenth century, pole carving spread farther south to the Nuxalk, Kwakwa̱ka̱'wakw, and finally the Nuu-chah-nulth (Malin 1986, 21).

THE ESSENTIAL TOTEM POLE AND ITS EXCLUSIONS

From the nineteenth century's beginning to its end, the conditions of the Alaska and British Columbia Native population changed from autonomy and prosperity brought about by the sea- and land-based fur trade to oppression, discrimination, and alienation from their traditional territories. Throughout the century, population decline resulted in the readjustment of indigenous hierarchies. As easy as it is to represent this often cruel and usually unjust imposition of change upon an indigenous group by their colonizers, it would be incorrect to perceive Northwest Coast Native people as simple victims, incapable of resistance and unable to adjust creatively to new and sometimes hostile challenges. Tragic as these encounters were, certain responses to colonialism by Northwest Coast groups should be looked at in a more positive light.

In some ways, the history of ideas about the totem pole parallels the history of anthropological approaches to aboriginal cultures. In general, early explorers attempted to record the exotic sights they saw, often scientifically but sometimes with wonder or disdain as well. Later, as more information on unfamiliar cultures emerged, attempts at systematic understanding were made, such as Boas' reconstruction of totem pole history. Boas endeavored to understand precontact cultures by occluding as many indications of Western influence as possible. It became standard, in anthropological, museological, and popular depictions of Native people, to present what was believed to be "pure" unadulterated culture. This attitude was in part responsible for the outcry against Barbeau's maverick theories about Native artwork inspired by non-Native people. By the 1960s, in sympathy with increasingly empowered Native people, some anthropologists focused on past injustices and criticized those whose work was judged to have, in hindsight, racist elements. This resulted in celebrations of Native creativity such as those promoted by Duff.

The works by these men, intended for largely academic audiences and published mostly in scholarly journals, reflected more general orientations shared by many nonprofessionals of their generations. Thus, Boas's concern for cultural authenticity, Barbeau's cosmopolitanism, and Duff's humanism can be understood in part as characteristic of their own cultures' changing views toward Native people. In general, there existed an underlying romantic, modernist nostalgia based on the perceived superiority of the indigenous past over the present, according to which changes endured as a result of contact, colonization, and settlement were to be lamented.

In recent years, anthropology has once again redirected itself, adjusting to new perspectives on the flaws of such modernist and essentialist perspectives on culture change. In an essentialist model, idealized types are held to be the basic unit of analysis, while variations on those types are dismissed as peripheral, derivative, and imperfect. The "essential" totem pole is that which is fixed in the contemporary imagination as what a totem pole *should be*: the tall, freestanding

3.12. Klinkwan (Kaigani Haida), 1897. Photograph by Winter and Pond. Alaska State Library, 87-0090.

column decorated with multiple images that convey the legends of its owners. To be deemed authentic, the essential pole must have developed prior to white contact, during some presumed Golden Age of cultural purity. That cultural purity by definition discredits most if not all hybridities, and disregards the dynamic nature of cultural interactions.[10] In their quest for ethnographic purity, scholars too often have sought a neat encapsulation of clearly defined types, and rejected or, at least, placed a lesser value on hybridized forms.

THE FLAGPOLE

In the context of totem pole history, one of these hybridized forms is the flagpole, a common sight on the Northwest Coast that has barely been mentioned in the literature. While photographs of Native people often shade their subjects with colonialist attitudes, some images show with great clarity things that viewers simply do not see. Among the hundreds of photographs that illustrate Northwest Coast villages and their poles are many that contain flagpoles and/or tall, thin, mast-like poles (figs. 3.1, 3.2, 3.3, 3.6, 3.12, and 4.6). Because they do not adhere to the preconceived notion of cultural purity, with its concomitant blindness to hybridized forms, such clearly Western items have been visually "edited out" of totem pole histories. That blindness to what is fully in view appears over and over again when publications fail to mention in captions or in text the flagpoles in photographs of Northwest Coast villages.

Throughout decades of contact with their trading partners and then colonists, Native residents of the Northwest Coast encountered symbols of alien power and importance that they assimilated into their own cultural vocabularies. Noblemen wore United States or Canadian military or law enforcement uniforms. Chief Kadashan of Wrangell built a large Victorian house. The Kwakwa̱ka̱'wakw mounted British flags on their canoe prows and atop the massive displays of gifts at their potlatches (fig. 3.13). Symbols of colonial power and authority signified far more than allegiance to the dominating authority if, indeed, they expressed that at all. For example, the Kwakwa̱ka̱'wakw actually appropriated the flag, transforming it into an indication of their own importance and status. The adoption of foreign emblems following intercultural contact was a

3.13. Alert Bay (Kwakwa̱ka̱'wakw) potlatch. Photograph by William Halliday. Courtesy of Royal British Columbia Museum, BC Archives, 10068.

logical extension of the local crest system, which displayed images referring to ancestral encounters. Here, overt displays of accommodation to colonial rule and local capitulation to government through the display of emblems of official authority—an act that the officials would have approved of—articulated resistance to that rule by assimilating these same emblems into illegal ceremonies (fig. 3.14). The overtones of resistance doubtless went over the heads of the colonizers.

Frequently the flagpoles found in coastal villages flew no actual flags. It is likely that residents began seeing flagpoles in non-Native settlements such as Spanish Yuquot and Russian Sitka, as well as around Hudson's Bay Company forts. They also saw ship's masts from which, at times, national or maritime flags hung. Perhaps the Northwest Coast people assimilated flagpoles, or the equally tall and thin masts of the ships that brought them such wealth, into the meaningful expressions of their own cultural values.

In some communities, flagpoles were more common than totem poles. For example, whereas the northern Tlingit erected no exterior carved totem poles, what appears like a ship's mast stands before a Tlingit house in an 1840 drawing of Sitka. Even the Haida, known for their well-crafted and intricately carved poles, sometimes made use of flags, such as the large standard that flutters from the top of the central watchman's hat in an 1881 drawing of a pole by Adrian Jacobsen (Jacobsen 1977, 24). Boas saw figures and flags on graves in his voyage to Newitti (Rohner 1969, 38), and had several photographed during his 1897 stay at Fort Rupert.

3.14. Mimkwamlis totem pole (Kwakwaka'wakw). Drawing made for Franz Boas. AMNH. "Boas Collection 1943" Courtesy of the Division of Anthropology Archives, American Museum of Natural History, box 2, folder 20.

Among the Mowachaht, flagpoles became popular in the early twentieth century, and by 1924 stood before five Yuquot houses.

In at least one case, a flagpole actually substituted for a specific totem pole. At a Tsimshian ceremony held in 1929, Ale'm-laxha' of the Ginax-angi'k tribe honored the memory of his brother, dead over twenty years, by raising not a totem pole—which would have aroused the wrath of the Indian agent—but a flagpole. Named "Pole of the Sand Place" after one of the chief's exclusive crests that had in the past been used on a totem pole, this flagpole was raised in the old way, with guests from clans opposite that of the chief pulling the ropes, and a feast complete with much oration and gift distribution (Garfield 1939, 212). Like the Haida tombstone and Kwakwaka'wakw flags, government authorities could find no fault with this flagpole, which they probably did not know was an element in a traditional ceremony that subverted the law.

As the nineteenth century progressed, flagpoles became more and more common in villages. But flagpoles have made virtually no entry into the totem pole literature, and even where they appear in published photographs they are ignored. There are several possible reasons for this, the most evident being that flagpoles, even if erected before a plank house, look like flagpoles of the white world. For essentialists, they have no business in a Native community. Moreover, flagpoles have nothing that declares aboriginality—no carving, no painting, no crests. Some simple poles, such as those at Fort Rupert, display a figure or copper, lending a modicum of authenticity, but many are plain and totally unadorned. As is so often the case, the largely non-Native people who have assumed the responsibility of presenting Native culture eliminated elements that could challenge the authenticity of their representations. As a result, they overlooked the complexity and ambiguity of colonial relations whereby Native groups might have been declaring their allegiance to some trading partners over others or ingratiating themselves to colonial authorities, while at the same time possibly accruing genuine prestige by flying the "crests" of powerful trading partners in the early years, and of governments later on.

A BRIEF HISTORY OF POLES

In most accounts, totem poles developed from shorter house posts or mortuaries among a particular ethnic group, the Haida being the most popular candidate for that honor. In fact, actual cultural history rarely proceeds along a clean and linear path. Totem pole history embraces many players. Most important of course are the Native artists who created them and the elite who displayed them. In the early period, as today, poles served as indexes of status and history. As fur trade brought more wealth, poles became more abundant and more complex. And, as villages amalgamated and populations declined, poles became expressions of identity and wealth in contested domains. For many Tlingit and Haida, they became temporarily vilified by Christian standards and abandoned or destroyed. For the Alert Bay Kwakwa̱ka̱'wakw, poles served as declarations of cultural sovereignty challenging those intending to destroy their culture; at least one flagpole served a similar purpose among the Tsimshian. Throughout the coast, families erected flagpoles as less notable yet significant objects that served as place markers for property and community. Other players in the totem pole story were academics who conducted debates about their origin, as well as the missionaries and assimilationist government officials for whom poles were symbols of all that was backwards about these potlatching Indians.

As we demonstrated in chapter 2, a variety of crest-depicting monumental artwork developed on the Northwest Coast prior to contact. Perhaps these different means of communicating family histories and status each contributed elements to the detached, full-size totem pole: the mortuary, a monumental carving that stands out-of-doors; the house post's columnar presentation of crests; and the more public display of crests on the house façade. Different communities held one or another of these artistic modes in higher esteem than others, but the exterior freestanding totem pole—which is a large columnar sculpture of multiple crests that stands outside—became more and more prevalent as time went on.

During the early nineteenth century, the Haida most extensively and enthusiastically produced that type of monument. It remained less significant to some other groups. The northern Tlingit favored house posts; the Nuxalk and some Tsimshian preferred façade painting; while the Salish remained content with funerary monuments. As we shall demonstrate in the following chapters, detached totem poles captured the imaginations of many non-Native people and, as a result, assumed a central position in their imaginations as *the* artistic achievement of the Northwest Coast. The Tlingit, Nuxalk, and Salish would probably have resisted the suggestion that a totem pole was in some way superior to their visual indications of rank and clan history.

We do not know for certain when the first freestanding, monumental totem poles were carved. We also do not know for certain where that occurred. We do know that prior to contact throughout the region, families communicated their position and history with large-scale public images, both painted and sculpted, in the form of house posts, funerary monuments, exterior poles, illustrated façades, and, after contact, even flagpoles. Northwest Coast groups traded extensively with each other, and observed or heard about their neighbors' means of expressing status. They also interacted with whites, sometimes appropriating their expressions of power. In the process, the totem pole as we know it developed—not as a pure, essential aboriginal creation but as an innovative product of an ongoing history of intercultural encounter. The role non-Native people played in establishing "the totem pole" above all other types of Northwest Coast art, as *the* singular monument of the region, becomes a major factor in pole history. In the next several chapters, we will discuss how tourism, expositions, museums, and even nationalism contributed to the growing dominance of totem poles in the popular construction of Northwest Coast cultures.

We began this chapter with the intentional destruction of Kake's poles, inspired in part by missionary zeal. We end with a more sympathetic Christian reaction to these carvings published in the October 29, 1902, edition of *The Christian Herald: An Illustrated Family Magazine*. Adah Sparhawk Young, in "The Indian Totems of Alaska," pointed out that poles provide samples of an "intelligent handicraft which seem far beyond the generally accepted ignorance of the Indians and the crude conditions of their life." After an accurate explanation of the significance of poles, Young comments on their attractiveness to tourists and predicts a natural demise of poles, which in turn provides her the opportunity for promoting Christian beliefs: "[Poles] are made of cedar, a very enduring wood, but many of them are defaced by time. Most of the religion of these Indians is of a material manifestation, which will perish with time. The finest pictures the artist puts on canvas will fade. Nothing done in matter is immortal, for matter is perishable, but he who works on the spiritual leaves impressions that shall endure forever" (Young 1902, n.p.). The notion that totem poles were on the verge of disappearance was to become a leitmotif repeated over and over again in the history of their representation. The imminent demise of poles became as much a part of their constructed identity as their very monumentality or presumed antiquity, pervading much turn-of-the-century literature that beckoned tourists north to "the land of the totem pole."

"PLACES OF TOTEMIC DELIGHT"

SIGNIFICANT SIGHTS/SITES ON THE NORTHWEST COAST

See Europe if you must—See America if you will, but see ALASKA FIRST! The totem-poles of Alaska are as different from everything else in the world as the scenery surpasses all other scenery; nowhere else such a combination of magnificent mountains, glaciers and picturesque fiords as in the land of the totem-pole.

—*ALASKA VIA TOTEM POLE ROUTE*, BROCHURE FOR THE PACIFIC COAST STEAMSHIP COMPANY, 1911

The appreciative individual, who would view the totems of Alaska as they were sculpted originally from the imagination and painted from the hues of fancy of those uncontaminated tribes, must lose no time. For this Adam has been crowded out of his garden, and he has ceased to speak in the breath of the woods or commune with the pines.

—TRAVELER LILLIE LE GRAND LOCKWOOD, 1906

In May 1879, just twelve years after the United States purchased Alaska from the Russians, naturalist John Muir left San Francisco on the steamer *Dakota*, not entirely certain of his Alaskan itinerary. His account of this and several other voyages, published in 1915 as *Travels in Alaska*, poetically depict the land and its animals, plants, and people as seen through the eyes of the great conservationist:

> To the lover of pure wilderness Alaska is one of the most wonderful countries in the world. No excursion that I know of may be made into any other American wilderness where so marvelous an abundance of noble, newborn scenery is so charmingly brought to view as on the trip through the Alexander Archipelago to Fort Wrangell and Sitka . . . .Never before this had I been embosomed in scenery so hopelessly beyond description. . . . Tracing shining ways through fiord and sound, past forests and waterfalls, island and mountains and far azure headlands, it seems as if surely we must at length reach the very paradise of the poets, the abode of the blessed (Muir 1915, 13–14).

With his statement that the scenery was "so hopelessly beyond description," Muir was just one of many travelers to bemoan the inadequacy of verbal expression. This trope of wonder and unrepresentability is reiterated often in contemporary travel literature in which authors, attempting to describe Alaska, insist that words cannot express its grandeur and beauty. The 1891 *All about Alaska*, published by the Pacific Coast Steamship Company, bubbles over with superlatives: "No artist's brush or poet's pen can adequately set forth the [glory] . . . " (27); "Neither pen nor pencil can paint the wonderful scenery . . . " (30); " . . . a thousand things which he [the tourist] can never describe—neither by mouth nor pen, nor brush" (31). Presumably, this purported failure of descriptive language was meant as a prompt to the direct eye-witnessing (and possibly photography) that results from travel.

Muir stayed in Wrangell, where he saw totem poles and described Native houses such as Kadashan's "as large and solidly built of logs and planks as those of Whites" (Muir 1915, 27). Through the Reverend S. Hall

Young, an important missionary in southeast Alaska, he met several high-ranking Tlingit, including the eminent Chief Shakes of Wrangell (fig. 4.1). At a feast hosted by Shakes, costumed dancers imitated porpoises, deer, and bears. In keeping with the progressive attitudes embraced by some Tlingit at that time, Shakes disavowed these ceremonies as pagan by claiming, "'This is the way we used to dance and play. We do not wish to do so any more. We will give away all the dance dresses you have seen us wearing, though we value them very highly . . . we have been long, long in the dark. You have led us into strong guiding light and taught us the right way to live and the right way to die'" (Muir 1915, 35–36). These words may have been sincere, or they may have been for the benefit of an audience that included three Presbyterian ministers and their wives. That the hosts may not have abandoned all their traditions became evident when, at the conclusion of the event that Muir himself identified as a potlatch, they distributed to their guests deer, sheep, marmot, and sable skins as well as carvings.

Sometime later, Chief Kadashan led Muir and a small party of whites to a deserted village seventeen miles south of Wrangell. The naturalist wandered among the posts and totem poles that he claimed to be a century old. Like so many newcomers to Northwest Coast art, Muir was "astonished" at the excellent workmanship of these well-preserved ruins. Employing the quantitative and objective language of the scientist, he described the sight:

> The carved totem-pole monuments are the most striking of the objects displayed here. The simplest of them consisted of a smooth, rough post fifteen or twenty feet high and about eighteen inches in diameter, with the figure of some animal on top—a beaver, porpoise, eagle or raven, about life-size or larger. These were the totems of the family that occupied the houses in front of which they stood. Others supported the figure of a man or woman, life-size or larger, usually in a sitting posture, said to resemble the dead whose ashes were contained in a closed cavity in the pole. The largest were thirty or forty feet high, carved from top to bottom into human and animal totem figures, one above another, with their limbs grotesquely doubled and folded. Some of the most imposing were said to commemorate some event of an historical character. But a telling display of family pride seemed to have been the prevailing motive (Muir 1915, 72–73).

Then, in terms similar to those used by travelers portraying the disintegrating ruins of vanished civilizations everywhere, Muir continued, "the colorful lichens and mosses gave them a venerable air, while the larger vegetation often found on such as were most decayed

4.1. Chief Shakes house, Wrangell (Tlingit), 1895. Photograph by Winter and Pond. Alaska State Library, P87-0117.

produced a picturesque effect" (Muir 1915, 73). With these words, the naturalist joined so many others of the late nineteenth century with predilections of romanticism toward decay, ruins, the picturesque, and a pervasive melancholy over loss.[1]

As Muir was contemplating this scene, he heard the sound of chopping wood, followed by a thud. Apparently, one of his party found a particular totem interesting and commanded the deck hands to cut it down and saw off the main human figure, a woman three feet wide at the shoulders. Muir termed this a "sacrilege" and conveyed the disapproval expressed by Chief Kadashan, to whose family this pole belonged: "How would you like to have an Indian go to a graveyard and break down and carry away a monument belonging to your family?" (Muir 1915, 75). Small presents and apologies managed to "mend the matter," although the ultimate fate of the artwork is not mentioned. (It went to Princeton University.)

Despite his apparently sympathetic attitude toward Native peoples, Muir was not quite ready to consider them equal to whites. In his description of Kadashan's old village, Muir asserts his ambivalence: "The magnitude of the ruins and the excellence of the workmanship manifest in them was astonishing as belonging to the Indian" (1915, 71). He nonetheless proceeds to praise the skill, thoughtfulness, and precision of the carvers that put to shame more "civilized" woodworkers. He continues, "The completeness of form, finish, and proportion of these timbers suggest a skill of a wild and positive kind, like that which guides the woodpecker in drilling round holes, and the bee in making its cells" (Muir 1915, 72). The excellence of the Native artists did not bring them to equal cultural standing with white carvers but instead, in Muir's estimation, lodged them more firmly in the world of industrious nature.

Although large numbers of poles left the Northwest Coast after the 1880s to become treasured museum collections (as we describe in chapter 7), many people visited Alaska and British Columbia in part to see what totem poles remained. As the West became settled, and railroads penetrated lands once dominated by Native peoples, travelers began taking excursions further from home. When the transcontinental railroad completed the link to the Northwest in 1882, the stage was set for the development of passenger steamship service to Alaska on the Inside Passage. Since then, Alaska has drawn tourists seeking its spectacular natural beauty, wilderness, and totem poles. Native art and culture enhanced the experience of early tourists, who quickly "discovered" the totem poles in certain southeast Alaskan villages and placed these monuments among the "must sees" on every touristic itinerary. Of all the vast American lands, Alaska was considered the wildest, most spectacular, most remote, and thus most appealing to those tourists wanting a "frontier experience."[2] Unlike early explorers, for whom voyages always contained elements of uncertainty and danger, the tourist easily and relatively quickly returns to safety, bringing both memories and material mnemonics—often in the form of photographs and souvenirs—back to civilization. Nature tourists, who often romantically associate Native peoples with the wilderness itself, often seek an experience with indigenous groups to recover what they believe is a simple way of life, more intimate with Nature.[3] The basic irony of such tourism is that the very process of encountering "unblemished" people and places results in their becoming encountered and blemished.[4] A profoundly ambivalent leitmotif runs through this history of tourism—indeed, through all of colonial relations with indigenous peoples—whereby fascination with primitive people, a disdainful or romanticized assessment of their backwardness, and laments for their modernization are expressed simultaneously.[5]

Most locations hoping to capitalize on tourist attention fix upon distinctive locales and place-specific images. No single image came to be more emblematic for the Northwest Coast than the totem pole, which helped transform the region from an unbounded geographical expanse into a specific tourist destination.[6] The tourist experience represented a new type of social encounter between Euroamericans and the indigenous people—or, more often, simply the Native material culture—of the region. Here we will explore both sides of this encounter. The new visitors to the coast (as distinct from the traders, settlers, missionaries, and government agents) brought their own knowledge and expectations to the region, and their own particular modes of representing and appropriating—both literally and literarily—the totem poles they found there. At the same time, the indigenous people, who were in some ways the object of the touristic experience, responded to and represented the whites, sometimes on poles. Thus continual developments allowed totem poles to react to, mediate, and symbolize the complicated nature of the tourist encounter.[7]

TOURISM TO ALASKA AND BRITISH COLUMBIA: WHITES, ON POLES

Muir's first trip to Alaska predated the massive influx of tourists who, during the 1880s, began traveling by steamer up the Inside Passage. Seeking greater profits, shippers—who sent provisions and equipment north and took Alaskan gold, fish, and lumber south—began filling their vessels with tourists. In 1882, General Nelson A. Miles took a group of excursionists on the *Dakota*, the same ship upon which Muir had sailed, formally inaugurating the Inside Passage tourist itinerary. Soon ships were leaving regularly from San Francisco or Seattle for the leisurely thirty-day trip, steaming north, often stopping in Victoria before commencing the long voyage to Ketchikan, Wrangell, Juneau, Skagway, and Sitka. In 1883, Captain James C. Carroll sailed the *Idaho* into the fantastic waters of Glacier Bay, which Muir had visited four years earlier, having been brought there by local Tlingit. This added spectacular tidewater glaciers to an already splendid itinerary.

To facilitate travel from the east, the Pacific Coast Steamship Company began collaborating with the Northern Pacific, Union Pacific, Canadian Pacific and Great Northern transcontinental railway lines to provide seamless connections among all the locations they served; a traveler could easily sail from Philadelphia to Banff and on to Alaska. Alaskan visits, which rapidly grew from 1,650 in 1884 to 5,007 in 1890, inspired curio shops, tours of missionary schools and mine operations, and, in the case of Sitka, marching or brass bands that welcomed and cheered docking and departing vessels (Hinckley 1996).

Some steamship lines began to publish their own brochures that served dual functions as advertisements and guidebooks. Indeed, before they were published for a broad audience, selections from Muir's writings appeared in a tourist brochure for the Northern Pacific Railroad (Kollin 2000, 47). One unabashed early usage of totem poles for commercial purposes is in the Pacific Coast Steamship Company brochures produced each year for its North Pacific excursions. An early brochure, published for the 1896 season (fig. 4.2), featured a drawing of the Kaigani Haida village of Kasaan. The 1906 brochure uses the Native carving to designate its itinerary—*Alaska via Totem Pole Route* (fig. 4.3). In the 1908 brochure, totem poles appear in twenty-two of the forty-nine illustrations. "An Easy Trip" stresses the importance of totem poles for the touristic experience: "Always there are new sights to see—totem-poles and gold mines, totem-poles and Indians, totem-poles and glaciers, and again, totem-poles" (Pacific Coast Steamship Co. 1908). Wrangell is one place to see poles, but the "totem-pole enthusiast will find his chiefest [sic] joy in Old Kasaan, the deserted Indian totem-pole village," which, according to this brochure, had 100-year-old poles standing and over 200-year-old poles fallen on the ground (fig. 4.4). The final page, illustrated with a large image of Kasaan, has the following text (quoted in the epigraph above): "The totem-poles of Alaska are as different from everything else in the world as the scenery surpasses all other scenery; nowhere else such a combination of magnificent mountains, glaciers and picturesque fiords as in the land of the totem-pole." Highlighting poles above all other Alaskan attractions indicates both the strength of early cultural tourism and the change in attitude toward Native peoples from that manifested a mere three decades earlier.

Then, as now, tourists appreciated reading about their destinations, so travel literature proliferated, some appallingly racist, some surprisingly sensitive.

4.2. Cover, Pacific Coast Steamship Company brochure, 1896. Alaska State Library, M68-1-01-01.

4.3. Cover, Pacific Coast Steamship Company brochure, *Alaska via Totem Pole Route*, 1906. Alaska State Library, M68-1-01-05.

4.4. Kasaan (Kaigani Haida), 1899. Photograph by Arthur Churchill Warner. University of Washington Libraries. Special Collections, Warner Archives 0451.

Virtually all guides for the region mention Alaska Native people and their totem poles. Eliza Ruhamah Scidmore, one of the few early women members of the National Geographic Society (founded in 1888), wrote the insightful and lively *Alaska, Its Southern Coast and the Sitkan Archipelago* (1885). The book recounts the region's scenery and culture from her perspective as traveler on the *Idaho* in 1883 (see McLean 1977). She gently teases both the Native peoples and the whites in her account of totem poles at the "show places of Fort Wrangell," which inspired the passengers to make "the hopeless plunge into Thlinket mythology and there flounder . . . aimlessly until the end of the trip," sometimes becoming quite inventive in their interpretations of poles. Scidmore also suggests that Native peoples themselves enjoyed "misleading and fooling" the inquisitive whites with their "theories and suppositions" (Scidmore 1885, 51). After these comments, she herself misidentifies the uppermost image on one pole as representing its builder.

Scidmore criticized some appalling behavior by tourists in Indian communities. In the summer, Fort Wrangell was relatively quiet, as Native peoples traveled to their fishing camps in June, leaving their houses locked. That locking was not always a deterrent to entry is suggested by the sign one house had over its door:

> ANATLASH
> Let all that read know that I
> Am a friend to the Whites. Let no

A CRUISE SHIP TOTEM POLE

BY NATHAN JACKSON, TLINGIT ARTIST

4.5. Nathan Jackson (Tlingit), totem pole on *Radiance of the Seas*, Royal Caribbean Cruise Line, 2001. Photograph courtesy of Nathan Jackson.

Back in 2000, Rebecca Mix brought some visitors out to the carving center in Saxman, where I was working at the time. Jack Williams, president of Royal Caribbean Cruise Lines, was one of those visitors. We talked about the possibility of a twelve-foot totem pole for the new ship that was being built. This was in the early summer. After that, we didn't hear anything for about four months, so I figured it wasn't going to happen, and then we got an e-mail from someone in Florida who was working with the London company and who was coordinating the artwork for the new ship. We started discussing the design of the pole, and they wanted something very untraditional . . . water, mountains, air, sky, etc.

After a lot of e-mails and a few phone calls, I was finally able to make it clear that it would be best to stick with a traditional format, so I began looking for stories to depict that would be suitable. I finally settled on two stories about Raven, one of Raven stealing the sun, moon, and stars, and one about Raven that is pretty much like a Jonah and the great fish story, where Raven is swallowed by a whale.

The pole stands twelve feet and is above the swimming pool, although there were several possible locations being considered at the time. Raven is the top figure, and he is sitting on a bentwood box, holding a copper moon in his beak. The bottom figure is a whale, not a killer whale, but a regular whale, since you should not have a killer whale and Raven on the same pole.[8] The whale has Raven peeking out of the blowhole. Around the whale's head at the base of the pole are swirls to depict water.

Royal Caribbean accepted the design, and the carving began. One of the big challenges of this project was the installation. It was to be installed in Ketchikan on the *Radiance of the Seas'* first trip there the following May, in 2001, but it was too tall to carry up the stairs to the twelfth or thirteenth deck, and too tall to fit into the elevators.

The only other solution was to bring it in by helicopter. It was a bit of a windy day, and definitely the most unique installation we've had. I really like this pole a lot, and it's probably one of my favorites that I have designed. I really like doing this kind of whale . . . it was the first time I had ever done a whale of this kind, and it was a lot of fun to do something different. I had several younger carvers working with me on it, and they really did a great job. As soon as it was finished, we all stood it up in the carving shed, and it was amazing! When you work on a pole in the horizontal position, there are things you really don't see until you stand it up. We were all there looking at it and saying, "Look at this . . . !" and "Look at here where it goes like this!" and so on. It had all kinds of really pleasant surprises. These are the kinds of things that make one want to keep on carving!

One molest this house. In case of my
Death it belongs to my wife (Scidmore 1885, 59).

Houses, even those occupied, were fair game for tourists, who walked in and made themselves at home, "scrutinizing and turning over everything they saw with an effrontery that would be resented, if indulged in kind by the Indians" (Scidmore 1885, 60). But apparently the Tlingit found opportunity here, and sometimes offered for sale whatever they had available, including "greasy baskets and broken spoons" if nothing better were available.

Scidmore had a special fondness for Howkan, a Kaigani Haida village at the southern end of Prince of Wales Island, with the largest number of totem poles she had seen (fig. 4.6). Scidmore describes how her vessel, the *Idaho*, had to anchor near a trading post one mile away from the community to avoid dangerous reefs, strong currents, and narrow channels. The passengers rowed to shore and met the post's five white residents, who guided them to the two crescent beaches of Howkan, offering historical anecdotes along the way. Scidmore found Howkan houses large, clean, and well-built, with impressive poles. Standing before the home of Chief Skulka were two poles, a flagstaff, and a "skeleton bell-tower" that were "the envy of all the Kaigahnees" (Scidmore 1885, 272). In addition to more recently carved poles, older poles stood before deserted houses on the beach; behind them, in the dense undergrowth, amidst grasses and ferns, were mortuaries, including fine carvings of Skulka's ancestors. Returning to the populated section of the village, Scidmore praised the elegance of the Haida canoes and became dismayed when the Haida offered one to her group for only fifty dollars, while other residents began bearing more treasures for sale (Scidmore 1885, 275).

More than a decade after publishing this travelogue, Scidmore wrote *Appleton's Guide-Book to Alaska and the Northwest Coast* (1898), among the first books specifically intended as an Alaska trip-planner that included British Columbia within its

4.6. Howkan (Kagani Haida), 1897. Photograph by Winter and Pond. Alaska State Library, 87-0050.

scope. The first Canadian Native people she mentions are Kwakwa̲ka̲'wakw from Alert Bay, where the "most southerly totem pole and the only one known to have been erected on the coast within ten years" stood. Scidmore noted that "missionaries have not been able to do anything with these people," and, if offered adequate recompense, they would perform dances for their visitors (Scidmore 1898, 22). She then proceeded to Fort Simpson, demonstrating significant ethnohistorical knowledge of the Tsimshian's original dispersed villages and their movement next to the Hudson's Bay Company post. She points out that the Native village had changed considerably in ten years, one-family houses having replaced large plank houses and totem poles having been removed, with "only a half dozen remaining from the forest that used to encircle the beach" (Scidmore 1898, 32). Scidmore found Massett similarly acculturated, its totem poles "tottering to decay," "the spirit of progress" having eradicated her favorite quality in a Native village—"picturesqueness" (Scidmore 1897, 36).[9] Nevertheless, she still directed the visitor to Cumshewa, Skedans, Massett, Skidegate, and "the finest collection of all at Laskeek on Tanoo Island." Scidmore's description of poles, with their "rude and monstrous heraldry, elaborate symbolism, a system of colossal hieroglyphics," likely resonated with the period's popular Egyptomania (Scidmore 1897, 38).

Alaska was next, and the villages of the Kaigani Haida and the Tlingit. In addition to Wrangell, Ketchikan, and Sitka, Scidmore portrayed her favorite village, Howkan. This Prince of Wales Island community was the destination only of small steamers that traveled from village to village and thus was rarely visited by regular ships. Howkan was, in Scidmore's words, "a place of totemic delight" (Scidmore 1897, 62). She even included Klukwan in the Chilkat region, explaining that each clan "had a splendid feast-house, with massive carved columns inside; and the graveyards are still an ethnographer's paradise" (Scidmore 1897, 94). Such adoration of totem poles likely encouraged tourists to have themselves photographed beside these trademark icons of the region (fig. 4.7).

4.7. Tourists next to Chief Kyan (Tlingit) pole, Ketchikan, ca. 1900. University of Washington Libraries. Special Collections, 27338z/AWC 1560.

Another woman traveler, Septima M. Collis, in *A Woman's Trip to Alaska, Being an Account of a Voyage through the Inland Seas of the Sitkan Archipelago in 1890*, was more critical of what Alaska had to offer. Wrangell—without sidewalks, horses, or vehicles—she pronounced "as uninviting a spot as any in the world," though it was redeemed by a few totem poles and graves as well as mission-run Indian schools (Collis 1890, 77).

> But I saw the totem poles; and since that time at various other places I have seen them, and pictures of them by the score, and although I confess there is little about these totem poles which is at all attractive from the physical point of view, they are interesting in so far as they illustrate

> the fact that all humanity, even in its aboriginal and its barbarous state, adopts for its own protection certain rules and laws of government . . . this totem-pole custom leads to extravagant display of family pride among those who are well off. It is as much an evidence of prosperity for Mr. Bear to erect a high pole surmounted by a poor imitation of his god-father and carved on all sides with rude effigies of his ancestors, as it is with us to live in a palace; and I wondered as I looked at some of these horrid sculpturings whether they did not beget the same neighborly jealousy and vulgar rivalry which possess those who esteem themselves more civilized (Collis 1890, 79–80).

For Collis, poles were not so much art as institutions, reflecting certain universals of human pride and prestige. She also indicates how prolific images of poles had become in the tourist literature of the time. Such repetitious illustration helped the totem pole become the central visual emblem for the region.

INDIANS, ON WHITES; AND WHITES-ON-POLES

We have been looking at how Euroamericans (mis) represented indigenous people through their views about poles. But totem poles also provide insights into how Indians tried to make sense of Euroamericans, in all their complexity. Great numbers of newcomers to the Northwest Coast provided Native peoples with increased opportunities to observe foreign behavior and appearances, which some artists portrayed on artwork. Early Alaskan tourists found one type of pole, largely confined to Prince of Wales Island, especially delightful—those that depicted whites. While white observers assumed such images honored their subjects, some such poles, in fact, mocked them. These may have developed from the existing tradition of erecting shame or rivalry poles to challenge other chiefs and enemies. Given the abuses of Native people doled out by many of their colonial interlocutors, it is no wonder that the First Nations sought public means with which to express resentment and challenge.

Poles criticizing the behavior of whites communicated their owners' defiant stance toward the colonizers. One pole carved in Tongass circa 1885 was intended to shame Secretary of State William Seward, the person most responsible for the purchase of Alaska. In 1869, Chief Ebbetts had hosted Seward at a lavish potlatch, which the American never adequately acknowledged or reciprocated (Garfield and Forrest 1948, 55–56). This carving, a copy of which stands today in Saxman Native village near Ketchikan, presents Seward as an ungrateful and boorish man marked (according to current Native tour guides) by his red ears. Another pole depicts the Russian Alexander Baranof with the Tlingit Chief Katlean, who destroyed the first Russian settlement of Sitka. The Russian's nakedness signifies his shame over losing that battle (although of course he soon recaptured Sitka). On the original Baranof pole, Katlean appeared on the top while the Russian stood at the bottom; when this pole was restored in the 1930s, the forest service insisted that carver George Benson alter the design so Baranof would be on top (Henrikson 2001, 43).

Opinion divides on the interpretations of other poles depicting non-Native peoples. In Kasaan, images of whites appeared on a pole owned by Chief Skowl. From top to bottom are an eagle, a figure pointing to the sky, an Indian's conception of the Archangel Michael, a Russian priest with hands crossed on his chest, a Russian eagle, and a human who could be Skowl's son-in-law, the early trader Vincent Baronovich. According to one early source, Skowl was famous for promoting old ways and resisting colonization, and expressed great disrespect by using images of priests to whom he would not listen and angels in which he did not believe. Thus, this pole ridiculed priests for failing to convert the Kaigani (Niblack 1888, 327). Garfield and Forrest (1948, 67–70) agree that the pole celebrated Haida resistance to missionaries. Other writers (Waterman 1923, 125; fig. 120; and Keithahn 1963, 143) offer the opposite interpretation, namely, that it commemorated the family's *conversion* to Orthodox Catholicism and baptism, with its images inspired by saints and cherubs depicted on cards given to the chief by the Russian Bishop. Wilson Duff (Duff, Wallen, and Clark 1969, 75) reported that according to Walter Baronovich Young, a direct

SKULKA'S HOUSE FRONTAL POLE

BY ROBIN WRIGHT, ART HISTORIAN

Thomas Skulka's house frontal pole fascinated visitors to Howkan in the nineteenth century. Elizabeth Skidmore reported an explanation of the figures she heard directly from Chief Skulka in the early 1880s, a story of one of his ancestors, a famous woman from the Eagle Clan, whose two children were carried off in "a Boston man" ship and were never returned. The bearded figure wearing a military uniform was understood to represent this "Boston Man," presumably to ridicule or shame him for the theft of the children. In the late 1880s George Emmons recorded a different story, that the bearded man was a military official of Sitka who had been kind to an ancestor of Skulka's (quoted in Barbeau 1950, 405).

It is interesting that there are two other accounts of children being taken away in ships from this area, one from the Spanish Arteaga expedition and one from Haida elder Robert Cogo in 1975. According to the journals of this expedition, in 1779 the Spanish explorer Arteaga purchased five children from Bucareli Bay in the vicinity of Prince of Wales Island with the purpose of "gaining a better knowledge of the people and their customs." There was apparently an exchange of goods for four of the children, but an older boy was invited on board as an interpreter (Gormly 1977, 13–14). Erma Lawrence recorded the Haida version of this encounter from Haida elder Robert Cogo in 1975. He said that the two Spanish ships were surrounded by the Haida in eighty canoes, and, being afraid, the Spanish fired their cannons, killing two Haidas, after which talks were held, peace was made, and gifts were exchanged. As part of this exchange, four Haida children were given to the Spanish, two girls and two boys. These children were taken away and never returned (Lawrence 1975, 26; Vaughan 1985, 29–30; Wright 2001, 29–30). Perhaps two of these children were from Skulka's wife's family, and this family remembered the loss of their children by carving the Spanish sea captain on their pole.

Though Scidmore said that Skulka was from the Eagle Clan, John Wallace identified him as from the Owl Clan (a Raven clan) and his wife as an Eagle. John Wallace explained the meaning of the figures on Thomas Skulka's Howkan house frontal pole to Viola Garfield in June 1941 at Hydaburg, Alaska. The pole combines figures from both Skulka's (sku'lkE) Owl Clan (a Raven clan) and his wife's (T'aul kīt kát) Eagle Clan. The two figures on the top belonged to the wife's father; the second figure is an Eagle, signifying the wife's crest (they chose to use an American eagle for this). He described the third figure down as a "White Russian from Sitka. This is a white person seen by the Haidas, probably the first one seen by this clan."

4.8. Chief Skulka house front pole, Howkan (Kaigani Haida), ca. 1923. Photograph by John Thwaites. University of Washington Libraries. Special Collections, NA3606.

A different explanation was offered by the school teacher in Hydaburg at the time, Mr. Miller, who said he was told that "the Russian was put on here because Russians took the land away from the Indians and did not pay them. The eagle stands on the Russian's head to hold them down until the land is paid for" (Garfield 1941, 5–6). The Burke Museum has a large model of this pole, with the name Skulka written at the bottom. The owl figure was initially identified by Bill Holm as an eagle, based on its hooked beak, before Garfield's notes were known. Holm also speculated that the model was probably made by the same person who carved the full-sized pole (Holm 1987, 156–57). Perhaps that man was Thomas Skulka himself.

descendant of Chief Skowl, the pole commemorated the baptism of Skowl in Sitka, not the ridicule of the priests. He agrees that the carvers (Gyinahwan and John Wallace's father from Klinkwan) were given pictures of saints to copy at the bottom. Most recently, Steve Brown (personal communication, 2003) commented, "When I worked on reconstructing this pole in 1980/81, and read the various interpretations, I tended to prefer the 'shame and resistance' position, but when the evidence mounted, had to concede that Walter Young was most likely correct." Brown now believes the pole commemorates Skowl's baptism.

Probably the most famous pole depicting a white person is the Lincoln pole of Tongass (fig. 4.9), which has been subjected to various interpretations over the years. Some facts are indisputable: Chief Ebbetts (the leader who hosted Seward and later erected the Seward shame pole) moved his village around 1869 from Cat Island to what became known as Tongass, where that same year an American fort and customs house had been founded. By the late nineteenth century, Ebbetts had erected a pole containing an image with the likeness of Abraham Lincoln. It is the interpretation of these facts and their historical reconstruction that have been consistently contested for a century. Judge James Wickersham, writing in *Sunset Magazine* (1924, 35), first asserted that the image originated when the government ship used to collect taxes, the *Lincoln*, was anchored near the new fort and custom house on Tongass Island. He claimed that the Tongass people had moved close to the fort site for protection from their Kagwantan enemies. Chief Ebbets associated Abraham Lincoln with the American's presence, and commissioned carver Thle-da to carve on a pole an image based on the president's picture. In addition, since members of their own clan had been enslaved by the Eagle Kagwantans, the pole celebrated Lincoln's freeing of *all* slaves.

4.9. Original carving of "Lincoln," from top of Lincoln pole. Tongass (Tlingit), nineteenth century. Alaska State Museum, Juneau, 2B-833.

Two widely distributed magazines, *Natural History* and the *Saturday Evening Post*, both uncritically accepted Wickersham's story (Eifert 1947; Powers 1950), as did Forrest and Garfield (1948, 52–55). This inspired Tlingit leader William Lewis Paul's letter to the *Post* (1950) contradicting Judge Wickersham's "commemoration of emancipation" story. According to Paul, Yahl-gee-yi of the Raven Clan erected the pole to validate his claim to have been the first to see a white man. When he asked the local soldiers for a picture of a white man that his artist could use as a model, they gave him Lincoln's; thus what appears to be the Great Emancipator himself was a generic white person to the pole carvers and owner. Paul also defends his Raven Clan ancestors against charges of slave-status—to this day a devastating insult—claiming that they were fierce warriors; he mentions, for example, when they attacked the British fort at Selkirk in 1852.

Paul's attempt to correct the record had limited success, as a major book on totem poles published in 1963 (Keithahn 1963, 67, 121, 154) reiterated Wickersham's story. Several years later, perhaps in response to that well-received book, Paul published a comprehensive, well-documented essay, "The real story of the Lincoln totem" in *Alaska Journal* (Paul 1971). Once again, he insisted that the "Proud Raven Pole," its name when Paul's Raven ancestors raised it at Tongass in 1883, represented the first white man seen by his people. He also suggests that Tongass village, which probably started up even a few years before the fort arrived, prospered economically by trading with the military post; the Tlingit neither sought nor needed any protection. Because of this new wealth, Tongass leaders raised new poles, some of which marked recent historical events—such as seeing the first white person. Paul added that in Alaska, slaves were only legally liberated later by Judge Lafayette Dawson, and that the revenue-cutter *Lincoln* played no significant role in the fort or in the peoples' lives. Paul again accused Judge Wickersham of having fabricated the story, claiming that only after Wickersham presented this story at a Lincoln Day Dinner in Washington, D.C., circa 1920, did he contact Paul for confirmation. Paul inquired among the elders and sent the judge the correct story, though Wickersham ignored it.

Despite this correction by a notable Native writer, the fiction continued. Quite recently, Native guides have said that the Lincoln pole (a copy of which stands in Saxman Village near Ketchikan) commemorated the peace of two rival Tlingit tribes that was facilitated by the intervention of the U.S. revenue-cutter *Lincoln*. The one prominent place that features Paul's story is the Alaska State Museum, where the fragile, old, and weathered original Lincoln figure is on exhibit. According to the label, Yahl-gee-yi, a Raven Clan Tlingit, commissioned the pole to commemorate the first white man seen by a Tlingit. The artist modeled it after a picture—which just happened to be of Abraham Lincoln—obtained from the army post on Tongass Island in the late 1860s. As photographs were extremely rare at that time, this was likely the only image they had.

This anecdote offers a cautionary tale about accepting a pole's explanation at face value. As Scidmore noted in her early writings, whites enjoyed fabricating stories about poles. It certainly appears that Judge Wickersham invented this one and perpetuated it even after he learned it was false. As Steve Henrikson, curator at the Alaska State Museum comments, "It's exactly the arrogance on the part of Caucasian people that allowed this story to be perpetuated to the present day" (quoted in Kizzia 1997, 28). Many non-Native people prefer the story of Lincoln the president being honored by a position on a pole rather than simply being an anonymous model for a Native carving. Indeed, a replica in fiberglass of the Lincoln pole proudly stood before the Illinois State Museum in Springfield, Illinois, to celebrate that state's great president (McMurty 1972, 7). They also find appealing to their sense of American-centric history the version in which a U.S. ship played a major role in subduing rival clans. But it would seem that, as was the case with the appropriation of flags and flagpoles, these images of whites served several functions, perhaps the most important of which was to enhance a Native chief's status.

THE ART OF TRAVEL: VISUALIZING THE "VANISHING RACES"

Totem poles were sometimes seen as aesthetic monuments to the fleeting vitality of the Native people. In 1906 Lillie LeGrand Lockwood wrote an article in *Sunset Magazine* entitled "Good Bye, Totem" (1906) extolling old poles and lamenting their demise. Lockwood celebrates Kasaan (see fig. 4.4) with florid phrases, "How musically [its name] clings to the auditory sense and resounds through the labyrinth and vestibule of the inner ear. Old Kasaan, the very sound of it suits the forest of stark, gaunt poles that have faced all sorts of wind and weather, a companion of the great White silence, as they face outward on Clarence straits from Prince of Wales Island" (Lockwood 1906, 338). She imagines the village and its proud inhabitants when fully populated, but then, bemoaning its abandoned state, sees "desolation weeping from the totems' protruding eyes and the heavy jowls bearded with lichens."

Regardless of such sentiments, tourism contributed significantly to the irreversible modernization of the Northwest Coast. Despite its Greek church, Russian cemetery, and historical structures, Sitka had held little enticement for Scidmore, who had complained, "There are no *totem* poles, or carved, grotesquely-painted houses to lend outward interest to the village, and the Indians themselves are too much given to ready-made clothes and civilized ways to be really picturesque" (Scidmore 1885, 175). In her opinion, sights of "civilized" Native peoples distracted tourists from their totem pole pleasures. Scidmore laments the decline of poles as the consequence of acculturation:

> With the advent of civilization the Indians are losing their reverence for these heraldic monuments, and some have been destroyed and others sold; for the richest of these Native peoples are so mercenary that they do not scruple to sell anything that belongs to them. The disappearance of the *totem* poles would rob these villages of their greatest interest for the tourists, and the ethnologist who would solve the mysteries and read the pictures finally aright, should hasten to this rich and neglected field (Scidmore 1885, 54).

Likewise, Lockwood urged readers to travel as soon as they could to Alaska, for in a short time she expected that there would be nothing of cultural interest left to see. In her account, the totem pole emerged from the unfettered imagination of Natural Man; those responsible for his Fall should hastily travel north to catch a glimpse of this temperate Garden of Eden that was soon to disappear, overwhelmed by the brutalities of civilization. Because a full-size totem pole "in its original proportions is quite an unmanageable feature in a collection," Lockwood noted that Indians had begun to create model poles to satisfy "the fascination with which the tourist regarded the hideous beauty of their totems" (Lockwood 1906, 340; on model poles, see chapter 6). She mourned the commercialization of Native culture that resulted from the tourist boom—especially as evidenced by what we now term totem pole kitsch—reserving her most critical comments for Ketchikan, where poles are "on wheels . . . in transit, passing into something else—at the mercy of the poverty or caprice of civilization." Having left their Native villages, totem poles now appeared as icons for barber shops and restaurants, "totem faces, with 'specs, advertising the leading oculist."

By the second decade of the twentieth century, thousands of tourists had sailed the Inside Passage, several gold rushes had taken place, and the world was about to undergo the massive transformation caused by the Great War. In 1915, a team of well-known and highly respected photographers of Alaska Native life and culture, Lloyd Winter and Percy Pond, published a small pamphlet, *The Totems of Alaska*, illustrated by photographs they took in 1895–96. The title on the cover (fig. 4.10) consists of whimsical letters composed of stylized Northwest Coast animals in the mode of medieval illuminated letters; the *T*'s all represent totem poles with horizontal animals perching at their tops. Accurate annotations accompany twelve photographs of poles, such as the Shakes and Kadashan monuments from Wrangell, the interior of the Klukwan Whale

House, a Chilkat shaman's grave with grave guardians, and two house posts from the Klukwan Frog House. In a striking, and even surprising, contrast with the veneration of old carvings so evident throughout the literature on poles, Winter and Pond write about recently carved poles: "The workmanship is of a higher order than that of the older carvings, which is probably due to the fact that modern tools were used in the execution of the work. The use of paint artistically applied adds to the attractive appearance of the totem" (Winter and Pond 1915).

Winter and Pond shared the conflicted attitudes of so many others of their era. They believed that acculturation was good for Native peoples but represented a passing of the glorious Native traditions that they themselves had photographed several decades earlier. Winter and Pond report that the Alaskan Native of the day was "totally indifferent" to the traditions of his forefathers, and would use his totem poles for firewood if necessary. The photograph entitled "The Last of the Totems at Howkan" laments the consequences of history while celebrating the civilizing influence of whites. Once a striking Haida community, Howkan was then "shorn of the rude symbols of [the Indians'] ancestors," for sidewalks, one-family houses, the government school, and sounds of phonograph music characterized the village. The photographers praised the "well-dressed, intelligent, industrious" Indians who exemplified the new order of contemporary Native life, but only at the cost of traditional custom.

The final photograph in this book, "Lovers Lane, Indian River Road, Sitka," depicts the totem-pole-lined path through the national historical park there. The romance of the ancient carvings has here merged with the romance of contemporary couples as they wander past totem poles through evergreen woods. The image shows three poles, each one more distant from the viewer. After Winter and Pond note that Sitka contains the "last evidence of the aboriginal method of recording history," they offer a poem, inspired by the thought of an Indian entering the Sitka grove, to complement the photograph:

May not the heart of Nature's child,
Thrill with the self-same pride,
That stirs the heart of those beguiled
To fickle Mammon's side.
The simple thoughts of lowly men,
And crude expressions wrought
In wood and stone, may speak of things
That higher Art cannot have taught,
In gilded palaces of kings (Winter and Pond 1915).

In a romanticizing vein common to their generation, Winter and Pond portray "lowly" Native peoples as simple-minded children of nature, creators of crude art. Despite such apparent inferiority, their very art embodies messages of great significance not present in more "advanced" art; the reference to Mammon implies that civilized society is replete with the avarice and envy lacking in more primitive groups. Like many colonial agents, the photographers—along with contemporaneous and later artists in other media—expressed keen nostalgia for those aspects of indigenous life that they were directly involved in displacing.

4.10. Cover, *The Totems of Alaska*, by Lloyd Winter and Percy Pond, 1915. Jonaitis collection.

THE LAMENTS OF EMILY

On the top floor of the Vancouver Art Gallery are several vivid paintings of Northwest Coast totem poles, including a 1912 impressionist-influenced depiction of a Kwakwa̲ka̲'wakw "old Indian house" from Gwayasda̲ms

4.11. Emily Carr, *Return from Fishing, Guydons,* 1912. Oil on paperboard. 38" x 26." Photograph by Trevor Mills. Collection of the Vancouver Art Gallery, Emily Carr Trust, 42.3.51.

(Gilford Island; fig. 4.11) that shows several canoes being unloaded of goods before an impressive sea monster pole. In contrast to this human activity taking place in the presence of a valued crest object, a 1930 painting of Skedans, *Vanquished* (fig. 4.12), shows a village with no humans, its abandoned poles at all angles, "conquered" by the encroaching forest. These are just two of the hundreds of Northwest Coast scenes painted over many decades by British Columbia artist Emily Carr, sometimes identified as that province's most beloved artist.

Today Carr's compelling images of the Northwest Coast function as both works of art and historic documents of certain locales at specific moments in time (Macnair and Stewart 1999). An awkward, unconventional British Columbian, Carr had early on identified with Native people, believing that they shared her alienation from mainstream Victorian society (Shadbolt 1990, 87). Like so many of her generation, Emily Carr often lamented the loss of the "disappearing Indian." She was thus receptive to the suggestion by artist Theodore Richardson, whom she met in 1907,

4.12. Emily Carr, *Vanquished*, 1930. Oil on canvas. 36.2" x 51." Photograph by Trevor Mills. Collection of the Vancouver Art Gallery, Emily Carr Trust, 42.3.

that she create as complete a catalogue of coastal poles as possible before they all vanished. Richardson, an American from Minneapolis who worked in Alaska during the summers from 1884 to 1914, believed that Native cultures were vanishing and in need of preservation by artistic images, so he traveled by canoe to remote communities and painted villages, houses, and poles. Carr was also influenced and supported by Marius Barbeau, who encouraged Canadian artists to depict totem poles as part of his effort to salvage national cultural heritage (see chapter 8).

Despite her intention to depict totem poles as accurately as possible for historical posterity, Carr found much to romanticize about the inner meaning of these poles. In her response we witness the tensions inherent in the modernist project, with its belief in scientific progress and its nostalgia for the pre- or anti-modern. Early in her career, she waxed poetic about the spirituality and honesty of Native art:

> Indian Art broadened my seeing, loosened the formal tightness I had learned in England's schools. Its bigness and stark reality baffled my White man's understanding. . . . The Indian caught first at the inner intensity of his subject, worked outside to the surfaces. His spiritual conception he buried deep in the wood he was about to carve. Then—chip! chip! his crude tools released the symbols that were to clothe his thought—no sham, no mannerism. The lean, neat Indian hands carved what the Indian mind comprehended (Carr 1971, 212).

Consistent with her romantic notion of both artist and Native, she felt totem poles to be the pure imaginative or spiritual expression of artists' deep-felt conceptions about nature and animals (Carr 1993, 51). (It is unclear if Carr understood the role of poles in competitive social display.) She also promoted what would later be termed "affinities" between the tribal and the modern (c.f. Rubin 1984); in one of her rare public talks, Carr pleaded for understanding of the modern artist. She pointed out that Indian images were spiritual in nature, something she wanted all art to be. She argued that Northwest Coast Native art was basically "modern" in its own right, in that it looks below the surface representation to the deep meaning, employing distortion and abstraction to better convey the spiritual truth within (Emily Carr 1927).

During her 1928 trip up the coast, Carr visited places she had painted over a decade before, including Alert Bay, the Queen Charlottes, and the Nass and Skeena rivers. No poles were left in Massett, only one stood in Skidegate and three in Alert Bay, and she found the Skeena poles poorly restored (Tippett 1979, 157). Unhappy to find economically depressed villages, fewer poles, and commodified art, she wrote,

> Everywhere I saw miserable change creeping, creeping over villages, over people. The Indians had sold most of their best poles. Museums were gobbling them. The recent carvings were superficial, meaningless; the Indian had lost faith in his totem. Now he was carving to please the tourist and to make money for himself, not to express the glory of his tribe (Carr 1993, 237).

She encountered fewer friendly Native peoples on this visit, probably adding to her disillusionment.

Carr expressed dismay that "the Indian had lost faith in his totem." But what exactly did that mean? Carr—and many others—assumed a causal relationship between beliefs and their visual depictions—in other words, the presumption that no poles meant no active traditions. Fewer poles stood, to be sure, but was there evidence that Native peoples had fully abandoned their cultural views? The potlatch was still illegal when Carr visited villages, and residents would likely have been reluctant to share with an outsider their beliefs and values. This surely did not mean they had none. Indeed, as we have described throughout this book, Northwest Coast First Nations maintained traditions while accommodating themselves to modernity.

A common trope in many turn-of-the-twentieth-century tourist documents and anthropological studies was the disappearing Native. Many totem pole representations were deeply embedded within this larger discourse. Carr's description of poles is filled with romanticism concerning the vanishing noble savage:

> [The poles of Skedans] were in a long straggling row the entire length of the bay and pointed this way and that; but no matter how drunken their tilt, the Haida poles never lost their dignity. They looked sadder, perhaps, when they bowed forward and more stern when they tipped back. They were bleached to a pinkish silver colour and cracked by the sun, but nothing could make them mean or poor, because the Indians had put strong thought into them and had believed sincerely in what they were trying to express (Carr 1993, 32).

> There were many fine totem poles in Cha-atl—Haida poles, tragic and fierce. The wood of them was bleached out, but looked green from the mosses which grew in the chinks, and the tufts of grass on the heads of the figures stuck up like coarse hair. The human faces carved on the totem poles were stern and grim, the animal faces fierce and strong; supernatural things were pictured on the poles too. Everything about Cha-atl was so vast and deep you shriveled up (Carr 1993, 58).

Like so many others who felt positively toward Native peoples, Carr presented Natives as innocent victims of progress, simple and plain like animals and children; she idealized their culture in a fashion similar to her romanticization of nature.[10] The harsh realities of a twentieth-century Native art that challenged such idealization and utopianism inspired further despair in Carr. Carr and others, like photographer Edward S. Curtis, were attempting to salvage what remained of the "vanishing Indian." As she wrote about Northwest Coast Native carvings, "These things should be to we Canadians what the ancient Briton's relics are to the English. Only a few more years and they will be gone forever, into silent nothingness, and I would gather my collections together before they are forever past" (quoted in Francis 1992, 31).

FROM LAMENTATION TO PROTECTIONISM

During the last several decades of the nineteenth century, different visitors to the Northwest Coast had strikingly different attitudes toward the Native inhabitants and their cultures. The missionaries who reported back to their home offices described the Indians most harshly, often with stereotypes of cannibalism, brutality, and savagery. Tourist brochures, in contrast, often went in the opposite direction, expounding the virtues of Native art and dance while emphasizing their higher degree of civilization than other aboriginal peoples. They offered the tourist an encounter with the unusual, even perhaps strange, "other" within a safe and contained environment. The guide books tended to fall somewhere between these two extremes, portraying a more honest and ambivalent picture of Native life.

By the first decades of the twentieth century, the missionaries had by and large succeeded in converting most Native people, and most traditional villages on or near the tourist routes were abandoned, many of their poles decaying. Visitors often considered the Native people they encountered (usually the ones most dependent on tourism-based income) as demoralized and degraded souls to be pitied at best or disdained at worst. Their cultures, influenced by years of interaction with Euroamericans, appeared as dismal mongrels unworthy of praise. Like the professional anthropologists, these outsiders lamented the ebbing of authentic Native culture, the destruction of the infinitely better "old ways."

In popular books and magazines, compassionate writers mourned the victimization of Native culture by the onrush of colonization and settlement. Ronald Campbell-Johnston, in his 1924 *The Story of the Totem,* writes "in deep sympathy for the hopeless passing-away of these . . . children of Nature, before the oncoming rush of the White man, who, with the ruthless heel of modern, supposed progress, has stamped so brutally on all obstacles in the path of his mercenary, economical trade advance" (Campbell-Johnston 1924, 7). In that same year, Aubrey Fullerton begins an essay entitled "The Last of the Totem Poles" with the statement, "The making of totem poles is at an end" (Fullerton 1924, 41). And J. R. Morrison, in his 1933 "The Significance of Totems," laments that "time's curtain is falling on the last act for [the Indian] and his; so he may well feel that the Totem and Faith of his forefathers are powerless against the new Totem whose followers are the disciples of avaricious and ruthless despoliation" (J. R. Morrison 1933, 8). These comments can be classified as "colonial laments," which, written after the end of aboriginal menace to settlers, mourned the deterioration of what was believed to have been an earlier, purer, more authentic way of life.

With such romantic modernism, Westerners who critiqued their own unstoppable progress toward modernity viewed indigenous lifestyles as desirable, if increasingly unattainable, alternatives. The Northwest Coast manifestation of the Colonial Paradox—in which becoming civilized is good, but losing traditional culture is bad—especially bemoaned the decline of totem pole carving and the deterioration of existing poles. As poles had become touristic emblems for the region, so too did their demise signal larger degrees of cultural loss. Something needed to be done. It was generally thought that First Nations cultures, indexed by their now-admirable artistic creations, had to be preserved and protected by well-meaning whites. During the first half of the twentieth century, individuals, museums, government agencies, and commercial entrepreneurs labored to preserve these monuments for posterity. The age of tourism during which totem poles were observed slowly changed into the age of preservation during which these monuments—as well as the global profile of the whole Northwest Coast region—became further transformed.

TOTEMS FOR TOURISTS

ON SALVAGE AND SALVATION

It might be said that the totem pole is the memorial of a people who are dead. Our Indians of today are being civilized according to the white man's definition of the word. Few of them can even read the totem poles that stand sentinel over their villages. Their fathers' ways are not their ways.

—HOWARD MITCHELL, 1925

Skill and resources of the white man must be employed to restore and repair the finest examples of this Indian magic, if the best illustrations of the skill of these ancient people are to be preserved.

—G.C. PORTER, 1926

Those responsible for [totem poles'] survival, and perhaps improvement, are the railways and the tourists.

—MARIUS BARBEAU, ANTHROPOLOGIST, 1931

Today's tourists to British Columbia and Alaska frequently consult guidebooks for advice on attractions. Those interested in Native culture—and, in particular, totem poles—are directed to numerous sites. Hillary Stewart's classic *Looking at Totem Poles* (1993) is a handy source for locating poles as one travels from the British Columbia–Washington border up to Juneau (see appendix A for further reference works). The two largest British Columbia cities are famous for their totem pole sites: Vancouver for Stanley Park and the University of British Columbia Museum of Anthropology, and Victoria for Thunderbird Park and the Royal British Columbia Museum. At Sitka's National Historical Park, the visitor can stroll through a magnificent old growth forest along a path lined with poles. A trip to Ketchikan becomes a totem pole aficionado's delight, with not just one but two totem pole parks—at the Native village of Saxman and out of town at Totem Bight—as well as at the Totem Heritage Center, which displays magnificent old poles and some new ones, and the new Potlatch Park attraction, with its reconstruction of a Northwest Coast village.

These are exceptionally popular tourist destinations. Today, Stanley Park's stand of totem poles attracts more than three million Vancouver visitors per year, making it the most popular attraction in British Columbia (Jensen 2004, 29; fig. 5.1). And in visitor surveys, the poles in Ketchikan consistently rate as the most popular cultural attraction in Alaska. It is interesting that Vancouver—as well as Victoria, Sitka, Seattle, and Juneau, other cities today associated with poles—had no poles before the twentieth century. Even Ketchikan, a city within the region of totem pole manufacture, had few poles until the 1930s. How is it, then, that these are now *the* places to see poles? Rarely mentioned at these impressive displays is the fact that they stand in parks or on museum grounds as the results of projects organized and controlled by non-Natives—with varying

5.1. Stanley Park totem poles, 2004. From left to right: Beaver Crest Pole, by Norman Tait (Nisga'a); Eagle Pole, by Ellen Neel (Kwakwaka'wakw); Wakas Pole, by Doug Cranmer (Kwakwaka'wakw); Sky Chief Pole, by Art Thompson and Tim Paul (Nuu-chah-nulth); Thunderbird House Post, by Tony Hunt (Kwakwaka'wakw); Breakfast on the Beach Pole, by Beau Dick (Kwakwaka'wakw); Skedans Mortuary Pole, by Bill Reid, with repairs by Don Yeomans (Haida). Photograph by Aldona Jonaitis.

degrees of participation by First Nations communities—who felt strongly that these monuments needed to be preserved. Today most of the villages where the poles once stood are known simply as notations on maps of old Indian sites. Their totem poles have been transported to larger communities where tourists can easily enjoy these monuments.[1]

By the beginning of the twentieth century, many Northwest Coast Natives had moved from their pre- and early contact villages. Sometimes entire groups abandoned traditional villages and moved closer to white towns for economic reasons. Others moved after diseases had destroyed their communities. In many of these villages poles remained, standing in silent rows before empty houses. Sometimes they were simply removed by unscrupulous visitors. The more responsible collectors for museums located the owners of poles and purchased the carvings (see chapter 7). In the meantime, residents of both British Columbia and Alaska became worried about the large-scale removal of these carvings to distant lands, and initiated projects to keep them in the region.

The role of non-Natives in these projects is of utmost importance, as whites who believed they were "saving" Native culture worked to preserve poles, often with the development of tourist economies in mind. While some projects imagined themselves to be "salvaging" poles, others used a language of "restoration." In a neutral sense, these terms can refer to two sequences in a single process ("salvage" indicating removal for protection; "restoration" suggesting subsequent treatment to ensure preservation). At the same time, however, there is an ideological basis for the terminology: salvage projects often assumed the moribund status of Native art and culture, while restoration projects were often approached as collaborations with indigenous pole owners and carvers. In practice, the two terms and concepts certainly blurred and overlapped. In any case, the totem poles thus created or altered during these projects are products of activities conceptualized, organized, and administered by usually well-intentioned non-Natives who largely imposed their own concepts of cultural accuracy and authenticity. The transformations of totem poles wrought by their incorporation into tourist economies encouraged neutralization of specific clan-based meanings and the development of stereotypical images through repetition and misidentification. As a result, most of the poles seen today by the majority of tourists are simultaneously genuine Native art works and artifacts of the colonial imagination—truly intercultural objects.

CHANGING TIMES FOR PEOPLE AND POLES

By 1910, Vancouver's population was over 100,000. With few exceptions, the growing white population of British Columbia, intent on exploiting its natural resources and farming its lands, felt little sympathy for the rights of its Native people. Moreover, because Native claims threatened development, land allotments required regularization, administration, and, ideally, territorial reduction. Unlike other indigenous Canadians, most coastal First Nations had never given up title to their lands and thus demanded fair and reasonable settlements for lands taken from them. After long and complicated negotiations between the provincial and federal governments, a special joint committee on Indian reserves appointed by the federal government ruled that the Indians had no claim on British Columbia lands, and that was thought to be that (Duff 1964a, 67–69).[2]

Concurrently, the Canadian government began to take seriously its self-appointed mission to encourage assimilation by destroying Native traditions. Parliament had outlawed the potlatch in 1884, but did not actively enforce the ban until the early decades of the twentieth century. For some groups, like the Haida, this prohibition meant little, as they had ceased potlatching anyway. Others, however, rebelled against the law. The Kwakwa̱ka̱'wakw defiantly continued potlatching openly until 1922, when a number of potlatch participants were sent to jail. After that, some potlatching continued, but more covertly than before.[3] Thus, totem pole relocation projects took place in the immediate context of federal policy promoting cultural assimilation and land expropriation.

Inequalities plagued Alaska Natives quite as much as their British Columbia brethren. In 1912, a group of twelve Tlingit and one Tsimshian founded the oldest continuing Native organization in the United States, the Alaska Native Brotherhood (ANB), dedicated to promoting Indian rights, especially citizenship. Three years later, the Alaska territorial legislature passed a law to allow Natives citizenship—as long as individuals disavowed their tribal affiliation, passed an examination, demonstrated that they had the endorsement of five whites, received approval by the district judge, and generally acted "civilized." Under such constraints, it is not surprising that only a few Natives became citizens at the time. The situation came to a head in 1922, when Chief Shakes of Wrangell and his niece, Tillie Paul Tamaree, were arrested for voting. William Lewis Paul, the first Native Alaskan lawyer, defended his great-uncle Shakes and his own mother, winning their acquittal. As a result, Alaskan Natives received the vote two years before other Native Americans got that right with the passage of the 1924 Indian Citizenship Act. The Tlingit—an increasingly formidable political force in the state—worked through the ANB and the Alaska Native Sisterhood (ANS), founded in 1923, to promote Native subsistence rights, to fight segregation that prevented Natives from entering public places reserved for whites, and to integrate the schools (finally achieved with the passage of the Anti-Discrimination Bill of 1945, twenty years before the desegregation of schools in the lower forty-eight states). A major issue in Alaska, as it was in British Columbia, was land rights, which the ANB had tried to address with lawsuits during the early decades of the twentieth century. In the 1950s, the ANB sued the United States, contending that twenty million acres of land (then the Tongass National Forest and Glacier Bay National Monument) had been illegally appropriated from the Tlingit and Haida. Resolution of this dispute would have to wait until 1971. As in British Columbia, discrimination, bigotry, and intolerance, coupled with callous appropriation of traditional lands, constituted one side of the Alaskan attitude toward Natives; the other side was marked by the increasingly treasured status of Native Alaskan art.

It is within the framework of the criminalized potlatch, colonial inequities, and deafness to legitimate aboriginal claims that the story of Alaska and British Columbian totem pole preservation projects should be understood. Well-intentioned people who admired these carvings but feared their deterioration initiated salvage programs to move poles to more populous locales. Properly maintained, the poles would be appreciated by the growing number of tourists to the region; indeed, it was hoped they would help draw travelers to these places and thus enhance the local economy. It was the rare individual who acknowledged the irony of denying Natives sovereignty for their land and prohibiting the potlatches so central to raising totem poles, all the while celebrating the very monuments displaying ancestral claims to crests that frequently functioned as validations of indigenous land title. The popular assumption that poles were of great antiquity, that they were ancient monuments not resulting from contemporary Native cultural production, helped release their aesthetic admirers from this political irony and injustice.

STANLEY PARK, VANCOUVER

In 1889, a group of British Columbian settlers founded the Art Historical and Scientific Association of Vancouver (AHSAV) to promote education, support art appreciation, and assemble a collection of Native objects "having value as Art, or historical material" (Goodfellow n.d., 11). Five years later, the association modified its structure and became more civically active, sponsoring lectures, supporting publications, and acquiring artwork and historical documents. In 1905, the group, in agreement with the City of Vancouver, opened the Vancouver Museum in the Carnegie Library Building on East Hastings Street.[4] By the early 1920s, the AHSAV had purchased four Kwakwa̱ka̱'wakw poles for Stanley Park—two house posts, one full-size pole by Charlie James, and the pole that stood attached to the façade of Chief Wakas's house in Alert Bay. Soon after all four poles were erected in Vancouver, the AHSAV published a pamphlet by the Reverend John C. Goodfellow, entitled *The Totem Poles in Stanley Park*, that interpreted "for the White man the strange relics of a vanishing race . . . the strange histories that are locked up in the Native hieroglyphics that adorn the totem poles" (Goodfellow n.d., 7). Although Goodfellow describes poles as strange in his preface, later he expresses a more positive judgment, stating that these carvings are "work[s] of art" made by "gifted carvers" (Goodfellow n.d., 23). And he concludes his introduction to totemism with the enlightened suggestion that this system of thought "seems to indicate that primitive people had glimpses of profound scientific truths. They may not have learned the 'why' and the 'wherefore' of all they practiced; but we shall do well not to consider them uneducated, though un-lettered" (Goodfellow n.d., 24).[5]

These four poles were to be the first carvings in an elaborate project envisioned by the AHSAV to promote knowledge and understanding of the indigenous cultures of British Columbia and to put Vancouver on the tourist map. AHSAV wanted to hire Native carvers, using traditional tools and methods, to fabricate an entire village. Goodfellow presents their initial vision: "The proposed village, and the totems already erected, will represent the work of the Kwakiutl Indians in particular, and the Coast Indians in general. The totem is an indication of an old and wide culture. It points to the past. The past illuminates the present" (Goodfellow n.d., 15). Despite this enthusiasm, the village was never realized, in part because the AHSAV had great difficulties raising the necessary funds for this project, and in part because the local Squamish objected strenuously to the establishment of a village (even if a simulation) representing their longtime enemies within their own territory (Jacknis 2002, 140). Nevertheless, the AHSAV did succeed in helping to make Vancouver a tourist destination by means of these poles. In 1936, when Vancouver celebrated its Golden Jubilee, three additional poles joined the Stanley Park assemblage at Lumberman's Arch: a Haida mortuary pole and two more Kwakwa̱ka̱'wakw poles. In addition, an unusual Coast Salish pole for the time, the "Thunderbird Dynasty Pole," by Squamish Chief Mathias Joe, was raised at Prospect Point (see chapter 12).[6]

So accustomed are most park visitors to museums—with their similar assemblages of objects from different provenances—that few likely wonder whether there is any connection between the individual poles, their status in their original locations, and the story of their transport to Vancouver. At most, visitors want to identify the images on the poles. For most people, what matters is neither original context nor aboriginal social significance nor the biographic history of the pole. Instead, what matters is seeing a tall, freestanding, usually colorful monument replete with mythic images made by the Indians of the region. By decontextualiz-

A TALE OF TWO HOUSE POSTS

BY MARY ANNE BARKHOUSE, KWAKWAKA'WAKW ARTIST

5.2. Mary Anne Barkhouse (Kwakwaka'wakw), in collaboration with Michael Belmore, *Reservoir*, partial installation views, Walter Phillips Gallery at the Banff Centre for the Arts, 1997. Salt, cedar, and casting resin. 48" x 96" x 36" each. Photograph by Michael Belmore. Courtesy of Mary Anne Barkhouse.

5.3. Detail of Thunderbird head cast from Charlie James house post.

As our extended family sat around the dinner table one wintery day, talk eventually meandered around to porcupines, a favourite subject of one particular uncle who has suffered much at the paws of the methodical and obsessive quill pig. Among the quill pigs' many offences were the destruction of trees through de-barking and chewing the brake lines out of cars in the wintertime whilst gnawing them for their salt content. On many occasions the beasts met an untimely end on account of their excessive quest for salt. This led to further discussion about the nature of the substance, its essential role in our diet, and also its toxic properties from overconsumption.

Many years ago I had heard that a mould had been made of a house post that my great-great-grandfather, Charlie James, had carved around the turn of the century. In 1927 the Art, Historical and Scientific Association of Vancouver had acquired a pair of house posts that Charlie had originally carved for Chief Tsa-wee-nok up in Kingcome Inlet, British Columbia. They were later displayed in Stanley Park, but when one of them had deteriorated due to age and decay, a fibreglass replica was made and the original put into storage at the Vancouver Museum. When the other one finally succumbed to decay, I understand that Tony Hunt was hired to carve a replica, which was painted with Charlie's original designs (see fig. 5.1). To further add to their drama, they had at one time been used as backdrop scenery in an Edward S. Curtis film, *In the Land of the Head Hunters* (see fig. 13.2).

In partnership with Michael Belmore, in the mid 1990s I created an installation, *Reservoir*, which featured (amongst other things) fragments of one of the house posts cast in salt. I had found one of the discarded fibreglass castings, a reject from the original casting processes those many years ago, in a garage in Burnaby and made my own moulds from portions of the posts. In creating work whose purpose was to provoke reflection upon personal and cultural histories, I felt it was important that the iconography originated from and was created by someone within my family. I wanted it to be clear that these were not items created by myself but by someone in my past, and that the work was reproduced in a substance that alluded to the fragile nature of understanding and the corrosive consequence of exploitation.

The original house posts have gone from being functional commissioned pieces to stage props to a tourist attraction to relics in a museum vault, and, lately, to installation artwork exhibited in contemporary galleries. And it probably will not end there. Many times, as I have perused the postcard racks in various cities and airports around North America, the familiar faces of the thunderbird, grizzly bear and the man held in the bear's paws peer out at me, documented at various stages of their lives . . . weathered and framed against a stormy sky, freshly painted against a backdrop of lush foliage in Stanley Park. For objects which are usually very stationary, out of necessity and circumstance, these particular posts have gone out and seen the world. I wonder where their travels will take them next?

ing individual poles in Stanley Park—and soon after in Victoria's Thunderbird Park, created in 1940 (see chapter 9)—"the totem pole" as an idea had been resignified in the province of British Columbia.[7]

SITKA

In the 1880s, Eliza Scidmore had disdained the modernism of Sitka and its lack of totem poles. During the first decade of the twentieth century, Lillie Lockwood praised that same town as a major site for "the most gigantic and impressive commemorative columns." Between the times these two women visited Sitka, the governor of Alaska, John Brady, had convinced chiefs of numerous villages to donate their poles to the state. These ultimately stood in a national park in that town, which as a result became a major center for totem pole tourism.

John Brady arrived in Alaska in 1878, encouraged by Reverend Sheldon Jackson to serve as a Presbyterian missionary. In addition to his evangelical work, Brady was a successful businessman and government official and, between 1897 and 1906, served as the appointed governor of the district of Alaska. He also frequently visited southeast Alaska Native communities and formed close, mutually respectful relationships with the Tlingit and Haida. One of Brady's most lasting legacies is Sitka National Historical Park, where impressive poles line a path through an immense spruce forest.

Like other sympathetic supporters of the time, Brady viewed with approval the American Indian's conversion to Christianity and assumption of a non-Native lifestyle. But this, he acknowledged, came at a loss: "The Natives are now fast giving up their old customs which I think is right for them to do, but it is well to preserve many of the old things so that the young people who are coming on may see how their forefathers used to live" (quoted in Patrick 2002, 57).

One way to preserve the "old things" was to collect totem poles and bring them all to Sitka for protection and preservation. When Brady visited various villages in 1900 to suggest this notion to the chiefs, none was interested in participating. However, Brady persisted, and in 1901 he convinced Chief Saanaheit of Kasaan to donate one large pole, four house posts, and a canoe. Brady rewarded the chief by appointing him town policeman, a prestigious position, and assuring the family that a metal plaque would provide visitors with the donor's name and information on the stories represented by the carvings. Once these treasures arrived in Sitka, Brady had them erected in what is now the National Historical Park (fig. 5.4). In 1903, Brady steamed around to other Tlingit and Haida villages, pleased that the chiefs were now willing to donate their poles as Sanaaheit had done. By the end of his travels, Brady had acquired at least nineteen poles.[8]

It is noteworthy that the Haida and Tlingit gave their carvings to Brady rather than charging him for them. At this time, American and Canadian museum collectors were scavenging the coast for any and all "traditional" objects they could find, the most treasured prize being a totem pole (Cole 1985). Many Native owners bargained skillfully with those collectors, never willing to accept a low price for so desirable an object. With Brady, however, no money changed hands. Brady, an atypical missionary, had enjoyed long-term relationships with the villages and obviously respected their traditions and art. He may have stood in contrast to the rapacious dealers, encouraging the chiefs to give him their poles. So one explanation is that these donations served as expressions of Native respect and admiration for at least some of their colonizers. That may be true from a Western perspective, for it is evident that Brady enjoyed considerable good will in the region. However, from a Native point of view, giving away something valuable enhanced a family's prestige and initiated relations of reciprocity. Just as a chief gained cultural capital through the depletion of material possessions at the end of a great potlatch, so were the totem pole donors empowered by what appeared to be great generosity. Moreover, the chief's pole would stand in a more populated community than his own, and be seen by many more people—thus increasing the number of witnesses to his depiction of status. The Brady poles thus served as articles exchanged in the Alaskan contact zone of both Native and non-Native worlds, each party benefiting from the activity within their own sphere of values.

5.4. Chief Saanaheit (Kaigani Haida) pole with four house posts, erected in Sitka National Historic Park, ca. 1910. Photograph probably by E. W. Merrill. Alaska State Library, P427-37.

Before Brady erected these poles in Sitka, he had them transported out of the state to be exhibited at the world's fairs in St. Louis (1904) and Portland (1905). (We will cover this component of their biographies in those cities in chapter 7.) They arrived back in Alaska in mid-January 1906 and were raised on a popular path alongside the Indian River that offered vistas of forest, mountains, and sea. Brady and his associates in Sitka had another goal for this exhibit, in addition to celebrating southeast Alaskan cultural heritage: to create an attractive destination for the burgeoning tourist industry. And thus Sitka, where tall exterior totem poles had never stood, became known as a major site for their viewing. Now, instead of seeing poles lined up along beaches in front of communal houses, as Scidmore had when she visited Kasaan and Howkan, the tourist sees individual carvings positioned within the spectacular Alaskan landscape. Connected neither to community nor clan, the Sitka poles were removed from participation in an ongoing cultural cycle that included carving, erecting, and potlatching to assume singular identities as objects of aesthetic and historical contemplation.

THE SKEENA RIVER PROJECT

Large-scale collecting activities from the 1880s to the 1910s greatly reduced the number of poles in situ throughout the coast. Only after World War I, when such rapacious acquisition had diminished, largely as a result of dwindling availability, did Canadians became concerned by the quantity of poles that had left British Columbia for the United States and Europe (see appendix D for a list of poles sent abroad). The situation came to a head in 1923 when the highly conservative Gitk'san, who had for years refused all offers for their poles, finally sold one to the American Museum of Natural History (Cole 1985, 272).[9] Canadians resented the notion that once again Americans were invading British Columbia, absconding with carvings that many citizens, with an emerging nationalist consciousness, felt were significant expressions of their country's distinct artistic patrimony. A 1926 article resonates with bitterness about this:

> Tourists go to Alaska . . . quite as much to see the totem poles as the Taku Glacier. Well, then, don't let any totem poles leave the country. "Oh, but we want some specimens," say the American museums. "Yes, indeed," replied Uncle Sam, "just step over to Canada and get all you want. The Canadians do not want them and the Indians will take a dollar a foot for the poles." And did they? You just bet they did! (*Resources* 1926, n.p.).

The author laments that Alert Bay, "one of the outstanding 'totem pole villages'" and one of the most accessible, had only three poles remaining. Even international celebrity Sir Arthur Conan Doyle wrote to Canada's Department of the Interior urging legislation to prevent the removal of poles from the country (Darling and Cole 1980, 30). In response to such petitions, the government amended the Indian Act in 1926 to prevent the "acquisition, removal or destruction of any Indian artifact without consent of the Superintendent General of Indian Affairs" (Darling and Cole 1980, 37). With this legislation, Canada supplied a federal mandate to consolidate totem pole sites for its own citizens and tourists.

Gitk'san poles had long stood in villages near the highly scenic Canadian National Railway (CNR) linking Jasper in the Rockies with Prince Rupert on the Pacific Coast. Recognizing that these decaying totem poles had great tourist potential, the CNR in 1925 initiated a plan to restore and reerect Gitk'san poles where railway passengers could see them. In contrast to Brady's plan—which had removed poles to Sitka, miles from their original villages—Gitk'san poles were to stay near their home communities, only be made more accessible to rail tracks. The CNR received funding from the federal government and help from several anthropologists associated with the National Museum of Canada to realize this project; thus national, commercial, and scholarly interests converged. Although the restoration of Gitk'san totem poles appeared to be an admirable gesture of historic and cultural preservation on the part of the railway, the principle motivation was economic, for the continued presence of totem poles on the Skeena River route promised a future as a major tourist attraction (fig. 5.5).

Anthropologist Marius Barbeau, whom we met in chapter 3, knew from firsthand experience how

5.5. Kitsegukla (Gitk'san) village from Canadian National Railway train, 1926. Canadian Museum of Civilization, 68489.

difficult some villages could be. In his report to the project planning committee, Barbeau recommended restoration work begin in the least hostile communities. He suggested Kispiox, a town he felt to have the friendliest and most agreeable inhabitants, as well as the greatest number of poles, as the first community to approach. Then should come Hazelton and Hagwilget. Only after successful projects had been completed in these villages should any attempt be made to restore the monuments at the conservative and contentious villages of Kitsegukla and Kitwanga. Completely ignoring Barbeau's recommendation, the Committee decided to start work at Kitwanga and Kitsegulka, communities closer to the railway, a decision that proved ill-advised.

Barbeau did not remain central to the project after his initial report, for Edward Sapir assigned Dominion archeologist Harlan I. Smith to "preserve the poles and other objects that will be of interest to tourists" (Darling and Cole 1980, 35). Sapir may have preferred Smith personally, or felt he could control this subordinate's activities more than those of the independent Barbeau. Unfortunately for the project, Smith—whose experience was limited to the Nuxalk and the Salish—had never worked among the Gitk'san and had little understanding of their culture. In 1925, Smith wrote a somewhat disingenuous letter to the chiefs explaining the nature of this work, promoting salvage and preservation, and asking permission to work on the totem poles (Dawn 1981, 32):

> To ALL whom it may concern,
>
> Mr. Barbeau, who was at Kispiox, Skeena Crossing, Hazelton and Hagwilget, as well as Kitwanga last year, went to Ottawa, where he lives, and told many of the good White people, members of Parliament and Dominion Government officials, about the Indians. There are a few other men who go to all parts of Canada to find out about the Indians, the way they live and the things they make, also to find out about the trees, rocks, stones, flowers, fish, animals and birds. These men return to Ottawa and teach people free of charge about these things as they are working all the time for the Dominion Government.
>
> The men who study the Indians all come to be good friends of the Indians. For many years these men have tried to get justice and help in sickness for all the Indians. It is the very same in the United States. It is very hard work, as

> some White people will not believe them. The bad people who want the Indian lands, or to get his furs too cheap, or to get him drunk and rob him, do not like these men and try to make trouble for them.
>
> At last these men have succeeded in a small way a little bit. So there is now a Dominion Government committee in Ottawa which is trying to help save the totem poles and help the Indians keep the totem poles on the places where they where [sic] where the Indians' children and their children's children can always see them and remember their fathers and the old customs.
>
> The White people also want to see the poles, learn how well the Indians could carve and paint, hear the stories and know the honor of the chiefs.
>
> As I have worked among the Indians since 1897 (twenty-eight years), and am known by all the Bella Coola Indians, Mr. Andre Paul and the Rev. Peter Kelly, I was sent by the Dominion Government to see if the chiefs wished me to help.
>
> I was given money for this work and have put it in the Hazelton bank. This I am to use if I can pay the people for their labor and to buy cement, oil and such things, to try and fix the poles so they will not fall down and be rotted by the rain and weather.
>
> First I must get permission from the chiefs. I will not touch a pole until I have permission to do so. Then I am to fix it below the ground so it will not rot. For this, cement and tar or paint will be used, but not so that it will show about the ground. Then I am to oil the pole like the one at Prince Rupert, so that it will not rot, and put color where it should be, but not too much color.
>
> Nothing must be done that the chiefs do not want. If anyone does wrong, come and tell me.

Smith presents himself as an anthropologist, in the most positive light, firmly committed to seeking permission for every action. Anthropologists, he explains, are scientists who collect information and material in order to teach others about Indian culture "free of charge" and therefore do not profit from their endeavors. A victory for Natives and anthropologists would be to restore the totem poles and keep them close to home. As "good friends," they fight the good fight against "bad people," who not only treat Indians with hostility but also disapprove of anthropologists for supporting them. Disregarding their privilege and status as educated whites, Smith actually equates the anthropologist's plight with that of the colonized Native. One wonders how the Gitk'san, among the most wary of outsiders of all Northwest Coast groups, would have received such an equation. Nowhere in this letter does Smith refer to the CNR's involvement in this project, or acknowledge its anticipated economic gain from increased tourism.

The newspaper coverage of this project applauded Smith's work. When the *Vancouver Province* reprinted his letter to the chiefs in full (H. I. Smith 1925, 2), its editors added a patronizing coda to remind their readers of the aggressive nature of several Skeena River communities: "It will be remembered that the Indians in this district about Kitwanga and Kitwancool have shown a disposition to resent any persons going through their domains, and last year several parties were turned back from the Kitwancool Valley. Dr. Smith is endeavoring to educate these people to the value of their own artistic monuments and is seeking their cooperation in the work." Government assimilation policies had long demanded that First Nations relinquish their ties to tradition. Now, instead of criticizing poles as expressions of heathenness, whites had to (re)educate Natives on the value of preserving their own artistic heritage. In reality, the Gitk'san, with their keen sense of their cultural values and ongoing potlatch tradition, had little need for an anthropologist—much less the provincial press— to give them such lectures.

On Sunday, December 6, 1925, the *Vancouver Sun*'s story "Aboriginal Art Is Lost: Belated Efforts Being Made to Save Remaining Indian Totem Poles" recast the carvings, originally intended as memorials to the dead, as tombstones for an extinct culture:

> It might be said that the totem pole is the memorial of a people who are dead. Our Indians of today are being civilized according to the White man's definition of the word. Few of them can even read the totem poles that stand sentinel over their villages. Their father's ways are not their ways. (Mitchell 1925)

5.6. Gitk'san carvers restoring pole, 1925. Photograph by Harlan Smith. Canadian Museum of Civilization, 65301.

And the same newspaper, in G. C. Porter's "Famous Relics of British Columbia to Be Preserved," later stressed the role of whites as saviors: "Skill and resources of the White man must be employed to restore and repair the finest examples of this Indian magic, if the best illustrations of the skill of these ancient people are to be preserved" (Porter 1926).

These articles reveal much about the popular sentiments toward Natives at the time. They place Indians—having once created "magic," an ability they lost—into the role of ignorant losers, unable even to understand the meanings of their own artistic creations. Whites, however, with technical skills necessary to preserve that magic and, heroically, maintain knowledge lost to Natives, could restore what had been lost and prevent further loss. Whereas missionaries fashioned themselves saviors of Native souls, now anthropologists and philanthropists imagined themselves to be saviors of Native culture.

During the first two years of work, restorations were relatively successful, and a total of sixteen Kitwanga poles were finished by 1926 (fig. 5.6). Yet, as Barbeau predicted, antagonism toward the project began to develop. In the National Museum of Canada's annual report for 1926, Smith presented what he understood to be the Gitk'san point of view:

> The White men had settled on their land and were pushing the Indians more and more to the wall; they had built canneries on the coast that were destroying all the fish; they were cutting all the best timber in the country so that within a few years none would remain for the Indian; they sold whiskey in government liquor stores and put the Indians in jail when they drank it. A few years ago, they prohibited the erection of totem-poles; why did they wish now to preserve them? (H. Smith 1928, 81).

The Gitk'san understood, perhaps more clearly than Smith realized, that the "loss" of their traditions was the direct result of official Indian policy that made some cultural traditions such as the potlatch illegal. Suddenly, mysteriously, and ironically, whites were celebrating Native creations made within the context of potlatching.

Although Smith ended his comments positively, stating that "in the end most of the difficulties were happily overcome" (H. Smith 1928, 81), his problems were, in reality, only beginning.[10] People in conservative Kitsegulka were especially suspicious of whites. When Smith arrived there to start his third season of work, the chiefs verbally forbade him to touch any poles and handed him a petition that asserted that the carvings were "the only honerable [sic] property that remains in our Hands" (Cole 1985, 275). Smith had no success changing the minds of these powerful men. The regional Indian agent, Edgar Hyde, described how an especially vociferous and contentious Gitk'san had worked to sabotage the project and criticize Smith himself: "The Indians of these parts are very suspicious of a person who tries to tell them what the Government is doing for them and in my opinion, Mr. Smith does talk too much" (Darling and Cole 1980, 40). This was not the first time Smith's personality had interfered with his fieldwork; years earlier, during the American Museum of Natural History's Jesup North Pacific Expedition, Franz Boas had had to sooth many feathers that the man had ruffled among both Natives and whites in British Columbia (Jonaitis 1988, 195).

In his 1926 report on the project, Smith expressed his insensitivity to Native concepts of ownership and respect:

> Several moulds showing a mask and details of some of the totem-poles were brought back to Ottawa. The figures reproduced from these moulds are useful as museum specimens, as advertisements in railway offices and depots, and as souvenirs to be used in the same way as animal heads. They also proved of value for architectural work, since the architect of the new Hudson's Bay Company's store in Winnipeg was recently searching for suitable totem-pole material to decorate the company's restaurant (H. Smith 1928, 83).

Smith finally resigned that same year, leaving an engineer involved with the project, T. B. Campbell, fully in charge of the restoration work.

During the 1927 season, Campbell enjoyed better fortune than Smith, successfully restoring eight poles in Kitselas. But when he approached Kitsegulka, the chiefs adamantly refused to cooperate, commanded Campbell to stay away from their property, and hired legal representation to formally protest these activities to the Department of Indian Affairs.[11] Campbell, wisely, backed away. By 1930, after thirty poles had been restored, all work on this project ceased. Even the initially cooperative Kitwanga became resentful; in 1931, a village committee wrote the National Museum that "the C. P. R. Co. is getting all the successful benifit [sic] out of it and us people, the sole owners, get nothing" (Cole 1985, 276).

Little of this project can be considered a success. Because no community members knew how to manufacture the kind of paint originally used, they had to repaint the poles with commercial pigments that even Smith, whose remarks on the project tended toward extreme enthusiasm, called "gaudy" (H. Smith 1928, 82). The very vividness that enhanced visibility to train passengers also decreased the poles' aesthetic appeal and cultural authenticity. Standing rigidly in straight lines and painted with intense, artificial colors, these poles did not represent Tsimshian art at its best. C. F. Newcombe sadly commented that these "restorations" made the poles' excellent sculpture unrecognizable, and Emily Carr criticized the poles for having "lost much of interest and subtlety in the process" of restoration and having "the heavy load of all over paint [that] drowns them" (quoted in Darling and Cole 1980, 46). The poles not only looked bad, they were poorly restored and, as a result, decayed rapidly. Because it is basic (nonacidic), concrete reacts chemically with wood and promotes decay. To add to these problems, bolts intended to maintain the poles' upright position created a structural instability that led to vertical cracking and produced rust that further encouraged decay.[11] Then in 1936 and 1937, major floods destroyed many of the bases of the poles; to save the poles, the Gitk'san had to cut them off their bases (Darling and Cole 1980, 45). Thus ends the story of the Canadian National Railway's totem pole restoration project, which Emily Carr scathingly judged as "too much catering to the 'beastly tourist'" (Darling and Cole 1980, 48). The one success of this project, completely overlooked in the literature, was the ultimate control the Gitk'san assumed as they successfully terminated, through their own efforts, an unacceptable appropriation of their culture.

But the idea of salvaging and reerecting Northwest Coast poles in northern British Columbia did not stop with the Gitk'san resistance. In 1935, the City of Prince Rupert, hoping to become the "totem pole city of the Coast," traveled to Haida Gwaii to request ten poles rather than approach the local Tsimshian. Fearing that foreign museums would purchase these Haida masterworks, the city commissioner, W. J. Alder, convinced their owners to part with them. The CNR, always willing to help with a tourist-related project, especially one at its western terminus, provided free transportation and secured T. B. Campbell, by then known as "Totem Pole Campbell" for his work among the Gitk'san, to assist in their preservation and correct positioning.

ALASKA TOTEM POLE PRESERVATION

It was not until the Depression that a New Deal restoration program propelled Alaskan poles into public attention once more. The Indian Civilian Conservation Corps (CCC), founded in 1933, provided work for increasingly impoverished and disadvantaged Natives. In Alaska, the first projects under this program, such as housing construction for teachers and nurses in Hoonah, worked to improve social conditions. In 1938, the Indian CCC, under the supervision of the U.S. Forest Service, began the highly visible and well-publicized Alaskan project that became one of their success stories—restoring and promoting totem poles as significant expressions of American artistic heritage. This was supported by another new federal organization, the Indian Arts and Crafts Board (IACB), whose mandate was to aid Native Americans in the creation and promotion of their art as part of larger social welfare efforts (see Schrader 1983).

In 1911, Native people who wanted citizenship in Alaska were required to move into "modern" communities and live in single-family houses. By that time, most Tlingit and Alaskan Haida had moved from their original villages to locations closer to white populations, leaving their poles in situ. The totem pole project workers transferred poles from these abandoned towns to more populated communities, restoring or replicating as necessary.

Like Brady, Forest Service personnel sought permission to do this from Native leaders, assuring them that they remained in control of the ultimate fate of these clan treasures. After much consultation, the restored poles were removed from their original villages: poles from Kasaan were moved to New Kasaan; from Klinkwan, Sukkwan, and Howkan to Hydaburg; from Tuxekan to Klawock; and from Tongass, Cape Fox, Cat Island, and Pennock Island to Saxman and Totem Bight, both in Ketchikan. In addition to copying extant poles, carvers also made some entirely new ones. More than 116 poles were restored or made anew during this project (Duff 1969). In addition, three houses, in Kasaan, Wrangell, and Ketchikan, were constructed to provide some kind of context for the poles.

Linn Forrest, architect for the Forest Service and supervisor of the entire program, described some of the restoration activities:

> First of all, you had to get permission from the people. The poles were considered owned by the community; they're not owned by the individuals—they're owned by clans . . . .The Forest Service had to do that before the government could spend money on restoring them, or moving them. I don't know of any instance where we didn't succeed, but it took a little care . . . To get the title to do the poles—the actual result in most circumstances was the older man, or heir to the chief, was given the job as head of the program that we were going to put in there [the carving program in that village]. . . . At Old Kasaan—there were numerous poles there—we brought what we considered the best poles and also the ones that were the best preserved. If a pole could be corrected, repaired, we tried to do that first. If a pole was especially fine because of some detail and was beyond repair, we made a copy. We would bring the original pole in and lay it down along side a new log and they would carve like the one that was adjacent. I think our luck varied in that respect. In some instances, I think we did just as well and [in others] I think we did much poorer that the original poles (Forrest 1971, 2, 16).

Prior to this project, few non-Natives knew Native artists by name. But, as Forrest makes clear, because the government bureaucracy required a hierarchy of head carvers to supervise teams of subordinates, individual artists emerged from anonymity. These "bosses" became known beyond their villages as totem pole carvers: John Wallace of Hydaburg, Jim Peele of New Kaasan, Tom Ukas and John Thomas of Wrangell, James Starrish and Charles Brown of Saxman, and George Benson at Sitka (fig. 5.7). As a result of this project, Ketchikan—a city that in 1924 had barely any poles—became the self-proclaimed "totem pole capital" of the world, with two major totem pole parks, one at the Native village of Saxman, the other at Totem Bight (figs. 5.8 and 5.9). The dedication of the restored Chief Shakes house was the occasion for a lavish potlatch attended by Native and non-Native people in Wrangell (fig. 5.10).

Sitka, which until that point had displayed the largest number of Alaskan poles, at the Sitka National Historic Park, also participated in the project, with salvageable poles being preserved and badly deteriorated ones copied. In addition, workers made many improvements that enhanced Sitka's attractiveness

5.7. James Starrish and Charles Brown (Tlingit) next to carved figure of Lincoln to be placed atop totem pole, Saxman, near Ketchikan, Alaska, 1940. University of Washington Libraries. Special Collections, NA3806.

5.8. Saxman Village, Ketchikan, 2006. Photograph by Aldona Jonaitis.

5.9. Totem Bight State Park, Ketchikan, Alaska, 2006. Photograph by Aldona Jonaitis.

5.10. Chief Shakes house dedication, Wrangell, 1940. Photograph by W. H. Case. Wrangell Museum Collection, P80.12.000.

to tourists. As a newspaper stated, "The hundreds of Alaskan tourists who walk through lovely forested Sitka National Monument to see these displays of Native art and legendry will find their visit anticipated by appropriately placed rustic benches, finely graveled footpaths, sanitary facilities, and resurfaced approach road and sidewalk from the boat dock. 'Sitka National Monument will be in its best dress to welcome Alaska's anticipated biggest tourist season,' declared custodian Miller" (*Cordova Times* 1940; see fig. 5.11).

The CCC project had certain parallels with the Skeena River restoration. Both were in part inspired by a genuine fascination with totem poles. Both hoped that restored poles would encourage increased tourism. Both were conceptualized and administered by whites with government support. Whereas the Skeena poles stood in or near their villages, some of which had an ongoing potlatch tradition, the Alaskan poles, erected in the totem pole parks, largely lost their intimate relationships with their places of origin, their connections to specific lineages, and their associations with the buildings that housed those lineages. Paradoxically, this project, which radically decontextualized the poles, inspired young Alaska Natives to renew ties to their culture and history that had waned over several decades. Native men working with their seniors learned about their heritage in a context that celebrated rather than belittled it. According to the project coordinator, moving poles from deserted villages to be restored and displayed in civic centers reinforced the Native ownership of poles and fostered among the Native population a reinvigorated cultural identity and pride:

> The object was to put people to work. . . . It was certainly logical; they had the timber and knowledge in that respect. . . . I just think the whole program was a wonderful thing for them. . . . The head men, the heads of these projects in various areas, were respected in their communities and they were boss. I think the rest of the people had a lot of respect for them—the workmen that is. I think it did an awful lot for the younger fellows that were part of the program, too. It gave them an interest back in their history that they probably would have lost. . . . These fellows were proud of their work; these meant something to them—I think much more to them after we started the project than it ever did before. And they would, of course, bring out . . . all kinds of relics and things stashed away. Like a Haida eye was shaped different than a Tlingit. Just a lot of things they knew (Forrest 1971, 9, 11).

It seems that in some ways, at least, the Gitk'san protected their totem poles by rejecting non-Native intrusion, and the Alaskan Natives by enjoying the new respect their poles generated.

5.11. Frog / Raven pole (Kaigani Haida) Sitka National Historic Park, 2007. Photograph by Aldona Jonaitis

The early decades of the twentieth century—with their economic depressions, world wars, and cultural prohibitions—were trying times for North America's Native populations. They were subject to profound ambivalence on the part of their non-Native neighbors and self-appointed administrators. Government assimilation and social welfare expanded, yet Native efforts to achieve citizenship and enfranchisement were stymied. Objects of maligned ceremonial culture were removed from communities only to be subjected to new appreciative discourses of fine art elsewhere.

Totem pole restoration projects provided a useful conceptual fulcrum between the conflicting poles of assimilation and welfare, between art appropriation and appreciation. Predicated on the salvaging of vanishing indigenous heritage, the projects recast colonial governments and agents as saviors of Native culture. Threatened totem poles were saved from indigenous indifference in the purported name of future generations of coastal Natives, but for the immediate benefit of the railways and of civic, state, provincial, and federal tourist initiatives.

Yet if these projects expressed and in some sense displaced the ambivalent discourses and practices of aboriginal administration, they also became venues in which divergent indigenous perspectives on the colonial encounter were articulated. The opportunity to cooperate with federal preservation programs challenged First Nations communities to reimagine their relationships to the state, to their own social units, and to their totem poles. While the goal here was to "restore" the pole in its original form, the opportunity to market First Nations art to visiting tourists presented both coastal artists and entrepreneurs with the context in which to materially reimagine the totem pole itself as an icon of destination-travel and as a souvenir for the transient tourist.

THE EXPANSION OF TOTEM POLE FORM

MINIS, MAXIS, AND MULTIPLES (OR, THE SMALL, THE TALL, AND THE KITSCHY)

The change in the population of southeastern Alaska is very marked . . . The primitive condition of the Native has almost wholly disappeared . . . log houses are rarely built; the Native dress has disappeared, replaced by cheap, ready-made clothing; Native manufactures, utensils, weapons, curios, all are gone, or made only in coarse facsimile for sale to tourists.

—WILLIAM DALL, "ALASKA AS IT WAS AND IS," 1895

Have you discovered the (totem) pole? . . . Have you collected Indian carvings and baskets? . . . Is Alaska represented in your den? Tourists visiting Alaska via "TOTEM—POLE ROUTE" have the opportunity to purchase directly from the Native makers, Baskets, Totems, and other curios at reasonable prices.

—PACIFIC COAST STEAMSHIP COMPANY, *ALASKA VIA TOTEM POLE ROUTE*, 1911

Although Kodak has long promised to ensure celluloid (now digital) memories of travel, most tourists love coming home with a material souvenir of a trip. Not surprisingly, totem tourists favor model poles as souvenirs.[1] Of the many varieties of models to chose from—some carved by Northwest Coast Native artists, some cast in foreign countries—by far the most common is a column with one or more animals, topped by a bird with outstretched wings. These can be found on bountiful display in tourist-oriented shops and airports throughout Alaska, British Columbia, and Washington State. Winged poles caught the fancy of non-Natives early on, and the tourism market responded by producing thousands of replicas of one particular type. The appeal of this type of pole extends into the realm of marketing, where business logos and travel advertisements for the Northwest Coast are replete with winged poles. Despite the fact that poles with outstretched wings were exceedingly rare in the nineteenth century, they have since become *the* iconic totem pole.

While the souvenir collector must be content with a miniature model, more ambitious collectors prefer that unique specimen at the other end of the scale—"the tallest totem pole." According to Susan Stewart (1984), miniature models have special appeal and respond to a deep psychological longing for origin, for place of being, for connection to the world. Using the human body as the standard for scale, Stewart suggests that the miniature serves as a metaphor for interior space and experience of the personal. The gigantic, in contrast, signifies authority, the state, and public experience.[2] The highest-ranking house in a Northwest Coast Native village would often endeavor to erect the tallest pole, so height had some cultural significance in Native cultures as well.[3] But the claim made by many tourist destinations to have the "world's tallest totem pole" falls into a different category. The importance of these poles derives from their status as tourist destinations.

The proliferation of model poles with wings and of hyperbolically tall totem poles is clearly a by-product of the intercultural tourist industry.

MODELS: THE MINIATURIZATION OF THE TOTEM POLE

When passengers on early steamships to Alaska disembarked at ports such as Sitka and Juneau, they encountered lines of Native people, most often women, selling baskets, jewelry, and model totem poles. Tourists who sailed up the Inside Passage, impressed by the full-size monuments they saw, enthusiastically purchased models from the Native people they encountered and from well-known curio shops, such as the Bear Totem Store in Wrangell and the Nugget Shop in Juneau (fig. 6.1). Soon curio shops took the lion's share of this lively business, and the sale of Northwest Coast souvenirs skyrocketed.[4]

Then, as now, shopping was an essential component of the travel experience. Steamship lines promoted this souvenir market by first praising the quality of the art found in situ in Northwest Coast villages, and then encouraging their clients to return home with Native-made souvenirs. For example, *All about Alaska*, the Pacific Coast Steamship Company's 1891 publication, explains,

> It is not often that one would want to call a tourist's attention to an Indian village, for the average encampment or habitation of the "noble red man" is not the most attractive sight or study. But in the T'linkit town we have no such hesitation, for the curiosities to be seen in their houses and surroundings, they are certainly one of the

6.1. The Nugget Shop, Juneau, 1925. Photograph by Winter and Pond. Alaska State Library, P87-0980.

> strangest people on earth. They are the artistic savages of the world. In front of each long-house, and often rearing its head much higher than it by two or three fold, are one or two posts, called "totem poles." . . . The savage sculptor exhausted all the resources of his barbaric imagination in cutting in hideous faces and figures that, with a hundred or so such terrible "totems" in front of a village, makes one think of some nightmare of his childish days (Pacific Coast Steamship Company 1891, 40–41).

Stressing the shopping potential of the region, the author praised Tlingit items that offered "romantic remembrances" of that splendid journey.[5] Although pointing out that the tourist could purchase directly from the Alaskan Natives who meet the steamer with furs, silver bracelets, and carvings, the guidebook warned that "as a rule, they have a high appreciation for their wares," and that better prices could be found at Sitka or Juneau stores (ibid., 18).

In the same vein as their competitors, the Alaska Steamship Company published a series of pamphlets entitled "The Totem Poles of Alaska and Indian Mythology" that not only described full-size poles but also directed sightseers to stores along the steamer route where miniature totem poles were available for purchase. One type of model pole stood out above all others in terms of quality—and compared "favorably with many of the productions of highly civilized sculptors"—and these were the Haida miniatures, which were crafted from argillite, a black, soft, grainless, and easily carved carbonaceous shale local only to Haida Gwaii (MacDowell 1906, n.p.; fig. 6.2).

6.2. Haida argillite model pole, late nineteenth century. 14.3" high. University of Aalaska Museum of the North, 75-049-0007.

Well before the outset of steamship tourism, the Haida had initiated the tradition of carving miniatures for sale to outsiders. Although there are some indications that the Haida carved argillite for their own uses prior to contact, sculptures in that medium proliferated after the 1840s.[6] The collapse of their enormously profitable fur trade had stimulated the resourceful Haida into developing new enterprises designed to provide novel sources of income. For example, the Haida produced exceptionally fine ocean-going canoes that they sold up and down the coast to other Native people. Recognizing the appeal that souvenirs had for foreigners who sailed into their territory, even before tourism became an important industry on the Northwest Coast, the Haida transformed argillite as well as wood into miniature carvings.

Early argillite carvings, intended for those who landed in Haida Gwaii on trading ships, depicted a variety of subjects, including Euroamericans and their vessels, but by the end of the nineteenth century, model totem poles had become the favorite souvenir of tourists. The earliest argillite poles, ranging from twenty to

6.3. Charles Edenshaw (Haida) carving model poles. Canadian Museum of Civilization, 88926.

forty centimeters, were evidently modeled after house frontal poles, for both shared one-to-one proportion of head to body, a shallow cross section, low-relief carving, and half-cylinder construction (Macnair and Hoover 1984, 113). By the 1880s, taller, thinner, and more deeply sculpted poles became popular. And while carvers maintained a full repertoire that included platters, pipes, candlesticks, and figures depicting mythic beings or Europeans, by far the best-selling argillite item in the late nineteenth century was the model totem pole.

In chapter 3, we saw how the Haida maintained elements of traditional culture by fusing them with borrowed traditions, such as their funerary activities. Argillite carvings functioned in a similar way. As the Haida ceased erecting full-size poles, argillite and wooden model poles began to appear, and their numbers increased in reverse proportion to the number of full-size wooden poles. Here was a source of income that also served as a means of perpetuating Haida culture through a form acceptable to the missionaries and "progressive" Natives. Argillite models brought the sophistication of Haida art—the elegance of their totem poles—literally around the world, becoming in the process a compelling mode of cultural endurance. The countless number of expertly carved argillite poles in museum collections around the world testifies both to their popularity and to the enormous drive that went into carving them. Of special note are the models by Haida master Charles Edenshaw, whose distinctive style is highly regarded by many (fig. 6.3).[7]

Although the most detailed and best-carved model poles were Haida argillite and wood, by the late nineteenth century, Native people from the Tlingit to the Nuu-chah-nulth were producing thousands upon thousands of model poles, most often of painted wood. Sometimes artists were creative in their choice of subject matter, especially when they knew the recipients of their carvings. For example, one Nuu-chah-nulth model is said to have been made for the Reverend Charles M. Tate, who did missionary work from 1870 to 1874, perhaps to illustrate not Native crests but Mary, Joseph, and the Child Jesus (S. Brown 1998, 137). Not unlike their British Columbia brethren, Alaskan missionaries encouraged Native people to become more economically self-sufficient by creating artwork in places such as the Indian Residential School at Wrangell and the Sheldon Jackson School in Sitka. Some models stand out as visually accurate representations, while others, crudely carved, satisfied the needs of indiscriminate tourists for cheap mementos of trips to a glorious part of the world. Some even came to serve important noneconomic functions within the cultures of their creators. For example, in his monograph *The Bella Coola Indians*, T. F. McIlwraith describes a Nuxalk memorial potlatch that he observed between 1922 and 1924, at which mourners for the deceased carried model totem poles representing his crests while an orator described the ancestral family legends that validated the carved figures (1948, 469–71).

ONE-STOP SHOPPING: CURIO STORES ON AND OFF THE COAST

As the guidebooks noted, tourists to Alaska could purchase model poles on the wharves from Native sellers or at the curio shops in various ports of call, such as the Nugget Shop in Juneau, H. D. Kirmse's shop in Skagway, and the Bear Totem Store in Wrangell. Those who did not make the voyage north or who had failed to purchase a model up the coast could do so at urban stores that conducted a lively trade in Native materials, such as two in Victoria, owned by Henri Stadthagen and Frederick Landsberg.

The most well-known turn-of-the-century American dealer was Joseph Standley, who founded Ye Olde Curiosity Shop in Seattle in 1899 and sold totem poles for every budget. In the middle of the second decade of the twentieth century, wooden poles ranged from fifty cents to seven dollars, while argillite poles sold for $1.50 an inch. In addition to walk-in trade, these shop owners discovered the profitability of mail-order business, selling poles to purchasers who may never have been to the Northwest Coast. This expansion of totem pole business demanded adjustments in supply. Although Standley acquired Haida argillite poles from Thomas Deasy, the Massett Indian agent, and Tlingit carvings from Alaskan shop owners John Feusi and Walter Waters, once he began selling by catalogue, he needed more volume than those northerners could provide. So Standley hired Sam Williams, a Nuu-chah-nulth born in 1880 in Nitinaht, on Vancouver Island, who moved to the Seattle area around 1900. Williams produced poles following Standley's preference for bold carving and bright red, blue, yellow, and green enamel paint. Williams's son Wilson also carved, and, by including whales and Thunderbirds, referred to typical Nuu-chah-nulth iconography. Williams's children, grandchildren, and great-grandchildren all carved for Standley, supplying him with approximately half of the poles he sold (Duncan 2000, 181). The Williams family today still carves model poles. A photograph of Rick Williams, for example, appeared in a *Seattle Times* magazine article, "Still Standing: From Fine Art to the Trinket Trade, A Native Tradition Survives" (Anderson 2003).

By hiring Native carvers, Standley could honestly label his wares as "Indian made," even if their connections to indigenous pole-carving traditions were tenuous. But when the Williams family and others could still not produce enough poles, Ye Olde Curiosity Shop and other stores in the area began selling inexpensive ivory or bone totem poles made in Japan. In the 1920s, Standley corresponded with the Tokyo Chamber of Commerce in order to find an ivory carving supplier and then forged a relationship with the Takenoya Brothers Company, which produced ivory totem pole pendants as well as painted walrus ivory model poles.[8]

By the 1920s, the totem pole had become unequivocally associated with the Native cultures of the Northwest Coast. But as model poles and images—as well as full-size poles—were increasingly decontextualized and circulated internationally, they became associated with "Indians" more generally. In response, some non-Northwest Coast Native people began to make totem poles to keep up with tourist expectations and commercial demand. Non-Natives dedicated to Native welfare sometimes encouraged such production. Among the eastern Arctic Inuit in the 1960s, artist James Houston distributed a handbook of craft forms—including model totem poles—to Inuit artists in order to spur their production and thus the sale of such items to a burgeoning metropolitan market in southern Canada. Today, model and full-size poles can be seen at or near many reservation "trading posts" across North America (see the following photo essay). For example, Frank Ettawageshik of the Little Traverse Bay Bands of Odawa (Ottawa) Indians, whose family owned The Indian Craft Shop in Harbor Springs, Michigan, describes helping his father produce poles in the 1950s:

> He carved them in various sizes, from large freestanding sizes to small pocket sizes. . . . At the age of seven, I was painting small totem poles in my father's workshop.

POLES AT NON-NORTHWEST COAST LOCATIONS

Trading post, Banff, Alberta.
Photograph by Aaron Glass.

Micmaq reserve, Nova Scotia.
Photograph by Aaron Glass.

Flathead reservation, Montana.
Photograph by Aldona Jonaitis.

Border Bob's, International Falls, Minnesota. Photograph by Aaron Glass.

Narrow's Gift Shop, Sioux Narrows, Ontario. Photograph by Aaron Glass.

Seminole Museum, Tampa, Forida, 1991. Photograph by Robin Wright. Courtesy of Robin Wright.

Santa Fe, New Mexico. Photograph by Zena Pearlstone. Courtesy of Zena Pearlstone.

WILLIAM SHELTON, SNOHOMISH TOTEM POLE CARVER

BY WAYNE SUTTLES, ANTHROPOLOGIST[9]

I remember going to the state fair at Puyallup, Washington, when I was a kid and seeing William Shelton sitting in his feather war bonnet in front of his teepee and his totem pole and lecturing on Indians. Later, as a student of anthropologist Erna Gunther [herself a student of Boas], I was given to understand that "Chief Shelton" was something of a phony—mixing traditions and creating an artificial past. Now I am inclined to believe that William Shelton was very sincerely trying to give whites an appreciation of Indian values (as he interpreted them) and an appreciation of the natural environment and to promote better relations between Indians and whites. He certainly had an impact—and I think a positive one—on a lot of non-Indians, as a file of newspaper clippings on Shelton show. But an obituary hailed him as "the last of the totem pole carvers," when the truth is [he] was probably the first of the totem pole carvers in our region. It may have been that irony that irked Erna.

Shelton said that as a child he saw "totem guardian spirits." Aboriginally, on Puget Sound, a man's "guardian spirit" could be represented on one of the posts in his section of the house. As far as we know, the Puget Sound people did not represent the "guardian spirits" of different people on the same house post or any post standing outside. The classic "totem pole" was a freestanding invention from the north. Shelton's adoption of this form may be seen as the normal consequences of diffusion that might have occurred by his time regardless of white presence. Or it might be seen as Shelton's innovative use of the Puget Sound tradition.

6.4. William Shelton (Snohomish Salish) carving totem pole, ca. 1920. Photograph by Webster and Stephens. PEMCO Webster & Stevens Collection, Museum of History and Industry, Seattle. MOHAI, 83.10.10, 923.2.

> I sometimes helped him by painting the basic colors while he did the finishing details. Each piece of his work was stamped with his name and labeled "Genuine Ottawa Indian Craft." On the other days we sat around a large box and folded the small pieces of paper on which the story of the totem was printed. We folded thousands and thousands of them, filling the box. We later attached a folded paper to the back of each totem with a tiny rubber band. In addition to selling his work in our own retail store, my father shipped thousands of items at wholesale to gift shops and museum stores across the country, including the American Museum of Natural History in New York and the Kansas City Museum (Ettawageshik 1999, 24).

Ettawageshik is comfortable with this use of a concept from the Northwest, pointing out that "totem" is an Algonkian word, and that small images of totems were placed outside Algonkian houses; "thus it is not the cultural stretch many scholars have believed for Indian people of the eastern woodlands to carve totem (*ododem*) poles" (Ettawageshik 1999, 24). By unpacking the earlier series of (mis)appropriations (i.e., scholars generalizing an Algonkian word and concept and applying it to the carved columns of the coast), Ettawageshik justifies his (re)appropriation of Northwest Coast material forms.

THE VALUE OF THE SOUVENIR

Some model poles were masterworks, but others displayed little understanding of the refined canons of Northwest Coast art. Model poles have all suffered from the pejorative label "tourist art," which presumes such objects to have little or no artistic or anthropological value.[10] It is believed by some that the transformation of a Native object into a commodity renders it culturally vacuous, a meaningless souvenir. Some of the totem pole models may be good works of art and others may not, but they nevertheless reveal much about both the Native carver and the non-Native owner and are thus significant documents of the intercultural encounter. Carvers understood and took advantage of the ready market for these items, which they knew would travel from the Northwest Coast to territories remote from their own, by people who had little understanding of the subtleties of their artistic and cultural heritage. That did not mean, however, that the carvers necessarily trivialized their creations, which functioned in several ways to express and promote Native survival. At the basic level, these carvings maintained artistic traditions during a period in which these traditions were thought to have been abandoned. The images on the models may have had considerable meaning to their makers, whose knowledge of cultural traditions and honoring of family prerogatives had not necessarily been eradicated. And, as indications of what endured despite the intrusions of whites, model totem poles became testimonials of Native identity and expressions of quiet resistance to those who would obliterate their culture but, in the end, could not.

Miniature totem poles embodied considerably different meanings for the consumers who brought home these models of exotic monuments from a remote and impressive place. Most non-Natives demonstrated little understanding of full-size poles, so there was little expectation by sellers that consumers would learn much about totem poles from the miniatures. Nonetheless, the model totem pole, a personal and portable reduction of the gigantic original, brought some of the wilderness back to "civilization" with its owner. Many travelers purchased and kept models as material souvenirs of their trips to a splendid region, projecting upon carvings the memory of the entire trip, not only the Native cultures they encountered.[11] The model, likely placed in a curio corner cabinet or on a mantelpiece, allowed the traveler to actually *possess* a version of a totem pole, as opposed to just gazing at one or taking a photo. This transformed the model pole into something very personal, reminding the tourist of his or her particular visit to the glorious Northwest Coast and of the Native culture she or he may have encountered there.

Whatever the tourist thought about Indians in general also became part of this model. It might have embodied a gamut of deeply held yet often contradictory attitudes: vanishing Indians and reborn Indians;

barbaric Indians and artistic Indians; uncivilized Indians and cultured Indians; traditional Indians and progressive Indians; authentic Indians and adulterated Indians. Outsiders came to the Northwest Coast, saw totem poles, and objectified their creators through the carvings, stereotyping them as barbaric, lesser-evolved people, noble savages, or members of a vanishing race. Those same people returned to their homes with portable poles that miniaturized these objectifications and served as mementos of whatever they imagined Northwest Coast Native peoples to be. Tourism created, and continues to create, a consumable experience of the totem pole in British Columbia and Alaska, enhanced by possession of the consumable objects. Commodified poles and their representations can be acquired and discarded at will, transformed into abstractions of some real or invented original that can render personal a source that is, by definition, not within the consumer's domain. Poles are therefore similar to the museums referred to by Susan Stewart (1984, 165), who notes that they substitute "the illusion of a relation between things" for actual social relations with the originating people (see also Kirshenblatt Gimblett 1998).[12]

THE GREAT APPEAL OF POLES WITH WINGS

One initiative of the Indian Arts and Crafts Board (IACB)—an organization we met in the discussion of Indian Civilian Conservation Corps totem pole projects in Southeast Alaska—was to promote model poles, among other types of Native American artwork, as decorations for the home. Two major exhibits of Native American art were organized by the IACB, one at the 1939–40 San Francisco World's Fair, the other in 1941 at the Museum of Modern Art, which showed many of the same works (see chapter 7). In order to foster consumer appreciation for Native art, both shows featured one gallery devoted to Indian art displayed within contemporary rooms to demonstrate how well such items fit into the contemporary home. By the late 1940s, *Better Homes and Gardens* urged, "To get sophisticated, brilliant color in your garden, install an authentic Indian-carved totem pole. The piquant faces, carved and painted to represent tribal spirits, have the charm of primitive art. *Totem Pole*, 3' to 12' high, each different; prices depend on size and intricacy of carving. A 3-foot totem pole is priced between $20 and $25, f.o.b."[13] This quote indicates a slightly different approach than that of the Victorian curio collectors, for now poles are identified as "primitive art." Primitivism in interior decorating became increasingly popular after World War II, perhaps as a desire for the simpler, less complicated, less worrisome, purer, preindustrial, closer-to-nature world in which romantics imagined primitive people to live.[14] Interior decorators were invited to write descriptions of individual poles they could purchase from Ye Olde Curiosity Shop in Seattle. What evidently appealed most to these interior decorators, as well as many others, was the now-familiar type of pole with outstretched wings.

An overwhelming number of representations, by both Native and non-Native people, depict winged birds standing atop poles. On closer examination of these images, it becomes evident that just a few specific poles appear over and over again—from the earliest photographs to the vast number of model poles sold in gift shops and airports throughout the Northwest Coast, and even to contemporary imagery on company logos and Web sites. The originals of these poles—or, more precisely, copies of the originals—stand today quite accessibly in Ketchikan, Wrangell, and Stanley Park. The fact that the winged poles are a minority in these assemblages seems to have made no difference to their selection as the quintessential Northwest Coast totem poles. A study of nineteenth-century photographs from various Northwest Coast villages reveals few poles with any elements projecting significantly from the column. But the majority of models depict winged poles, as do a large percentage of advertisements that illustrate poles.

A small group of Alaskan poles have projecting wings. Several can be seen in Saxman Totem Park, Ketchikan. For example, the Tlingit Sun and Raven Pole depicts a raven face encircled by a sun disk, with three anthropomorphic figures on its chest, and vertical appendages painted with feathers that represent folded

6.5. Photographer Ray B. Dame with camera and tripod photographing Sun and Raven Pole in Ketchikan, Alaska (Tlingit), 1938. Photograph by Schallerer. Anchorage Museum of History and Art, b75-175-685.

6.6. Raven pole, Wrangell (Tlingit), raised either for Chief Shakes's wife or sons, ca. 1900. Photograph by Winter and Pond. Alaska State Library, PCA-87.

wings (fig. 6.5). In Wrangell, Chief Kadashan's two poles carry eagles with folded wings. Also in Wrangell, a pole associated with Chief Shakes shows Raven-at-the-Head-of-the-Nass, wearing a hat with basketry rings and standing on a box that represents the box in which daylight was kept; under him is Raven with a sun halo about his head and folded wings (fig. 6.6).

Promotional literature about Alaska favors images of totem poles featuring birds with three-dimensional wings, despite the relative infrequency of these on the Northwest Coast. A photograph of the Wrangell Raven Pole appears in the 1908 brochure for the Pacific Coast Steamship Company, and multiple drawings of it grace the cover and interior of the 1911 brochure. The pole is also illustrated in *Totem Lore of the Alaska Indians and the Land of the Totem* (Corser 1932), a booklet written for the Inside Passage tourist, and on the cover of Lloyd Winter and Percy Pond's *Totems of Alaska* (see fig. 4.10).[15]

When Glass interviewed tourists in Vancouver about totem poles, he inquired as to their favorite, and 75 percent said they liked the brightly painted Kwakwa̱ka̱'wakw poles with extended wings the best. Given the history of selective and recursive representation, this should not surprise us. One particular pole type started appearing in the tourist literature in the early twentieth century and rapidly became its star: a short Kwakwa̱ka̱’wakw house post depicting a Thunderbird or eagle with outstretched wings atop a bear holding a human. A few examples of this type were found throughout Kwakwa̱ka̱’wakw territory, but four individual poles have been repeatedly depicted. Two virtually identical carvings, originally intended as interior house posts for a structure never completed, stood on the street in Alert Bay from the early 1900s until at some point they moved to the St. Michaels Residential School in Alert Bay, where fragments of one remain today (fig. 6.7). This set is strikingly similar to Charlie James’s poles, which were carved for a Kingcome Inlet chief but apparently never erected in that village. This second set was relocated to Fort Rupert, used in the 1914 Edward S. Curtis film *In the Land of the Head Hunters*, and ultimately erected in Stanley Park, where they (or their subsequent replicas) remain among the most photographed poles in the world. James—second only to Charles Edenshaw in early-twentieth-century artistic name recognition among coastal carvers—profited financially by producing numerous model poles, many of which depicted the topmost Thunderbird or eagle with its wings outstretched (fig. 6.8). This dynamic motif, now almost synonymous with the totem pole itself, was perhaps James’s invention; if not, his multiple models contributed significantly to the public’s familiarity with it, as did those of his granddaughter, Ellen Neel (see chapter 8). This pole design—often a conflation of the

6.7. Chief Tlah-Co-Glass house posts, Alert Bay (Kwakwa̱ka̱’wakw), 1909. Photograph by John Cobb. University of Washington Libraries, Special Collections, NA2767.

6.8. Charlie James (Kwakwa̲ka̲'wakw) model pole. Wood. 15.5." Photograph by Jessica Bushey. Museum of Anthropology, A5329.

6.9. Brochure cover, Alaska Steamship Company, 1936. Jonaitis collection.

two James poles in Stanley Park and the two in Alert Bay—was soon to become *the* quintessential image for *all* totem poles, appearing in innumerable tourist publications, postcards, travel advertisements, and souvenir spin-offs.[16]

It is not surprising that the Canadian Pacific Railway, in an advertisement for its Alaskan route, utilized this British Columbia pole. Yet, oddly, Alaskan businesses also made—and continue to make—extensive use of the Alert Bay/Stanley Park pole. The 1932 edition of Corser's *Totem Lore* depicts on its cover two mirror images of the Wrangell Raven totem pole, but the title page and back cover illustrate the Alert Bay Thunderbird pole. Corser even devotes a page to what he calls "the Alert Bay Indians," who live at the southernmost boundary of totem pole territory. Without citing the drawing, Corser misinterprets the Alert Bay pole as containing the image of a Thunderbird that "gave a man strength to build houses" and a bear "with what appears to be a mummy of a man in a coffin" (Corser 1932, 100).[17] Likewise, an advertisement for Juneau's Nugget Shop contains a photograph of the store showing a full-size copy of the Alert Bay/Stanley Park pole outside (see fig.

6.10. Lion's Club totem pole, Ueno Park, Tokyo. Photograph by Dean and Ruth Hartley. Courtesy of Patricia Partnow.

6.1 above). A 1936 brochure for the Alaska Steamship Company illustrated a far-larger-than-life-size Alert Bay Thunderbird pole surrounded by men crouching before a fire; in the background are indistinct images of what appear to be real Alaskan poles (fig. 6.9). Early twentieth-century postcards and vast numbers of contemporary tourist souvenirs indiscriminately employ the Alert Bay/Stanley Park pole as a symbol of Alaska. One postcard, for example, even contains the caption "Alaskan totem pole." Bumper stickers, refrigerator magnets, model poles, and even backscratchers, all with the word "Alaska" clearly imprinted, show the same British Columbia pole (see following photo essay). Even in a recent publication, *A History of Alaskan Totem Poles* (Chandonnet 2003), the Alert Bay/Stanley Park pole is shown on the inside cover, standing between two genuine Alaskan poles.

Versions of the Alert Bay pole appear in some of the strangest circumstances. An advertisement for (now defunct) Isadora's Restaurant in Vancouver depicts a pole made entirely of different foods (see page 154). When the Tokyo Lion's Club wanted to erect a totem pole in a Tokyo Park, they chose this stereotypical version (fig. 6.10).

Why have these particular Alaska and Alert Bay/Stanley Park poles assumed such a prominent place? Birds with wings majestically outstretched, perhaps about to take flight, are singularly dynamic when compared with the more simple columns. Moreover, they are photogenic, as Bill Holm has suggested (1998). Poles are notoriously difficult to photograph, as these tall, thin carvings with shallow-relief images rarely produce vivid, interesting, and easily read pictures. Moreover, due to their height, poles often appear tilted in photographs. Some are also difficult to "read," with beings whose iconographic identities are not immediately evident. The Alert Bay/Stanley Park poles solve these problems. Being shorter, they fit nicely into a rectangular picture frame. The main images—the mythic Thunderbird or eagle and that most human personification of the wilderness, the bear—are easy to identify. The Thunderbird, whose beating wings create thunder and whose eyes flash lightning, appeals to those intrigued by romantic stereotypes of American Indians. In silhouetted advertisements and logos, the winged poles read more clearly as "totem poles."

There is another element of the Alert Bay/Stanley Park pole that might contribute to its appeal: it has the shape of a cross. Perhaps this universally understood symbol subliminally suggests Native American spirituality. This association is made explicit in an illustration in Jock Macdonald's 1937 *Indian Burial, Nootka* (fig. 6.11) that shows Christian crosses in the foreground and totem poles in the background. And even those viewers not favoring a Christian perspective might find a comfortable connection between the exotic and alien totem pole and such a familiar icon. The twin processes of decontextualization and frequent reproduction helped turn these individual totem poles—direct indexes of particular lineages in specific villages—into generalized icons of the entire region, if not of the notion of indigeneity itself.

HIGH SITES: THE WORLD'S (MANY) TALLEST TOTEM POLES

Most totem poles standing on the Northwest Coast today are artifacts of various intercultural practices: indigenous status display, scientific preservation of old monuments, national and regional symbolizing, and economic support for impoverished Native people. The most visible goal of those who erected totem poles in civic places was to develop tourism and promote territorial economic growth. Poles were physically transported and assembled in parks close to tourist routes in

6.11. Jock Macdonald, *Indian Burial, Nootka*, 1937. Oil on canvas. 36" x 28.3." Photograph by Trevor Mills. Vancouver Art Gallery, 38.1.

WINGED POLE SOUVENIRS OF ALASKA

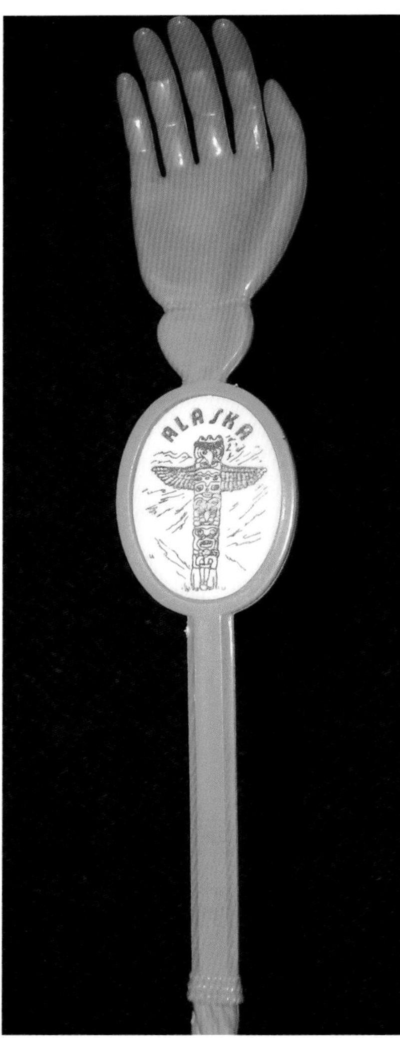

Backscratcher. Aldona Jonaitis collection.
Photograph by Aldona Jonaitis.

"Greetings from Alaska" envelope. Aldona Jonaitis collection.
Photograph by Aldona Jonaitis.

Postcard. Aldona Jonaitis collection. Photograph by Aldona Jonaitis.

Bottle opener. Aaron Glass collection.
Photograph by Aaron Glass.

Dish. Aldona Jonaitis collection. Photograph by Aldona Jonaitis.

Playing cards. Aaron Glass collection.
Photograph by Aaron Glass.

Refrigerator magnet. Aaron Glass collection.
Photograph by Aaron Glass.

THE WORLD'S THICKEST TOTEM POLE

BY RICHARD HUNT, KWAKWAKA'WAKW ARTIST

I remember driving up to Duncan to have a look at a log that the city wanted to have carved into a totem pole. On my drive up the island, I passed the log on the back of a logging truck. The log was huge! I quickly did a U-turn and followed the truck, and once I had a closer look, I knew this was a project I wanted.

The totem project committee wanted the log, donated by MacMillan Bloedel, to be the world's largest (in diameter) totem pole. The log ended up being over 800 years old, 12 meters [39.5 feet] tall, seven feet around at the top and six feet at the bottom, and weighed seven tonne (7.7 tons). The committee had never seen a log that massive, and I had never seen a log that massive, and I decided this was a challenge I could not pass up.

6.12. Richard Hunt (Kwakwaka'wakw), Cedar Man Pole, Duncan, 1992. Photograph courtesy of Richard Hunt.

I wanted to leave as much of the log as I could so that people could see how big it was. The figure that came immediately to my mind was Cedar Man. Cedar Man was on a memorial pole in Alert Bay that was carved for Mungo Martin when he passed away. I wanted to carve the figure and have him emerging from the tree, leaving the natural wood as the hairline.

I proposed carving a maquette done in the scale of one inch to one foot. This gave the committee the chance to see what Cedar Man would look like, and the maquette made my job easier, as I was able to transfer the measurements.

The project began, and each day I made the hour drive to Duncan. The city had put the log in the centre of town under a large army tent, and I was carving for the public to view the progress. I maneuvered over the site with the help of bleachers and ladders. I had never worked on anything so big! The face of Cedar Man was six feet tall and his eyes were eighteen inches through. The talking stick was twelve feet long and one foot square. I had to stand on top of the log and eyeball my measurements. I was also aided by my four-foot calipers, which helped keep everything uniform.

When I worked at the Royal British Columbia Museum, I made minimal use of chainsaws and power tools. I used more traditional tools. Chainsaws were loud, and I was afraid of using them. My worst nightmare would be that the chain would break. I quickly realized, however, that I could not do this project without one. I had a tiny sixteen-inch chainsaw in my basement and I attempted to cut the hairline of Cedar Man with this saw. It was evident that I needed bigger tools.

I decided to carve the log upside down so that it would have a bit of a V shape. I wanted the head of the pole bigger than the bottom. On the back of the pole, I could see that maybe a hundred years ago or so, someone had taken a piece of board from this log. Once the sap wood and bark are disturbed, the tree won't grow in that area. I could see how they had taken the board out, and it was kind of neat.

This was such a beautiful piece of wood. It hardly had any knots, and it had no rot. I wasn't able to use any of my carving knives, and instead I had to use big chisels, big axes, big adzes, and a variety of chainsaws.

The figures I chose for the talking stick are Kulus (my Hamat'sa headdress), Killer Whale (said to be the spirits of our great chiefs), and Chief (to represent my ancestors).

I carved Cedar Man entirely on my own, and the project took about four months. It was a once-in-a-lifetime project for me, and I am grateful to the City of Duncan for believing I could do it.

impressive stands unconnected to their actual village origins. Non-Natives appropriated these traditional items of material culture and transformed them into artifacts that complicate our understanding of authenticity. Many tourists who admire and photograph poles in totem parks assume that this is the way they always were—since, perhaps, "time immemorial."

Poles with wings (both full-size and miniature) may be the most popular, transportable poles, but the most sought-after in situ poles are the tallest ones.[18] The gigantic has long held sway in global visual culture, as it showcases human technological, political, and cultural achievement. A recent manifestation of this and a hallmark of North American road trips, the "world's biggest [insert any possible object]" has brought hopes of tourist dollars to many a small prairie, woodland, mountain, desert, or coastal town. Consider the largest ball of twine in Cawker City, Kansas, or the competitor for that title in Darwin, Minnesota. For years, a monument claiming to be the world's tallest totem pole was found in the unlikely location of Foyil, Oklahoma, created between 1937 and 1948 by a local teacher, Ed Galloway. This bizarre edifice made of concrete over a sandstone and scrap-metal skeleton and decorated with Plains Indian images has no obvious association with the Northwest Coast; in this case, "totem pole" has come to mean any tall sculpture decorated with any sort of Native imagery.[19]

On the Northwest Coast, there have been many poles claiming to be the world's tallest. The first of these was carved by the Kwakwa̱ka̱'wakw master Mungo Martin, along with his son, David, and Henry Hunt at the British Columbia Provincial Museum (now the Royal British Columbia Museum) carving shed in Thunderbird Park (fig. 6.13). Stuart Keate, publisher of the *Victoria Times*, which sponsored the pole, devised an ingenious fund-raising scheme: for a share of fifty cents, an individual could view the pole being carved and have his or her name on a scroll that would be buried under its base. More than 10,000 shares were sold to support this carving, which illustrates the legendary origin of Mungo Martin's lineage. The 127-foot 7-inch pole was dedicated on July 2, 1956, as a tribute to Native Canadian World War I and World War II veterans (Light 1966, 7). After more than forty years, this monument had deteriorated, and it was taken down in 2000. After a restoration that took more than a year, the pole was raised again on Victoria's Beacon Hill in 2001.

Several years later, another "tallest pole" was erected—not in B.C. or Alaska but in the Columbia River community of Kalama, Washington. This pole's carver, Don Lelooska, was skilled in Northwest Coast style, but his ethnic affiliation was Cherokee. The Kalama Chamber of Commerce uses the pole as its emblem, as it is the most visible and striking monument in town. Lelooska's 140-foot pole is also a tourist draw. Cowlitz County's tourism brochure explains its significance as follows: "Easily visible for miles, the totem poles give a sense of long-ago Native American lore and tradition to the beaches and recreation areas along the modern

6.13. Mungo Martin (Kwakwa̱ka̱'wakw; right) and the "world's tallest totem pole" in the Thunderbird Park, Victoria, carving shed, 1956. Courtesy of Royal British Columbia Museum, British Columbia Archives, I-26790.

scenic Columbia River" (where, of course, there never were totem poles).

The people of Kake, Alaska, also wanted to have a "tallest pole," and originally conceived one as a commemoration of the 1967 Alaska purchase centennial, but found no funds to support it. In 1969, the non-Native owner of Alaska Indian Arts (AIA) in Haines, Carl Heinmiller, revived that idea when he had carved and then sent a 132-foot 5-inch pole to the Alaska display at the 1970 Osaka World's Fair. After the pole returned from Japan, it was erected in Kake (Hazen 1969, 22–23). Well advertised in tourist literature, this pole is the main attraction of the small town and brings a fair number of visitors there each year.

Alert Bay's entry to the field, two joined logs 173 feet tall with thirteen figures representing the various bands of the Kwakwaka'wakw, was raised in 1973 to draw tourists to Alert Bay. It was carved by James Dick with the assistance of Benjamin Adam, William Dick, Gordon Matilpi, and Mrs. Billy Cook. The pole, tethered by guy-wires, stands adjacent to a ceremonial bighouse—opened in 1965 to aid in cultural revitalization and economic development—which housed dance performances for cruise ship passengers in the 1960s and '70s. Even today, one can see the tall pole rising like a beacon from the island's hill. Since Alert Bay has many totem poles as well as an excellent museum, this is only one of many attractions the community has to offer. Even so, this "world's tallest totem pole" receives a good deal of space in B.C. guide books and Web sites.

In 1994, the Commonwealth Games were held in Victoria, enhanced by considerable First Nations participation in the form of performances and art making. One of the more impressive Native art works celebrating that event was a 180-foot 3-inch pole called "Spirit of Lekwammen (Land of the Winds)," carved by a team from various First Nations, including Art Sterritt, Bill and Alex Helin, Richard Krenz, Jessel Bolton, Heber Reese, and Nancy and Anthony Dawson (fig. 6.14). This monument was part of the larger Spirit of Nations project that brought together First Nations groups from Vancouver Island to perform cultural events, carve, and sell art to the public. It was intended as an intertribal representation of the local peoples. Host chief Norman George of Songhees spoke about the pole with the following words: "When the Commemorative Pole is standing, it will give significance to the sacred site our forefathers established decades ago. . . . Our last potlatch was held here, on this site in 1895, and the land belonged to my grandfather. The reserve system changed everything for my people but we've got to carry on and make life better for ourselves by sacred events like this" (*Katou News* 1993, 2). The pole was raised with much ceremony in Victoria's Inner Harbour. Because of its massive height, steel brackets anchored it to the ground with guy-wires, although its engineers insisted that it would stand without them. In addition, a blinking light was placed on the peak for passing seaplanes. (This pole did not remain the tallest for very long. The community judged the cables unsightly, and the city feared the pole might pose a risk; in 1997, its top section was removed.).

Which is the tallest totem pole? That is not an easy question to answer. Technically, the 1994 Victoria commemorative pole was once the tallest, but with its partial dismantling, it is no longer so tall. In addition, it was made not from a single tree, as are most others, but from three trees attached to one another with steel brackets. The Lelooska pole was not made by a Northwest Coast Native, invalidating it in some people's eyes. In terms of sheer height, a purist might argue that the Alert Bay pole still holds the title as the "world's tallest totem pole." An argument against that would be that it is not made from a single log. Of course, this whole question is an artifact of contemporary tourism, part of the enduring quest for the singular and the spectacular. The concept of the "world's tallest" would have been meaningless to a chief using poles to display his status; all he may have needed was for his to be higher than his neighbor's monuments.

The growth of the tourist economy in the twentieth century resulted in the continued material transformation of the totem pole. Preservation projects altered a pole's surface, coloration, and location to make it more accessible and appealing to travelers. Miniature versions were mass-produced to provide

6.14. Art Sterritt, Bill and Alex Helin, Richard Krenz, Jessel Bolton, Heber Reese, and Nancy and Anthony Dawson. Commonwealth Games Pole, 1994. City of Victoria Archives, PR74.

visitors with souvenirs. Gigantic poles were erected (one cannot escape the phallic connotations) to mark the distinctiveness of (multiple) destinations. Specific pole arrangements—especially the winged bird perched atop a bear holding a human—emerged as iconic stereotypes. From repeated visual representation and material reproduction, these poles became decontextualized emblems of the region. Thus many agents—governments, anthropologists, entrepreneurs, advocates, advertisers, and tourists, as well as First Nations—all participated in and benefited from the commoditization of the totem pole. Through all of these processes, the most widely circulated representations of the totem pole (the preserved, the miniature, the gigantic, the logo, the winged pole, the pan-Indian stereotype) were also the least representative of actual poles in both appearance and distribution. Thus emerged a generalized, regional icon from what were specific family- and clan-based objects. These physical transformations of poles into new material forms within the touristic context parallel a different sort of transformation that occurred as full-size totem poles were removed from the coast altogether. In the next set of chapters, Part Two we will trace the national and international movement of poles from Alaska and British Columbia, and see how different non-Native concepts contributed to their ongoing conceptual—if not physical—transformation. Of course, the novel and multiple values adhering to "the totem pole" would return to the coast and to First Nations communities, where they were integrated into emerging contexts for carving and raising new heraldic monuments.

PART TWO

THE GLOBAL CIRCULATION OF TOTEM POLES

TRANSFORMING EMBLEMS AT MUSEUMS AND EXPOSITIONS

POLES IN THE GLOBAL VILLAGE

Rudely carved into a series of hideous monsters one on top of the other, painted in crude colors . . . [with anthropomorphic forms] having huge noses projecting like pump-handles.

—ATLANTIC MONTHLY, ON A TSIMSHIAN TOTEM POLE AT THE 1876 PHILADELPHIA CENTENNIAL EXPOSITION

The most striking single feature is the totem pole realistically carved, in totemic designs indicating the descent of its owners.

—OFFICIAL GUIDEBOOK TO THE ABORIGINAL CULTURES GALLERY AT THE 1940 SAN FRANCISCO WORLD'S FAIR

After Euroamericans settled Native lands and transformed the autonomous Northwest Coast peoples into dominated minorities, full-size totem poles became increasingly urbanized and miniature versions increasingly domesticated. Poles migrated from Northwest Coast villages to North American and European cities. While most poles outside British Columbia and Alaska are today in and around museums, the first poles most Americans had the opportunity to see were at a world's fair, the 1876 Philadelphia Centennial Exposition. These poles often generated such pejorative but searching reactions as that expressed in the first quote above. This process of removing poles from their original sites and sending them to distant places transformed poles from declarations of lineage affiliation within villages into regional emblems displayed the world over, from signifiers of a Native family's wealth and history into objectifications of non-Native perceptions about Native people.[1]

Over one hundred years before Buckminster Fuller's conception of the "global village" or Walt Disney's EPCOT Center, Victorian-era world's fairs brought nations together to tout their material resources, technological innovations, and cultural expressions with lavish exhibits.[2] Totem poles appeared at many world's fairs over the past century and a half in display contexts ranging from evolutionary object lessons to regional advertisements to exhibitions of fine art. The shifting values applied to poles reflected and further encouraged changes in attitude toward their indigenous makers.

MUSEUM COLLECTING

By the late nineteenth century, some well-intentioned settlers attempted to "civilize" Native people through conversion and education, although they also ruthlessly eliminated aboriginal languages and traditions in the process. Less benign government policies encouraged segregation, discrimination, and even cultural genocide. Virtually everyone—both those sympathetic to and those antagonistic to Native Americans—believed that aboriginal cultures were vanishing. This expected disappearance of Native cultures stimulated museum collectors to salvage for science whatever was available. Informed by the emerging discipline of anthropology, which endeavored to record and understand cultures irrevocably changed by colonialism, ethnographers and museum collectors combed the Northwest Coast for artifacts that would make compelling exhibits in distant museums. They took it as their mission to record what they believed to be the last vestiges of these dying cultures.

Between 1880 and 1920, European, Canadian, and American museums engaged in what can only be described as a voracious scavenge for artifacts up and down the coast.[3] The most desirable prize for these collectors was a totem pole, which every museum wanted to have proudly displayed in their lobby or atrium, alongside other gigantic specimens of natural and cultural history, including elephants, whales, dinosaurs, stone monoliths, and dugout canoes. As with other artifacts of indigenous cultures, totem poles ended up in natural history museums—one more symptom of the Victorian predilection for associating Native people more with nature than with culture. The Smithsonian Institution's United States National Museum (now the National Museum of Natural History) began acquiring poles as early as the 1870s, and the Berlin Royal Museum of Ethnology followed suit a decade later. During the late 1890s and early 1900s, the American Museum of Natural History sponsored, under the leadership of Franz Boas, the Jesup North Pacific Expedition, which collected material culture and ethnographic information in British Columbia and Siberia, including a considerable number of Haida, Kwakwa̲ka̲'wakw, Salish, and Heiltsuk poles.[4] Soon the Field Museum of Natural History in Chicago, the Victoria Memorial Museum (later the National Museum of Man, now the Canadian Museum of Civilization) in Ottawa, the Pitt Rivers Museum in Oxford, and the British Museum in London, among others, could boast tall, well-carved poles (see appendix D for a list of poles in museum locations abroad).[5]

In the vast lobby of the Field Museum, totem poles soar. In the Pitt Rivers Museum, a Haida pole's bottom stands on the main floor of a large atrium space, while its top peeks over the balcony of the second story. In many buildings—such as the Royal Ontario Museum in Toronto, the National Museum of Natural History in Washington, D.C., the British Museum, the University of Chicago's anthropology department, and the Eiteljorg Museum in Indianapolis—poles stand in stairwells so that visitors circle around them as they rise toward the topmost figures. In contrast, at the American Museum of Natural History, the Brooklyn Museum in New York, and the University of British Columbia's Museum of Anthropology, tall poles are sometimes divided into sections, which are either displayed together or distributed around the galleries. What was once a single expression of family status has become separate carvings presented as individual art works, the original losing not only it social meaning but also its material and cultural integrity.

INTERNATIONAL EXPOSITIONS

Ideally, museums are permanent institutions committed to preserving their collections. International expositions are transitory, less overtly educational, and designed to be highly entertaining. World's fairs originated and developed in Europe as public spectacles glorifying the economic benefits of colonialism. In 1851, the Crystal Palace opened its doors to throngs of visitors to the first world's fair, London's Great International Exposition, which celebrated the channeling of raw goods from the colonies into economic prosperity for Britain. Sixteen years later, the 1867 Paris exposition added archeological and ethnographic displays, thereby contrasting the natural bounty of the colonies with their cultural backwardness, and justifying both the exploitation of Native resources and the civilizing of indigenous people. In 1889, the next Paris exposition introduced another striking innovation—exhibits of living people from the French empire. One hundred and eighty-two Africans and Asians wore aboriginal garments, lived in "traditional" houses organized into "native villages," and performed authentic, if staged, ceremonies for fairgoers. Europeans were invited to experience for themselves the "resources" of the colonies that were waiting to be exploited by the "superior" civilizations.

A POLE FROM TANU

BY BILL HOLM, ART HISTORIAN AND ARTIST

In 1902, Dr. Charles Newcombe, collecting for the Field Museum in Chicago, bought a magnificent sixteen-foot interior house post in the Haida village of Tanu. The post traveled to Chicago, to New York State, to Los Angeles, and finally to Quebec, the most distant location since it left its home in Haida Gwaii. The pole now stands in the Canadian Museum of Civilization's Great Hall, facing a row of houses replicating traditional dwellings of the Native peoples of the British Columbia coast—a much more fitting setting than the New York camp where it stood for many years, covered by successive coats of bright paint, which fortunately protected its surface from the ravages of weather! Through careful work by conservators, it can be seen much as it once was, although without its original setting of the interior of a great six-beam Haida house. An unusual speaker's staff resembling the tusk of a narwhal was an original feature of the pole, and now the two have been reunited through the generosity of the Field Museum.

Although Newcombe, a medical doctor, lacked anthropological training, he was a meticulous chronicler who recorded valuable information about the objects he collected. He noted that the post illustrated the crests of the wife of a house chief and were crests of a Skedans family. The upper figure represents the Wasgo, an undersea monster, part wolf or grizzly bear and part killer whale, recognizable by the pectoral fins pendant from forelegs and a fluked tail curled up over its abdomen. Upright formline designs between the forelegs probably represent dorsal fins, brought around to the front. A small whale's head appears between the creature's ears, through which are thrust the whale's pectoral fins. Wasgos often appear with whales, their prey, caught between the ears. All these fins, flukes, and joints are rendered in massive formlines that may offer clues to the identity of the maker.

7.1. Wasgo and Grizzly Bear house post, Tanu (Haida). Photograph by Bill Holm. Courtesy of Canadian Museum of Civilization, V11-B-1797a.

The fierce faces of the Wasgo and the grizzly bear set the pole apart from most Haida monumental sculpture. Broad, arched eyebrows; large, rounded eyes on full orbs; curled nostrils; wide, grinning lips; and formidable teeth were standard features of Haida bear imagery. But almost all Haida monumental totem poles fit these features much more within the confines of the original half-cylindrical shaft. In this they differ from the figures in late nineteenth century argillite model poles, begun with a slab of material rather than a cylindrical trunk of a tree. The sculptured faces in this pole are much more like those of argillite. Full, rounded foreheads; deep, smooth dip at the bridges of the protruding snouts; massive, full-sculptured canine teeth are all examples of this style. Deep sculpture of the intersecting and overlapping fins, flukes, and tail joints of the Wasgo are also argillite-like.

I've been tempted to relate this masterpiece to the work of an unidentified Haida artist whose formlines and some of his associated sculpture resemble this pole. We've given him a fictional name, "The Master of the Chicago Settee," after a masterful chief's seat in the Field Museum, collected by Dr. Newcombe in the same period. Whether this perceived relationship will stand or fall depends on more examination and reexamination of the objects, old photographs, archival and genealogical records, and past interpretations. Whatever the outcome, the Wasgo and Grizzly Bear house post of Tanu stands as one of the great masterpieces of Northwest Coast sculptural art.

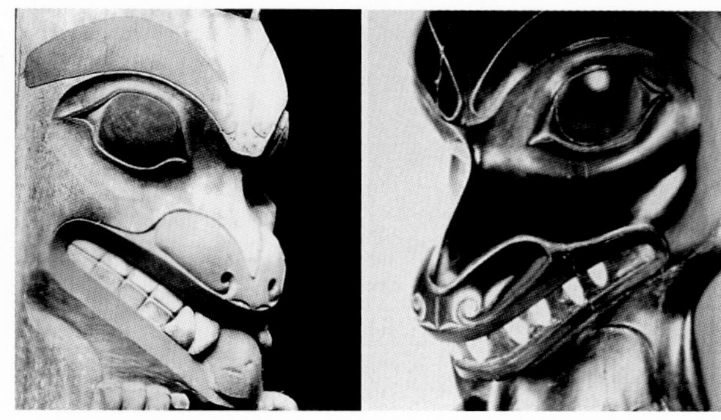

7.2. Tanu house post grizzly bear compared to a grizzly bear on an argillite pole, perhaps by the same carver. Private collection. Photograph by Bill Holm. Courtesy of Canadian Museum of Civilization, V11-B-1797a

Fairs in the United States were funded and organized by wealthy industrial capitalists and were legitimized by scientists across various fields. Like their European counterparts, the first American world's fairs reflected the prevailing ideology that the races had evolved at different rates, with dark-skinned "primitives" standing low on the ladder of evolution and light-skinned people of the North having advanced much further.[6] (It is tempting to draw a parallel with the trope of the devalued "low man on the totem pole").

At international fairs in the United States, this social Darwinism (the application of theories of biological evolution to race and culture) merged with an expanding global capitalism to create a utopian, white-dominated vision for the future that buttressed American nationalism, supported evolutionary theory, and "scientifically" legitimated imperialism and segregation.[7] At some fairs, anthropologists from institutions such as Harvard and the Smithsonian organized ethnographic displays meant to bestow academic respectability upon the notion of "primitives" as being lowly and whites as superior. While some serious academics hoped that ethnographic villages would enlighten visitors about racial and cultural differences, to most fairgoers, Native people were simply inferior aliens whose appearance, behavior, and artifacts reinforced prevailing attitudes about race and culture. (See appendix E for a list of poles at expositions.)

THE PHILADELPHIA CENTENNIAL EXPOSITION, 1876

The first public presentation of a totem pole outside the Northwest Coast was at the 1876 Philadelphia Centennial Exposition (fig. 7.3). Like all such expositions, certain messages were meant to be conveyed; the overarching message at the 1876 exposition was that America—only a century old—was solid as a rock, would thrive in the future, and must assume the lead in the international march of progress. American scientific and intellectual achievements were presented by the Smithsonian Institution in a massive 20,600-square-foot building. In addition to an array of American natural resources, the Smithsonian building was to

A THIN LINE CONNECTING THE VISUAL TO THE INVISIBLE

BY ROBERT DAVIDSON, HAIDA ARTIST

In myth time it is believed that there is a thin line that connects our soul to our body. It is illustrated in a story: when the husband left for fishing, he was connected by a thin line to his home; when the thin line stopped going out, his wife knew that he was on his way back home. Because she wanted him to die, she cut the line. On his way home he died.

The totem pole is that thin line crossing generations, telling our history. There is a totem pole standing in the great hall at the Museum of Civilization in Ottawa. It once stood inside a house at Tanu (see fig. 7.1). This totem pole embodies all the principles of a universal sculpture in the Haida style. It is one step beyond the classical totem pole style of the mid-nineteenth century, demonstrating that artists were continuingly striving to be the best.

This totem pole is the peak of perfection, balance, composition, bursting with energy, ready to leap out. It has a unique style bordering between the classical wooden totem pole and the developing argillite style of the time. This totem pole's life began as a house pole validating the house chief's place in society. Its birth was at a time when activity was at its height of discovery, new technologies, new ways of expressing, new materials resulting in a new economy.

When I sit and contemplate this totem pole, I am brought back to that time where there was no word for art. Art was one with everyday life, was to be experienced, was to be used in cooking, eating, storing food, in ceremony, in dancing, in singing, marking our place in society, documenting our place in history.

Evidence of this once-accomplished art form from the nineteenth century can be seen in totem poles, carved and painted boxes, and carved mountain goat and sheep horn spoons and bowls collected and now housed in museums.

These objects are the thin line allowing artists of our generation to study and imitate the principles and ideas achieved through countless generations of artists. The thin line connecting the past masters to our generation of artists is now a thick rope. As we relearn their standards and expand on this knowledge, we are reclaiming an ancient way of expressing our values.

We are facing a new challenge now that we have artists who can create the same standard of our forefathers in these totem poles. The old growth cedar forests are being clear-cut at a rate exceeding the regrowth of the trees. The old growth trees have the straight and fine grain, free of knots, making this an ideal material for totem poles. In a very short time, perhaps my generation, we will no longer enjoy creating new totem poles.

A thin line will be the connection to the future generations as they discover the totem pole and realize that it was carved from a single tree trunk.

present "an exhaustive and complete" display of "the past and present condition of the Native tribes of the United States, or its anthropology" (Rydell 1984, 23). The people of British Columbia (at that time part of the United Kingdom, as was the rest of Canada) were included in this survey, a curious incorporation for a country celebrating its separation from Britain.

Otis T. Mason, then a professor at Columbian College University (later George Washington University), organized collectors for the Smithsonian's exhibits, instructing them to acquire artifacts that conveyed the life of "savage tribes of men [who] are rapidly disappearing from our continent, and that, ere another century . . . will have disappeared forever" (Rydell 1984, 23–24). Mason assigned James Swan of Port Townsend, Washington, the task of acquiring Northwest Coast materials for Philadelphia. Swan's Smithsonian-sponsored collecting activities, begun in spring 1875, represented the first systematic acquisition of ethnographic material in the region and would offer large numbers of people outside the Northwest their first opportunity to see totem poles (Cole 1985, 22).

7.3. Philadelphia Centennial Exposition, 1876. National Anthropological Archives, Smithsonian Institution, RU95b61f5, neg #76-4541.

Swan traveled north to the amalgamated village of Fort Simpson, where he met the Methodist missionary Thomas Crosby, who was working diligently to convert the Tsimshian and encourage them to renounce their traditions. For Crosby, totem poles represented "old heathen ways" and needed to be removed if their owners were to become truly "civilized." Some converts had burned their poles, while others gave their offensive carvings to Crosby for what, in reality, became his private museum. From this collection, Swan purchased a forty-foot totem pole as well as a forty-foot-wide house front painted with a sea bear and killer whales. For transport, the house front was disassembled into its constituent planks, but the unwieldy pole had to be cut in half (Cole 1985, 23). At Prince of Wales Island, Swan wanted to purchase a pole, but the residents roundly refused Swan's offer, insisting that their valued memorials to the dead were not for sale. So Swan commissioned one.

When the Philadelphia Centennial Exposition opened in May 1876, fully one third of the Smithsonian Institution's vast hall showed Native American weapons, tipis, house models, photographs, pots, manikins dressed in aboriginal clothing (the first such figures displayed in America)—and totem poles. Disassociated from Native villages, totem poles now appeared among artifacts of other Native people—Southwest pots, Plains quillwork, California baskets, and models of Native houses—as well as garlands of American flags. No longer the heritage of a particular Kwakwaka'wakw, Tsimshian, or Kaigani Haida family, these became symbols of a generalized American Indianness. Here, then, was a source of the cliché that Indian culture in its

THE SWAN POLE

BY ROBIN WRIGHT, ART HISTORIAN

7.4. Swan pole, Kasaan (Kaigani Haida; left) at the Philadelphia Centennial Exposition, 1876. Smithsonian Institution Archives, record unit 95, SIA 2008-2344.

The first known person to commission a full-size pole for an outside audience was James G. Swan, on his Centennial Exposition collecting trip to Alaska in 1875. Having failed to purchase an existing pole on his trip, he wrote a letter on

July 15 to the trader Charles Baronovich, who had a store at Karta Bay that he had visited near the village of Kasaan on Prince of Wales Island. In the letter, Swan ordered a new pole to be carved and sent to him in Port Townsend. This pole is now on exhibit at the National Museum of Natural History, Smithsonian Institution, where it went after the fair in Philadelphia.[8] It tells the Tlingit story of Ku.l qe, who had an encounter with land otters. This is the same story recorded on a pole carved by Dwight Wallace for Kusqwa'i, John Wallace's mother's brother, that once stood in the village of Sukkwan. John Wallace brought this Sukkwan pole with him to the fair in San Francisco in 1941, and it eventually went to the Denver Art Museum, where it is on exhibit now.[9] It is likely, given both the story and the similarity in carving styles, that Dwight Wallace was the carver commissioned by Baronovich to carve the pole for Swan. He may also have carved a smaller model of this pole that is now in a private collection in Seattle. His son, John Wallace, would have been about fifteen years old at the time of this commission, and may have assisted his father. John Wallace also carved a copy of this pole in 1941 for Mud Bight Park north of Ketchikan (Wright 2001, 199–203, 206–9). This Mud Bight pole has since deteriorated and has been replaced with a replica carved by Nathan Jackson.

entirety could be embodied by a few choice icons: the feather bonnet, the tomahawk, the "peace pipe," the tipi, and, most important for this study, the totem pole.

The rhetorical role of artifacts at the fair was to exhibit the "savagery" of Native Americans who were denied participation in the progress and cultural achievements of their colonizers based on presumptions about their deficiencies. At that time, few white Americans associated Indians with anything positive; in 1876, most considered the "Red Man" a problem at best and a villainous enemy at worst. Plains Indians were still fighting the cavalry; indeed, the Battle of Little Bighorn took place just weeks after this fair opened. In addition to continuing military action against Native people, in 1883 the U. S. government would attempt to destroy Indian culture by outlawing the Sun Dance and other Native religious ceremonies (the year before the Canadian government followed suit with the potlatch prohibition). The Dawes Severalty Act of 1887, which offered incentives for Native people to reject tribal affiliations and assimilate into white society, would make it easier for whites to acquire Indian reservation land. The Smithsonian's exhibition hall also contained natural specimens that conveyed to the visitor the "raw" nature of both American resources and aborigines—the former to be exploited, the latter destroyed in a phenomenal westward expansion governed by the concept of Manifest Destiny.[10]

Given the prevalent attitudes of Americans toward Native Americans, negative evaluations of Native art were certain to follow. Indeed, the epigraph of this chapter contains a quote from an *Atlantic Monthly* article describing the Tsimshian house front (now considered one of the masterpieces of northern two-dimensional painting) as barbaric and crude, "daubed with the most grotesque and barbarous devices, among which a lidless, browless eye recurs with disquieting frequency." As for the poles, the article considered them "rudely carved into a series of hideous monsters one on top of the other, painted in crude colors" (Cole 1985, 30).[11]

Not all writers were so contemptuous, and some even tried to understand the cultural significance of poles. For example, James McCabe, in *The Illustrated History of the Centennial Exhibition,* tries to explain their function, though he submits to stereotype in the end:

> Here, too, are two large "totem posts" from the Pacific coast. These posts are common among the Indian tribes of that region. To the uninformed, these "totem posts" look like rude idols of wood, reared in front of, and towering high above the houses of the Native people, but in reality they are nothing but a sort of illustrated pedigree or family tree, or more simply, "name posts." . . . The northwest coast Indians still further illustrate their names and family

> history by erecting in front of their houses tall posts of cedar, cut into combinations of human and animal forms. Each of those representations illustrates a generation in the pedigree of the owner. These posts are not worshiped, though they are supposed by the Indians to exercise a protecting influence over their houses (McCabe 1876, 557).

It would be interesting to know how many fairgoers took the time to understand these poles instead of viewing these alien carvings with fascination or disgust. After the Philadelphia Centennial Exposition was dismantled, all of the Native American materials were sent to the Smithsonian Institution, where today they rest in the National Museum of Natural History's collection.

THE CHICAGO WORLD'S COLUMBIAN EXPOSITION, 1893

Four hundred years after Columbus landed in North America, the people of Chicago sponsored an ambitious fair that presented a utopian vision of the world and of America's dominant place within it. As in Philadelphia, the theme of the fair was progress: the general progress from savagery to civilization; the impressive progress the United States had made in industry, agriculture, arts, and culture; and the progress Chicago was making in establishing itself as an American civic center rivaled only by New York. According to its executive director, Colonel George R. Davis, the fair would "celebrate the opening of a hemisphere for the benefit of humanity, for the progress of civilization and the advance of the Christian religion" (de Wit 1993, 63). One way to achieve this was through scientific exhibits explicitly intended to serve as object lessons for making better citizens of the masses.

Ground was broken in 1892, the actual quadricentennial, but the fair opened in 1893. The main exhibitions were located in the carefully planned, neoclassical complex with lakes, fountains, broad avenues, and white buildings—thus the moniker "White City." Here the masses could learn about the order of the world, the value of education, and the greatness of the country to which they belonged. Perpendicular to these elegant beaux-arts buildings (the sole remaining one of which houses the Field Museum of Natural History) was the Midway Plaisance, the fair's entertainment zone, with food vendors, commercial operations, exhibits of global exotica, and the world's first Ferris wheel. People flocked to the exposition; in the nine months that it was open, more than 27,500,000 visitors explored the Chicago fair.

To celebrate American advancements, it was necessary to demonstrate their distance from primitive origins—hence the importance of anthropology at the Chicago fair. The exposition's administrators hired Frederic Ward Putnam, director of Harvard's Peabody Museum of Archaeology and Ethnology, to head the ethnology department, charging him with acquiring collections for exhibition. Unlike in Philadelphia, where ethnology shared a building with natural science, the Chicago exposition devoted an entire building to human history. In an article entitled "Anthropology at the World's Fair," anthropologist Frederick Starr asserted, "Every great international exposition is, in a certain sense, a practical study in anthropology. Recent world's fairs have, however, shown more and more a tendency to make an especial exhibit in anthropology and kindred sciences" (1893, 610). For Starr, the Chicago exposition was especially impressive, for "we have a great object lesson in anthropology: a museum of somatology, archaeology, and ethnology; a picture of ethnography; a laboratory of unusual completeness" (Starr 1893, 621).

In fact, Putnam hoped to use the fair to introduce the discipline of anthropology to the American public; a colleague later likened him in this role to "Einstein at a Barnum and Bailey circus." To help him assemble a truly great anthropological collection, Putnam hired Franz Boas to coordinate a team of collectors; as a result, the Northwest Coast tribes were among the most fully represented in Chicago. Boas planned to focus on the Kwakwa̱ka̱'wakw, whom he still considered the most interesting Northwest Coast group, and illustrate their culture as completely as possible with a display of objects as well as actual people. He worked closely with George Hunt, his longtime collector and collaborator regarding the study of Kwakwa̱ka̱'wakw culture. Comparative material from other tribes would demonstrate the cultural history of the Northwest Coast. As he had done in his history of totem poles, Boas represented the Kwakwa̱ka̱'wakw as the originators of virtually every element of Northwest Coast culture. As Boas explained,

> It was my plan to illustrate the culture of the tribes of Fort Rupert most fully, because they have exerted an influence over all the tribes of the North Pacific Coast. It is my belief that the peculiar culture of this whole region has had its origin among the tribes of Fort Rupert, the Kwakiutl. This is proved most fully by the fact that the names of all the ceremonies which play so important a part in the customs of these tribes are borrowed from the Kwakiutl language. For this reason I also desired to bring a number of representatives of this tribe to Chicago, and I succeeded in doing so through the efforts of Mr. George Hunt" (quoted in R. Johnson 1897, 344).[12]

Putnam had attended the tenth International Congress of Anthropology and Prehistoric Archaeology in Paris in 1889 (the same year that the Paris exposition displayed artifacts and living people to considerable acclaim). Putnam had been most impressed by the colonial city, and decided to have similar living exhibits in Chicago. As a result, a "small colony of Indians"—including seventeen Kwakwa̱ka̱'wakw from Vancouver Island—lived at the fairgrounds and spent the summer presenting dances in the "ethnographic vil-

7.5. Northwest Coast poles and houses, World's Columbian Exposition, Chicago, 1893. Digital collections, Paul Galvin Library, Illinois Institute of Technology, 0003/4010.

lage."[13] Their houses, near the Anthropological Building as well as the Leather and Shoe Trades Building in a remote part of the fair, faced a pond upon which the Kwakwa̲ka̲'wakw could paddle their canoes (fig. 7.5). They not only enjoyed themselves but also made sufficient money for some to host lavish potlatches on their return to British Columbia.

Most visitors to the fair had their first opportunity to see the impressive structures built by the Native people of the Northwest Coast: a forty-five-square-foot house replete with a painted façade (where the Kwakwa̲ka̲'wakw stayed) and a smaller twenty-nine-square-foot Haida house from Skidegate. Flanking these structures were poles from the Haida, Tsimshian, Nuxalk, Salish, and Tlingit. Jacknis (2002) points out that this was the first of many composite Northwest Coast villages that decontextualized individual tribal objects in exchange for a larger totemic tableau. (The current Great Hall of the Canadian Museum of Civilization represents perhaps the latest of these). In fact, at all of the fairs mentioned here, in fair literature Northwest Coast people and objects were assigned to Alaska, the United States, or Canada seemingly at random—and were thus deterritorialized discursively as well as physically.

As the fair organizers saw it, these living exhibits would serve an important didactic function—to educate Americans about the world's different races—which would in turn become an object lesson on how far whites had progressed. The official guidebook to the fair suggested that visitors first explore the White City, with its celebration of progress, and then see the contrasting Midway Plaisance, with its masses of primitives and barbarians organized along clear evolutionary principles. Despite this advice, the midway—designed as a commercial location that represented the sideshow of the less evolved human—actually turned out to be more popular and attracted more visitors than the civilized, proper, and austere White City. Although not on the midway proper, the position of the Northwest Coast village subtly communicated evolutionist concepts, for it stood between the replica of Maya ruins—with their own monumental columns—and a model Indian boarding school exhibited by the Bureau of Indian Affairs that displayed how the U.S. government was "civilizing" the Indian through education. Maya ruins represented the Indians of the pre-Columbian past, and the boarding school, the Indians of the colonized future; the highly artistic Kwakwa̲ka̲'wakw were placed en route.

The Chicago exposition opened only three years after the U.S. Army had massacred men, women, and children at Wounded Knee, South Dakota, in the last major incident of the Indian wars. The poor living conditions of the Native people at the fair, where there were outbreaks of measles and smallpox, and the colonialist attitudes of the fair organizers can be considered an apt (if unintentional) testimony to one side of Columbus's impact on the New World. In Chicago, Indians were no longer a threat, merely an administrative burden and an opportunity for science. In contrast to the general disdain and occasional outright hatred of Native people expressed in Philadelphia, in Chicago Indians were inferior and outmoded yet colorful and creative. Indeed, as historian Robert Trennert points out, "The 1893 Exposition actually helped make Indian lifeways more interesting to the public," something that would become more and more evident throughout the next century (1987, 212). Only after Native Americans were no longer a political threat did they become "interesting" to science, and "colorful" to proper American citizens.

LOUISIANA PURCHASE CENTENNIAL EXPOSITION, ST. LOUIS, 1904

In 1904, St. Louis commemorated the Louisiana Purchase of 1804 by hosting the largest American fair up to that time. Once again, visitors would receive a message of tremendous progress, framed by an imperial vision of the United States within an expanding context. The St. Louis fair's anthropology section—the most comprehensive thus far—was managed by the Smithsonian's W. J. McGee, a committed evolutionist. It was designed to present a "Congress of Races," with numerous Native peoples from around the world living in "natural" settings. McGee, already well known in

THE ORIGINAL "CHEESY" TOTEM: THE KRAFT/LINCOLN PARK POLE

BY AARON GLASS, ANTHROPOLOGIST

When I first arrived in Alert Bay in June 1993, there was an old, decaying totem pole lying on the grass in front of the U'mista Cultural Centre, the local museum, archive, and repository for repatriated regalia. One of my first assignments as a volunteer for the centre was to remove the few still clearly visible figures from the pole, to salvage intact hardware from its surface for reuse, and to facilitate its "return to the Earth" (a romantic though not inaccurate euphemism for dragging it into the sea). As I worked, visiting tourists questioned my activity— especially as a non-Native—and lamented the lack of local concern for this seemingly obvious cultural treasure. I tried to explain that under traditional Kwakwa̱ka̱'wakw custom, poles that had served their display purposes and fallen were left to decay. Sometimes new poles were erected in their place; they may have presented visual analogues, with similar sets of images, but rarely were they direct copies. After a number of visitors inquired as to the origin and history of this pole, I consulted the U'mista Cultural Centre files and found that it had traveled and transformed many times in its considerable lifetime.

The pole originally lived a few hundred meters down the main road in Alert Bay. Carved around 1900, the pole stood before the house of its owner, Chief Waxawidi. It likely displayed crests and figures related to an ancestor of the chief: from top to bottom, a Thunderbird (a common crest atop poles from Alert Bay); a baleen whale with a spear-carrying man astride its back; and a grinning sea monster. A photo from around 1910 shows the pole in situ, in front of the chief's house bearing a sign reading "Chief Klakwagila of Kingcome Inlet BC broke a copper valued [at] 11,500 Blankets" (fig. 7.6).[14] Famed Canadian artist Emily Carr then painted the pole in 1912 (fig. 7.7).

In the mid-1920s, James L. Kraft (famous cheese magnate) traveled along the Northwest Coast and by 1926 had secured the purchase of two poles from Alert Bay; his

7.6. Kraft/Lincoln Park pole (Kwakwa̱ka̱'wakw), in situ in Alert Bay, 1910. Courtesy of Royal British Columbia Museum, BC Archives, PN2711.F.

7.7. Emily Carr, Chief Klakwagila Pole, 1912. Oil on canvas. 27" x 14.2." McMichael Canadian Art Collection, McMichael Gallery, 1974-18-4.

records suggest that these belonged to Chiefs "Waxawidi" and "K'wamaxalas." He sent the latter pole to a private estate in Wisconsin and in 1929 donated the Waxawidi pole to the City of Chicago on behalf of the city's school children; it was erected in Lincoln Park (on the corner of Lake Shore Drive and Addison Street) under the watchful eyes of "American Indians" dressed in feathers and buckskin. At its base, a plaque completely muddling its history and identity read:

> The "Kwa Ma Rolas"—Historic Haidan Indian totem pole from the Queen Charlotte Islands, British Columbia, Presented to the Commissioners of Lincoln Park by J. L. Kraft, June 20, 1929. The "Kwa Ma Rolas," carved from a single yellow cypress, forty feet high and five feet in diameter, tells the tribal history and legend of one of the oldest civilizations in the world. The figures carved upon the pole from top to base represent the Kolus, great sister to the Thunderbird; founder of the tribe, the Steelheaded Man; and the Killer Whale. Dedicated to the schoolchildren of Chicago, the "Kwa Ma Rolas" stands in Lincoln Park to repeat forever in its carvings this saga of the American Indian.

Ironically, in the sense that the plaque completely misrepresented the pole's indigenous origins, this final statement bears a sad semblance of truth. In fact, over the years that it stood in Lincoln Park, the pole was abused and altered many times. Its name was an Anglicization of the name of the second pole Kraft bought, K'wamaxalas. The Thunderbird's head was missing its curved horns, likely lost in transit or sent to Wisconsin. A pair of wings and horns originally attached to the Wisconsin pole were added to this one, but (absurdly) on the torso of the Whale and at the feet of the Thunderbird, respectively (fig. 7.8). The pole was repainted in 1953, at which time it was claimed by the Kraftsman newsletter to be "more than 500 years old." In 1958, the human figure was recarved, with the hand now covering his eyes; in 1966, conservators recarved and repainted the pole extensively, completely altering its original two-dimensional designs. In 1972, the pole was set afire by vandals (according to one report, by members of the American Indian Movement); in 1973, responding to a query by a reader, the *Chicago Tribune* explained the pole as telling the story of a princess who saved her tribe by slaying a sea monster; in 1979, it was completely covered in fiberglass and epoxy paint. Finally, in 1982, Native and non-Native advisors to the Field Museum deemed the pole a valuable example of Kwakwa̲ka̲'wakw sculpture. The city returned the badly decayed pole to British Columbia in 1985 and hired Tony Hunt (along with his son, Tony Hunt Jr., and John Livingston) to carve a replica of the original, which was

7.8. Pole in Chicago, 1929. Chicago History Museum, DN-0088619.

dedicated in Lincoln Park on May 21, 1986, with considerable fanfare, including a dance performance by the Hunt family and an art contest for school children to draw totem poles for their own families. The pole was renamed—more accurately, to reflect an origin story of the 'Namgis people of Alert Bay—"Kwanusila, the Legend of the Thunderbird" (fig. 7.9).

The original pole remained at the University of British Columbia Museum of Anthropology in Vancouver for a few years until it was designated as beyond viable restoration, and it was shipped back to Alert Bay and placed on the beach in front of U'mista. The little man, sans spear, is now in deep storage at U'mista, while fragments of the sea monster's face stand outside an Alert Bay carving shed.

7.9. Replicated pole in Chicago, 1994. Photograph by Aaron Glass.

7.10. Fiberglass Thunderbird, Alert Bay, 2000. Photograph by Aaron Glass.

7.11. Pole on Boy Scout patch, 1950s. Photograph by Aaron Glass.

The fiberglass Thunderbird was given to Tommy Brown, the grandson of Tlakwagila, and today it stands before his son Harry Brown's house on Front Street (fig. 7.10), mere meters from where the original stood a century ago.

After I learned of the pole's provenance, I asked my father, who grew up in Chicago, if he remembered a totem in Lincoln Park. He enthusiastically recalled using it as a meeting point for friends gathering from around the city. Recently, he even found his old Boy Scout district patch, which pictures the Lincoln Park pole, complete with the extra pair of wings on the whale's body (fig. 7.11). My father now proudly displays a file about the pole on the mantelpiece of his Los Angeles home, along with a small chunk of mostly rotted wood that I "salvaged" from the original monument before launching it into the Pacific Ocean.

7.12. Alaska Building, Louisiana Purchase Exposition, St. Louis, 1904. Missouri Historical Society, St. Louis, neg. 15775.

the academic world for his theories on social progress, advocated the notion that "cephalization"—the increased brain capacity of the "higher" races—and "cheirization"—increased manual dexterity along the same lines—led naturally to the advance of culture. He once wrote, "It is a matter of common observation that the white man can *do* more and better than the yellow, the yellow man more and better than the red or black" (Rydell 1984, 160). McGee verbalized a remarkable call to action for Anglo-Saxons in "National Growth and National Character": It is the duty of the strong [i.e., white] man to subjugate the lower nature, to extirpate the bad and cultivate the good among living things, to delve into earth below and cleave the air above in search of fresh resources . . . to halter thin vapors and harness turbulent waters into servile subjection, and in all ways to enslave the world for the support of humanity and the increase of human intelligence" (quoted in Rydell 1984, 161). This represented a general anxiety directed more toward waves of immigrants to the United States than toward concerns about absorbing its indigenous populations.

Various ethnic groups were brought to the fair in order to demonstrate the hierarchical racial diversity of the world. In his inventory of ethnic groups at the fair, McGee (1905, 822, 824) noted that the Kwakwa̱ka̱'wakw and Nuu-chah-nulth—"singularly light-colored fisherfolk"—who performed at the fair were complemented by a presentation of "totems or animal tutelaries [that] helped maintain law." He was referring to a large array of totem poles that stood outside the Alaska Building (fig. 7.12). When plans for the St. Louis fair were announced, Alaska governor John Brady seized the opportunity to promote his goal of statehood. At that time, the territory had too few (white) residents to be a state, and needed ways to attract immigrants. Recognizing that Alaska needed a large-scale infusion of settlers, Brady tried, in his exhibits, to challenge common misconceptions of Alaska—such as its being a frozen wasteland—and to make the region appealing to new settlers. One way to do this was by assembling interesting exhibits about this fascinating region, and surrounding the Alaska building with striking and artistic monuments—totem poles and two plank houses. Brady announced,

> The two Native houses together with the totem poles all put in order will be as unique an attraction as any building on the grounds. Say what we will, these strange carvings have a great power of attraction, as we can see by the marked attention given them by the tourists year by year. With this attraction to the building we feel that thousands will visit it who would not come near it were it destitute of these features. In fact, a plain American building would lack the real Alaskan flavor (quoted in V. Wyatt 1986, 18).

Brady had already begun to acquire poles to erect in a Sitka park but first wanted to send them to St. Louis. In all, Brady sent fifteen poles, two carved planks, four interior house posts, a canoe, and two complete houses. Several Native men traveled to Missouri to raise the houses as well as repaint and erect the poles, but union rules prevented them from doing any work on the fairgrounds. One could imagine their horror when several of the union workers erected some poles upside down! Ultimately, the error was corrected, and five poles stood on one side of the Alaska Building, with nine on the other (Feldman and Scherer 1994, 44).

One wonders how much Brady succeeded in his quest to bring favor to Alaska during the fair, but he was sufficiently pleased with his exhibit to write, "The totem poles are doing the work intended. They draw the people" (V. Wyatt 1986, 21). Apparently wanting to share his excitement and pleasure with the totem poles' donors, he later wrote, "This morning's *Republic* has a full page devoted to totem poles on one end of our building. I have bought 20 copies to mail—mostly to Native peoples who gave them" (V. Wyatt 1986, 22). In *The Book of the Fair*, Marshall Everett illustrated a picture of nine poles and a house with the caption, "Erected in front of the Alaska buildings was a quaint array of totem poles. The carved figures of bird, beast and man tell the family and tribal history of the Red Men of the North. They are also believed to be used as receptacles for the ashes of the dead, and represent, as a whole, a most interesting exhibit of primitive life" (Everett 1904, 187). In the narrative section on the Alaska exhibits, Everett comments, "Totem poles always form a striking sight. They are gaudily painted in the rude coloring of Native artists. The oldest Alaskan inhabitant cannot remember the origin of these poles, but they are believed to be as old as 150 years" (1904, 361). Thus the totem pole was situated as a prehistoric artifact.

Although Brady sent fifteen poles to St. Louis, only fourteen stood by the Alaska Building. During transit, one pole had broken into pieces and was considered unrepairable. Nevertheless, it caught the attention of "Captain" Dick Crane. This entrepreneur, who had lived in Alaska during the gold rush, managed the "Esquimaux Village," a concession on the Pike in which a group of Alaskan Eskimos and their dogs lived behind a façade covered with papier-mâché icebergs. Crane approached Brady to request the damaged pole, which he reassembled and erected in the Eskimo village (fig. 7.13). The resulting scene represented a hodgepodge of Alaskan ethnography: a miniature lake; scenes of Eskimo life (dogs with their sleds, "native sports, marriage ceremonies, and burial rites," a simulated "combat between esquimaux and polar bears [which] brings the exhibition to a thrilling climax"); an Alaskan gold mining camp in Athabascan territory with log cabin, railroad tracks, and sluice; and the broken Brady totem pole, repaired, with electric lights placed on the lowest figure's eyes (Feldman and Scherer 1994, 46). Fully disregarding ethnic differences in Alaska, Crane amalgamated the three major Native groups—Eskimos, Athabascans, and southeast Native people—into one peculiar, if popular, assemblage. After the fair closed, Brady sold one pole to the Milwaukee Public Museum for five hundred dollars. He also sold the Eskimo village pole to a St. Louis business, which gave it to prominent Indianapolis industrialist D. M. Parry, who erected it on his private estate. The other poles traveled first to Portland for another fair, then back to Alaska to be installed in the park at Sitka.[15]

7.13. "Esquimaux Village," Louisiana Purchase Exposition, St. Louis, 1904. Missouri Historical Society, St. Louis, neg. 16341.

The St. Louis fair embraced the evolutionism prevalent in Chicago, but, at least in the Alaska exhibit, it displayed a somewhat more enlightened attitude toward Native people. For example, one fair brochure (District of Alaska 1905, 57–58) explained the meanings of the poles and identified some of their donors, transforming them from timeless and anonymous "Indians" back into individual, contemporary human beings: "A Thlingit at Klawack named 'Chief Tom' presented one of the poles elaborately carved. . . . One of these Thlingit poles was given by Yennate, who is now a very old man. He said he made it in honor of his mother. . . . All these poles, together with two Native houses and a large war canoe, and the carvings on the inner posts of the houses, were graciously donated by Native people." This was the first time Native owners of Northwest Coast artwork were identified by name in

official fair literature, and Native people appreciatively acknowledged. Yet Native art was still transformed into an emblem of the territory. In St. Louis, totem poles became metonyms that "stood for" Alaska as a particular geographic place within the national imagination, a significance only fueled by the regional tourist industry at the time.

THE DEPRESSION YEARS AND INDIAN WELFARE

During the Great Depression, a more benevolent attitude toward Native Americans became official U.S. governmental policy with the initiation of the 1934 Wheeler-Howard Act, often referred to as the "Indian New Deal." Inspired by the passionately pro-Indian-rights Commissioner of Indian Affairs, John Collier, who worked tirelessly for its passage, this bill was designed to improve the conditions of American Indians and encourage public sympathy toward their plight. It supported greater Indian self-government, gradually closed boarding schools, ceased the allotment policy of the 1887 Dawes Act, promoted greater knowledge of the contributions Native people had made to the United States, and encouraged the preservation and development of Native arts and crafts. This major shift in governmental attitudes reversed the nineteenth-century Indian policy of assimilation and celebrated Native culture, promoted religious freedom, and supported artistic expression. It was during this period that a major government-supported project for totem pole restoration and replication brought renewed public interest in Alaskan totem poles (see chapter five).

Collier believed that art could play a significant role in Native American economic, social, and cultural initiatives. To that end, Congress established the Indian Arts and Crafts Board (IACB) to encourage, support, and market Native art (Schrader 1983). Under general manager René d'Harnoncourt (who later became the director of the Museum of Modern Art in New York City), IACB encouraged Native self-sufficiency by promoting Native art. D'Harnoncourt also believed that exposing the public to the recognizable excellence of Native American art could contravene the deeply entrenched racism of American culture. Furthermore, in d'Harnoncourt's view, indigenous art could be instrumental in distinguishing a uniquely *American* culture in opposition to Europe. He professed, "I personally believe that the Indian artist has enough to contribute to American civilization to make it worthwhile to spend a great deal of time and effort to give him every chance for a free development of his potentialities. I sincerely believe that Indian art . . . may become a powerful fresh factor in American art" (quoted in Rushing 1992, 199). This effort to demonstrate and fabricate national cultures distinct from Europe—and the strategy of using indigenous arts to achieve this goal—was shared with Canada, and would accelerate after World War II in the context of the Cold War.

THE SAN FRANCISCO GOLDEN GATE INTERNATIONAL EXPOSITION, 1939

In the years directly before the United States entered World War II, two fairs on either coast welcomed hundreds of thousands of visitors—one in New York City, the other in the Bay Area. Although two winged Kwawa̲ka̲'wakw poles stood outside the Canada Pavilion in New York's Flushing Meadow Park, Native culture was almost entirely subsumed by the 1939 fair's futuristic celebration of progress. The first opportunity for the IACB to promote Native American art—and totem poles—on a large scale occurred during the 1939 San Francisco Golden Gate International Exposition. Like other fairs, this one celebrated progress in the form of two major public works, the Golden Gate and the San Francisco–Oakland Bay bridges. The exposition's theme, "Empire of the West," revolved around the promise of economic recovery from the Depression and the consequent development of flourishing consumerism. This fair also presented a considerable amount of Native American art under the IACB's auspices.

It would be wrong to think that racist attitudes toward non-whites had been eliminated, despite the change in official policy. Indeed, the San Francisco fair was noteworthy for its introduction of eugenics into popular consciousness, the result of an increasing xenophobia spurred by fears of "racial degeneracy" in the 1920s and 1930s. The legacy of nineteenth-century evolutionism, coupled with the influx of southern and eastern European immigrants into the United States, inspired the founding of the Race Betterment Foundation, which sponsored the Second National Conference on Race Betterment at the fair. Ironically, the official image of Native Americans projected at this fair differed dramatically from all previous ones, and contradicted the eugenicist model. D'Harnoncourt believed that the Native art exhibit organized by IACB would promote a greater appreciation on the part of the American public for the value of Indian heritage and the contemporary vitality of Native arts: "It is the contention of the organizers of the exhibit that the American Indian has in the past shown an admirable ability to cope with his physical surrounding, to build a well ordered society and a highly specialized culture even in the most unfavorable environments and that his achievements are of such value that were they more generally known they would become a real contribution to our contemporary life and would thus give the Indian his deserved place in the contemporary world" (d'Harnoncourt 1939, 164). To learn of these achievements, visitors could explore an entire building dedicated to American Indian materials, first entering the introductory Hall of Indian History, and then rooms exhibiting art from culture-areas such as Eskimo, Plains, and Southwest. Two rooms held Northwest Coast art. The Northern Fisherman room, a large, dark space with a glowing fire pit in its center, evoked the interior of a Northwest Coast bighouse. One of its walls was partially open, revealing the totem pole room, in which stood "trunks of towering totem poles and the monumental grave sculpture in a diffused gray outdoor light" (fig. 7.14; d'Harnoncourt 1939, 11). As mentioned in chapter 6, outside the building was a retail exhibit where consumers could outfit their homes with contemporary indigenous wares.

7.14. Totem pole in Northwest Coast exhibit, San Francisco Golden Gate International Exposition, 1939. Bancroft Library, University of California, Berkeley, 1992.034.3.24-alb.

Forty Native Americans came to the fair as "living pages from history, who were at the exposition to demonstrate their superiority as artisans producing for an international market" (Rydell 1993, 89). One of these was Kaigani Haida John Wallace, whose pole d'Harnoncourt had seen and admired in Waterfall, Alaska. Wallace brought along for exhibit at the fair two poles from Sukkwan that belonged to his family (*Ketchikan Chronicle* 1939a, 1939b). And, in what may have been the first public presentation of full-size totem pole carving outside the Northwest Coast, Wallace and his son Fred together created a thirty-foot pole in San Francisco, which was then erected in the courtyard between the Indian and Government buildings. Such totem-carving demonstrations are now standard fare at public exhibitions of Northwest Coast art.

7.15. John Wallace (Kaigani Haida), totem pole outside Museum of Modern Art, 1941. Photograph by Digital Image. Museum of Modern Art, ART343200. Museum of Modern Art/Licensed by SCALA/Art Resource, New York.

TO THE MUSEUM OF MODERN ART, 1941

D'Harnoncourt was not satisfied to limit his Native art promotions to the Bay Area, and so he invited representatives of various museums to visit the San Francisco fair, hoping to interest them in sponsoring a major exhibit back East. The artwork especially impressed officials of the Museum of Modern Art, the bastion of modernism in New York City. Indian Art of the United States opened there in 1941, filling the entire MoMA building with much material that had been in San Francisco. In contrast to the disparaging comments elicited by earlier fair visitors, responses to the Native art in this major eastern museum could not have been more glowing. *Newsweek* reported that the opening night attendees "wedged four-deep around the dramatically lit showcases testified to the brilliance of the exhibit"; for *Art Digest*, this was the "definitive exhibit of Indian arts and crafts"; the *New York Times* called the exhibit "the most significant recognition to date of the aesthetic gift of American Indian artists" (quoted in Rushing 1992, 216).

Totem poles once again held center stage. As d'Harnoncourt wrote, "The proportions and lighting of the main part of the Northwest Coast room suggest the interior of a huge wooden house of the region, with its central firelight and deep shadows.The visitor will see a weird forest of grave posts rising out of a dim light just before he enters"[16] (1941). Wallace's pole, carved in San Francisco, was sent to New York, where it stood on 53rd Street outside the museum entrance, complementing the other poles inside, which rose "like a surrealist forest" (Rushing 1992, 207; fig. 7.15). A totem pole in front of the most influential modern art museum in the world certainly signified its aesthetic coming-of-age, and the most respect Northwest Coast artists had yet achieved. Indeed, the Northwest Coast art on exhibit elicited special praise. George Vaillant, writing in *Art Bulletin*, called this tradition "an incredible artistic expression blending religion with family pride and social dignity. Totem poles, chests, masks, all in wood, form a powerful and definite art, the most imaginative achievement of the North American Indian" (Vaillant 1941, 168).

Northwest Coast art appealed especially to those searching for surrealistic elements in aboriginal works. European artists had "discovered" African and Oceanic art at the turn of the century, bringing attention to the aesthetic qualities of the "primitive" art that influenced their own works. Similarly, surrealists, such as Max Ernst, "discovered" Native American art when they escaped Nazism in the United States during the 1930s. One of the chief spokesmen for the surrealist movement, Wolfgang Paalen, in his essay "Totem Art," praised Northwest Coast art works as exceptional visions of the subconscious (1943). The general appeal of surrealism is reflected in the press surrounding the exhibit. Vaillant saw otherworldliness in the Northwest Coast exhibit, enhanced by the mysterious-looking, spot-lit sculptures: "The supernatural forces, with whom the Indian has always been in such intimate and uncomfortable contact, seemed dramatically concen-

THE KAIGET POLE AT THE MUSÉE DE L'HOMME

BY MARIE MAUZÉ, ANTHROPOLOGIST

The unveiling of a heraldic pole at the entrance of the Musée de l'Homme on January 20, 1939, was a striking event for Parisians. It was reported in an article by the French surrealist poet Benjamin Péret appearing in Paris-Soir under the sensational title "Krikiett, the Tallest Totem Pole in Europe" (Péret 1939). The sixteen-metre-high pole, once standing on the ridge of the Bulkley Canyon in the Wet'suwet'en Village of Hagwilget (British Columbia), was acquired in September 1938 by the Swiss surrealist painter Kurt Seligmann.

The first European artist to visit this part of the world, he undertook a trip to the Upper Skeena region with the firm intention to bring a totem pole back to Europe. Seligmann shared with his surrealist friends a passionate interest in Northwest Coast art and aesthetics, and was also fascinated by Indian mythology and its interrelations with totemic thought (Seligmann 1995; Hauser 1997, 147, 153–54, 409). With the moral support of the ethnologist Marius Barbeau, well known for his inventory of Gitk'san totem poles (1929) and his involvement in the Tsimshian pole preservation and restoration project in the Skeena District (Cole 1985, 271–278; Jonaitis 1999b, 112–13; Dawn 2001, 224–37), Seligmann spent a few weeks in the Gitk'san community of Hazelton. He chose to acquire the oldest and best preserved of the two heraldic posts still standing in Hagwilget, remarkable for "its beautiful silver grey to copper brown changing patina" (Seligmann 1939, 124).

The Kaiget pole was erected in the late 1860s in front of the house of Gitdumskanees, the then chief of the House of Many Eyes (Ginehklaiyax) of the Laksilyu Clan (Small Frog Clan) of the Wet'suwet'en (Barbeau 1929b, 72–74; Jenness 1943, 486; Seligmann 1939, 121).[17] Carved by Samali of Hagwilget and Tsibasa of Gitsegukla, the pole portrays in different guises the mythical monster Kaiget, which was adopted as a clan crest by the Laksilyu;[18] it also shows the crest of Gitdumkanees (Mountain Man), represented as a human being with a cedar bark neck ring, usually worn in winter ceremonies, and that of an otter, supposedly the crest of a noble of the house (Jenness 1943, 499; Barbeau 1929b; Seligmann 1939, 125–26; Chapman 1965).

7.16. Kaiget pole at Hagwilget, 1923. Photograph by Barbeau. Canadian Museum of Civilization, 59526.

The pole was secured by Seligmann with the help of the Indian agent at Hazelton, G. C. Mortimer, who organized a meeting attended by the descendants of Gitdumskanees. After lengthy talks fuelled by various ownership claims over the Kaiget pole, the deal was concluded with a payment of one hundred dollars, divided among six individuals of the Laskilyu Clan according to their rank (Seligmann 1939, 126–27; Hauser 1997, 149, 510). To ward off the dramatic events which surrounded the removal of the pole, Seligmann was symbolically married to a deceased woman of the clan (Hauser 1997, 149). Mortimer took care of the export certificate, granted in five days by the Department of Indian Affairs (Seligmann 1939, 128). The pole remained on loan until the death of Seligmann's widow, who bequeathed it to the Musée de l'Homme in 1992. Today the Kaiget pole is erected for the third time at the new Quai Branly Museum.

trated here, overawing even the case-hardened New Yorker" (Vaillant 1941, 168). In *Art News*, Jeanette Lowe wrote, "The carved raven, killer-whale and devil fish may strike that eye, more accustomed to such fauna in the world of Surrealism, as symbols of the unconscious mind." This association of surrealism with Native art opened the eyes and minds of many who may have previously dismissed these carvings as "hideous." The trope of aestheticization took center stage at this time, and would remain prevalent for decades as indigenous art, including totem poles, made the slow transition from the curio shop and natural history museum into the art museum and gallery.

TOTEM POLES IN GLOBAL AWARENESS

As anthropologist Fred Myers points out, "The conditions of transnationalism under which most people in the world now live have created new and often contradictory cultural and economic values and meanings in objects—that is, in material culture—as those objects travel in an accelerated fashion through local, national, and international markets and other regimes of value production" (2002, 3). Museums and world's fairs provided venues for totem poles that suffused these artwork with meanings never intended by their makers.[19] The totem pole's expression of family history and status became secondary to its embodiment of contemporary attitudes toward aboriginal people, its signification of various geographic locations, and, sometimes, its expression of concepts entirely unrelated to Indians. Over the decades, tens of thousands of people experienced poles and went away with dramatically different messages. As most exhibits provided little specific information on their original context, viewers were encouraged to perceive them as generic types and not as specific tokens of particular societies, much less of individuals, families, or clans. The erasure of this kind of ethnographic knowledge was essential to the revaluing of Native artifacts as "art" within a modernist construct, as aesthetic productions unmoored from their specific cultural meanings and thus amenable to a universal mode of appreciation or apperception.

Over the years discussed in this chapter, poles have communicated different messages about Northwest Coast art and architecture. In Philadelphia, poles stood in a vast structure that gave no sense of the arc of houses on misty shores—they were simply tall, upright, strangely carved pillars. In Chicago, Boas, who thought exhibits should contextualize artifacts, lined the poles before two pitched-roof houses that faced the "shore" of a pond, amalgamating carvings from hundreds of miles of coastline. In San Francisco and at the Museum of Modern Art, the designers erected the poles in spaces a visitor could enter after walking up a flight of stairs and through a pitched-roof-shaped entrance inspired by Northwest Coast house forms. This aestheticized the presentation and created a compellingly beautiful array of poles from different groups, but one that conveyed little about the poles' cultural contexts.

Exhibits embody the values of the cultures that create them. From the perspective of the twenty-first century, much can be found to criticize in these displays and museums. Putting Native people on exhibit, as was done in Chicago and St. Louis, can be seen as degrading, yet in various cases Natives managed to impose *their* values on the non-Natives. For example, when Swan approached the Kaigani Haida, they refused to sell their poles but agreed to make one to order—for money. The performers in Chicago and St. Louis demonstrated who they really were to visitors; the observers may have *thought* these Native peoples were their inferiors, but the Northwest Coast people controlled the entire performance and earned good money that they later distributed at potlatches. If Natives "played primitive," they did so largely on their terms. In addition to financial remuneration, participants were offered the opportunity to travel, a key mode of achieving status back home. The troupes took further advantage of a ready-made stage to advertise their cultural riches over those of their neighbors. Thus, according to their own value system, they may have enjoyed great success. As owners of the St. Louis poles, the Alaska chiefs became recognized by name as individuals. In San Francisco, a respected carver shared his skill with appreciative audiences, profiting from the exposure and reinforcing the individuality and contemporaneity of totem pole carving.

During these fairs and at museums, non-Native visitors got the opportunity to see both indigenous people and their cultural treasures. Native people got the opportunity to contradict prevailing racialist beliefs. Some visitors were blind to these messages, but others found them compelling. It would take decades before those who accepted the equality of Native people outnumbered those who did not, but the process of changing non-Native attitudes can be thought of as beginning in part with the development of international expositions and museum exhibits.

"MONUMENTS IN MULTICHROME"

TOTEM POLES AND THE PROMOTION OF PLACE

It has already been said by one critic abroad that the only form of art that can be called Canadian is that of the West Coast tribes . . . the Awakening is already with us. Our painting, as an original contribution to the history of art, is already gaining recognition abroad. Art to many Canadians is no longer a luxury, but a means of self-expression, a step toward a culture that will some day be distinctly our own. The manifestations of Canadian art, both ancient and modern, are of vital significance. They speak of the country that is ours.

—MARIUS BARBEAU, ANTHROPOLOGIST, 1927

In 1909, the monumental south entrance to Seattle's Alaska-Yukon-Pacific Exposition (AYPE) featured a pagoda-style lintel supported by four plaster totem poles, two on each side. Electric light bulbs brightened the eyes of every figure carved on the poles (fig. 8.1). This particular fair celebrated expansionism, especially in the trans-Pacific region. It made good use of the totem pole as an icon of Seattle, a city itself named after Suquamish Chief See-alth in a common colonial appropriation and transformation of indigenous names. One particular totem pole stood out in all the advertisements and souvenirs of the fair: a Tlingit monument known as the "Seattle Totem Pole" that still stands in Pioneer Square in downtown Seattle. The pole was illustrated in the center of the cover of the official fair publication, *Seattle, the Gateway to Alaska and the Orient*, as well as in many advertisements for the fair (fig. 8.2). Fairgoers could find an abundant number of spoons with a Seattle pole image on the handle, silver totem pole brooches, and totem pole lead pencils (Duncan 2000, 71–72). This treasured Tlingit clan possession had morphed into the signifier of a distant metropolis.

During the twentieth century, the totem pole has become the symbol of many different places—Seattle, Vancouver, Alaska, British Columbia, and even Canada itself. Efforts to mobilize totem poles as local, regional, and national icons of place were in part a response to the massive export of poles to eastern and European museums. Some of these efforts involved the physical movement and material transformation of the poles themselves, as many were removed, restored, and reerected in largely urban settings. Many of these projects were strategies to salvage remaining monuments, extensions of the activities that led to the placement of poles in Stanley Park and the restoration and relocation of Gitk'san poles on the Canadian National Railway (CNR) line. In addition to the physical re-presentation of totem poles, American and Canadian artists also represented totem poles as subjects of their own artistic visions, which were often tied to government support for the development of distinct national aesthetic styles. Like the earlier totem poles projects, conflicting interests and motivations animated the salvage efforts surveyed here, including scientific preservation, regional or national symbolizing, advancement of the tourist economy, aesthetic inspiration, and concern for the welfare of Native populations. Although indigenous

8.1. Entrance, Alaska-Yukon-Pacific Exposition, Seattle, 1909. Photograph by Frank Nowell. University of Washington Libraries, Special Collections, Nowellx1900. Alaska Yukon Pacific, 280.

craftspeople were frequently involved in the projects, the non-Natives who engineered them engaged in a clear discourse of superiority and custodianship; that is to say, they presented themselves as the benevolent patrons and saviors of a First Nations heritage otherwise doomed to oblivion. In the settings discussed here, the totem pole's role as a beacon for tourists is extended as it becomes a concrete symbol—a "totem," one might say—of particular places.

SEATTLE AND TOTEM POLES

The story of the Seattle Totem Pole begins in 1899, when the *Seattle Post-Intelligencer* newspaper and Seattle's Chamber of Commerce sponsored an excursion to Alaska for 165 Seattle businessmen and their families in order "to promote relations with the merchants and business organizations of the north" (*Post-Intelligencer* 1899a). By the last decade of the nineteenth century, Seattle's population had grown to more than 80,000, and the city sought to establish itself firmly among major American cities. Seattle's proximity to Alaska, a land of abundant resources, offered great business opportunities, such as providing transportation, equipment, and supplies during the 1898 Klondike gold rush. Businesses connected to Alaska constituted a considerable proportion of Seattle's income. To strengthen these ties, the Chamber of Commerce tour left Seattle on August 17, 1899, aboard the steamer *City of Seattle* to visit New Metlakatla, Ketchikan, Wrangell, Juneau, Skagway, Glacier Bay, Killisnoo, and Sitka.

On their return trip, the Seattlites removed a totem pole from what was judged to be an abandoned village. The *City of Seattle* had anchored at Tongass, where many noteworthy poles still stood (fig. 8.3). Only one person, "probably a vagrant fisherman, who refused to come out of his hut," could be seen in this village, suggesting to the travelers that Tongass was indeed abandoned, and its monuments free for the taking. A group decided on one pole, almost fifty feet in height, felled it, and then cut it in half, brought it to the ship, and simply sailed away. The day after the ship returned to Seattle, the *Post-Intelligencer* carried a story that described how the excursionists had seen many totem

8.2. Cover, Alaska-Yukon-Pacific Exposition official brochure, 1909. UW21287. Alaska Yukon Pacific, 546.

8.3. Tongass (Tlingit), 1898. Photograph by Louis Shotridge. University of Washington Libraries. Special Collections, NA3676.

poles along their route and had agreed to bring one back as a "municipal landmark." In its September 3 edition, the paper declared that "Seattle is to have an official emblem that will probably be the most unique possessed by any city in the world" (*Post-Intelligencer* 1899b). This represents perhaps the first time a totem pole was used as a symbol not of a Native family or community nor Native of Alaska or British Columbia but instead of a city hundreds of miles from the nearest totem pole village.

A committee of businessmen identified the best place to erect this pole, a triangular patch of grass on First Avenue and James Street. The front page of the September 3 *Post-Intelligencer* displayed a drawing of the pole and announced the decision to place it in Pioneer Square. Although the customary adjectives "unusual," "weird," and "odd" modified descriptions of the pole, the writer praised the pole's potential for enhancing Seattle:

> Seattle will have probably the most unique municipal decoration of any large town in the United States. The pole is fifty feet high and carved in a manner that might almost be artistic. . . . Aside from the value attaching as a curio to such a creation, there is a fitness in its erection in the heart of this city. . . . So thoroughly is Seattle identified with Alaska that it is generally felt no more appropriate municipal decoration could be set up than this magnificent emblem of the north land. Someone, in discussing the advisability of so decorating the city, has urged that it would look too much as though this were an Indian village. An answer to this lies in the very name of Seattle. (*Post-Intelligencer* 1899b)

Having already adopted an indigenous moniker, further symbols of Seattle's ties to Alaskan heritage were deemed entirely appropriate. The article proceeded to describe the pole's imagery with relative accuracy, noting that poles commemorate individuals and represent "family arms" as well as events in family history. It ended by praising the fortune of the excursionists in finding so magnificent a carving, "as these interesting tribal emblems are becoming rare."

THE SEATTLE TOTEM POLE UNVEILING CEREMONY

BY ALDONA JONAITIS

8.4. Seattle Pole (Tlingit), Pioneer Square, Seattle, 1899. Photograph by Anders B. Wilse. University of Washington Libraries, Special Collections, NA1509.

On October 18, the Seattle Totem Pole was unveiled with great ceremony on Pioneer Square. Excursionist W. H. Thompson, representing the Art and Decorative Association of the City of Seattle, presented the pole, and W. V. Rinehart, president of the Seattle City Council, accepted it. The *Post-Intelligencer* published both of their addresses in full. Thompson, who had taken part in the excursion, summarized the pole's significance as "a symbol and exemplification of totemism . . . the wild men's history, tradition, folklore, mythology and religion combined and interwoven into one" (*Post-Intelligencer* 1899c). Thompson cautioned the audience against judging Indians as unintelligent because they adhered to totemic beliefs, and he likened Native American totemism to the ancient Egyptian practice of embalming ibises and bulls. He described the Greeks, and even the Romans, as being "far more superstitious" than the American Indian, and claimed that they believed in myths "a thousand times more voluminous and illogical than that of the child of the American wilderness." Then Thompson waxed poetic and romantic as he described the pole:

> The shadow of the wilderness is in its deep barbaric lines. The wild man's bizarre coloring adds a strange strength to its rugged outlines. It was fashioned and grew out of his love and reverence for the birds and beasts and the wallowing leviathan of the deep; out of his feeling of affinity and nearness to the trees and brooks and the whispering winds; of perfume, and bloom, and the songs of birds; of the strange voices of the dark and gloomy forests, and the awful silence of the northern lights. He toiled at it lovingly, and reared it in perpetuation of his name and fame. It will here voice his deeds with surer speech than if lying prone in the moss and fern on the shores of Tongass Island. (Applause.) (*Post-Intelligencer* 1899c)

After alluding to the wilderness, Native oneness with nature, and the value of preservation, Thompson, to more applause, officially presented the pole to the City of Seattle.

City council president Rinehard took the podium, addressing the audience in Chinook, a language he had learned as commander of Fort Klamath, Oregon. The *Post-Intelligencer*'s report translated Rinehard's speech, which thanked the donors, complimented Thompson's oratory, and predicted that many visitors, Native and white, would come to see the pole. As if speaking in a Salish voice, Rinehard asserted, "Indians talk thus, 'All the deer have gone from here. Great Chief Seattle is dead. Good woman Angeline, is gone. But this totem pole will stay, remain. Great Seattle has a great totem pole, yes, friends'" (*Post-Intelligencer* 1899c).

William J. Lampton, another prominent Seattlite, then stood up and read his poem, which assumed the voice of the pole standing in Pioneer Square:

> *I am the only*
> *Civilized totem pole*
> *On earth,*
> *And civilization fits me well*
> *I am the city's pride,*
> *And in the whole wide world*
> *No city has*
> *An ornament like me.*
> . . . .
> *Seattle is Seattle still*
> *And I'm her totem pole.*
> *For centuries I hid my light*
> *Beneath a bushel, now*
> *It gleams and glistens*
> . . . .
> *A monument in multichrome,*
> . . . .
> *Better fifty days of Seattle*
> *Than a cycle of Siwash*
> . . . .
> *So here's farewell to all my past*
> *And welcome to the things that are,*
> *With you henceforth my die is cast,*
> *I've hitched my wagon to a star.*
> *And by the Sacred Frog that hops,*
> *And by the Bird that flies,*
> *And by the Whale and by the Bear,*
> *I'll sunder all my ties*
> *That bound me to the ancient creed*
> *That holds my people flat,*
> *And I will be a Totem Pole*
> *That knows where it is at. (Post-Intelligencer 1899c)*

Lampton's poetic logic decreed that all other totem poles were barbaric, decaying in abandoned villages, forgotten by their makers; this one, affiliated with a great city, had been "civilized" and anthropomorphized. Transformed into an accessory to the booming metropolis of Seattle, city of progress and modernity, the pole delighted in the prospect of appreciative masses of people. The pole burst with pride at having severed its connections to its superstitious Indian past; indeed, the totem pole was no longer Native.

As the pole was being prepared for erection, some Seattlites expressed concern about the unethical nature of its acquisition. In his speech, Thompson noted that some "fragile folk of over delicate sensibilities" had worried that the pole was stolen, and that sacred burying grounds had been desecrated (*Post-Intelligencer* 1899b). Thompson reassured the audience that the pole's village had indeed been deserted, that no one owned the pole, and that the excursionists' actions saved it from certain destruction. He claimed that they had protected the pole from being destroyed, either by missionaries who encouraged Native peoples to burn their poles or by the forest fires that constantly threatened abandoned villages such as Tongass. And, comparing his colleagues' activities to recent well-publicized British archeological discoveries at Nineveh and the transportation of Assyrian carvings to London, Thompson argued that "no one has ever questioned the propriety or value of this precious salvage" (*Post-Intelligencer* 1899b). The "White savior" trope continued to be the justification for plunder of archeological and ethnographic material worldwide, and would be applied throughout the twentieth century in cases of other deteriorating and "abandoned" totem poles.

According to the official story, the pole had been removed honestly and with noble intentions. Yet, apparently, that was not the attitude of some of the trip's excursionists. Thompson himself revealed a different point of view than that expressed at the unveiling in his poem "The Voyage," composed and read on board during the steamer's return trip. The poem's narrator states, "Let another tell the story/ Of our lovely voyage homeward,/ . . . Of the forays to deserted/ Cities of the ancient people, / Of the ravening of their graveyards,/ Bearing off the stolen totems!" (*Post-Intelligencer* 1899c).

8.5. Golden Potlatch Parade, Seattle, 1912. University of Washington Libraries SEA 313.

The raising of the Tongass pole in Pioneer Square was but one initiatory moment in Seattle's long association with totem poles. Several years after the 1909 Alaska-Yukon-Pacific-Exposition, Seattle held its first civic "potlatch" as a means of advertising the city's natural and cultural resources—what the press materials referred to as the "Seattle Spirit."[1] In addition to appropriating Native ceremonial terms and concepts, ordinary citizens were encouraged to further their symbolic association with regional Natives by donning indigenous costumes and referring to their civic leaders as "tyees" (chiefs) or shamans. For the 1912 Golden Potlatch, hundreds of plaster totems festooned city streets, and the event logo, the "Potlatch Bug," was a chubby cartoon totem pole. The event even featured a parade in which walkers wore huge totem pole costumes, creating in effect a transient forest of poles circulating through the streets of Seattle (fig. 8.5; Boswell and McConaghy 1996).

DIFFERENT MYTHS FOR DIFFERENT AUDIENCES

When David E. Kininnook of the Gaanax.adi Clan, who had lived at Tongass before moving to Ketchikan, discovered his family's pole had been removed from Alaska by Seattle businessmen, he reported its loss to Alaska governor John Brady, then demanded and eventually received recompense. In 1904, University of Washington anthropologist Edmond Meany published Kininnook's explanation of the pole's imagery (from top to bottom): Raven, Human, Frog (who married the man), Mink (who married Raven), Killer Whale (whom Raven then married after Mink), and the father of Raven. The specific episode in the Raven cycle alluded to on this pole is Raven's stealing of the sun and moon (Higginson 1908, 79–80). In 1905, anthropologist John Swanton received from Boas's Native collaborator, George Hunt, a longer version corresponding closely with Kininnook's account, which he published in the *Journal of American Folklore.* Hunt's Tlingit mother, Anisalaga (Mary Ebbetts Hunt), belonged to the Gaanax.adi Raven Clan, which is why Hunt happened to have information on this pole. It had been raised at Tongass in 1870 as a memorial for Anisalaga's mother. Swanton's article illustrates not only the Seattle pole, but also another from Fort Rupert, which—although carved in the volumetric and vividly painted style of the Kwakwa̲ka̲'wakw—clearly depicts the same crests (fig. 8.6). Hunt (who identifies himself as "Geo. Hunt, History Collector") is quoted in the article as stating, "This is the totem pole at Fort Rupert, imitation of that taken from Alaska and now in Seattle, put up by its true owner, Mrs. Robert Hunt, who put it over her dead mother as a tombstone" (Swanton 1905, 110).

8.6. Charlie James (Kwakwa̲ka̲'wakw), Fort Rupert variation of Seattle Pole, 1914. Photograph by Edward S. Curtis. University of Washington Libraries. Special Collections, NA437.

Anisalaga's grandson, David Hunt, had commissioned sculptor Charlie James to erect the pole in memory of his grandmother. The Fort Rupert variation of the Seattle pole is thus a polynational or truly intercultural pole—a Kwakwa̱ka̱'wakw copy of an Alaskan pole made for the mother of a Tlingit immigrant to British Columbia and described by her half-Tlingit, half-English son (himself raised as a Kwakwa̱ka̱'wakw). Yet few of these biographical details traveled with the Alaskan pole itself, its initial Seattle owners preferring to imagine its romantic origins. Once it was discovered that a Tlingit had a well-founded claim of ownership, according to one later apologist for the pilfering businessmen, "It was honorably purchased for presentation to the city. . . . Any stories of theft or desecration are barnacles of myth and fable which have incrusted themselves around these simple facts to the obscuration of truth" (Llwyd 1909, 5).

The Seattle pole stood in Pioneer Square until 1938, when arson and rot rendered it beyond repair. After unsuccessfully seeking a local carver to replicate this symbol of Seattle, city officials accepted the United States Forest Service's offer to replicate it in Alaska as part of the Civilian Conservation Corps' efforts. They shipped it to Ketchikan, where a team led by carver Charles Brown copied the pole, which was then returned to Seattle (Garfield 1996, n.p.). About thirty years later, Tsimshian artist Jack Hudson from Metlakatla, Alaska, restored and repainted this Depression-era pole. Today, the Seattle totem pole still stands in Pioneer Square and claims status as a National Historic Landmark. The official Web site of the National Park Service, which oversees the landmarks at Pioneer Square, offers a history that confirms the theft of the pole yet suggests that, once the "mistake" had been realized, the city reimbursed the original owners properly:

> The Totem Pole first appeared in 1899, after members of the Chamber of Commerce, vacationing in Alaska, stole it from Tlingit Indians. The men gave the object to the city as a gift, but the tribe justly sued for its return and $20,000 in damages. The courts found the men guilty of theft, but fined them only $500 and allowed the city to retain ownership. In 1938, the pieces that remained after vandals set the Totem Pole on fire were sent back to Alaska, where Tlingit craftsmen graciously carved a reproduction. The new pole was soon dedicated, with tribal blessings, at a Potlatch celebration and has since remained unharmed on Pioneer Square. It now stands as symbol of the complicated relationship between American Indians and European Americans. (National Park Service, n.d.)

The verification that the pole was stolen, the unwillingness of the courts to provide fair settlement for the clan treasure, and the acknowledgment of the "complicated relationship" that exists between Native and non-Native people all reflect a contemporary attitude very different from that expressed at the turn of the twentieth century. Now the pole not only signifies Seattle but also brings attention to the problematic colonial past. The comment about the totem pole representing the complexity of the colonial encounter is perhaps one of the single most valid statements ever publicly made about these monuments. The Seattle totem pole has traveled quite a distance, from Tongass to Puget Sound (and back and forth again) and now to cyberspace, its meanings and mythologies evolving accordingly.

POLES AS CANADIAN ICONS

While Seattle was trying to identify itself within an expanding American economic context, the United States' neighbor to the north was engaged in a contest with much higher stakes. In the early decades of the twentieth century, Canada was struggling to establish a national identity separate from Great Britain and France, countries to which it was still in some ways colonially beholden. There was considerable support at that time for federal endeavors to help articulate this identity, and the production of "culture" (taken colloquially as "fine and performing arts") was seen as a primary mode of doing so. In the 1920s, the loosely knit association of innovative artists known as the Group of Seven sought to define a new Canadian identity and to develop a uniquely Canadian art style by synthesiz-

8.7. A. Y. Jackson, "Skeena Crossing, B.C. (Gitsegukla)," 1926. Oil on canvas. 20.9" x 26." McMichael Canadian Art Collection, 1968.8.27.

ing art nouveau and Scandinavian postimpressionism with images of Canada's vast landscapes and cultural treasures.[2] Many of these artists' works expressed a unity with nature and a mystical oneness with "place," which they believed to be especially characteristic of their country. The catalogue of the Group of Seven's 1926 exhibition contained a declaration by the artists: "The Group of Seven realize that subject is not necessarily an ingredient in a work of art. Nevertheless it also feels that the Canadian environment is the most potent stimulus to Canadian creative genius" (quoted in Hill 1995, 32). The National Gallery of Canada, directed by Eric Brown, supported the Group of Seven and actively encouraged awareness of and respect for Canada's art. Although best known for their compelling landscapes and scenes of Canadian life, some members of the Group, as well as some artists affiliated with them, chose totem poles as subjects for their work and as symbols of their country (fig. 8.7).

Marius Barbeau, whom we met previously in the context of controversial totem pole origin theories and the Skeena River pole restoration project, played a significant role in bringing Northwest Coast art into the awareness of these primarily eastern artists. He shared with the Group of Seven the quest for a unique national cultural identity and believed that totem poles could play a role in defining Canada. Over the course of several years, Barbeau brought artists such as Edwin Holgate, Langdon Kihn, and A. Y. Jackson from eastern Canada to the West Coast, where they painted landscapes and, significantly, totem poles. Barbeau repeatedly supported the visual if not material appropriation of Native sources for emerging national art styles: "It had become clear to all that the Skeena and West Coast were a new country for Canadian art, so far unknown, unrevealed, and full of promise. . . . Their [artists'] search for truth and beauty had not been idle. They carried off with them new riches that had become their own [including] profiles of carved house posts and poles that exult in style and barbaric splendor" (Barbeau 1929b, 30). By embedding totem poles in a larger language of landscape, the Group of Seven and Emily Carr (who was increasingly under the group's influence by the 1920s) helped naturalize and nationalize (and, one might add, neutralize) Native imagery.

These eastern artists embraced the nostalgic evaluation of disappearing cultures. Upon returning from the Skeena River, Edwin Holgate reported, "I felt we were witnessing the rapid decline of a splendid race of creative and well-organized people. There persisted a brooding gloom which I found it impossible to dispel" (Thom 1989, n.p.). Langdon Kihn, in an article on his experience with the Gitk'san that was illustrated with his portraits, accepted the stereotypical "vanishing races" rhetoric. Yet his attitudes toward the Gitk'san he met were complicated; he called them "suspicious, shrewd and sometimes sudden . . . emotional and highly keyed . . . keenly intelligent" (Kihn 1926, 173). Kihn's conclusion to his article is an excellent example of imperialist nostalgia:

> This wonderful world, with its touch of the supernatural, is rapidly disappearing. This fine spirit, this exotic colorful life in most localities of the great Northwest has gone—passed out . . . the new generation will not carry on. They titter and poke fun at the old men . . . when the summer breaks they hire them to the large fish canneries on the coast to "make um some money all the same White man." And with this comes all the sordid life of aimless souls. When the old women and men die, there shall be little left. We shall go to the archaic, empty halls of our museums and gaze with wonder at what they knew and did. But what we see will be lifeless—dead. It will lack the spirit that gives it life. They will have entered the realm of specimens (Kihn 1926, 176).

Once the connection between poles and Native culture was thought severed, "the totem pole" became available for appropriation—literally, in the case of thefts; commercially, in the case of tourism; and aesthetically, in the case of romantic artists. Totem poles had come to be considered monuments to a past, almost-extinct culture that benevolent whites had to record before it was gone. Thus indigenous culture was indelibly marked as moribund and was transformed into Canadian heritage.

Attempts to foster a unique Canadian artistic identity encompassed, in addition to the fine-arts realm of painting, the translation of Northwest Coast images into industrial designs, interior decorations, and applied art, especially in the system of hotels that served travelers experiencing Canada's vast wilderness via the national railways.[3] In 1929, during the Skeena River restoration project sponsored by the Canadian National Railroad, Holgate designed the Jasper "Totem Pole" Tea Room in Ottawa's CNR-owned Chateau Laurier Hotel. He based the room's decor on his Skeena experience and included generalized totemic columns (loosely Tsimshian in style), totems as lamp bases, Chilkat designs, and masks. Canadian writer Merrill Dennison deemed this room "the most Canadian room in Canada," with the columns "treated as totem poles rich in pagan symbolism and primitive colorings" (quoted in Dawn 1981, 44). Barbeau called the room "a decided departure from the beaten path, a step forward in Canadian art and culture that will lead us a long way. It is an eloquent symbol, the symbol of our growing aspirations toward a nationhood and a culture that will be our own, our contribution to the world at large" (1929a, 33). In another CNR hotel, at the western rail terminus, British Columbian painter Jock Macdonald produced a mural in the main dining room of the Hotel Vancouver in 1939 that depicted generalized poles amidst a cubist-inspired landscape. The silence on the part of the white artists about the Native artists who originated the designs they borrowed suggests the general acceptance that Northwest Coast cultures were dead, with only their artistic creations remaining, ripe for the taking. Moreover, those creations could no longer be considered solely Native, as they had been absorbed into the visual fabric of Canada.

AFFINITIES OF THE TRIBAL AND THE MODERN (THE 1927 VERSION)

To highlight the "Canadianness" of Northwest Coast art as well as the home-grown indigeneity of Canadian art, it was necessary to exhibit in both eastern Canadian population and political centers. In 1927, Marius Barbeau, along with Eric Brown, organized an ambitious show at the National Gallery of Canada, Canadian West Coast Art, Native and Modern, which presented Northwest Coast Native artwork along with paintings of the coastal region by Langdon Kihn, A. Y. Jackson, Edwin Holgate, Paul Kane, Walter Phillips, Annie Savage, Peggy Nicol, Florence Wyle, and, to her enormous satisfaction, Emily Carr. Indeed, the professional turning point for Carr had occurred when Barbeau told Brown about her "Indian pictures" and sought her participation in the exhibit. In addition to showing her paintings and ceramics in the exhibit, Carr designed the cover of the catalogue, signing it Klee Wyck ("Laughing One"), the name Salish friends had given her. Her self-identification with a specific Native moniker is an apt metonym for the national uses to which this exhibit put First Nations motifs.

This exhibit was a centerpiece of emerging national consciousness grounded in "uniquely Canadian" Indian motifs. It is noteworthy that the show's venue was an art museum, for at that time most Native works appeared in natural history or anthropology museums. The catalogue's preface, by Brown, asserted the importance of British Columbian Native artwork: "[It is] one of the most valuable of Canada's artistic productions . . . an invaluable mine of decorative design which is available to the student for a host of different purposes and possessing for the Canadian artist in particular the unique quality of being entirely national in its origin and character" (Hill 1995, 192). In the same catalogue, Barbeau wrote, "A commendable feature of this aboriginal art for us is that it is truly Canadian in its inspiration. It has sprung up wholly from the soil and the sea within our national boundaries" (Nemiroff 1992, 23). In a public lecture associated with this exhibit, Barbeau again stressed the patrimonial availability of Northwest Coast art:

> It has already been said by one critic abroad that the only form of art that can be called Canadian is that of the West Coast tribes . . . the Awakening is already with us. Our painting, as an original contribution to the history of art, is already gaining recognition abroad. Art to many Canadians is no longer a luxury, but a means of self-expression, a step toward a culture that will some day be distinctly our own. The manifestations of Canadian art, both ancient and modern, are of vital significance. They speak of the country that is ours (Hill 1995, 192).

Brown and Barbeau collaborated to promote Canadian nationalism, with Barbeau illuminating Native cultures and Brown outlining an artistic heritage for Canada through the integration of modernism. As Lauren Harris, who would become the most famous of the Group of Seven painters, said, "We are about the business of becoming a nation and must create our own background" (quoted in A. K. Morrison 1991, 4). This process was served well by Native culture, the "ancient" expression of a uniquely Canadian art. Although clearly regarded with high esteem by those who helped forge this national identity, Northwest Coast art was not, for these artists, a vibrant aboriginal tradition as much as the ancestral underpinnings of a new tradition. The living, forward-looking art inspired by such Canadian visual art would be carried forth not by inheritors of those indigenous traditions but instead by artists who were not of Native origin. Northwest Coast art was explicitly claimed both as the material heritage of Canada and as the source of visual inspiration for the nation's defining artists.[4] The original

TOTEM POLES AS LOGOS

Intracorp brochure, University of Alaska.

Isadora's Restaurant (defunct), Vancouver, British Columbia.

Ketchi Candies, Ketchikan, Alaska.

Totem Ocean Trailer Express, Seattle, Washington.

Totem Printing, Ltd.

Leckie's Tree Planter Boots, Vancouver, British Columbia.

meanings of totem poles were replaced by meanings based on presumed antiquity, uniqueness of place, and desires for a national patrimony.

CREATION OF THE TOTEMLAND POLE

Since the late nineteenth century, totem poles had been associated with the Alaskan Inside Passage. As we have seen, during the first half of the twentieth century, poles had expanded their geographic significance and were embraced by the city of Seattle and the nation of Canada. Soon Vancouver relocated poles to celebrate their history, building on the display set up in Stanley Park in the late 1920s. During that city's 1936 Golden Jubilee, an Indian Village was set up in Stanley Park, complete with local Coast Salish carvers and Salish and Kwakwa̲ka̲'wakw poles. At the 1946 Vancouver Diamond Jubilee, a group of Kwakwa̲ka̲'wakw presented Viscount Alexander, the governor general of Canada, with an honorary name as well as a totem pole carved by Mungo Martin, who was soon to become a famous culture broker. That same year, the Canadian Citizenship Act was passed, which for the first time differentiated Canadian from British subjects. Three years later, in 1949, the Canadian government initiated the Massey Commission, which would investigate the state of culture in Canada and make specific recommendations on how best to encourage the emergence of a unique national culture through financial support to individuals and institutions across the country (Litt 1992). Aboriginal art—visual and performance-based—would loom increasingly large in the federalist project (see appendix F for a list of poles at British Columbian and Canadian celebrations).

In 1950, promoters of tourism to British Columbia decided to use totem poles as the major symbol of the province, building on the precedent of the urban totem displays in Vancouver and Victoria as well as in the Skeena River restorations. A group of citizens, along with Vancouver mayor Charles Thompson, formed an association and formally adopted the name "Totemland" to trademark British Columbia. In their efforts to promote tourism and bring attention to these emblems of the region, the group encouraged the use of totem poles on license plates, stamps, and, especially, in advertisements. So receptive was the community that a local newspaper wrote optimistically, "The BC totem may become as famous as the Idaho potato" (quoted in K. Phillips 2000, 1). The goals of this group were as follows:

> To collect in writing and disseminate the legendary history, customs and philosophy of our Native Indians; also to encourage and preserve their ancient weaving, painting and sculptural arts; to promote the use of a Thunderbird Totem and the slogan Totemland as the symbol of the colour and romantic interest of the British Columbia Indian together with their singular totemology and unique wood-carving art; to advise, encourage and support the British Columbia Indians in overcoming obstacles that may stand in the way of their attainment to the enjoyment of full citizenship (quoted in K. Phillips 2000, 25).

Note that this statement recognizes the historical value if not the contemporary vitality of Native culture and makes optimistic reference to the improving condition of British Columbia First Nations, thus synthesizing sheer economic exploitation and cultural appropriation with at least a stated interest in Native welfare.

The Totemland Society asked a well-known Kwakwa̲ka̲'wakw artist, Ellen Neel, to design the model pole that would become its official emblem. Neel was the granddaughter and student of Kwakwa̲ka̲'wakw artist Charlie James, and had been selling model poles to visitors in Alert Bay since she was a teenager. In 1943, she moved from Alert Bay to Vancouver, and in 1946 began carving and selling model poles to help support her family after her husband had a stroke. With the assistance of her six children, Neel carved large quantities of small, modestly priced models for department stores and souvenir shops. In 1948, the Vancouver Board of Parks commissioners granted Neel permission to set up a carving studio and sales shop in an abandoned military building in Stanley Park. Although Neel did make full-size carvings—including a sixteen-foot pole that she and her husband donated

8.8. Ellen Neel (Kwakwa̱ka̱'wakw), *Totemland Pole*, 1950. Cedar. 24". Photograph by Phil Nuytten.

to the University of British Columbia (see chapter 9) and a large pole for the Pacific National Exhibition (an annual Vancouver-area fair)—she worked principally on models. When business was good, Neel and her family filled an order from the Hudson's Bay Company for 5,000 poles (Nuytten 1982, 57).

Neel, intrigued by the commission to design the Totemland pole, created a unique two-foot model pole that depicts a Thunderbird atop an egg-shaped globe prominently depicting western British Columbia and Vancouver Island, with a human figure kneeling underneath (fig. 8.8). In this carving, Neel integrated some Northwest Coast traditions with some decidedly non-Native concepts. Maps were not part of the artistic vocabulary of Northwest Coast artists, but Neel here incorporated a distinctly Western geographical representation into the carving. Furthermore, while full-size totem poles are not strictly narrative, Neel responded to the non-Native's desire to know the "story" of any pole. She therefore explained the Totemland pole as a narrative of Thunderbird giving British Columbia to the first man, much as in her own 'Na̱mgis traditions, the great bird helped raise the house beams of the first people of the band. Neel herself reproduced this vividly painted, highly original pole a number of times as official gifts, while her popular Totemland image appeared on society letterhead, scarves, T-shirts, ties, and a Royal Albert china dinner service.

Non-Native Vancouverites had high regard for Ellen Neel. Newspapers identified her as "one of Canada's outstanding authorities in the art of totem carving," praising her cultural authenticity, connection to tradition, and artistic achievements. But, as Kimberly Phillips (2000, 57 ff.) points out, this was a time when some B.C. Native people were becoming more vociferous with their political demands, especially in terms of land claims. Because Neel expressed no political agenda and rarely appeared in Kwakwa̱ka̱'wakw regalia, she presented no risk of turning her projects into a cause for Native rights. Indeed, Neel appeared to be an unthreatening, accessible, and fully modern homemaker and mother, in addition to being a totem pole carver.

The Totemland pole could be judged as a "degradation" of a treasured aboriginal artistic tradition, now appropriated by the colonizers, but that reading would be misguided. Neel knew exactly what she was doing, and took delight in her creation for white businessmen. As her friend Phil Nuytten (1982, 47) commented, Neel, who never took herself too seriously anyway, "laughed a lot about the Totemland Poles." According to Nuytten (personal communication, 2003), Neel's artist uncle, Mungo Martin, half-seriously, half-jestingly referred to it as a "white man's pole," but then agreed with his niece that "a white person wouldn't know the difference [between a pole based on tradition and one made for non-Natives] anyway," over which they shared a good laugh. Moreover, despite appearances, Neel was not completely apolitical. She presumably recognized the underlying fatuousness of the commission. But a serious message underlies the work as well, for the globe on the Totemland Society's pole depicts *only* Vancouver Island and the nearby mainland—not even the entire totem pole region of British Columbia. In the middle—at the center of the world—is Kwakwaka'wakw territory, Neel's own tribal land (K. Phillips 2000, 69–70). Nuytten (2003) also points out that the human underneath the globe has an uncanny resemblance to the European concept of Atlas with the world on his shoulders. Neel not only appropriated the idea of a map from Western culture but also took an image from Western mythology, subordinating both to her own cultural values. Moreover, she centered her people in historical and contemporary narratives of provincial development. Every official who proudly displayed this pole, every T-shirt emblazoned with its image, every piece of Totemland china declared to a largely white audience that may very well not have understood, the fundamental centrality of the Kwakwaka'wakw, their traditional ownership of the land, and their management of Eurocanadian symbols and sensibilities.

1958 BRITISH COLUMBIA CENTENNIAL: PROMOTING AND CONFLATING NATURAL AND CULTURAL RESOURCES

British Columbia, proud of its settler history, made good use of the totem pole during three centennials it had within a thirteen-year period. In 1958, the province celebrated the centennial of the mainland's becoming a crown colony, achieving equal status to Vancouver Island (which had been a crown colony since 1849). During this highly feted anniversary, the totem pole became a central element of the province's self-image. By the late 1950s, British Columbia had become a prosperous province, with an economy among the strongest in the nation. The centennial lionized the booming forestry and mining industries for producing prosperity and carving a modern nation out of the wilderness (Baird 1995, 9).

The celebration's official publication, *B.C. Centenary*, published in 1958, is replete with images of poles embellishing even those stories unrelated to Northwest Coast Native culture. One particularly striking totem pole image appears in an advertisement in the centennial edition of *Maclean's Magazine*—the whole issue is rife with totem pole imagery—where "Twentieth century totems . . . symbols of British Columbia's century of progress" honor the Bank of Montreal, B.C.'s first permanent bank, which opened in 1887 (fig. 8.9). On a hill stand two children and their dog, staring up at a monument that declares on its base with bold carving, "MY BANK to 2 million Canadians, B of M." Rising from this plinth are two hard-hatted men, a miner carrying a drill and a logger with a chain saw. Above the logger's head leaps a salmon, while above that an

8.9. Advertisement for Bank of Montreal, *Maclean's* centennial edition, May 10, 1958, p. 9.

airplane with wings quotes the outstretched wings of the Thunderbird. References to success and progress conflate natural and cultural resources on the familiar nineteenth-century totem pole, transforming it into a monument of the generative future; although this may or may not have been intentional, the drill is phallic, while the saw looks priapic. Here totem poles (as cultural resources) are being identified with industry and the extraction of natural resources.

British Columbia Native people themselves were almost entirely ignored during the 1958 centennial celebrations—with the exception of Kwakwa̲ka̲'wakw artist Mungo Martin. The province commissioned Martin to carve two identical hundred-foot poles, one for Queen Elizabeth and the other for Vancouver, where it still stands in Hadden Park near Kitsilano on the grounds of the Vancouver Maritime Museum. On March 23, 1957, at the ceremonial inauguration of his regal carving project, Martin guided the lieutenant-governor of Canada, Frank Ross, to make one of the "first cuts" on the log in the British Columbia Provincial Museum carving shed at Thunderbird Park in Victoria. Martin made a speech, giving the Queen his greetings, while Helen Hunt translated his Kwak'wala into English:

8.10. Mungo Martin (Kwakwa̲ka̲'wakw) and the Queen Mother, Windsor Park, UK, 1957. Courtesy of Royal British Columbia Museum, British Columbia Archives, I 51777.

> We are honoured that [the Queen] would accept this totem pole. Totem poles are things that we make—no one else in the world makes them. We are happy that Her Majesty will accept this pole and will put it up in one of her parts of England. Your Honour, I have made many totem poles, I have carved totem poles for over fifty years, but this will be a very special one. I have never made one for such a high personage before. I am honoured that I was chosen to carve this pole and that the work of my hands will stand in London for many years to come. This will be a real totem pole. I designed it to show the family stories of my tribe, the Kwakiutl. This is the way we show our history. This pole will show the crests of ten tribes (Nuytten 1982, 104).

The seventy-eight-year-old Martin then traveled to England to attend the dedication ceremonies in Windsor Park and meet the Queen Mother (fig. 8.10). This trip served several purposes: for its patrons, it signified that British Columbia was a province loyal to the British royalty, and for Martin, it demonstrated the importance of Kwakwa̲ka̲'wakw history and sovereignty, much as Ellen Neel's Totemland pole had done.

Totem poles circulated iconographically during the celebrations. The commemorative centennial dollar coin proudly displayed a relief of a Skidegate carving (fig. 8.11)—a nice encapsulation of the emerging currency enjoyed by Northwest Coast art in the national and provincial imaginations. A series of postcards, specially created for B.C.'s centennial year by G. M. Abrams-Lytton, carried the greeting "Kla-how-ya (hello) from Totem Pole Land 1858—B.C.'s Centennial Year—1958." Despite the attempt to represent B.C.'s aboriginal population, these cards blur tribal distinctions and convey the trope of the vanishing Indian (fig. 8.12). Each card prominently features a Haida-esque village serving as a background for one of a number

8.11. British Columbia centennial coin, 1958. Courtesy Bill Holm.

8.12. British Columbia centennial postcard, 1958. Photograph by Aldona Jonaitis.

of different totem poles from the Kwakwa̲ka̲'wakw, Nisga'a, Haida, Nuxalk, and Tlingit (Baird 1995, 5). Text on the reverse side identifies each pole and its original location and imagery, and explains that "Kla-how-ya" means "hello" in the Chinook trade jargon widely spoken on the Northwest Coast in the nineteenth century.

The card makers wanted the same words of greeting for all the cards, and thus resorted to a language that, having originated in Oregon in the early years of the fur trade, was not even Canadian. They also chose to depart from ethnographic accuracy and place all poles in front of the same generic Haida village—which nonetheless has two Kwakwa̲ka̲'wakw-style Thunderbird poles interspersed among the Haida ones. The Nisga'a card contains this text: "The swift rush of civilization has destroyed what this pole stood for. It is, however, preserved at the University of British Columbia." By means of image and text, this First Nations culture is simultaneously rendered extinct, demolished by progress, transformed into the amorphous identity of the British Columbia Native, and preserved for posterity in a museum. Only the very public activities of master carver Mungo Martin suggested that aboriginal culture in the province was not entirely dead.

1966–67 BRITISH COLUMBIA AND CANADIAN CENTENNIALS

Totem poles and their living carvers played even greater roles in the 1966–67 celebration of the hundredth anniversary of Vancouver Island's joining with the mainland as a single colony (1866) and the subsequent centenary of Canadian federation (1867). At these centennials, Northwest Coast art took center stage at civic, provincial, national, and even international levels, and poles were used iconically throughout. Canada was selected to host Expo '67, in Montreal, where Wilson Duff coordinated the carving of totem poles in the Indian Pavilion.[5] At the same time, a major exhibition of Northwest Coast art, Arts of the Raven: Masterworks of the Northwest Coast Indian, opened at the Vancouver Art Gallery to celebrate the past and present the artistic heritage of British Columbia coastal Native people. Curated by Bill Holm, Wilson Duff, and Bill Reid, this impressive exhibit was designed to present Northwest Coast carvings as fine art rather than ethnology. One of the centennial-related newspapers was even called *The Totem*.

In January 1966, centennial festivities got off to a "rousing start" as 1.5 million onlookers and 150 million television viewers in North America and Europe watched the Pasadena Tournament of Roses Parade in which B.C.'s float won the International Trophy (*The Totem Pole* 1966, 2). Roses on this large float spelled out "A Royal Welcome Centennial 1966" and "Beautiful British Columbia Canada." Emerging from a (literal) bed of roses were two classic Thunderbird-style totem poles (fig. 8.13). While these flower-festooned symbols were accompanied by other provincial images, they stood as the *only* component of the float fully unique to British Columbia.[6]

8.13. British Columbia float, Pasadena Tournament of Roses Parade, 1966. Courtesy of Pasadena Tournament of Roses Archive.

By this time it was becoming clear that Native art was *not* "disappearing" but instead emerging more fully into public awareness. Non-Natives started to recognize both the continuity of traditions and new flourishings of creativity—especially in terms of totem poles, increasingly visible in nationwide popular culture. And, since totem poles had for so long been attractive to tourists, the provincial government decided to take advantage of this expanding productivity and awareness of Native art. To coincide with the centennials, the British Columbia Indian Advisory Act, under the management of director R. J. McInnes, initiated a large-scale project to place new poles along several provincial automobile and ferry routes: from the border crossing at Blaine, Washington, to the Horseshoe Bay ferry terminal in Vancouver (fig. 8.14); from Victoria to Port Hardy (at the southern and northern ends of Vancouver Island); and at Port Simpson and Prince Rupert on the northern mainland. At first this assemblage of poles was to be called the "Route of the Haidas," to commemorate those who in the nineteenth century had traveled seasonally to Victoria to trade. Wilson Duff (1965) considered this most unwise, arguing that the route traversed territory owned not by the Haida but by their regular enemies and victims, the Kwakwa̱ka̱'wakw and Coast Salish, who would doubtless object to using that name. The general manager of B.C. Ferries, M. F. Aldous, recommended the name "Route of the Totems," suspecting that this would enhance its advertising potential (Duff 1965). That not all British Columbians approved of the initiative is evident in a confidential note from the assistant manager of BC Ferries, R. B. Worley, who—partially at the request of the premier, "who [did] not wish to have the route referred to in such a manner"—recommended "Direct route to northern British Columbia and Alaska," (Duff 1965). "Totems" prevailed, and artists were invited to carve poles 12 feet high by 3.5 feet wide, all of which were to depict a grizzly bear at the base. Each artist would determine his pole's other images and was to interpret the imagery for an explanatory plaque. Most logs for the project were donated by MacMillan Bloedel lumber company. Anthropologist Wilson Duff and Nuu-chah-nulth writer and artist George Clutesi evaluated the submissions, awarding $750 to the carvers of poles accepted for erection along the route and $250 to the carvers of rejected poles. With this procession of monuments up the coast, totem poles became firmly bonded to B.C. tourism. (See appendix F for a list of these poles and their carvers and locations).

FURTHER ROUTES OF THE TOTEMS

In 1971, to celebrate the entrance of British Columbia into confederation a century earlier, the province commissioned even more poles, to be given as presents to the other provinces.[7] Once again, McInnes oversaw the project, which gave every province a fifteen-foot-high pole. The B.C. Council of Forest Industries donated the logs. The committee charged with selecting poles included Kwakwa̱ka̱'wakws James Sewid, William Scow, and Simon Baker, as well as Clutesi and Duff. Carvers whose poles were accepted received $1,200, with Kwakwa̱ka̱'wakw artists James Dick, Henry Hunt, and Daniel Matilpi being singled out for special recognition prizes of $200, $300, and $500, respectively. All of the poles were first erected in front of the British Columbia Provincial Museum in Victoria before being sent east (*Victoria Times*, 1971). Prospective recipients were given "Hints for the New Totem-Pole Owner," provided by the Ethnology Division of the Provincial Museum, which described, among other vital details, optimal display arrangements: "Photographers will be unhappy if the sun is behind the pole or if some obstacle (such as a building or flowerbed) prevents them from stepping back far enough to include it all." With these additional poles, the entire country of Canada would become a "route of totems," with the totems pointing to British Columbia. (See appendix F).[8]

8.14. Tony Hunt (Kwakwa̱ka̱'wakw) Haida-style bear pole at Horseshoe Bay ferry terminal, Vancouver, 1966. Photograph by Aaron Glass, c. 2003.

While the province and nation were jumping on the totem bandwagon, some towns in the region thought to capitalize on what they considered their territorial prerogatives. In 1983, the town of Duncan—located on southeastern Vancouver Island firmly in Coast Salish lands, south of the "traditional" totem pole zone—declared itself the "City of Totem Poles." The community hired mostly less-well-established Kwakwa̱ka̱'wakw carvers as well as local Cowichan and Nuu-chah-nulth artists to line their main street along the Island Highway (the only route to the North Island) with poles intended to draw tourist traffic (fig. 8.15). A Maori artist even carved a pole for Duncan, the sister city to his hometown in New Zealand. The poles in Duncan vary according to tribal styles and fidelity to nineteenth-century design principles, and include the world's thickest totem pole, carved with great effort by Richard Hunt (see sidebar, page 112). Although many coastal cities are known by their impressive stands of

8.15. Duncan, "City of Totems," 2007. Photograph by Aaron Glass.

totem poles, Duncan is the only one to have claimed legal title to the designation.[9]

Today, totem poles still mark a traveler's route through the Northwest Coast via airports. In one of these, poles signify a new message about place. The Vancouver International Airport displays several monumental carvings, including a pair of welcome figures by Musqueam artist Susan Point (see fig. 12.21) and another by Nuu-chah-nulth artist Joe David. The presence of Native-made art in the Vancouver International Airport emphatically asserts that the original inhabitants of the region claim the place. Certainly this act has precedents, and in fact reasserts the aboriginal function of poles as specific place and property markers. As we have seen, Ellen Neel used commercial commissions to make a subtle statement about Native ownership of the place her carvings symbolized. Her uncle, Mungo Martin, repeatedly carved personal, family, village, and "tribal" crests on his poles, which advertised Kwakwa̱ka̱'wakw identities around the world. By the 1966–67 centennial, the Native artists who played a role in the creation of the totem route carved poles more iconographically connected to their own heritage than those they had been making for tourist markets. The indigenous people of the Northwest Coast were beginning to reappropriate the totem poles placed in public, civic, regional, national, and international spheres.

As will be discussed further in chapter 12, the presence of Susan Point's welcome figures at the Vancouver International Airport represents a paradigmatic shift in the meaning of poles at travel destinations: they state with assurance and strength that the land they stand on is neither Canada nor Vancouver nor even generalized Native land but instead *Musqueam* territory. But to claim this political position, totem poles had to emerge from the archaic burial ground they were located in, had to be seen as meaningful as well as spectacular monuments; in short, totem poles had to reenter contemporary indigenous history. The activities of one individual, anthropologist Wilson Duff, helped lay the groundwork through which such a transformation could occur in the public imagination, and on which such a powerful statement could now be expressed. It is toward Duff's contribution to the history of totem poles that we now turn.

BEYOND RESTORATION

THE WORK OF WILSON DUFF

In a way it was a depressing scene. Here were the bleached bones of a proud way of life that was dead. . . . But it was also an awesome and stirring scene. There was strength and strange beauty in the boldly carved figures of grizzlies, beavers and whales staring from these poles. The art had been developed on this rugged and tempestuous coast, by a hardy and vigorous people attuned to its harsh rhythms, and like all great arts, it reflected the spirit of its time and its makers.

—WILSON DUFF AT THE VILLAGE OF NINSTINTS, 1957

Art styles, it would seem, have greater viability than the cultures that produce them. The old Indian cultures of the coast are dead, but the art styles continue on in new and modern contexts. The Kwakiutl style never did suffer a full eclipse. . . . The Haida style, kept barely alive for many decades by a handful of slate carvers, has recently been rediscovered and revived by Bill Reid, Bill Holm and others, and finds a promising future in the hands of young Robert Davidson. But now these are arts in a different sense. Though truly enough of Indian descent, they are now Canadian art, modern art, fine art.

—WILSON DUFF, *ARTS OF THE RAVEN* CATALOGUE, 1967

It was a long road from salvage-oriented restorations of poles as markers of non-Native places to the appreciation of poles as examples of Native fine art—even a living art. This transition involved a shift in non-Native attitudes and agendas, the emergence of Native political mobilizations, and the developments of commercial markets. The transition took a whole social network of artists, professionals, and institutions, both Native and non-Native. At the center of many of these projects was Wilson Duff. A complex, passionate man whose devotion to Native people was immeasurable, Duff's contributions to the preservation and promotion of totem poles on the Northwest Coast constitute an entire chapter in this history.

Early on, Wilson Duff combined his dedication to British Columbia Native people with solid scientific, ethnological, and ethnohistorical training. His academic credentials featured bachelor's and master's degrees in anthropology from the University of British Columbia (UBC) and the University of Washington, respectively. His teachers included Audrey Hawthorn, Harry Hawthorn and Erna Gunther, all long central to the emerging Northwest Coast art world. Duff went on to train students at both schools and to hold curatorial positions at both the Museum of Anthropology at the University of British Columbia (MOA) and the Royal British Columbia Museum (RBCM). In his later career, the poet-scholar departed from empiricism and embraced a more subjective approach, especially in terms of analyzing Northwest Coast art. His 1975 exhibit catalogue, *Images, Stone, B.C.*, wove together psychoanalytic and structuralist interpretations in an attempt to decipher the deep, underlying meaning of ancient stone carvings. In fact, Wilson Duff's own career trajectory mirrors—and actively helped constitute—the shifting of popular and scholarly attitudes toward totem poles and their indigenous creators.

WAS MUNGO MARTIN *REALLY* "THE LAST GREAT TOTEM CARVER"?[1]

After World War II, Canada's pursuit of a national identity accelerated when it embarked on an effort to represent itself as independent of the United Kingdom. To this end, in 1949, the government formed the Royal Commission on National Development in the Arts, Letters and Sciences, also known as the Massey Commission (after its chair), to study the health of the arts in Canada. As Marius Barbeau and the Group of Seven had recognized several decades earlier, an important component of this identity was to be the art of the uniquely Canadian First Nations. The commission assigned Harry Hawthorn, the newly appointed director of the UBC Museum of Anthropology, to prepare a report on "Canadian Indian arts and crafts" and suggest ways to improve the marketing of these items (Litt 1992). Hawthorn asked his wife, anthropologist Audrey Hawthorn, to research this topic. She reported that Eastern woodlands and Plains people still produced significant quantities of art, while "the artists and craftspeople of the Coast, in spite of their great tradition, were now producing very little and for a very unsatisfactory market. A few workers in silver jewelry, argillite, and still fewer in basketry were the only ones making anything other than souvenirs" (Hawthorn 1993, 7). It is worth noting that Hawthorn disregarded those very souvenirs that, as we pointed out earlier, played a significant role in perpetuating Northwest Cost artistic traditions.

Hawthorn seized the opportunity to make MOA a center for Northwest Coast art in general and totem poles specifically. The university already had a special connection to the totem pole, for since 1914 the totem pole had been the university's unofficial symbol and had lent its name to the title of its annual publication,

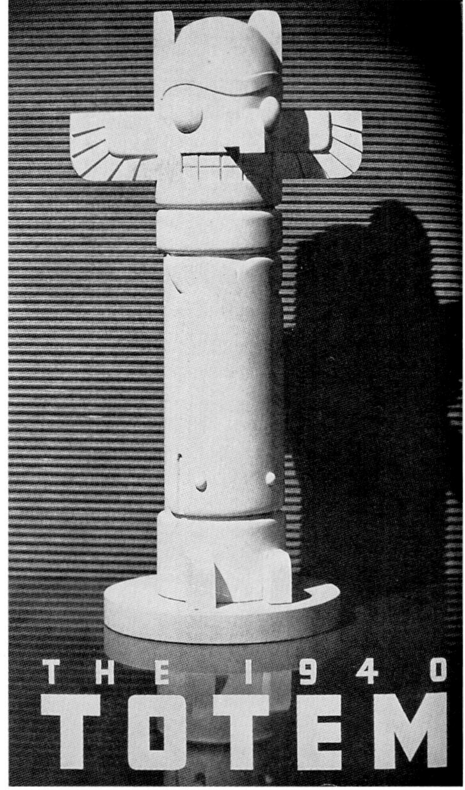

9.1. *The Totem*, University of British Columbia annual yearbook publication, 1940. Courtesy of University of British Columbia Library.

The Totem (fig. 9.1). The university also used the image of Totie—a cartoon totem pole mascot—in creative ways, such as in the *Totem*'s 1942 wartime issue depicting three Toties: a worker, a soldier, and a nurse (fig. 9.2).

In 1948, William Scow, a Kwakwa̱ka̱'wakw chief and political leader, retroactively bestowed on the university regents the rights to the Thunderbird image, thereby attempting to legitimize their longtime use of the mascot. At the same time, Ellen Neel carved a new Thunderbird totem pole for the UBC campus; entitled "Victory through Honour," the pole was funded by the student body and dedicated to the university's athletic teams. In 1949, the university funded Marius Barbeau's acquisition of Kwakwa̱ka̱'wakw poles, house posts, and an eleven-piece house frame. A Totem Pole Committee composed of several faculty members, the university president, and Harry Hawthorn decided to restore,

9.2. "Totie goes to war," *The Totem*, University of British Columbia annual publication, 1942. Courtesy of University of British Columbia Library.

repaint, and ultimately erect the poles and house frame on campus. Audrey Hawthorn writes, "We envisioned obtaining a section of forest [on campus] where at least four main styles of carving and architecture indigenous to the region could be shown—an outdoor museum" (1993, 9).

The museum needed a Native carver to restore these poles and hired Mungo Martin, who was later credited with the revival of quality Northwest Coast Native art. Martin was born around 1880 in Fort Rupert. His father's name, Yanukwalas, translates as "nobody leaves his house without a gift," indicating a record of lavish potlatches. To ensure that her child would become a great artist, his mother, Nagayki, is said to have brought Mungo to the carver Yakutglasomi, who made a paintbrush for him of porcupine bristles and four of Martin's eyelashes. After his father died, Martin's mother married Charlie James, with whom Martin apprenticed, ultimately developing into a major Kwakwaka'wakw artist.

Though frequently hired to carve or sing for underground potlatches, Martin had to fish to support his family: his first wife, his son David, and his daughter Lucy—and, after he was widowed, his second wife, Abaya Hunt, with her daughters Grace and Agnes and her son Tommy. Despite the potlatch prohibition, Martin was well-versed in his cultural traditions and ultimately earned the honorific title Nakap'ankim, which means "Ten Times a Chief." From 1949 to 1951, Martin was in residence at MOA, where he helped the museum assemble a large collection of Kwakwaka'wakw ceremonial objects, restored his own *Raven-of-the-Sea* pole from Alert Bay (among others), and carved two new poles with his family's crest figures. In 1951 the museum erected Mungo's poles, the internal frame of an old-style house, and three other poles at a three-acre site near Southwest Marine Drive that had been set aside as the location for a totem park (Hawthorn 1971, 21; fig. 9.3). During this period, Martin also starred in a few important films, including *Carving a Totem Pole* (Hawthorn and Hill-Tout 1951) and *Wooden Box*, both intended to salvage and record manufacturing techniques (see chapter 13).

From his curatorial seat at the British Columbia Provincial Museum (BCPM), Duff watched the activity in Vancouver with interest.[2] In keeping with the initiatives of the Massey Commission, the British Columbia minister of education, W. T. Straith, wanted to promote Northwest Coast art at the Provincial Museum, the other major provincial repository for Northwest Coast objects. In 1940, the BCPM had erected some of its totem poles outside the museum building, where two Northwest Coast style houses were also constructed, the larger of which blended Coast Salish, Kwakwaka'wakw, and Haida elements, and the smaller being an amalgamation of Kwakwaka'wakw and Nuu-chah-nulth components (Jacknis 2002, 146). This totemic assemblage, known as Thunderbird Park, was Victoria's main contribution to the growing number of such tourist-oriented sites in the province (fig. 9.4). In

9.3. Mungo Martin at University of British Columbia totem park, 1951. Museum of Anthropology, 2005.001.645.

1951, Duff laid out a plan for preserving the museum's deteriorating monuments and suggested that the BCPM follow MOA's example and hire Martin to carve in the park. The following year, Martin started working in Thunderbird Park in a program that, in addition to replicating fine old carvings, was intended by the museum to accomplish two secondary goals: to preserve the art of totem-carving and to serve as a unique tourist and educational attraction (see Hawker 2003). Once again, the museum was presenting itself as the savior of a disappearing culture.

Martin could not do all the restoration and replication work by himself, and so brought his son David to Victoria to serve as his assistant until 1959, when David died in a fishing accident. Martin also worked with and trained his adopted daughter's husband, Henry Hunt, and Hunt's son, Tony Hunt. Bill Reid, a silversmith of Haida ancestry who was to become one of the most highly regarded Northwest Coast artists, worked alongside Martin in 1957 on Reid's first pole, a monument that now stands at the Douglas border crossing near Blaine, Washington (fig. 9.5). Over the ten years that Martin was chief carver at the BCPM, his team replicated twelve old poles—three Kwakwa̲ka̲'wakw, three Tsimshian, two Nuxalk, and four Haida. As Steve

Brown (personal communication, 2003) points out, "Each [of these] maintains the subtle stylistic properties of the original poles as well as has been done anywhere." During his tenure, Martin also carved two original Kwakwa̱ka̱'wakw poles for the BCPM, as well as numerous poles for civic promotions, provincial markers, and federal gifts to foreign dignitaries and nations. Thunderbird Park became the locale for replicated and new poles, while the originals ended up within the museum building. By the late 1950s, Martin was regularly—and somewhat paradoxically—singled out as both the last of the totem carvers and the initiator of a wave of revival in Northwest Coast art (Glass 2006a).

We have seen throughout this book how non-Native attitudes and perceptions have molded the meanings of totem poles. Many non-Natives involved in even the earliest restoration projects adhered to the trope that coupled the vanishing Native with the anthropologist-as-hero. The durability of this trope becomes evident in a pamphlet explaining the carvings at Thunderbird Park. Duff writes that it had become clear that if the old poles in the park had remained outside, they would have soon decayed: "It was decided to obtain skilled Indian carvers to carve exact copies of the best old poles, and some new ones, to replace the old exhibits and produce a permanent and representative outdoor display of this unique art for the benefit of future generations. By employing Native craftsmen and having them work in public view in the park, the programme accomplished the added aims of keeping alive Native art and providing a public educational attraction" (Duff, "Thunderbird Park," n.d, 29). It was the museum, not the Native person, who "kept the culture alive." This is not to say that Duff necessarily believed that Kwakwa̱ka̱'wakw culture was dying in the villages, but he knew that the metropolitan public was likely to share that common assumption. Martin, promoted as "one of the few surviving authorities in the old ways of life" (Duff, "Thunderbird Park," n.d., 29), soon became a major attraction himself. Both Martin and his wife Abaya were personable and they charmed the visitors to MOA and the BCPM.[3]

9.4. Thunderbird Park, Victoria, ca. 1949. Courtesy of Royal British Columbia Museum, BC Archives, AA-00274.

9.5. Mungo Martin and Bill Reid (Haida) pole at the Douglas border crossing near Blaine, Washington, 1957. Photograph by Aaron Glass, 2006.

9.6. Ellen Neel (Kwakwa̲ka̲'wakw), White Spot Totem Pole, 1957. Originally installed in the Delta, British Columbia, restaurant; currently installed in the lobby of the White Spot corporate office, Vancouver, British Columbia. Courtesy of White Spot Limited.

By being an elderly male potlatch host who sang in Kwak'wala and spoke heavily inflected English, Mungo Martin fit beautifully into the myth of the vanishing Indian, a myth that harmonized nicely with the myth of the totem pole as an ancient tradition on the verge of disappearance. Although Martin was undoubtedly the star of the MOA and RBCM totem pole projects, several versions of the story of his selection exist. According to Phil Nuytten (1982, 9–10), UBC's Totem Pole Committee first approached Kwakwa̲ka̲'wakw artist Ellen Neel (who, as we have seen, conducted a thriving business carving model poles in Stanley Park), asking her to restore their poles.[4] For Neel, this collection had special meaning, as one of the poles had been carved by her grandfather, Charlie James, and another by Martin, who was her uncle. During the summer of 1949, Neel restored four poles from Fort Rupert, including James's. After one summer of work, Neel lost enthusiasm for this project, both because her business had suffered during her absence and because she, as an artist interested in creating new works, found replication uninteresting. To release herself from this task, Neel asked her uncle, Mungo Martin, who was in Vancouver visiting her, if he would like a job copying poles. He apparently was delighted by this suggestion and MOA soon hired him (Nuytten 1982, 52–53). Audrey Hawthorn, however, offers an entirely different story, stating that Marius Barbeau suggested Martin from the very beginning, and that MOA approached Neel to be his assistant; "She was not, however, in a position to assist Mr. Martin on restoration work at that time" (1993, 9–10).

Regardless of which account is true, Ellen Neel, despite her considerable productivity, never became a significant player in the official history of British Columbia's totem pole projects, perhaps because she did not adhere to the stereotype favored by anthropologists and the public. Her English was excellent, and she did not wear ceremonial regalia at events, instead dressing in clothes more appropriate for a 1950s housewife. Moreover, having married a white man, according to Canadian law, she lost her Indian status. Instead of promoting herself, as did Martin, as a high-status aboriginal, she presented herself as a modern mother, supervising six of her seven half-native children as totem-carving apprentices. Her art, while capable of being quite "traditional," at times ventured into the unexpected, as in her Totemland pole. Her light-hearted attitude toward her craft is well exemplified by a pole she carved for the Delta White Spot restaurant; at the top of the pole is a smiling chicken (the chain's mascot) with the outstretched wings of the Kwakwa̲ka̲'wakw Thunderbird (fig.9.6).

Ellen Neel's art—so unapologetically commercial—did not allude to the golden age of authenticity, and she herself, as a Canadian woman, did not fit nicely into the category of "disappearing Indian" so favored by the museums. She is rarely mentioned in the literature. Indeed, *The Legacy* (Macnair et al. 1980), a major exhibition and catalogue of contemporary Northwest Coast art, fails even to mention Neel but does comment favorably on Charlie James and Mungo Martin. Neel has been, in effect, erased from the history of Northwest Coast art, while her uncle Mungo Martin—selectively but not inappropriately—has been transformed into one of its stars. Only Phil Nuytten, a personal friend of Neel's, and Kimberly Phillips have written extensively about this "modern" Northwest Coast carver.[5] In the 1940s and 1950s, Neel could not (obviously) adhere to the then prevalent gender stereotype of the powerful male artist. With the rise of feminism, Neel now has a more secure place in the history of Northwest Coast art.

WERE THE CULTURES *REALLY* DYING?

Virtually everyone who thought about Northwest Coast Native people at midcentury accepted as true the belief that rapid acculturation had destroyed their cultures, which only a small handful of older people remembered. It was up to institutions like museums to preserve and, if possible, perpetuate the lost traditions. The Kwakwa̲ka̲'wakw, despite Duff's claims that Mungo Martin was the "last" authentic member of their group, actually maintained strong traditions throughout the first part of the twentieth century. Mungo Martin was by no means the only maintainer of his people's traditions, and the Kwakwa̲ka̲'wakw were by no means the only coastal people to claim active, accomplished artists. Because of the series of high-profile public projects surveyed here, however, he and they were uniquely promoted.

When the Kwakwa̲ka̲'wakw got the opportunity to demonstrate their cultural endurance, many people, including Wilson Duff, were surprised. In 1953, with provincial support, Martin built a plank house in Thunderbird Park at the BCPM. The house name, Wawaditla, translates as "He orders them to come inside," an expression of tremendous authority and power within the potlatch system (fig. 9.8). According to Jacknis (2002, 151–57), this house represents an amalgamation of two houses, the Fort Rupert structure in which Martin was born and another house from New Vancouver. Martin owned the privileges of the beings depicted on Wawaditla's four house posts as well as that of the supernatural sea creature which he painted on the house's façade. The pole that stood outside the house did not, however, represent Martin's privilege, for it depicted crests of four high-ranking Kwakwa̲ka̲'wakw groups, from Village Island, Blunden Harbour, Alert Bay, and Fort Rupert.

To validate this building, its imagery, and the exterior pole, Martin hosted a splendid three-day potlatch in the house on December 14–16, 1953. Two years previously, the potlatch prohibition had been eliminated from the Indian Act, making potlatches legal once again, and Martin's opening ceremony for this house represented the first legal public potlatch since 1884. The first day of the potlatch, December 14, only Native people and a small number of special white friends attended the ceremonies. There were speeches, feasts, and distributions of gifts and money. On the next day, invited non-Native guests were treated to an incredible presentation of dances and masked ceremonies owned

ELLEN NEEL

BY PHIL NUYTTEN, SUBMARINE DESIGNER AND CARVER

I was fortunate to have Ellen Neel as a mentor when I first began learning to carve and paint in the Kwakwaka'wakw style. It was in the early 1950s. I was very young, and very eager. I devoured her lessons as though I were starving. I learned from Ellen along with her three sons, but for me it was only on Saturdays during the school year: just one day a week. The rest of the week, I practiced every day, making endless model poles, letter openers, single figures for bookends, tray handles, small masks, paddles, plaques, and on and on. I raised a bumper crop of blisters that slowly turned into tough calluses as I reduced large pieces of cedar into small pieces of cedar. Months and years later, those pieces of wood finally came to have some small, vague resemblance to Ellen's then distinctive style.

Later in my life, I came to know about Ellen's own early efforts to produce good work; that is, work that was not only saleable but also satisfied her as an artist. I learned about her progress by collecting her signed and dated pieces. The work she produced in the mid 1940s lacked the sophistication of weighted form and fine balance that she began to achieve only a short time later—a half decade or so. She was teaching herself. There were nuances of technique and elements of style that she somehow missed or was not old enough to fully appreciate when, as a child, she watched and learned from her skilled grandfather, Charlie James (Yakuglas). So she taught herself through books, the Vancouver Museum, visits back home to Alert Bay, and by asking questions of Mungo Martin when he came to Vancouver every few months. I knew nothing of this, since she was very good at her work by the time I met her in 1952. I thought her work was wonderful then, and more than half a century and a lot of learning later, I still feel the same way.

I have a favorite Ellen Neel piece. It's a tourist wall mask depicting the forest giantess called *dzunuk'wa*—the female Sasquatch or Bigfoot. The mask is made of red cedar and it was roughed with a chisel, the eye and cheek hollows gouged, and the rest knife-finished. The mask was then lightly charred over its entire surface by turning it over the open flame of a gas cooking stove. The soft wood between the lines of the grain burn deepest and the piece was then wire-brushed to make the vertical grain stand out. That's it: form only. No incised lines, no eye-holes—nothing. Just form and shadow. I've had this piece for a long time and I believe that it is a true work of art.

9.7. Ellen Neel (Kwakwaka'wakw), *dzunuk'wa* mask, ca. 1955. Cedar. 9" x 7.5" x 6.1." Nuytten collection. Photograph by Phil Nuytten.

I was asked to loan some masks to a traveling exhibit mounted by the Vancouver Art Gallery a few years ago. It was called "Down from the Shimmering Sky—Masks of the Northwest Coast." It was conceived as an exhibition of masterworks of Northwest Coast artists, both contemporary and those who had long ago "gone home." One of the curators came to pick out two masks, and he was curious to know why I had put this simple tourist piece beside powerful works by master carvers like Willie Seaweed, Mungo Martin, Henry Hunt, and others. I said, "Because I believe it stands up well as a piece of Northwest Coast art." He looked at it for a long time and said "You're right . . . it's very powerful."

So Ellen's little sightless tourist piece joined the intricate, multiple-faced transformation masks and the huge *hamsamtł* crooked-beaks, and traveled all over North America for several years. Shortly after it was returned to me, the National Gallery of Canada wrote and requested the loan of it for a major display. They were so taken by Ellen's mask that it appeared as the cover of their museum quarterly, *Vernissage*—the magazine of the National Gallery of Canada. Thousands of people have gazed at Ellen's mask and seen a special kind of life in the eye hollows and the puckered lips ready to make the *dzunuk'wa*'s cry: "Whoooooooo" . . . the sound of the rain-forest wind. Many of these people are moved and feel that they have seen something special; just as I did, so many years ago.

9.8. Mungo Martin (Kwakwa̱ka̱'wakw), Wawaditla house and totem pole, 1953. Photograph by Aaron Glass c. 2003.

and largely performed by Martin's extended family. On the third day, another, abbreviated presentation was produced for the general public, who lined up to witness the historic event.[6]

In the past, anthropologists such as Franz Boas had attended potlatches and produced scientific accounts of ceremonies that they expected would vanish. For the celebratory opening of his new house, Martin—who understood the value of anthropological documentation—invited anthropologists (including Duff, the Hawthorns, and Erna Gunther) to record the event.[7] It was audiotaped (including preliminary meetings with other chiefs) and photographed, and the documentation was saved in the archives of the RBCM. Even Wilson Duff was surprised at the vitality of Kwakwa̱ka̱'wakw culture. Despite all the accounts to the contrary, Kwakwa̱ka̱'wakw culture had not disappeared, and Martin was not the last and only culture-bearer. Although Martin may have suggested that his would be the last "real" potlatch, instead it marked the beginning of a ceremonial resurgence among Kwakwa̱ka̱'wakw chiefs, many of whom had attended his event.

OPPORTUNITIES ON HAIDA GWAII

One group whose artistic culture Duff was certain had deteriorated was the Haida. He believed Haida art to be the finest on the Northwest Coast, and he devoted much time and energy to preserving it. In 1953, he traveled to the Queen Charlotte Islands to survey the village sites of Cumshewa, Skedans, Tanu, and Skidegate. In addition to taking copious notes, Duff made films of each village. Soon after, he wrote,

> As a museum man accustomed to handling every object of Haida art with care and respect, I was appalled at what I saw. Magnificent totem poles which I knew from old photographs lay broken and disintegrating on the ground. House timbers lay askew, covered with a lush, wet growth of moss, grass and vegetation. A spruce forest had overrun each village, masking the ruins and partially shielding the few poles that still stood. At each village I took movies, of the house ruins, the shattered remnants of the fallen poles, and especially of the few poles that remained sound. These few, I decided, should be taken out and preserved (Duff 1954a, 12).

Once again, in the context of the vanishing Indian, the anthropologist presents himself as a benevolent hero, preserver, and savior of a disappearing heritage.

INTERIOR HOUSE POSTS BY MUNGO MARTIN, THUNDERBIRD PARK

BY IRA JACKNIS, ANTHROPOLOGIST

In 1953, Mungo Martin (Kwakwa̱ka̱'wakw) was commissioned by Wilson Duff, curator at the BC Provincial Museum (now RBCM), to construct a new house and an original pole to replace the several composite houses in Thunderbird Park. After about ten months of work by Martin, his son David, and a staff carpenter, the house was ready, and on December 14–16, 1953, Mungo Martin dedicated it with a series of potlatches and performances.

Unlike the earlier Native houses in the park, Martin's new building was to be a "real" Kwakwa̱ka̱'wakw house. As Duff commented, "This is an authentic replica of a Kwakiutl house of the nineteenth century. More exactly, it is Mungo Martin's house, bearing on its house posts some of the hereditary crests of his family. This is a copy of a house built at Fort Rupert about a century ago by a chief whose position and name Mungo Martin had inherited and assumed—Nakap'ankim [Na̱kap'an̲ka̱m]. The house of old chief Nakap'ankim was twice as large, but its general style of construction and the carvings on the house posts have been faithfully copied" (1963, 20). Martin was reportedly (Nuytten 1982, 86) born in the house of old chief Nakap'ankim, the uncle of Martin's mother. However, when this house is compared to the old house, Duff's definitive statement about an "authentic replica" becomes ambiguous.

One important trait of a "real" house is having a name. Chief Nakap'ankim owned two house names, of which Martin picked Wawaditla, or "He orders them to come

9.9. Mungo Martin (Kwakwa̱ka̱'wakw) Wawaditla house post , 1953. Courtesy of Royal British Columbia Museum, BC Archives, H03376.

inside," meaning that "the chief in this house is so powerful that he can order anyone else to come in and be his servant" (Duff 1963, 21). At Martin's dedicatory potlatch, Chief Tom Omhid explained the importance of the name: "You all recognize this house, chiefs. This house is not just a made-up house. Take a look at this, and that, and that [the carved house posts]. It is a copy of the first house that all you tribes used to gather in; the house that belonged to my chief; the house that belonged to Naqa'penk'em. That is the reason he can't take just anything up. After all, this house was planned long ago. This house has a story."

If one had only these words to go on, one would think that the two houses were essentially the same. However, using historical photographs of Nakap'ankim's house, one can see that while the creatures on Martin's house posts are the same as in Nakap'ankim's house, they *look* quite different. First, the artist has reversed some of the figures. Nakap'ankim had a pair with *huxwhukw* (a cannibal crane) on top and grizzly holding a copper on the bottom. The opposite pair had a *dzunuk'wa* (wild woman of the woods) on top and a grizzly holding a man on the bottom. In Martin's house, the grizzly holding the copper has been matched with the *dzunuk'wa,* and, correspondingly, the grizzly with the man is under the *huxwhukw*. Second, whereas the man is held upside down in Nakap'ankim's house, he is right side up in Martin's. Finally, and perhaps most significantly, the visual style of the two houses differs radically. This can especially be seen in the painting on the wings, which in Martin's version are in the more florid style popular in the first several decades of this century. Numerous differences can also be seen in the eyes and jaws of the grizzlies.

We can reconcile these seeming discrepancies by considering alternate conceptions of the authentic. For a positivist Western historian, the real physical differences between the two pairs of poles means that Martin's Thunderbird Park house was neither an "authentic replica" nor a "faithful copy" of the Fort Rupert example. However, from a Kwakwaka'wakw perspective, they were the same, because they represented the same crests in a house that carried the same name and was, in a real sense, owned by the same person.

I was attracted to this example for several reasons. It is a Kwakwaka'wakw pole, the subject of my extensive research (Jacknis 1990 and 2002), and was created by Mungo Martin, the most important Kwakwaka'wakw culture broker of the twentieth century, widely regarded as the "slender thread" of his people's artistic tradition. These posts are examples of what I call "museum poles," commissioned by and made for display in a museum. At the same time, they are a kind of replica pole, one in a series of linked forms, created to keep the past alive in the present. Finally, I was attracted methodologically to an instance when photographs became critical historical evidence.

9.10. Pole at house of Chief Nakap'ankim (Wawaditla), Fort Rupert, ca. 1850. Courtesy of Royal British Columbia Museum, BC Archives, PN10027.

9.11. Skedans (Haida), 1902. Courtesy of Royal British Columbia Museum, BC Archives, PN 10.

Two villages on the east coast of Moresby Island, Tanu and Skedans, had especially fine poles (fig. 9.11). To salvage six poles from these communities, Duff organized a "rescue" expedition sponsored by the BCPM and MOA, and financed by the Powell River Company. He first secured permission from the owners, who lived in Skidegate, then returned to the Queen Charlottes with the silversmith and Canadian Broadcasting Company (CBC) radio announcer Bill Reid, Jimmy Jones (a Haida whose family originally came from Tanu), and a work crew to crate and remove the poles. The originals were to be displayed indoors at the two museums, with copies made by Mungo Martin exhibited outdoors in Thunderbird Park (Duff 1957).

Not satisfied with this success, Duff dreamed of salvaging the exceptional poles that stood in remote Ninstints on Anthony Island, in the southernmost region of the Queen Charlottes. The linguistically distinct Kungit Haida who inhabited this region of the archipelago had developed a reputation as one of the most aggressive Northwest Coast people, conducting periodic raids on their Haida enemies in Tanu, Skidegate, and Massett. However, like virtually every other Haida village, Ninstints's population plunged after the 1862 smallpox epidemic. In the late 1830s, 308 Kungit lived in seventeen houses, while by 1884 only thirty people inhabited twenty houses. The survivors of Ninstints finally joined so many other Haida and moved to Skidegate, town of their former enemies.

Although for many years Duff had unsuccessfully attempted to travel to Ninstints, after the positive results of his 1953 work in Tanu and Skedans, he finally made it to Anthony Island in 1956. As the first step in this project, Duff and some museum staff examined the poles and planned for their removal. On the beach that surrounded a small, protected cove were more than thirty still-standing poles. These included house posts, mortuaries twenty feet high, tall memorials, and house frontal poles. In keeping with his salvage paradigm, Duff and UBC anthropology professor Michael Kew describe "the moldering remnants of once-magnificent carved posts," yet in appreciative, relativist, humanist terms:

> What was destroyed here was not just a few hundred individual human lives. Human beings must die anyway. It was something even more complex and even more human—a vigorous and functioning society, the project of just as long an evolution as our own, well-suited to its environment and vital enough to participate in human cultural achievements not duplicated anywhere else (Duff and Kew 1957, 63).

Unlike the earlier lament, which assumed a passive cultural death, this quote implies a more active—and presumably colonial—force of destruction. The team's own current salvage activities may have been seen as an active if partial attempt to remedy the past injustice by working to preserve what had been nearly destroyed.

In the spring of 1957, Duff consulted with the Skidegate Band Council and with families of Kungit ancestry who owned the poles, receiving permission to conduct a salvage operation to bring some to Victoria and Vancouver for safekeeping. The pole owners were to receive a payment of fifty dollars per section of pole removed. In June, the crew that included Duff, anthropologists Wayne Suttles and Michael Kew, Bill Reid, cameramen, assistants, and several Haida sailed to the site in a chartered fishing seine boat, accompanied by three Native men (fig. 9.12). Once on the island, work progressed quite quickly. The team first roped shorter poles to standing trees, cut though their bases, and gently lowered them onto supports, where they were crated. Then they sawed the taller poles into three pieces, as the poles were thought to be far too massive to be safely transported intact. Sometimes the men needed to be inventive. The mortuary of Chief Kanskinai was immense—twenty feet tall, four feet in diameter at the base, and weighing at least two and one-half tons. Even with a portion removed, this pole, once lowered to the ground, could not be moved. So the team took blocks and tackle from the seiner and used them to slowly and carefully drag the pole over a track of driftwood logs to the shoreline—an operation that took over two difficult hours. In 1799, Captain Roberts used ship tackle to help Kiusta Chief Cunneah raise his pole; in 1957, anthropologists used similar technology to take a pole down.

After working for over a week, the crew successfully crated eleven poles for safe transportation. To move them from the site to the anchored *Laymore*, a naval auxiliary vessel loaned for this occasion, the team pushed the crates down to the water's edge and roped them together in a single line (fig. 9.13). At high tide, a motorboat pulled the long row of floating boxes to the ship, where, secured by cables, they were carefully winched onto the deck. The ship's first stop was Victoria, where poles destined for the BCPM were unloaded and trucked first to the warehouse for drying, and ultimately to the museum itself for restoration and display. The remainder traveled to MOA in Vancouver (Smyly and Smyly 1975).

In 1959, the CBC produced *Totem*, a film about the salvage expedition to southern Haida Gwaii undertaken two years prior. Bill Reid, already a well-known CBC announcer, narrated the film. The lament of destruction runs like a leitmotif through the production; early on, for example, Reid states, "Think also of what had been lost; not only the poles and other material things that had been destroyed, or been allowed to decay through neglect, but all the rich pattern of legend and ceremony

9.12. Wilson Duff (left), Harry Hawthorn of UBC (center), and Bill Reid (right), Ninstints (Haida), 1957. Courtesy of Royal British Columbia Museum, BC Archives, I-28960.

9.13. Removing poles from the island, Ninstints (Haida), 1957. Courtesy of Royal British Columbia Museum, BC Archives, 15316.

that lay behind these massive expressions of a rich and powerful way of life" (quoted in R. Morris 1994, 90). His narration reinforces the finality of this event: "Though the White Man brought disruption and eventual destruction of these people, he also brought . . . new wealth and . . . new tools. . . . So for a little while during the first two thirds of the last century, creativity on the West Coast flourished as it never had before—and perhaps never will again . . . forgotten history. . . . sudden disaster . . . end of a society" (quoted in R. Morris 1994, 91). The camera lovingly pans the old poles, then records the sawing and segmenting, crating, and floating away of the rescued portions. As Morris notes in *Totem*, Native people are not just disappearing, they have already gone (R. Morris 1994, 92). Their poles, rotten as they are, represent all that remains of a once-glorious culture. Such elegiac declarations, while representing a real-enough assault on indigenous vitality, were almost always made from outside the First Nations societies under observation.

9.14. Ninstints (Haida), 2004. Photograph by Aldona Jonaitis.

Like other global sites with significant "ruins," Ninstints has repeatedly attracted considerable historical interest. In 1957 Anthony Island became a Class "A" Provincial Park and the subject of further ethnological and archeological research, which greatly increased knowledge of Ninstints and the poles that the Duff team had left standing the previous year. Over the next twenty years, as relic hunters disturbed the site and removed artifacts, the provincial government recognized the need for more careful oversight of the park, in 1979 declaring Anthony Island an ecological reserve, and in 1980 an archeological and heritage site. One problem was the state of decay of the poles. They needed conservation, for the forest that flourished in that damp and lush environment had slowly moved closer to the shoreline and surrounded the poles, and, in some cases, cast seeds onto the poles so that saplings grew from the carved heads of the crest images. In 1978, the Skidegate band asked the BCPM to help conserve the poles that remained by preventing further encroachment of the forest into the site. The federal government then became involved, and through its efforts, in 1980, Ninstints was designated as a UNESCO World Heritage Site. Today the island is monitored by the Haida Watchman Program, as Native bands have gained control over tourist access to their heritage sites (see chapter 11). These totem poles finally enjoy local, regional, provincial, federal, and global recognition and protection (fig. 9.14).

KITWANCOOL AND TOTEM RESTORATION AS LAND CLAIM

In addition to his work among the Haida, Wilson Duff devoted considerable effort toward preserving Gitk'san poles. In 1952, prior to his Haida salvage efforts, Duff had visited five Gitk'san villages (Hazelton, Kispiox, Kitsegukla, Kitwanga, and Kitwancool) in order to survey the poles that remained standing. In his judgment, fifty well-carved poles still stood along the Skeena River, "Fine, deeply carved sculptures, never painted or with their original paint weathered away . . . now bleached, mossy and cracked with age"

(Duff 1952, 21). He felt that the kind of project conducted in 1926 would probably no longer be successful due to the "insurmountable" objections of the Natives. Yet Duff singled out the poles at Kitwancool (fig. 3.11) as being among the finest in existence, so he approached the Kitwancool leadership to discuss allowing some of their poles to be preserved.

Among the Gitk'san, the significance of totem poles had subtly increased, partially in response to ongoing problems with the government. Village leaders Albert Douse and Walter Douse soundly refused Duff's proposal, not so much on artistic or cultural grounds but instead on political grounds related to land title. The band members of Kitwancool asserted that they had never signed a treaty, never relinquished their ownership of their lands, never accepted the government's authority to take away land and create a reserve, and they wanted nothing to do with any government body, including the Provincial Museum, unless it acknowledged their claims to the land. Duff, whose passion lay in the artistry of the totem poles, discovered an equal passion among the Gitk'san concerning their poles' histories and political implications. The Kitwancool poles communicated a new, collective message beyond their clan-based affiliations, a declaration intended not so much for Native people as for whites: "The land these poles stand on is ours as Gitk'san."

After his success with the Haida in Ninstints, Duff returned to Kitwancool in 1958, once again anxious to preserve its treasures. This time he offered to have replicas made in Victoria and shipped back north so that the community could maintain access to its monumental history. The townspeople proposed a counteroffer: in addition to the replicas, the BCPM would publish a Kitwancool history to demonstrate traditional Kitwancool ownership of the land. On March 24, 1958, Duff, Chief Wiha, Chief Gamlakuyelt, and Walter Derrick, chief councilor of the Kitwancool band, signed an agreement declaring a common desire to preserve totem poles "for the use and benefit of future generations of both white and Native people" as well as asserting the Kitwancool people's demand "that their authentic history, the stories of their totem poles, their social organization, territories and laws be written down, published and used in the highest educational institutions of the province to teach future generations of white and Native students about Kitwancool" (Duff 1958). The document states that the people of Kitwancool agree to allow three poles—the small pole of Chief Guno as well as the "Split Person Pole" and the "Mountain Eagle Pole," both of Chief Wiha—to be removed to Victoria, and to provide the information necessary for the production of the aforementioned publication.[8] The BCPM agreed to replicate the poles, to transport the copies back to Kitwancool and erect them, to fund an individual acceptable by both parties to record the histories, to issue the publication, to provide copies of the information to the University of British Columbia, and to supply the university with sufficient copies of the publication for professors and students. The document included this statement: "Furthermore, [BCPM agrees] to recommend to the officials of the University that these materials be extensively used in teaching the coming generations of students about Kitwancool. And furthermore, to inform the officials of the University that the people of Kitwancool would welcome suggestions for the improvement of their legal position and welfare; and in future may ask the University and the Provincial Museum for information and advice on matters within their competence and concerning the people of Kitwancool" (Duff 1958).

As the museum's press release put it, "Through the years the Kitwancool . . . have fought to keep their territories and tribal life intact. . . . Now they have turned their faith to education—to educate the White men by having their history published" (Duff 1958). That same release proudly asserts that "the first three totem poles ever to leave the famous village of Kitwancool . . . arrived in Thunderbird Park today," to be replicated according to a historic agreement (fig. 9.15).

In 1959, the museum honored its other promise, publishing *Histories, Territories, and Laws of the Kitwancool*, edited by Wilson Duff. An excerpt from that publication, on the Ha-ne-lal-gag Pole, demonstrates the close connection that poles and territory have for the Kitwancool. The story describes an ancestor's travels:

9.15. Replicated totem poles, Kitwancool (Gitk'san), 1961. Courtesy of Royal British Columbia Museum, BC Archives, PN 12985-3.

> The reason they were traveling so much was that they were making their map, and on each piece of land when they stopped they had left their mark and their power, making it theirs . . . . The poles gave them their power . . . and gave them the right of ownership of all the lands, mountains, lakes and streams they had passed through or over and camped or built villages in. The power of these poles goes into the lands they had discovered and taken as their own (Duff 1959, 24).

This historic book remains today a major document of the rich possibilities resulting from collaborations between museums, governments, and Native communities. Duff obtained the poles he craved, and the Gitk'san secured something intangible but essential to their political and cultural sovereignty—validation of their land claims. In a potlatch, attending the ceremonial display of regalia and accepting distributed gifts signifies acceptance of a leader's claim to status; here, the acknowledgment of these histories and the public distribution of a book signified an analogous achievement within the world of the Gitk'san's colonizers.

Duff's activities represented a fundamental shift in the language of social relations from the earlier Skeena River project of the 1920s, for he recognized and promoted Native ownership of land as well as poles. It is noteworthy, however, that Duff's progressive actions occurred during the same decade as the British Columbia Centennials, during which the appropriation of Native culture was the dominant mode of relation. Then (as now), different attitudes, multiple and often conflicting paradigms, and distinct patterns of relation existed simultaneously vis-à-vis Native cultures. Just as the totem pole itself exists in many different forms and expresses different meanings at any single point in time, so does its reception by Native and non-Native people.

SAVING STATE HERITAGE IN SOUTHEAST ALASKA

Duff also played a major role in Alaska pole preservation. As early as 1946, René d'Harnoncourt of the

Indian Arts and Crafts Board had sent art writer and curator Katherine Kuh to survey extant Alaskan Native art—including totem poles—to determine the potential for federal support, although nothing came of her work (Kuh 1966). During the summer of 1966, the staff of the Alaska State Museum (ASM) in Juneau, along with Erna Gunther, University of Alaska anthropology professor, surveyed totem poles in Tongass, Village Island, Old Kasaan and New Kasaan, Klawak, and Hydaburg, acquiring clear evidence of their physical deterioration. The next year, the Alaska State Council on the Arts funded the 1967 Southeast Alaska Native Artifacts and Monuments conferences, held July 13–15 in Juneau and November 17 in Anchorage. These meetings, cosponsored by ASM, the Alaska Native Brotherhood (ANB), the Alaska Native Sisterhood (ANS), the Tongass Historical Society, and the U.S. Forest Service, focused on the present conditions of Tlingit and Haida totem poles extant in remote villages and the need to preserve these cultural treasures. This effort represented an unprecedented degree of cooperation between local, state, and federal officials as well as statewide Native organizations, in addition to specific totem pole owners. Topics included the question of ownership, the need for a comprehensive survey of totem poles, and potential sources of funding for their restoration. The Smithsonian Institution's representatives assured the group that once the survey was conducted, it would give financial support for preservation.[9]

Verbalizing the difference between the response of a white person who appreciated poles as art and the Native family for whom poles embodied significant history, Erna Gunther, at the November 17 meeting in Juneau, urged intercultural understanding:

> What we have now is a meeting of two cultures. To the White man the totem is a monument, but the basic reason for a totem is not that. . . . Its purpose is to enhance the prestige of the family which puts it up. The pole itself is secondary in value. People like to see them, but in the culture to which they belong, they have deeper meaning. This is very important to consider when talking to people who own the poles. They would not consider it of value to re-erect a pole because they could not afford to put on the ceremony that would go along with it. We must be able to give them some idea of what we want to do with them. What we are doing is trying to share their heritage (Gunther 1967, 6–7).

Philip Ward, of the BCPM, emphasized that project managers should present themselves as facilitators to the proper pole owners in order to avoid any sense of outsider expropriation.

As a result of this meeting, Jane Wallen of the ASM; Joe Clark, wood pathologist of the U.S. Forest Products Laboratory; and Wilson Duff, here in the role of "Research Associate of the Smithsonian Institution," embarked on a survey of Southeast totem poles from June 8 through 31, 1969. Included in the final report, "Totem Pole Survey of Southeast Alaska: Report of Field Work and Follow-up Activities, June-October 1969" (edited by Wilson Duff, with Jane Wallen and Joe Clark) were the names of those Haida and Tlingit who accompanied the team in the actual villages: Walter Baronovich Young, George Keegan Williams, Joe Demmert, Sr., and Forrest DeWitt, as well as Dennis Demmert, a Tlingit student in the American Indian Program at Harvard University. The team visited and mapped villages, photographed and took detailed notes on their retrievable poles, and recorded narrations by the Native consultants. They met with several groups of ANB and ANS members to discuss the survey and what kind of preservation activity could result from it.

The report begins with a brief history of totem pole loss, noting that collectors began purchasing poles for museums outside Alaska as early as 1875, when James G. Swan bought carvings for the Philadelphia World's Fair. The early twentieth-century John Brady acquisition, the report continues, "might be considered the first official restoration project," as it ultimately kept poles in the state. Poles continued to decay until the 1930s and the Indian Civilian Conservation Corps projects, which removed numerous carvings considered salvageable. "The poles left for us to find on our survey, therefore, were those which had been considered beyond saving by the standards of 1940." Nevertheless, "we were able to find about forty poles or fragments that still display the strength and beauty of the old sculptural styles" (Duff, Wallen, and Clark 1969, 16). The survey is extremely thorough, with extensive information on every one of the forty-one retrievable poles as well as detailed maps of villages with the largest numbers of poles: Village Island (eight), Tongass (six), and Old Kasaan (nineteen). There were, in addition to these, two poles from Cape Fox Village, and one each from Howkan, Sukkwan, Tuxekan, Tebenkof Bay, and Klawak Creek. The team recommended that those poles be transferred to a sheltered location, dried, treated, and maintained in a permanent, secure environment. The team also visited the totem pole parks, noting that with the exception of Sitka, the communities responsible for the maintenance of their poles had been unable to maintain them adequately due to lack of funds. The team composed detailed lists of all the poles in each park, along with maps, notations on whether they were originals or copies, and references to published illustrations. Also covered were poles standing in the cities of Juneau, Ketchikan, Wrangell, and Sitka.

In his Alaska report, Wilson Duff promoted the "correct way" to restore poles. For example, the section "The Artistic Use of Paint" bemoans the many layers of paint that have covered so many restored poles:

> In earlier times, poles were created and appreciated primarily as works of sculpture. Any paint that was used (we are referring here mainly to Haida poles) served only to accentuate carved features such as eyes, mouths, and ears. Colors were few and never glossy. The larger areas, such as bodies of animals and spaces between figures, were usually left unpainted. During the 1880s, *just before the end of the totem pole era*, there does seem to have been an increased use of paint by the Haida and others. Partly this was a result of the fact that paint was more easily available from the White men; partly it was associated with the new subjects such as Russian priests which were occasionally being shown on the poles; and partly, it represented a decline of the art as painting began to be substituted for carving. . . . The unfortunate results can be seen today in Juneau, Wrangell and Ketchikan, Hydaburg and Saxman, and New Kasaan (Duff, Wallen, and Clark 1969, 85–86; our italics).

Duff even criticized the work of John Wallace, stating that he was "an accomplished carver" but took "liberties" in his copies, where "the artistic quality . . . is good, but definitely inferior to the originals" (Duff, Wallen, and Clark 1969, 51). One problem with the Wallace works (and virtually all the other CCC carvings) was their use of "garish" bright paint, which Duff said should, in the future, "be used in more authentic and tasteful ways."[10] One of the poles that was ultimately salvaged, the Chief Skowl pole from Kasaan, was resplendent in this kind of bright paint.

Replicated poles were to be painted only as brightly as they would have been in the nineteenth century, then allowed to weather and never be repainted. Since it would have been impractical to remove all of the paint from existing poles—although Duff clearly would have approved of so doing—the paint was to be allowed to weather, and, when appropriate, the pole was to be repainted according to proper canons. The report listed "guidelines" for repainting poles:

> Colors should be limited to a flat black, red, blue-green and white. Black was traditionally used for eyebrows, eyelids, and the large circular irises of the eyes . . . Beaks and the formlines outlining ears were also usually black. Red was used for lips, tongues, nostrils, and the inner parts of the ears. The hollows around the eyes were often blue-green. Teeth and the whites of the eyes were often painted white. In general, the painting should be kept as simple and bold as possible. To avoid the fussiness that obscures the boldness of the carving, no details should be painted in unless they are already outlined by carved lines. Bodies, foreheads, limbs and the long cylindrical hats should usually be left unpainted.

Tlingit poles, the report continued, were originally more heavily painted than Haida ones, but not with the brilliant tones seen at that time throughout southeast Alaska. "We can only suggest that a conscious effort be made toward a more restrained use of color, so that the poles are shown as *works of sculpture* rather than as the garish stereotype which has come to represent the totem pole in the popular mind" (Duff, Wallen, and Clark 1969, 87–88; our italics). This text was part of Duff's efforts during the 1960s to recast Northwest Coast carvings as "fine art," in part by delineating their formal rules and conventional styles. His own aesthetic taste—for the unpainted poles of the northern coast over the elaborately painted poles of the Kwakwa̱ka̱'wakw—was quite evident.

At the same time, however, Duff increasingly acknowledged the political engagement of coastal First Nations in managing their own affairs, and he demonstrated keen reflexivity about the clash of cultural values involved (often echoing Gunther's statements at the initial 1967 planning conference). For example, in Duff's lecture on totem pole salvage projects to his anthropology class in October of 1971, he began: "This is an emotional, *personal trip* I am laying on you today. (If any of you really object to profs. laying on personal trips, you can leave.) Yet it has something to do with relations—with our redefinitions of Haida art." Later he confronted his students directly. "Who collected QCI [Queen Charlotte Islands] totems? *Whites*. Why? We defined them as art. Who is collecting Alaska poles? The ANB [Alaska Native Brotherhood]."[11] In personalizing his statements, Duff was also acknowledging how his own trajectory of participation in totem salvage projects mirrored the increasing assertion of First Nations control over them.

Over several months following the conference and survey, Jane Wallen and Dennis Demmert met with various groups (both Native and non-Native), appeared on television, discussed the project, developed support among the communities of southeast Alaska, and ensured that all parties had the opportunity to contribute to the discussion about how to proceed. They also visited Gitk'san communities along the Skeena River, as well as K'san Village, in order to assess similar British Columbian projects. The consensus was that poles should be retrieved from abandoned village sites and preserved. To guarantee adherence to Native traditions and protocol, the Tlingit and Haida formed the Southeastern Alaska Indian Arts Council, which would assume ownership of the poles if their rightful owners could not be identified. As Demmert wrote in 1973, this project was unique because white people asked Natives for permission to do this work, resulting in "support and participation by the Indian people [that] added another dimension to the project: it showed that they, as an ethnic group, are becoming aware that their heritage is something of value" (Demmert 1973, 33).

During the summer of 1970, fourteen poles made their way from abandoned sites to Ketchikan, and Demmert made a public request for old mattresses to be used to transport the poles (Ketchikan *Daily News* 1970). The Southeastern Alaska Indian Arts Council oversaw the removal of thirty-eight poles and fragments from the villages, and brought them to Ketchikan, where they were stored in a fish cannery while a suitable building was constructed. That same year, the Alaska State Museum and the Ketchikan Native Brotherhood instituted a training program both to revive the art of totem carving and to foster public awareness of the quality of Tlingit and Haida traditional art. Tlingit master Nathan Jackson, along with non-Native artists Bill Holm and Duane Pasco, taught a course in Northwest Coast art, generating considerable interest in the community. In 1976, the Totem Heritage Center opened in Ketchikan, displaying the fine old poles, storing others, and sponsoring an active curriculum of Native art workshops. Today, this facility, one of the main attractions of Ketchikan, welcomes thousands of visitors a year, its various poles—old and new—a testament to this transforming art form.

WILSON DUFF: FROM SALVAGER OF ARTIFACTS TO PROMOTER OF ARTWORK

Wilson Duff played an indispensable role in the restoration, preservation, and creation of many British Columbia and Alaska totem poles. Unfortunately, his insistence upon the nineteenth-century art historical canon and poetic requiems to Native culture overshadowed his appreciation of ongoing cultural activities that included the erection of new poles. He adhered to a Boasian salvage paradigm that assumed that cultural change compromised authenticity. For example, when he visited Skeena River villages in 1952 to survey poles, he reported that from the 1850s to 1890s, fifty-three poles had been raised; from 1900 to 1925, eighteen new poles were erected; and since the 1920s seventeen new poles had been raised and eleven more restored (fig. 9.16). These new and restored poles were erected with all the necessary ceremonies that involved feasting, gift giving, displays of prerogatives, and expenditure of considerable amounts of money.[12] However, Duff considered these recent poles aesthetically inferior and so failed to appreciate the "authentic" cultural work that likely went into their creation and erection.

Despite these indications of cultural continuity, Duff remained profoundly pessimistic about Gitk'san artistic culture (Duff 1952, 26). For him, the flourishing of totem poles from the 1920s to 1952 was not a *continuation* of tradition but instead, "in a very real sense, a *revival* of the Native culture," due in part to the earlier Canadian National Railway project that had "awakened" the Gitk'san to the value of their heritage. Duff, uncritically accepting the trope of anthropologist-as-hero, assumed that their concern for preservation was "learned from, or at least reflected, the strongly expressed opinion of almost all the Whites with whom the Native people have had contact in recent years" (Duff 1952, 26). Duff's firm commitment to the idea of Northwest Coast culture dying blinded him to the agency the Gitk'san demonstrated in maintaining their traditions. During the period of the most severe cultural oppression, the Gitk'san, like the Haida, erected grave monuments according to clan rules and accompanied by gift giving. For Duff, the Gitk'san had simply forgotten their heritage and had needed non-Native people to stimulate lost traditions. Furthermore, Duff noted that the only carver active in the region, seventy-four-year-old Arthur McDames, probably "the last of the Gitskan carvers," was training no successor (Duff 1952, 27). Smitten by nineteenth-century, northern-style Northwest Coast art and informed by the cult of authenticity and antiquity, Duff conflated loss of canonical styles with loss of art as cultural production. Art of poor quality had, according to this point of view, little cultural meaning. The crude Gitk'san poles raised after 1920 and the model

9.16. Gitsegukla (Gitk'san) pole raising, 1930. Canadian Museum of Civilization, 97526.

poles crafted for sale to tourists meant little or nothing to most anthropologists. For Duff, as for many others, the great art of the past had died. Contemporary studies of the Gitk'san, as well as of other Northwest Coast groups, concentrate less on what has been lost, rather focusing on what has been maintained or cleverly transformed to accommodate the contemporary world (e.g., see Anderson and Halpin 2000). Duff's lamentation of decline has been replaced by an optimistic, and politically strategic, assessment of cultural negotiation and endurance.

Because of Duff's belief that the culture resided in the aesthetic canon, he was thrilled when, starting in the 1960s, Northwest Coast Native artists such as Bill Reid and Robert Davidson began to create new artwork that adhered to those stylistic tenets. In 1967, Duff had the opportunity to promote the artistry of quality Northwest Coast art when, along with Bill Holm and Bill Reid, he curated the Vancouver Art Gallery exhibit that claimed to be the first true *art* exhibit of these pieces, Arts of the Raven: Masterworks of the Northwest Coast Indian. Doris Shadbolt, curator at the gallery, asserted in her preface to the catalogue, "This is an exhibition of art, high art, not ethnology."[13]

The works of Doug Cranmer, Bill Reid, Robert Davidson, Henry Hunt, Tony Hunt, Don Lelooska Smith (Cherokee), and non-Native Bill Holm appeared in an art museum alongside masterpieces of historic Northwest Coast art. As will be described in more detail in the next chapter, this aestheticization of Northwest Coast art bestowed upon it an enhanced value, both economic and cultural, in the eyes of art appreciators. This was yet another major contribution of Wilson Duff to the ongoing history of Northwest Coast art.

TOTEM POLE RESTORATION PROJECTS AND THE LEGITIMIZATION OF COLONIAL RULE

Wilson Duff was one in a line of twentieth-century totem pole project directors, all connected in some way to the government. After effectively colonizing Alaska and British Columbia, why did governments invest such large amounts of funds in restoring the totem poles that had earlier been subjected to such disdain? Surely, devoted admirers such as John Brady, Harlan Smith, John Collier, the Hawthorns, and Duff invested time and energy into activities they judged to be important toward understanding and perpetuating Native cultures. But why would the state be interested in supporting such projects? What was there that supported or endorsed this agenda? To answer this question, we briefly consider the problems Northwest Coast Native people posed to authorities.[14]

Throughout the twentieth century, both Alaska and British Columbia Native people continued to demand voting rights, an end to discrimination, and, most importantly, the rights to their traditional lands and to self-determination. The governments slowly acquiesced to some of these demands but, until quite recently in Canada, held firm on land claims. It could be said that these totem projects served to divert attention from the more serious demographic and political consequences of settlement. The state looked good if it publicized its commitment to care for Natives (legally and ethically construed as wards of the state) and preserve their (preferably ancient and defused) culture for the benefit of all humanity. In their position of increasing dependence and subordination, the Natives thus require the involvement of the state to survive. As the state becomes the savior of minority cultures and the educator about Native heritages, indigenous people themselves assume a subaltern position. This process, by which the dominant society's power structure assumes control, communicates a powerful message: Northwest Coast cultures were once great, but they are no longer. This, in effect, can silence those living Native people petitioning for improved conditions and better treatment. In effectively archaizing "authentic" Native culture, the state justified its collection and promotion of material culture-cum-fine art. A similar dynamic was (and remains) at play when major timber corporations donate logs to prominent totem carving projects, thereby appearing to be supporters of the First Nations whose unceded land they may otherwise be exploiting for great profit. Such neoliberal patronage of multicultural arts projects is one primary way in which corporations and states often deflect attention from long-standing inequity and disenfranchisement.

We have seen already how cities and regions—during world's fairs and centennials, and in the context of the tourism industry in general—appropriated totem poles for their own purposes, usually unrelated to Native cultures. This transformation of a cherished material statement of a family's history and worth into a tourist attraction can be considered another facet of the state's efforts to occlude the real situation of Northwest Coast Native people and their claims. Reconstructed poles became tourist spectacles: repainted, repositioned, surrounded by neat lawns, and explained (or not) by carefully worded plaques. "Museumized in this way, they were repositories as regalia for a *secular* colonial state" (Anderson 1983, 180–82). In projects such as these, the state takes over Native culture and presents it as its own, further legitimizing its control over the Native people who created the objects in the first place. Soon the state begins to regard these monuments as *its* predecessors, *its* ancestors. The colonial possessive pronoun is still frequently deployed by government officials who celebrate "*our* Native peoples," "*our* indigenous heritage," "*our* cultural treasures."

Of course, this is not to say that all partcipants in totem restoration projects or exhibits promoting Northwest Coast art were consciously engaged in such obfuscation. To the contrary; many of the projects profiled here were undertaken both collaboratively with indigenous carvers and communities and with the latter's best interests in mind. However, when we examine the larger sociopolitical contexts and relations under which such projects get funded and realized, we must acknowledge that all players operate under historically specific systems of power, regimes of value, and patterns of discourse, with all of their inclusive ambiguities and potential contradictions.

THE DEATH OF WILSON DUFF

After 1967, Duff's fascination with the visual and symbolic aspects of Northwest Coast art took a decidedly poetic turn. He immersed himself in classic northern style art and began to imagine conversations with Haida chief Albert Edward Edenshaw and Charles Edenshaw, men he greatly admired. Influenced by psychoanalytical and structuralist theory, Duff began using sexual terms to interpret the deeper meanings of Northwest Coast art, identifying phallic and vulvic forms in numerous objects. For example, according to Duff, the monumental frontal pole on the Edenshaw house in Massett was phallic, the open hole at its base vulvic. Furthermore, the bear at the base, which is eating an upside-down anthropomorphic figure, had even more complex sexual significance:

> So, in addition to being a crest, if that is what the bear is, I read this bear-eating man figure as a vulvic symbol on the base of the pole . . . [it also appears on] a Haida mortuary with the little human part almost invisible, but the whole is smaller than the part; the whole is literal; the part is metaphoric and the whole thing is a vulvic symbol. Here we have this bear vulvic symbol as a tomb, and if you think that the clang relationship in our own language between womb and tomb is accidental, I think you are wrong (Duff 1981b, 221).

This conceptual chain of reasoning, based upon simple sexual metaphors having little to do with Haida culture, had become idiosyncratic and obscure and, for many, difficult to comprehend.

Duff spoke these words at a symposium on the prehistory of Northwest Coast art held at Simon Fraser University in May of 1976.[15] He had chosen an intellectual path that infuriated many people, including those First Nations friends to whom he had dedicated his life, which was taking a downward spiral. The anger toward and incomprehension of his ideas deeply saddened him. He believed that long-dead master artists sent him messages. His painful poems revealed a driven, depressed genius.[16] Life became unbearable, and on August 8, 1976, Wilson Duff shot himself.

Duff's accomplishments were many—his enthusiastic retrieval and restoration of poles, his encouragement of contemporary carvers, his promotion of Northwest Coast art as *art*, his provocative suggestions as to the meaning behind this art's form, and his passionate promotion of the social, intellectual, and spiritual equality of First Nations people. He had the misfortune, however, of living through a paradigm shift of Native/non-Native relations. When he started his career, he shared the prevalent belief that Northwest Coast cultures were disappearing, so he dedicated his life to preserving what remained. While acknowledging the ongoing vitality of some groups, his admiration for the classic northern art style blinded him to the ongoing production of noncanonical art. What he was not prepared for was the reaction of contemporary Native people to his imposition of Western theories onto their cultures. By the 1970s, Native North Americans were rebelling against colonial control—Duff's increasingly imaginative ideas were, unfortunately, badly timed. No longer would First Nations without complaint allow whites to speak for them, appropriating their creations and explaining their culture. On the Northwest Coast, retaking ownership of their heritage meant bringing art back under their own control. It is sadly ironic that, despite his controversial relationship with the First Nations late in life, Wilson Duff exerted an unquestionable influence upon what would become known as the Northwest Coast Renaissance.

HIGH ART FROM RAINY PLACES

THE "RENAISSANCE" OF TOTEM CARVING

It is sad to relate, but it is true, that the day is not far distant when there will not be a single totem pole in British Columbia. I believe I am safe is saying that another one will never be erected.

—GEORGE DORSEY, MUSEUM COLLECTOR, 1898

I've been making art since I was a kid, and did miniature poles. Then I learned to carve larger poles and began receiving commissions. Some were as far away as Kobe, Japan! I'm always trying to understand my tradition, my artistic heritage, more deeply. It's great that there are so many good younger carvers (I've trained some, actually). Some maintain traditions, some are innovative. . . . But the art flourishes.

—NATHAN JACKSON, TLINGIT ARTIST, 2003

The recurring (and greatly exaggerated) news of the death of Northwest Coast culture filled pages of newspapers, popular books, and anthropological texts from the nineteenth century until the 1960s. Even communities that were actively engaged in ceremonialism—such as the Gitk'san, who raised poles for decades; the Kwakwa̲ka̲'wakw, who kept potlatching; the Nuu-chah-nulth, who maintained a feasting tradition; and the Coast Salish, who engaged in spirit dancing—were lamented by sympathetic observers such as Wilson Duff. That decline of Northwest Coast culture, the theory went, was manifested in part by the degradation of the refined nineteenth-century art style, which had been replaced by crude imitations of a glorious tradition. Then in the 1960s, according to the dominant narrative, those great traditions were revived during what has been termed the renaissance of Northwest Coast Native art. In a classic scenario, rebirth followed a period of cultural morbidity.

In the 1960s a movement developed whereby scholars and artists articulated the canons of northern art, and a generation of Native artists—inspired by their impressive nineteenth-century traditions and supported by wealthy and academic patrons—began producing art of considerable formal merit. It is unquestionable that after 1960, new Northwest Coast art was more refined, adhered more closely to nineteenth-century canons, and became more widely recognized in the marketplace as "fine art." What is *not* true is that prior to this time art making had been abandoned, or that cultural integrity had been entirely compromised. Indeed, this "renaissance" had much more to do with the visual than the cultural components of Northwest Coast art, and drew not only on the new understanding of its traditional canon but also on the involvement of institutions like museums and art galleries that encouraged the production of stylistically conservative art. Moreover, the initial positive reception on the part of consumers had as much to do with widespread changes in attitudinal trends on the part of the dominant culture (and the rising public appreciation at that time of all things Indian) as with shifting patterns of Native production. Thus, while describing the expansion of the market for totem poles as fine art, and the concomitant revitalization of certain cultural activities within indigenous communities, we want to avoid—and explicitly critique—the dominant renaissance discourse in which such transformations have been couched.[1]

This chapter surveys the development of a Northwest Coast art world—a social network of artists, patrons, educators, critics, dealers, institutions, and clients that facilitates the production, circulation, and critical reception of material valued as "art"—and the resulting impact on totem pole creation and appreciation.[2] We suggest that the emerging acceptance of totem poles (and all Northwest Coast material culture) as fine art resulted from the coordination of activities and strategic efforts by many players (both Native and non-Native), each of which had a different level of investment in the issue—political, financial, intellectual, and cultural. In tandem, they helped negotiate new terms of social relations and new categories of value surrounding totem poles and other kinds of indigenous creations. These efforts ranged from developing new contexts for artistic production (museum projects, private and public sponsorship, the return of active potlatching in communities) to redefining the terms of public reception (critical evaluation, aesthetic appreciation, art-historical understanding, and sophisticated connoisseurship). With the eventual collapse of the "vanishing Indian" trope came a recognition of the reality of contemporary First Nations cultural production, and a concomitant shift in the criteria for evaluating the "authenticity" of Native art. As such, new efforts were made by Native people to regulate access to their artistic vocabulary and to limit some of the kinds of artistic appropriation that had occurred in the past. Increasingly, the universalist language of high modernism—applied in the mid-twentieth century to promote the appreciation of non-Western art—expanded to include culturally and ethnically specific ways of knowing and depicting the world. Thus, any recounting of the rise of a specifically artistic consciousness surrounding totem poles must occur in the context of larger developments in the struggle for First Nations self-determination and cultural and political sovereignty.

THE RENAISSANCE MEN AND WOMEN: UNDERSTANDING THE NORTHERN CANON

When speaking publicly, a Tlingit introduces him- or herself by first devoting considerable time to the detailing of clan, house, and crest affiliations as well as other significant components of history and genealogy. Similarly, to understand post-1960 Northwest Coast art, one must acknowledge several different lineages that contributed to the new proliferation of artistry and the reengagement with the northern stylistic canon. These intellectual genealogies can be traced through two academic and institutional families, one in Canada, the other in the United States. At the University of Washington and the Washington State Historical Museum (now the Burke Museum) in Seattle, anthropologist Erna Gunther (who studied with Franz Boas) taught Bill Holm about Northwest Coast culture. Holm in turn worked with art historians Steve Brown and Robin Wright, both of whom, like Holm himself, are artists as well as scholars. On the other side of the border, at the University of British Columbia (UBC) in Vancouver, Harry Hawthorn and Audrey Hawthorn taught anthropology to Michael Ames and Wilson Duff—who in turn instructed Peter Macnair and Marjorie Halpin—while promoting Northwest Coast art through the Museum of Anthropology. Working with these anthropologists were the artists at MOA and the British Columbia Provincial Museum, starting with Mungo Martin, who taught fellow Kwakwaka'wakw Henry Hunt and his son Tony, as well as Doug Cranmer.[3] Bill Reid, a Canadian Broadcasting Company broadcaster of Haida descent who was affiliated at different times with both Canadian institutions, helped train Robert Davidson, among others. These few individuals formed the core of people most responsible for orchestrating the so-called renaissance through numerous exhibits, books, talks, classes, commissions, projects, and opportunities to publicize a new aesthetic awareness.

Wilson Duff's doctrine of "proper" restoration, discussed in chapter 9, conveyed the anthropologist's concern for a canon based on analysis of historic masterworks in museums, and Duff—as well as the Hawthorns—specifically promoted the production of archaic styles among Native clients and collaborators. Non-Native artist and scholar Bill Holm similarly spent long hours in museums, studying works created during the "Golden Age" of northern Northwest Coast art (early to mid-nineteenth century), analyzing the complex component parts of two-dimensional design. As Holm states, "My motivation for this was to learn to *make* things that looked right. Each thing I make adds to my understanding" (Holm 2003). The result of Holm's meticulous work was *Northwest Coast Indian Art: An Analysis of Form* (1965), which remains to this day a highly insightful stylistic study of northern art. Numerous catalogues and exhibits then disseminated Holm's scheme, starting with Arts of the Raven in 1967. Historians often give Holm credit for helping to motivate what they call the "Northwest Coast Renaissance" by clearly delineating the stylistic rule of the "classic" art form. While it is true that after 1965 many coastal artists turned away from the poorly executed works of their recent predecessors and drew inspiration from the nineteenth-century masterpieces analyzed by Holm, the contributions of the above-mentioned network of individuals should be recognized here as well.[4]

Although Mungo Martin was the first to be celebrated as such, Bill Reid would become the world-famous artist most closely associated with the renaissance. The son of a Haida woman, Reid, already a talented jeweler trained in the Western tradition, started carving wood in the Northwest Coast style when he briefly assisted Martin in Victoria in the late 1950s. Like Holm's, Reid's formal education in this style came from his careful study and replication of older pieces in catalogues and museum collections. In 1958, MOA, where Wilson Duff was working, hired Bill Reid to replicate some of its Haida poles, which he did in collaboration with the Kwakwa̱ka̱'wakw carver Doug Cranmer (fig. 10.1). Both men worked until 1962 to create two Haida houses and an array of poles, now one of the highlights of a visit to the UBC campus (fig. 10.2). A house frontal pole in MOA's collection that Reid had first seen on his 1957 Ninstints voyage inspired his first complete pole, which stands before the new mortuary house. Because the mortuary house was smaller than the house before which the original had stood, Reid reduced his replica's scale by one-third. Before the other, full-size replica of a nineteenth-century Haida structure stands a pole inspired by a Skidegate carving. Reid and Cranmer also made a mortuary pole, a double mortuary pole, and a memorial pole. At the opening of the Haida section of UBC's Totem Park on June 25, 1962, in addition to speeches by university officials, the official ceremony was performed by Kwakwa̱ka̱'wakw chief William Scow, whom we met earlier validating the university's use of the Thunderbird image. This entire project was a collaborative effort between the univer-

10.1. Doug Cranmer (Kwakwa̱ka̱'wakw; left) and Bill Reid (Haida; right) carving at the Museum of Anthropology, University of British Columbia, 1958. Museum of Anthropology, 2005.001.401.

10.2. Bill Reid (Haida) and Doug Cranmer (Kwakwa̱ka̱'wakw), Haida houses and poles, 1958–1962. Museum of Anthropology, University of British Columbia. Photograph by Aaron Glass, 2007.

sity, its museum anthropologists, a classicist Haida artist, and politically vocal Kwakwa̱ka̱'wakw leaders.

Reid clearly benefited from his involvement in these MOA totem pole restorations. He had grown up in the non-Native world, and only in adulthood became connected to his Haida heritage. But once he embraced that heritage, Reid's works were included in nearly every major exhibition of Northwest Coast art as well as many critically successful solo exhibits and art catalogues. Reid became acknowledged as a distinguished fine artist, achieving celebrity status far beyond British Columbia. An artist with deep understanding of the principles underlying classical Northwest Coast art, his creativity functioned elegantly within the constraints of those conservative principles. As a radio broadcaster, he possessed the communicative skills needed to impart a universalizing aesthetic approach to audiences unfamiliar with Northwest Coast design principles.

While Martin lived within an ongoing potlatch tradition, Reid's connection to Haida culture was not nearly as firm as his affinity for its visual art. He admired the creativity of his ancestors, and the inseparable bonds that existed between art and their life, but judged contemporary efforts at cultural revival false and pretentious. He simply insisted that Haida culture was incapable of being resuscitated. Nevertheless, others credited him with generating a cultural as well as artistic revival. So, despite Reid's own statement, "I never believed in this so-called renaissance of Northwest Coast Indian culture" (Wyman 1986, 51), no less a luminary than Claude Lévi-Strauss declared that Reid had "tended and revived a flame that was close to dying . . . thanks to Bill Reid, the art of the Indians of the Pacific Coast enters into the world scene; into a dialogue with the whole of mankind" (W. Reid 1974, n.p.). Karen Duffek (1986) suggests that Reid stood between the innovative, competitive individualism of the Western tradition and the highly conventionalized tradition of his Haida forebears.[5]

Wilson Duff admired Reid and wrote passionately about the artistic nature of his MOA carvings:

> The poles of the Haida village in Totem Park have still not received their due recognition as fine modern sculpture. To me, they are the clearest markers of the intersection—Haida art and modern art, both at the same time. In there too, the distinction between "original" and "copy" loses all of its usual force. Bill chose to combine, in varying measure, the roles of performing artist and original composer. None of the poles is a simple copy, although some are repetitions of older compositions, either those salvaged from deserted village sites and stored as bleached and fragile chunks in the shed of Totem Park, or others known only by photograph. I remember the ruins in the rain on Anthony Island in 1957, and Bill's adoration of the spongy remains of Chief Ninstint's frontal pole, and the care with which we saved them. Bill's scaled-down interpretation of that fine pole, of the front of the little mortuary house, was his overture to the concert of modern Haida artistry in Totem Park [quoted in W. Reid 1974].

Thus, counteracting the colonialist lament was a new artist who could actually comprehend the achievements of the past while creating new versions of old masterworks. Reid was an innovative sculptor and a public persona who could place the art firmly in the then-prevalent realm of modernism. But, at least according to Duff, allowing the Indian into the ranks of modernity proved a difficult transition, as "authentic Indian art" was and is still in large measure defined and valued by its formal replication of "tradition."[6]

"DISCOVERING" INDIANS AND THEIR ART

The period known as the Northwest Coast Renaissance, with its reapplication of canonical styles to new artwork and broader public appreciation of the art, paralleled the more widespread "discovery" of the values of Native culture in the United States and Canada. Throughout this history of totem poles, some non-Natives, such as Franz Boas and Governor John Brady, demonstrated support for and kindness to Indians. Far more prevalent among the general population was the opinion that the restriction of Native rights, disdain for Native traditions, and outright discrimination were appropriate modes of colonial relations. But by the 1960s, such attitudes toward Native people were undergoing a qualitative change. While discrimination and intolerance were by no means eradicated, no longer were Indians considered lowly and incapable of determining their own destiny. Recognizing the insidiousness of racism, governments designed policies to enhance the social and economic conditions of people of color.[7] The general sympathy with the oppressed that characterized the 1960s expressed itself in part by invigorated engagement with Native Americans and enthusiasm for their political agenda. Native peoples, by virtue of *being* Indian, possessed a kind of cachet based in large measure on their subjection to colonial victimization and racism by the dominant culture.[8]

By the late 1960s, Northwest Coast art finally began to achieve unprecedented prominence in art museums. Since the beginning of the twentieth century, occasional spurts of activity promoted the "artistry" of Northwest Coast art: the scholarship of Franz Boas, the 1927 exhibit at Canada's National Gallery, and the 1941 Museum of Modern Art show. After those exhibitions closed, however, the aesthetic value of Native art was by and large forgotten. But with the 1950 publication of *Art of the Northwest Coast Indians* by Robert Bruce Inverarity, the first widely available catalogue of images and objects, familiarity with these works began to grow. Buttressed by the enhanced appreciation of all (or most) things "native" in the 1960s, Native art—especially from the Northwest Coast—finally acquired permanent recognition in the world of fine art.[9]

Although the Denver Art Museum had been framing Native American material culture as art since the 1930s, after 1950 several museums presented Northwest Coast art as art. Audrey Hawthorn was invited to install some of MOA's new collection at the Vancouver Art Gallery in 1956; despite the fine art venue, the resulting People of the Potlatch exhibit and catalogue retained an ethnological rather than aesthetic approach. In 1964, the Chicago Art Institute, a venerable institution with outstanding collections of European and (non-Native) American art, hosted Yakutat South: Indian Art of the Northwest Coast, curated by Alan Wardwell, an art historian. A man with an exceptional eye for quality, Wardwell selected many of the finest artwork available in museums in the United States, Canada, and Europe. As distinguished as this exhibit was, it neglected contemporary art. Historical and contemporary works were displayed together in a major exhibit in 1967, when the Vancouver Art Gallery presented Arts of the Raven: Masterworks of the Northwest Coast Indian (discussed in chapter 9). Northwest Coast art also appeared during the 1970s alongside other First Nations artwork in a series of outstanding exhibits at prominent fine art museums such as the Whitney Museum, the Walker Art Center in Minneapolis, and the Nelson-Atkins Museum of Art in Kansas City. With its validation by major museums and its lavish exhibition catalogues, Native art became more desirable to collectors and the price of nineteenth-century works rose dramatically.

Northwest Coast art became a good investment. The first issue of *American Indian Art Magazine*, a journal geared principally toward collectors, was published in 1975. In New York, art dealers George Terasaki, Julius Carlebach, and Merton Simpson, all known for carrying "primitive art," began displaying larger numbers of Native American pieces (Bernstein 1999, 60). Private commercial galleries in Vancouver, Victoria, and Seattle began to specialize in Northwest Coast art, catering to enthusiastic consumers willing to pay significant sums for "traditional" Northwest Coast works. The market soon opened for contemporary works that had theretofore been restricted to souvenirs, such as model poles. Quality contemporary art by Bill Reid and other artists, such as Robert Davidson, became major investments. In an attempt to regulate the quality and price of new work, some Native artists established their own galleries, such as the Arts of the Raven Gallery in Victoria, owned and operated by Kwakwa̱ka̱'wakw carver and printmaker Tony Hunt with his non-Native collaborator and fellow Northwest Coast–style artist, John Livingston. With the nascent public celebration of ongoing Native cultures, and the growing appeal of contemporary Native art, carvers found a rich market for full-size totem poles in both public and private spheres. No longer was their patronage limited to government welfare programs, universities, natural history and anthropology museums, or tourist-minded civic associations. New totem poles sprouted all over the coast, both within First Nations communities and as commercial endeavors.

TRAINING ARTISTS AT HOME AND AT SCHOOL

Some artists learned from established masters in the tradition of apprenticeship. Tony Hunt (fig. 8.14), for example, learned carving at the side of his father, Henry Hunt, and uncle, Mungo Martin. As a young boy in Massett, Robert Davidson watched his father carve wood and his grandfather carve argillite for the tourist market. When he was thirteen, Davidson's father carved one side of a model pole, instructing his son to carve the other side. He later recalled,

> The learning process that an apprentice goes through is to copy another person's style. Because I learned by copying totem poles that Tsinii [his grandfather, Robert Davidson Sr.] or Dad had carved, mine were actually copies of copies—they were third generation carvings. Dad and Tsinii, like other carvers in Massett in the late 1950s and early 1960s, were inspired by fuzzy photographs of argillite carvings in three books written by Marius Barbeau. . . . He helped to inspire some carvers to start carving argillite by coming out with those books (Steltzer and Davidson 1994, 16).

In 1966, the young artist received the Senior Special Grand Prize in the Native art contest sponsored by the education subcommittee of the British Columbia Centennial Committee. Davidson went to high school in Vancouver and became captivated by the art (both Native and non-Native) he encountered in the city's museums. He also met Holm, Duff, and Reid during these years. Reid both guided the young artist to increasingly outstanding work and urged him to learn how to draw in art school. Davidson enrolled in the Vancouver School of Art (now the Emily Carr Institute), and now asserts that Reid's suggestion to receive formal training was "the best advice he ever gave me. Drawing enables me to capture the images that flash through my mind" (Steltzer and Davidson 1994, 20). Bill Reid so respected Davidson's abilities that in 1968 he recommended the young Haida as an instructor at the newly opened Kitanmaax School of Northwest Coast Indian Art at 'Ksan (Shadbolt 1986, 36).

In fact, the Kitanmaax School, in the village of 'Ksan in Hazelton, B.C., has since trained a number of artists. The history of this school is inseparable from the story of the village itself, for 'Ksan emerged from the ongoing efforts in northern British Columbia to preserve the same Gitk'san totem poles that had so impressed the Canadian National Railway, Marius Barbeau, Harlan Smith, and Wilson Duff. In the mid-1960s, many valuable poles remained at risk, so amateur antiquarian Stan Rough of Kitimat and a group of dedicated volunteers continued Duff's efforts to preserve them. Rough successfully lobbied the provincial legislature, which soon appropriated twenty thousand dollars for the Skeena Totem Pole Restoration Society (STPRS), a new organization incorporated from Rough's informal group. The STPRS contacted Wilson Duff, requesting that he act in an advisory capacity to the organization's board of directors.[10]

In the late 1960s, after completing restoration of the Kispiox, Kitwancool, and Kitwanga poles, the STPRS then embarked on an ambitious project: to build a replica Gitk'san village to be named after the word for the Skeena River, 'Ksan. The incentive for this project went beyond heritage conservation. At that time, the town of Hazelton had a mixed population of Gitk'san and non-Gitk'san residents and a pattern of social problems damaging to the whole community. The developers of 'Ksan, both Native and non-Native, believed that good relations could result from the understanding by all residents of the cultural complexity and aesthetic sophistication of Gitk'san culture ('Ksan 1972, 12). Moreover, the Native community could improve its economic condition by selling art, while the entire community would benefit from increased tourism. Travelers on Highway 16, a spectacular road from the interior of British Columbia to the coast, were an untapped resource for economic development. In part funded by money earmarked for 1967 centennial projects, 'Ksan was located on land donated by the Hazelton Indian Band Council, which also agreed to manage its operations.[11] 'Ksan opened in 1970, and eventually included a museum, a café, a gift shop, an ethnographic exhibit on past lifestyles, and the school for Native artists (fig. 10.3).

The Kitanmaax School of Northwest Coast Indian Art claims to have been "the first to offer Northwest Coast Indian art in formal instruction."[12] Early teachers in

10.3. 'Ksan village (Gitk'san), Hazelton, British Columbia, 2006. Courtesy of 'Ksan Historical Village and Museum, DSCN0389.

10.4. Alaska Indian Arts, Inc., Haines, Alaska, 2007. Photograph by Aldona Jonaitis.

this four-year program included Kwakwa̲ka̲'wakw Tony Hunt and Doug Cranmer, Haida Robert Davidson, and non-Natives Bill Holm and Duane Pasco. Poles went up, house façades were painted, and new artists developed a distinctive style that has come to be known as the "'Ksan style." This was, according to Holm, based on the style Pasco was working in at the time (Holm 2003). A clear mark of the traditionalism that accompanied the early years of artistic "revival," the 'Ksan style was frequently criticized for not adhering strictly enough to the canonical style outlined by Holm and promoted by Duff and Reid. Many found it too florid and overtly narrative (especially in silkscreen prints). Moreover, it was at times difficult to distinguish the hands of the individual artists, as the collective style was so dominant. In this sense, the artists of 'Ksan fell into a nether zone between the anonymous masters of the traditional style and the clearly individuated creators of contemporary work. Nevertheless, the houses and poles of 'Ksan remain a major stop on scenic Highway 16 (Dawn 1981, 124–28).

Another institution at which some artists were trained was Alaskan Indian Arts (AIA), Inc., in Haines, Alaska (fig. 10.4). AIA was inspired by the vision of one white man, Carl Heinmiller (whom we met in the earlier section on the world's tallest poles). In 1947, World War II veteran Heinmiller came to Haines and, with the assistance of several friends, purchased Fort Seward. Fascinated with local Native culture, he used his position as leader of the local Boy Scout troop to promote Tlingit traditions. In 1957, the Haines scout organization decided to send a group of boys and two scout leaders to Valley Forge, Pennsylvania, for the National Scout Jamboree. As half his troop was Native, Heinmiller suggested that the boys perform a Tlingit dance at the jamboree. When he first approached the elders for their permission to do this, they resisted, uncomfortable with a white person appropriating their privileges. But Heinmiller persisted, finally convincing the parents and then the grandparents that their children would benefit from reinforced connections to their cultural heritage. Tlingit silversmith and carver Dan Katzeek, along with his wife, Margaret Katzeek, consented to teach songs and dances to the children. The new nonprofit organization, Alaska Youth Inc., that resulted from this not only provided instruction in performance but also initiated a project of carving and regalia-making and built a new tribal house. Under the aegis of Alaska Youth, Inc., the Chilkat Dancers performed for audiences consisting largely of tourists. In 1962 the name of the corporation was changed to Alaska Indian Arts, Inc.

The most senior and well-respected contemporary Tlingit artist, Nathan Jackson, worked at AIA. Born in Tenakee Springs, Alaska, Jackson had spent much time as a teenager watching his uncle carve small totem poles, but did not think of doing art full time until 1962, when he spent time in the hospital with tuberculosis. Part of his therapy included working yellow cedar, which he transformed into small totem poles. Discovering pleasure in carving, Jackson became involved with AIA to learn even more about his traditions. He traveled to see more old-style Tlingit art and learned a great deal from Bill Holm, who did some teaching at AIA in the 1960s. Jackson ultimately became established as a master carver who in turn has influenced an entire generation of outstanding young Alaskan artists. He has carved over fifty poles that are at least ten feet tall. They stand in Alaska as well as in remote places such as Zurich, Bremen, and Japan. Jackson's success, and the carving legacy he helped inspire in younger Alaskan artists, is in part a testament to the reach of projects such as AIA, which started with Native and non-Native negotiation over the reproduction of indigenous visual and performative culture.

WHAT DO YOU DO WITH NON-NATIVE AND NON-NORTHWEST COAST CARVERS?

In the 1960s and 1970s, an object's being considered a Native "artwork" meant that it could stand alone as a visually interesting creation, equal in value to works from the Western artistic tradition. In this context, a totem pole's ethnographic meaning became less relevant than its form. Of course, this art's "nativeness" could never be ignored; in fact, it was essential to its aesthetic, spiritual, and market value. Yet the shift of attention and appreciation to the formal qualities of the art object opened a space for slippage between the material form and the identity of its maker. White artists had been representing poles since the late eighteenth century, and non-Natives had been manufacturing souvenir poles since the early twentieth. But now that a market existed for fine Northwest Coast art, and manuals and catalogues were published outlining the visual vocabulary of classical Northwest styles, an increasing number of non-Native artists (some of them scholars and art historians) began producing high quality, stylistically accurate pieces, many of which were capable of fetching top prices in the gallery and auction markets. This raised the question of the locus of authenticity in the Northwest Coast art object: is it the ethnic identity of the artist or the formal qualities of the object that determines its status as "native art"?[13]

Non-Northwest Coast Native American carvers further challenge the boundaries of authenticated identity. The popularity of totem poles and the portability of souvenirs have led a good many noncoastal Native people to start carving poles, big and small. For example, the Cherokee sell a totem pole with extended wings attached by a nail; this allows the wings to rotate ninety degrees to make the souvenir more portable. Its self-proclaimed authenticity is verified by a seal on the back saying "Hand made by the Cherokee." We have already discussed Frank Ettawageshik's family totem pole business in the Great Lakes Region. The ubiquity of poles on Native reservations beyond the Northwest Coast (such as the Shinnecock on Long Island, the Miccosukee in Florida, and the Crow in Montana) might be a response to tourist expectations that to be "Indian" means having totem poles. All the poles in such contexts that we have seen are made either in a crude imitation of the Northwest Coast style or in no discernable style; all that connects them to totem poles is the depiction of one figure stacked on another.

In contrast to these poles that do not look like Northwest Coast carvings, in the 1960s, Don Lelooska Smith, a carver of Cherokee ancestry, and his family began carving poles and masks of considerable artistic merit on their compound in Ariel, Washington. As discussed above, Lelooska carved one of the several "world's tallest totem poles." Lelooska had gotten to know Kwakwa̱ka̱'wakw chief and politician James Sewid, who hosted the family at potlatches and formally bestowed on them names and dance privileges. The family built a ceremonial house in Ariel and for decades has invited regional school groups and tourists to spend a few hours learning about Northwest Coast art, listening to myths, witnessing dance performances, and buying original carvings (Friday 2003). Does the fact that Lelooska is a descendant of an indigenous (though not Northwest Coast) tribe make his art equally "authentic" as works by Tlingit, Haida, and Kwakwa̱ka̱'wakw carvers? Or, at least, is his art more authentic than that made by carvers with no Indian heritage?

A number of highly talented white carvers have had close relationships with Native people. As part of his analysis of style, Bill Holm created replicas (and eventually original pieces) himself. Through his studies, he became close with many Kwakwa̱ka̱'wakw families (including that of Mungo Martin), was granted ceremonial names and dance privileges, and participated in various potlatches. Duane Pasco started out as a hobbyist trying to make Northwest Coast–style works, and, with the help of Bill Holm, taught himself northern-style carving. He taught at 'Ksan, where the Gitk'san honored him with a *naxnox* (or "spirit being") name. John Livingston grew up in Victoria and became so close with the Hunt family that he was almost considered a sibling; he got involved in their ceremonies and learned to carve in Kwakwa̱ka̱'wakw style. Carl Heinmiller established Alaska Indian Arts, Inc., in Haines, and his son, Lee Heinmiller, still maintains control of that operation, which supports artists, including Tlingit Wayne Price, non–Northwest Coast Alaska Native John Hagen, and non-Native Greg Horner. Steve Brown learned Northwest Coast art with Bill Holm, worked with the Makah Indians in Neah Bay, and lived for many years in southeast Alaska, where he was given the name of a great artist, Kadjisdu.áxch, by the Wrangell Tlingit. Many contemporary artists, including Nathan Jackson, Joe David, Walter Harris, and David Boxley, have expressed considerable debt to these white artists for helping train them.

The involvement of non-Natives in totem pole creation, as well as in the Northwest Coast art world in general, raises difficult questions. One concerns authenticity: what do you do when technical knowledge can be acquired regardless of ethnic affiliation? Another involves economics: what are the consequences to Native people of market competition from whites? Yet another question emerges from history: how much of this activity continues the legacy of appropriation seen throughout this history of the totem pole? These are far from simply academic queries; they are essential to the management of political relations between indigenous and settler societies.[14]

Certain circumstances bring to the fore the problematic nature of white artists doing Northwest Coast art. For instance, in 1976, as part of the celebrations for the United States bicentennial, Sitka National Historic Park sponsored a design competition for a pole. The winner of this competition was the non-Native carver Duane Pasco. His concept was meant to be read as a linear narrative from bottom to top: the image of a Tlingit prior to contact; a raven and eagle, symbolizing the two Tlingit moieties; a white man with a gun and a cross, representing colonial intervention; and, on top, a Tlingit of today who holds two staffs, one richly carved, the other an unfinished piece of wood. The completed carving refers to the rich artistic and cultural heritage of the Tlingit, while the uncarved piece signifies uncertainty about what the future will bring. Today, this pole stands directly in front of Sitka National Historic Park's visitor center, with a plaque explaining its imagery but omitting the non-Native status of its carver. The participation of such non-Natives in the contemporary history of the Northwest Coast totem pole forces us to address the question of how to evaluate carvings by these artists, many of whom have a deep understanding and genuine respect for the genre and its indigenous practitioners.

Many discerning consumers prefer that artists, in order to validate their work, have authentic knowledge about and experience participating in Native ceremonies, as did Hunt and his colleagues. Many commercial galleries today keep extensive biographies on their artists, and many catalogues of Northwest Coast art include auto-biographical statements about artists' participation in their cultural traditions (see, for instance, G. Wyatt 1994 and 1999). Regardless of knowledge about a culture or skill in producing stylistically accurate objects, it is this connection through inheritance to a long-standing artistic tradition that distinguishes a Native from a non-Native artist, who cannot legitimize their work in this fashion.

Some Native artists, such as Tony Hunt, forcefully assert that non-Natives cannot and should not make Native-style art. At a workshop on Native art that coincided with the 2006 Juneau Celebration, several participants objected to the presence of non-Natives among the participants. Others are less critical and acknowledge the debt they have to certain individuals. Nathan Jackson, for example, is agreeable to non-Natives making Northwest Coast art, as long as they are respectful of the culture. "The problem happens when white people don't care about the culture. People who do Northwest Coast art but don't understand its meaning—that's not right" (Jackson 2003). Joe David and Marvin Oliver both worked with Pasco and were influenced by his stylistic innovations. Perhaps the most historically balanced perspective on this issue of non-Native involvement with Northwest Coast art was the response a young carver gave when asked why he was carving with Steve Brown on a canoe project: "It is white people who were largely responsible for the unraveling of our culture. . . . It's only right that some of them help us put it back together!" (Brown, 2003).

POLES WITH WHITES, REVISITED (AND REFIGURED)

In 1986, Pepsi-Cola hired Robert Davidson to carve three poles for its Donald M. Kendall Pepsi Sculpture Gardens in Purchase, New York. Assisted by Reg Davidson and Glen Rabina, he created the largest works of his career so far, *Three Variations of Killer Whale Myths*. In honor of the Americans who had commissioned him, Davidson placed an eagle on the central pole (Davidson and Seltzer 1994, 83–84). Before the poles were shipped east, the Semiahmoo Salish, in whose territory Davidson's studio was, hosted a ceremony to publicly validate the poles. The Davidsons referred with humorous irony to the destination of these poles. Claude Davidson said, "We teach our carving. It was dying out, but now it is coming back. We get orders from far away." Then Robert Davidson declared, "The White man is now interested in our art. At one time White people made us take our totems down" (*Katou News* 1986, 13).

During the early years of tourism, some Tlingit and Haida carvers referred to whites on their totem poles, sometimes positively, sometimes negatively. Davidson's American eagle is a statement of respect. While most contemporary references to non-Natives are respectful, some can be critical. For example, to celebrate the centennial of Alaska in 1980, Nathan Jackson (with Steve Brown) received the commission to carve two poles for Juneau's Centennial Hall. One pole, which depicts Uncle Sam at the top, refers to the early history of the Wooshkeetaan Clan of Angoon, who were bombed in 1882 by the United States Navy. The Wooshkeetaan, through Jackson, wanted the world to see that the U. S. government, in the form of Uncle Sam, had never paid restitution for this massacre. A more positive take on the government appears in Jackson's *Honoring Those Who Give*, a pole raised in 1999 at the Totem Heritage Center in Ketchikan, which celebrates the individuals and groups who contributed to the center's founding and prospering. An eagle is meant to represent several federal government entities: the Smithsonian, the U.S. Forest Service, and the Department of Commerce. A salmon symbolizes the city of Ketchikan; an Alaska flag, the state itself. Interestingly, Jackson chose to depict Native people in twentieth-century garb: a couple at the top wearing suits represent the Alaskan Native Brotherhood and Alaskan Native Sisterhood, while three figures at the base depict the center's instructors and students.

Sometimes a Native carver honors a non-Native individual by clothing him or her in Native garb. An example of this is the 2001 pole at the Pilchuck Glass School in Seattle that celebrates this distinguished institution's thirtieth anniversary and honors its three founders—glass artist Dale Chihuly and supporters John H. Hauberg and Anne Gould Hauberg (see Singletary sidebar, page 198). Tlingit glass artist Preston Singletary, along with several carvers from AIA and elsewhere, created this mixed-media monument. The figure representing Chihuly himself (identifiable by his eye patch) carries the raven that brought light into the world and signifies the creation of Pilchuk. The donors bear Native signifiers of wealth. John Hauberg holds a copper, on which is a cast-glass replica of a Tlingit steel dagger once owned by the Haubergs and repatriated to its original owners, the Daklaweidi Clan; Hauberg also wears a Daklaweidi headdress that indicates his adoption by that clan when he returned the dagger. At the top, Anne Gould Hauberg wears a Chilkat robe and a glass hat with nobility rings. This pole bridges historical conventions and contemporary innovations with an almost postmodern sensibility, as traditional concepts and new materials blend seamlessly. Most poles are made by a master with perhaps several apprentices; here a large team of artists from various ethnicities col-

THE PILCHUCK FOUNDERS TOTEM POLE

BY PRESTON SINGLETARY, TLINGIT ARTIST

In the Spring of 2000 I was visiting with David Svenson in Haines, Alaska, when he mentioned that the Pilchuck Glass School should have a totem pole in honor of the founders. I met David at the school in 1986, and he had noticed my interest in doing NW coast designs in glass and encouraged me to pursue my research. David had been affiliated with Alaskan Indian Arts in Haines for fifteen years, which has been instrumental in continuing Tlingit carving traditions. David had shifted his focus from wood carving to glass and neon, and had worked previously with AIA on incorporating a glass casting in a totem pole.

Pilchuck is an international glass school founded by John Hauberg, Anne Gould Hauberg, and Dale Chihuly, located in Stanwood, Washington. The school's mission has always been finding new ways to showcase the material of glass. We thought that the school might like to expand on the theme of glass castings inlaid in the pole, and we would backlight them with neon. The school was going into its thirtieth year, and we thought that they might be ready to commemorate the event with a tribute to the founders.

John Hauberg was a passionate Northwest coast Native art collector. He had been adopted by a family in Angoon, Alaska, for repatriating a ceremonial dagger to them, and given a Tlingit name. We asked permission from the family to carve a replica that could be cast in glass and used as an element for the pole. John and Anne Hauberg had donated the tree farm that Pilchuck is situated on, and John was the heir to Weyerhauser, a timber company in Washington State. For these reasons, a cedar pole with glass inlays on the campus seemed like a symbolic monument to the founders of the school.

The idea was quickly supported by the board. My close connection with the school and the momentum I had with my own art made me feel that I was in the perfect position to drive this project. I worked with Pike Powers, the artistic director of the school, to put together a class that David and I would teach, where the students would assist and witness the finishing touches on the pole. In the winter of 2000, the carving team in Haines (including John Hagen, David Svenson, Greg Horner, Clifford Thomas, Daisuke Nakajima, and Wayne Price) started the production of the pole. They would work on it all winter, and in the summer of 2001 it was shipped to the campus. The pole was set up outside of the glass studio and the carving team put the finishing details on it. As we as a class produced the castings, the carvers incorporated them into the pole.

We had asked Steve Brown, an artist and former curator of the Seattle Art Museum, to make the dagger. Marvin Oliver and Joe David, who were close with John Hauberg as well, were asked to make carvings that could be cast and inlaid into the pole. Lee Heinmiller, the director of AIA, suggested that I make a large blown-glass rain hat for the pole, and that was produced with the help of Elio Quarisa, an Italian master glass-blower who was also teaching during the session we were there.

The class of ten students included six people of Native decent, two of whom had never worked with hot glass before. One of the students, Clarissa Hudson, a Tlingit Chilkat weaver, was asked to design the blanket that would adorn the top figure on the pole. Shaun Peterson, a Salish carver, helped with the carving details, and many of the other people attending the session helped in various ways, including the final painting of the pole, which was completed in twelve hours.

Joe David was also in attendance. Joe had become a mentor to me just the previous year, when he adopted me and shared his name with me. He helped the carving team with the finishing details and he also conducted some sweat ceremonies for us to prepare ourselves and commemorate the event. We asked the local Swinomish, whose ancestral lands Pilchuck is situated on, to attend and welcome the pole to their lands. The Tulalip were invited as well. Lee Heinmiller and his wife, Judy, came down with elders from the village of Klukwan to help with the raising of the pole.

On the day of installation, the fog rolled in and the whole installation site was alive with the spirit of what we were going to do. A red-tailed hawk circled the site, and

10.5. Preston Singletary (Tlingit), with team that worked in both Haines, Alaska, and Stanwood, Washington, Pilchuk Founders Totem Pole, 2001.

the fog dissipated. The deer were alert to our actions, and the elders spoke in Tlingit, and then the drums started. The whole school took part in lifting the pole to the installation spot. A lot of speeches were made, and we prepared ourselves to lift up the pole. Once erected, David and I climbed up a ladder and placed the glass hat on top of the twenty-foot pole. A button blanket was placed on my back, and I had my first dance around a newly raised totem pole.

For some it was the first experience with hot glass; for me it was a rite of passage; for some it was a vision coming to pass; and for others it was a once-in-a-lifetime experience. After the installation, we feasted on salmon and other traditional food, and then distributed gifts to all the people who witnessed the event. As the sun started to set, the neon shimmered like the northern lights or the abalone inlays in the carvings. It was a great day.

laborated from the start. Tlingits Singletary and Wayne Price, Yupik John Hagen, Salish/Pueblo Marvin Oliver, Nuu-chah-nulth Joe David, and non-Natives Dave Svenson, Greg Horner, and Steve Brown all contributed to this project.

TOTEM POLES IN THE ART WORLD(S)

Totem poles sell, and they sell their sellers. That is, as poles spread around the world through markets driven by tourism, government and museum patronage, and/or fine arts, they also advertise the location and ethnic identity of their makers, buyers, and brokers. As one would expect in the Internet age, Web sites exist that offer original poles to global markets. A few individual artists have their own Web sites, while many commercial galleries illustrate their wares on the Net. The commercial AIA, where both Native and non-Native carvers have worked since 1957, has produced over seventy totem poles ranging in size from 5 to 132 feet, which have made their way to locations in the United States, Japan, China, Korea, Canada, Germany, and South America. On its Web site, AIA offers the opportunity to order poles:

> Large totems (over 5') are $2500.00 per foot for the carved portion (1'-2' base, painting, and oil/wax finish is included in this price). Medium totems (under 5') are $1500.00-$2000.00 per foot for the carved portion. The price depends on the detail of the totem and any additional embellishments. One quarter of the purchase price is required when carving begins, 50% due when the totem is half finished, and the balance due upon completion. The customer is responsible for freight and crate charges.[15]

The consumer specifies the size of the pole and its imagery, and sometimes receives a unique, personalized artwork. In 1994, Tlingit Wayne Price carved a pole for a gardener who collects Delft china. The artist encircled the base with a row of daisies and covered the whale's concave blowhole with a beautifully painted blue-and-white floral design. The artist integrated non-Native images into his creation, which, exhibited by its purchaser as art, draws from an aboriginal tradition of presenting visual images that identify the owner. The line between "traditional" artifact and "contemporary" artwork is obscured.

In 1996, the Legacy Gallery in Seattle sent out a large postcard with a photo of Kasaan accompanied by the words, "The first exhibit solely of contemporary Northwest Coast totem poles since this village was young." This was an invitation to a new exhibit, Monuments in Cedar: Totem Poles of the Northwest Coast, which exhibited and sold six- to twelve-foot poles from various coastal bands. The press release made it clear that poles had a place in contemporary private collections: "As with all sculptures of consequence, this display among other things should demonstrate the difference between size and *scale* while remaining true to forms which are devotedly non-negotiable, and suggests a viable future for totem poles (pointedly *not* maquettes, but rather legitimate, fully resolved pieces) placed in settings other than commodious institutional buildings" (Legacy Gallery 1996). The artists included Wayne Price and Rick Beasley (Tlingit), David Boxley (Tsimshian), Don Yeomans (Haida), Calvin Hunt and Tom Hunt (Kwakwa̲ka̲'wakw), Art Thompson and Tim Paul (Nuu-chah-nulth), Andy Wilbur (Skokomish Salish), and one non-Native, John Livingston.[16]

The works ranged from exquisite aesthetic statements, such as Yeomans's pole carved from a near-perfect piece of old cedar, its graceful and dramatic carving complemented by the grain of the wood, to the highly meaningful and symbolically rich expressions of Wilbur's Salish tradition. The artists at the opening also presented themselves in different ways. Andy Wilbur explained that he started working in northern styles but has in recent years turned to his own southern tradition, using his grandfather Henry Allen's stories as inspirations and working in a self-taught Salish style. Tim Paul insisted that Nuu-chah-nulth poles were ancient, and that his pole was a continuation of a long precontact tradition. Wayne Price explained, "Poles are our books. I have done many poles with Duk-toolth [a Tlingit hero]. I just wrote another on the same idea."

David Boxley asserted, "We are like vessels that the culture rides in . . . . The name of my pole is 'Culture Bearer.' That's what I am, a culture bearer."

This exhibition represented in microcosm the full diversity of contemporary pole carving. The Hunts were proud of their unbroken tradition of carving that continued throughout the twentieth century when other groups had supposedly lost theirs. Other artists in the group had learned the "rediscovered" canons from masters, books, and museum collections. Some poles were primarily presented as works of art, others as expressions of deeply held cultural traditions; all maintained some combination of both interpretive frames. Some depicted often-retold stories in the public domain, others illustrated images their carvers had inherited rights to. Most were by Native artists, and all were made for sale, most likely to non-Native buyers. The long legacy of melding tradition and commodity continues, contributing to the economic success of Native carvers who would have been unable to survive on their art alone four decades earlier.

While the market for such carvings tends to privilege their traditionality—in formal style, materials, and, to a large extent, content—some Northwest Coast artists choose to work in more contemporary artistic milieus by examining totem poles in the context of their own "nontraditional" artistic concerns. Many have been trained at art school and have chosen to work in contemporary media such as easel painting, mixed media sculpture, and installation.

As she describes in her sidebar (page 82), Kwakwaka'wakw artist Mary Anne Barkhouse transformed her great grandfather Charlie James's famous poles by casting them in salt, a material that is used as a preservative for food but is also highly corrosive, and a potent metaphor for both tears and memory. Her sculptural installation, *Reservoir,* became part of her exploration of her own genealogy as well as the cultural legacy of representing and preserving First Nations' art in museums.

Brian Jungen is a Dunne-Za (non-Northwest Coast Native from northern British Columbia) and Swiss Canadian artist known for his interrogation of specific materials and mass cultural representations. He appropriates popular non-Native misrepresentations of Northwest Coast art to suggest the various stages at which visual imagery can mediate colonial relationships. For his Totems exhibit, held at the Charles Scott Gallery, Vancouver, in 2000, Jungen created an installation of wall murals in which he scaled up cartoon images depicting stereotypical Northwest Coast Native imagery that he had elicited from Vancouver pedestrians; foremost among them were winged totem poles (fig. 10.6). Building on his previous art world success with Northwest Coast-esque masks fashioned out of Nike running shoes, Jungen has recently created a series of totem poles fabricated from disassembled golf bags (fig. 10.7). These sculptures reference both the iconicity of sporting equipment logos and the ongoing land disputes between First Nations and developers eager to create golf courses (or highways or strip malls).

An important predecessor to Jungen, noncoastal First Nations artist Mike MacDonald, of Mi'qmak, Beothuk, and Scottish descent, early on recognized the sculptural potential of video and the refreshed emphasis that new media can bring to well-established artistic and advocacy goals. In *Electronic Totem* (1987), five vertically stacked video screens play continuous loops, each about nineteen minutes long, consisting of the

10.6. Brian Jungen (Dunne-Za and Swiss Canadian), *Totems 1,* 2000. Wall murals. Photograph by Linda Chinfen. Courtesy of Charles H. Scott Gallery, Vancouver, British Columbia.

10.7. Brian Jungen, installation view, Catriona Jeffries Gallery, 2007. Works from left to right: *1970* (2007); *2000* (2007); *1960* (2007); *2010* (2007); *1980* (2007). Golf bags, cardboard tubes; dimensions variable. Photograph by Scott Massey. Courtesy of Catriona Jeffries Gallery, Vancouver, British Columbia.

testimony of elders submitted as evidence in support of the Gitk'san Wet'suwet'en land claim in northern British Columbia. As befits an oral tradition, claim testimony is made performatively; on the sculpture's screens, the elders are seen in their traditional territory fishing, gathering berries, singing, and drumming—enacting their cultural persistence through the flickering reiteration that animates the images on this pole. *Electronic Totem*, with its multiple images in vertical relationship, updates the formal and communicative essentials of the totem pole as recording device and proprietary claim.[17]

Videos and totem poles come together as well in the work of Tlingit Nicholas Galanin. Galanin uses art to address how books and museum exhibits fictitiously represent Native people by denying them their ongoing history: "People write about culture and then go into wormholes of history, and don't really look at what's happening now" (Galanin 2006). For his 2006 MFA in indigenous visual arts at Massey University, New Zealand, he created an installation, What Have We Become? In addition to masks of individuals and supernatural beings made of pages from books, such as Frederica de Laguna's *Under Mount Saint Elias* and the Bible is a video entitled *Talking Totem Poles*. Unexpectedly, the video shows no carved monuments at all, just a bored and boring person with a dry voice reading from a 1970s book on totem poles. Instead of any reference to the vitality of totem poles in the contemporary world or discussion of the multifaceted importance of historic poles to real people, the narrator embraces the text as the "truth" about these carvings. Galanin criticizes how in many cases people—both non-Native and Native—accept that truth from books that appear to dictate the nature of Native culture (Jonaitis 2008).

NEO TOTEM BY LAWRENCE PAUL YUXWELUPTUN

BY CHARLOTTE TOWNSEND-GAULT, ART HISTORIAN

A vertical pileup of gaudy, empty elements, *Neo Totem* seems to be a pastiche of the vertical multiplicity of messages that makes totem poles what they are. And at first glance it might look like a one-idea painting, an eye-catching declaration that the meaningful has become meaningless. Yet, like most totem poles, it turns out to be an abstraction of many meanings.

Yuxweluptun, a contemporary artist of Coast Salish and Okanagan ancestry, is well known as a politically engaged critic of the consequences of the colonial oppression of Native people. His canvases are typically large scale, vivid, neo-surrealist, moral narratives of what has gone wrong with the human relationship with the earth, and why; among them, *Throwing Their Culture Away* (1988), *Red Man Watching White Man Trying to Fix Hole in Sky* (1990), and *Scorched Earth Policy: Clear-cut Logging on Native Sovereign Lands, Shaman Coming to Fix* (1991) have been widely reproduced.

Yuxweluptun trades in the allure of the visual spectacle, a technique by which the older versions of the cultures of the fabled Northwest Coast awed their social inferiors, scared their enemies, humiliated their rivals, and incited in newcomers to the land a potent mix of desires to possess and dispossess. The allure is intensified by Yuxweluptun's dexterity with Western art history's modes, and his awareness of the modernist search for pure, nonreferential abstraction, which turns out again and again to have precedents in indigenous cultural forms—ovoids, for example. *Neo Totem* is part of an ongoing, parallel series of paintings dealing with what he terms "Ovoidism." Parodying the "isms" of modern art, Ovoidism critiques the formal analysis of Northwest Coast Native art, an analysis which revealed the "ovoid" as an element of a consistent formal language, but inadvertently fixed the art as a static, dead style, making it, in Yuxweluptun's view, both a travesty of tradition and a restriction on contemporary Native artists. Ovoidism also probes the non-Native fascination with a mythological past and a distorted mythical present. Through a complex maneuver his paintings of voided ovoids declare

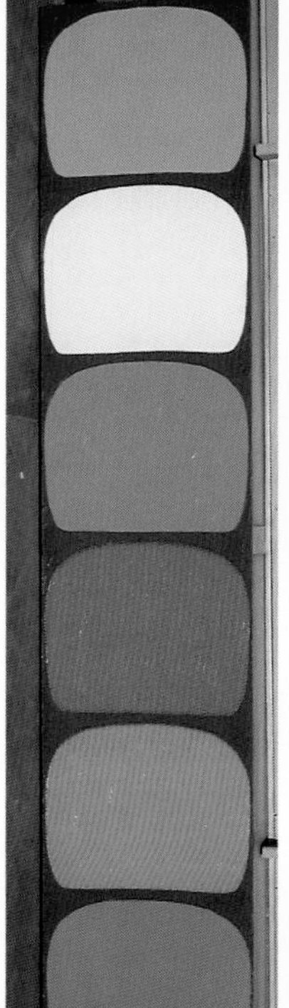

10.8. Lawrence Paul Yuxweluptun (Cowichan-Okanagan), *Neo Totem*, 2001. Acrylic on canvas. 68" x 32." Photograph courtesy of the artist.

both that "mythology is dead" and, at the same time, block access to it—Salish cosmology being not dead at all but in need of protection. In its mix of anger, despair, and active protectionism, Ovoidism reveals the tensions between demonstrating the vibrant adaptability of Native culture and fearing that it is in danger.

Whether *Neo Totem* works as an abstract painting or is merely blank is at the heart of the matter. If, on the other hand, it is taken up for its distasteful kitschiness, *Neo Totem* may be saying something about the lower register of totem pole variants, that dwarfish mob arranged in phalanxes by height and price in many a souvenir emporium. For they too may be deceptive. Who can be sure that they do not meet needs beyond the profit motive? In one account they are travesties of the originals, polluted by commerce. In another, they play their own role in the public imaginary, as this painting tries to do, a disturbing schizophrenia between desire for "the Native" and disdain.

Far from being quick nihilism, *Neo Totem* allows for a slow disclosure of the reasons why anyone should pay attention to totem poles. A vertical stack of blank colours probably also suggests traffic lights. Like totem poles they are the kind of symbol whose meaning depends on a social consensus rather than on resemblance. Unless you know what they mean, or do not mean, you are in trouble. If traffic lights run in the wrong sequence, in the wrong colours, if, that is, they are not working properly, then everyone is in danger. The same may be true for totem poles.

One of the most aggressively critical and outspoken regional artists is Coast Salish Lawrence Paul Yuxweluptun, who has become famous for his acerbic paintings and biting performances that comment on the history of colonial relations in British Columbia. Consciously and strategically appropriating both northern design elements and surrealist landscapes and colors, many of his paintings depict denatured landscapes severed by towering, totem-like stacks of human figures. Other works depict poles directly—*Alcoholics on the Reservation* (1988) includes a Native figure contained inside of a beer bottle attached to a totem pole, and *Throwing Their Culture Away* (1988) pictures an automobile atop a pole. All of these artists take advantage of the totem pole's iconic status to comment—from their personal perspective as indigenous artists choosing to work within contemporary art modes, venues, and markets—on the role of Northwest Coast imagery in mediating historical and modern relationships in the not-yet-postcolonial context of Canadian cultural politics.

Totem poles displayed and sold as fine art would have been unthinkable a century ago. That this is now widespread is a testament to Native carvers who kept the practice alive and adapted it to new circumstances, as well as to non-Native scholars and patrons who helped promote widespread public aesthetic appreciation for the work as art. The two groups regularly collaborated in efforts to produce a Northwest Coast art world through training programs, exhibits, books, civic displays, private commissions, and commercial markets. The history of poles-as-art is a history of changing intercultural relations, complicated dynamics of appreciation and appropriation, and shifting criteria for authenticity in Native art as well as culture.

Bill Reid, his predecessor Mungo Martin, and his student Robert Davidson are the three best-known Native cultural "saviors." Each had his own somewhat different mode of participation in cultural revival, and each is celebrated as the "genius" of the so-called renaissance at different moments in time. Basically, each man articulates the relationship between modernity and traditional aboriginality in a unique way; or, it may be more accurate to say, each man had different versions of and values for that changing relationship projected onto him in subsequent decades. The fame of each artist is also connected, in differing degrees, to their involvement with and promotion by non-Natives. In the 1940s and '50s, Mungo Martin was said to have done everything from carving and potlatching to training apprentices in "the old way," turning his back on modernity. He was celebrated as a traditional chief and as the last great totem carver, in large measure because the public was made aware of him through Wilson Duff and others at MOA and the Royal British Columbia Museum. In the 1960s and '70s, Reid attempted to integrate classical Native forms with a modernist sensibility by presenting his works more as contemporary artwork and less as culturally rich signifiers of an ongoing indigenous tradition (despite Duff's comments to the contrary). He was celebrated as a truly modern, universally appreciated artist who could tap into this wealth of cultural vision to infuse his clean (and conservative) artwork with a spirituality lacking, presumably, in much of modern life and modern art. Brought up outside the Haida community, Reid moved easily in the dominant society and its art world. Davidson, the youngest of the three, both attended an art school and trained with Reid, benefiting from two modes of instruction. He functions comfortably in the modern art world, and yet integrates ceremony, community, and cultural meaning into his creations. He was celebrated in the 1980s and '90s as an ethnically authentic practitioner of his culture as well as a highly skilled and refined visual artist.

Unlike Martin, whose Kwakwaka'wakw ancestors and descendents maintained much of their ceremonialism, Davidson has created new versions of Haida ritual, composed new songs, and choreographed new dances—in short, created new cultural contexts for his contemporary "traditional" art works. Such a contemporary fusion of high modernist aesthetic ideals and traditional cultural practice has been accepted by other artists who feel less strictly bound to the past, yet desire to acknowledge their important heritage. Thus, today, in the era of postmodern pluralism and identity politics, Northwest Coast artists adhere to many different models. Some consider themselves primarily fine artists, while others adhere strictly to what they believe are their unique cultural protocols.

New contexts bring new boundaries. The benefits of participation in a global art world feed back to local artists and their diverse communities. Artists can now choose from among various modes and markets, an option not open to most of them fifty years ago. Some firmly believe that only Native people should make Northwest Coast–style art, while others are more flexible. Some believe in invention and innovation, others feel uncomfortable experimenting. First Nations artists and communities are active players in their own struggles for artistic, cultural, and political sovereignty. The possibilities for the contemporary artist and for commercial development are wide-ranging; like their predecessors, contemporary totem poles have become entrenched in numerous modes of exchange. The emergence of a distinct Northwest Coast art world was not the only or final transformation affecting totem poles at the end of the twentieth century, for—as a century earlier—tourism to the coast continues to influence the production and reception of poles, as we shall see in the next chapter.

PART THREE

CURRENT CULTURES OF THE TOTEM POLE

11

BEYOND FAIRS

CONTEMPORARY CULTURAL TOURISM AND ETHNOKITSCH

Kwakwaka'wakw Indians are at home on the sea. . . . They get their food from the sea and they can cover enormous distances in their canoes. Dolphinarium Harderwijk has invited the Kwakwaka'wakw to show us in their own unique way how special the sea is. The legend of Kumuge, the lord of the Undersea World, illustrates the message that there must be harmony between human beings and nature, both above water and below it.

—INTRODUCTION TO THE TOTEM POLES AT THE DOLPHINARIUM OCEAN THEME PARK, HARDERWIJK

In the early twentieth century, travelers to the Northwest Coast lamented the deterioration of once-great cultures. In the early twenty-first century, travelers learn of the vitality of Northwest Coast cultures and the current productivity of Native artists. The dynamism of cultural tourism in today's global ethnic marketplace is more than simply evidence of the failure of total colonial assimilation and the error of the "vanishing races" trope; it is central to First Nations' strategies of visibility and self-determination. Contemporary visitors to museums and cultural centers in British Columbia and Alaska often "encounter" carvers in the process of creating new poles and "discover" that artists (and all Native people) today exist within the contemporary world while maintaining their cultural traditions. Native guides take tourists through Saxman Totem Park in Ketchikan. Haida Watchmen meet those who make their way to the remote site of Ninstints. Kwakwaka'wakw residents of Alert Bay stage dance performances for visitors in the shadow of the world's tallest totem pole. Guidebooks encourage travelers to take advantage of tours led by indigenous people, whose "families have lived for more than 10,000 years on these lands, [and] tell the best stories we've ever heard. There are creation myths, countless stories about Raven and Coyote, and hilarious tales of human error . . . native people know their culture, their art, their land as no one else does" (Halliday and Chehak 1996, ix). This is a far cry from the century-old guidebooks that promoted visits to totem pole villages *despite* the presence of actual Native people.

Like the nineteenth-century travelers contemplating a trip to southeast Alaska, who consulted books by Eliza Scidmore and studied the brochures of steamship companies, contemporary tourists can select from a myriad of guidebooks and tour companies. But of all the possible sources for information on the region, the most immediately and widely accessible are on the Internet. Totem pole aficionados can plan their vacations, chart travel routes, visit museums, and conduct research on these carvings, all while sitting in front of a computer at home. A search using the term "totem poles" yields several different categories of Web sites: commercial galleries that sell them; tourist-related businesses and organizations such as chambers of commerce that promote them; museums that exhibit them; and photographic archives that contain images of them. The Internet has proven the most recent technology for facilitating the now-virtual transportation and transformation of totem poles worldwide. But it is only one node in a continuously expanding network of cultural or ethnotourism, which has material as well as electronic manifestations. As the World Wide Web again threatens to unmoor totem poles from their coastal origins, subjecting them to endless, unmonitored (mis)representation, Native bands are reclaiming control over the local representations of their cultures as tourists come to them.

This chapter examines the convergence of multiple aspects of the current climate of cultural tourism—from digital media and souvenir kitsch to global theme parks and Native-run businesses—and explores the shifting dynamics of appropriation and appreciation in the entangled and contested realms of art, commerce, place, and aboriginality. For over a century, totem poles stood as relics of disappeared civilizations; now they have come to represent for tourists the authenticity of vital, contemporary Native societies.

GLOBAL TOTEMS ON THE WORLD WIDE WEB

The Internet has allowed vast quantities of images, illustrations, and information to be made available virtually instantaneously via technological confluences of commerce, culture, and communication. Commercial sites abound, with information on where to see poles, as well as how to order them. Museums and archives have been energetically placing their photographic collections online, to the great benefit of all. Canada's Digital Collections, which "showcases over 400 web-sites celebrating Canada's history, geography, science, technology and culture," draws on federal institutions, such as the National Library, the National Archives, and the Canadian Museum of Civilization (CMC). The Royal British Columbia Museum provides access on its Web site to its totem pole collection, in "Totem Poles; Glass House." Here, images of poles in the museum's great glass-enclosed totem pole display are accompanied by field photographs of their original locations. Curator Martha Black provides a useful overview of poles. A very large totem pole database is provided by the U.S. Library of Congress, in "American Memory," which contains a gateway to rich primary sources. The specific information on totem poles is located in the "American Indians of the Pacific Northwest" section, which contains 2,300 photographs and 7,700 pages of text drawn from the University of Washington Libraries, the Cheney Cowles Museum/Eastern Washington State Historical Society, and the Museum of History and Industry in Seattle. A search using the term "totem poles" in the winter of 2008 produced 261 images. Much of this information is included on the University of Washington Web site, which also features an illustrated essay on totem poles by Robin Wright and links to various related Web sites.[1]

Geographic destinations for totem pole seekers also offer information on the Internet. Stanley Park, Saxman Park, and Sitka National Historic Park maintain Web sites featuring their poles. The Museum of Anthropology at the University of British Columbia (UBC), long known for its innovative work with First Nations, has ventured into the world of cyberspace. As mentioned earlier, Bill Reid, along with Doug Cranmer, carved several Haida poles on the Museum of Anthropology (MOA) grounds. By the 1990s, one pole had so deteriorated that it had to be brought indoors. Haida master Jim Hart (the present holder of the title "Chief Edenshaw") replaced that pole, which was raised in 2000 with great celebration. The Web site "The Respect to Bill Reid Pole" goes far beyond straightforward text and photographs, although a well-documented timeline is illustrated with information on the Haida, on Bill Reid and his work at MOA, and on the selection and carving of the pole. What provides this site with an entirely new dimension are three video clips of people assembling on pole-raising day, the pole blessing, and the actual raising of the poles. The Internet has the ability to add movement and sound to the virtual totem pole experience. It also has the flexibility to present information through hypermedia—the complex networks of links, nested pages, and cross-references—that challenges straightforward, linear histories (Museum of Anthropology n.d.).

In addition to a Web presence, the Canadian

Museum of Civilization produced its own CD-ROM, *Totem Poles: Myths, Magic and Monumental Art on the Pacific Northwest Coast*, in 1997 (Canadian Museum of Civilization 1997). The animation opens with a mustachioed man bearing a resemblance to the young George Hunt, strolling along a shoreline. He points to an image of the CMC, incongruously standing in a forest, then, farther along, to a stand of totem poles from various nations assembled in front of the Kwakwa̱ka̱'wakw house of Chief Wakas. This guide finally arrives at a clearing where a pole is being carved. After this fanciful introduction, the CD presents extensive information on poles, organized according to ethnic group, museum location, and pole type. The information available on some poles presents the history of acquisition, on others, the "short story" of their meaning. All poles include information on the figures as well as an "index card" with details on the museum catalogue number, collector, year of acquisition, and original village, if known. Extensive field photographs supplement the data on the poles themselves. Considering that this is a straightforward documentation of ethnographic material, the use of the term "magic" in the title is curious; presumably those who titled the CD sought to appeal to prospective purchasers. Once again, connections are forged for non-Native peoples between poles and magic, associations suggesting that the romanticizing of the totem pole remains strong, even in the publication of a research-oriented museum.

Thus far, all the examples we have cited are of a serious nature. One can also find on the Internet more amusing references to poles. By searching the term "totem poles," one can find the previously mentioned "world's largest totem pole" at Ed Galloway's Totem Pole Park in Oklahoma and even join "Friends of the Totem Pole" online (Roadside America n.d.). Then there is eBay, which has transformed the world of collecting art and artifacts. The site frequently hosts the sale of totem poles. At 2:45 Alaska time on February 12, 2009, you could purchase a Haida argillite model pole for $1,000, a Rufus Moody argillite totem pole for $3,000, an eight-foot Thunderbird totem pole "not carved by Native Peoples of the Northwest Coast" (for "full disclosure") for $879, and a jade totem pole on a gold necklace for $70. You could also acquire a bewildering array of totem pole kitsch: a nine-and-a-half- inch-tall wooden pole "nicely and brightly painted, it says 'Chief and Bear' on the back," a skateboard with a totem pole image, a "rare Camp Moosehead 'totem pole' beer tap handle," a pair of clay totem pole salt shakers, an eighteen-inch totem pole lamp, a totem pole quilt pattern kit, a totem pole folding knife, and a copy of the Chevrolet ad ("as trouble-free as a totem pole") illustrated in figure 1.6. The diffusion of totem poles on the Web is today virtually limitless.

TOTEM POLES AND THEME PARKS

World's fairs, and their descendants, theme parks, have made great use of totem poles since they first appeared in public at the Philadelphia Centennial Exposition in 1876. When Vancouver hosted Expo '86, totem poles and totem carving, not surprisingly, took center stage. Two welcome figures by Nuu-chah-nulth Joe David greeted fairgoers, while three Gitk'san poles by Earl Muldoe, Brian Muldoe, and Walter Harris (as well as copies of Nuxalk, Haida, and Gitk'san poles) graced the British Columbia Enterprise Pavilion (*Katou News* 1988a). Tony Hunt and Henry Hunt also demonstrated carving.

The most popular totem pole representation at Expo '86 was not one of these carved poles but instead the set and props of a theatrical illusion in the General Motors pavilion called "Spirit Lodge." Long lines of visitors waited hours to see this nine-minute show created in collaboration with the U'mista Cultural Society in Alert Bay. Although the theme of the show centered on transportation (appropriate for an automobile company), what drew the crowds was the apparent "magic" of the production, in which holographic beings seemed to transform into others, a canoe emerged from the smoke and paddled away, and supernaturals appeared and disappeared.[2] The show was set in a nineteenth-century Kwakwa̱ka̱'wakw bighouse, framed by carved house posts with outstretched wings, in which an actor impersonating an old storyteller (lip-synching a prerecorded narrative) conjured his mythical characters out of the smoke of the central fire pit. As scholar Nick Stanley notes, "The tradition of [Kwakwa̱ka̱'wakw] showmanship, begun at the 1893 Chicago Exposition, continues in a new format with a range of shows" (Stanley 1998, 161). We would only qualify that by saying that while 1893 may have inaugurated an *intercultural* "tradition of showmanship," the Kwakwa̱ka̱'wakw and other Northwest Coast groups have a much longer tradition of producing theatrical, artistic, and ceremonial spectacles at home.

In 1994, a new version of Spirit Lodge, called Mystery Lodge, opened at Knott's Berry Farm, a Los Angeles area theme park. The farm had a history of interest in Native Americans. In its earlier years its depictions of Native Americans presented them as either classic Indian foils to the cowboys or as thoroughly colonized and successfully converted California Native people in the context of Spanish mission history (memorialized at Knott's with a series of miniature models of missions). The park has long made itself available for school fieldtrips (which coauthor Glass was subjected to in grade school) in order to educate California children about the nineteenth-century history of the "Old West." This was primarily a history of resource extraction (the gold rush), settlement, and civilization efforts.[3] In the early 1990s, Knott's embarked on a program of more "sensitive" portrayals of Native Americans. Their first effort was completed in 1992, when the Indian Trails tour opened. It featured presentations on Native cultures from the Northwest Coast, Plains, and Southwest, as well as artist demonstrations and dance performances. The coordinator of Indian Trails, Beverly Manning Mills, was quoted in the *Los Angeles Times* (Slate 1992) explaining the thinking behind this new section: "We're known for being real, [for] bringing an authentic representation of history. . . . [President] Terry Van Gorder had always felt that to really bring our Western theme full circle, we [needed] the essential element of the Native people, which we were missing. We just felt this was the proper time to do it." Despite these claims for authenticity, the entrance to Indian Trails is marked by a twenty-seven-foot-high pole, carved not by Native people but by two Knott's Berry Farm woodworkers (fig. 11.1). Its imagery refers to the settler West—with a gold miner, a covered wagon, and a burro.

11.1 Totem pole at entrance to Indian Trails, Knott's Berry Farm, California, 2001. Photograph by Aaron Glass.

11.2. Tourist souvenir, Dolphinarium, Harderwijk, The Netherlands, 2003. Photograph by Aldona Jonaitis.

The centerpiece of the newer Native attractions at Knott's is Mystery Lodge, which opened in 1994. This attraction was produced by the same team that created Spirit Lodge in Vancouver. President Van Gorder had seen the Vancouver production and wanted a similar show at Knott's. However, because the prevalent ideology of the theme park is "family values," the new production focused on love of family and home. Much like its predecessor, this attraction uses mirrors to depict masked spirit beings dancing, smoke from a fire transforming into different animals, and the narrator disappearing except for his mouth. As the executive vice president of BRC Imagination Arts, the development company that designed and produced Mystery Lodge, said, "It's ancient art meets state-of-the-art" (Woodyard 1994). Again, the theater was built within a Kwakwa̱ka̱'wakw-style bighouse, complete with house frontal painting and carved winged interior posts. For a conservative theme park desiring to improve its representation of Native Americans, Knott's imported a group of safe, picturesque Indians from Canada with whom Americans had no active political relationship (another parallel, perhaps, to the consistent appropriation of British Columbia Natives by U.S. government displays at turn-of-the-last-century expositions).

Responding to Van Gorder's wishes, Mystery Lodge reinforces the importance of family. Its plot revolves around an old man who knows he is about to die. The producer of the show, Bob Rogers, claims that "it's something that's a universal message that happens to come from a Native American culture. . . . As the guy starts thinking over his life, he begins to think about what was really important to him. He wishes he'd spent more time with his kids, [and] that's exactly what our audience is doing" (*Los Angeles Times* 1994). Here, once again, this Northwest Coast icon has been far removed from its original context, emplaced in a colonial history of California and made the vehicle for communicating a conservative message.[4] But does Knott's Berry Farm's use of totem poles and "magic" to convey the park's fundamental messages make much sense? Furthermore, when asked about this production's connection to Kwakwa̱ka̱'wakw self-presentations at their local cultural center, Gloria Cranmer Webster—who was an advisor on the project—responded, "There is a clear distinction that we make: Mystery Lodge is for white people, U'mista is for us. Comparing the two doesn't make a lot of sense" (quoted in Stanley 1998, 164).

Farther afield yet, in Harderwijk, the Netherlands, is a major tourist attraction called the Dolphinarium, a marine theme park built around an artificial lake. Its central attraction is a large saltwater lagoon for dolphins as well as other marine mammals. In addition to the expected sea creatures, Kwakwa̱ka̱'wakw totem poles as well as a Northwest Coast house greet the lagoon visitor. A monumental welcome figure with outstretched arms beckons the visitor into this building, which has three separate Northwest Coast–style façades facing different directions: one depicts K̲umugwe, Lord of the Sea; another the double-headed serpent Sisiutl; and the last a broad frontal face not unlike that on the Mungo Martin house in Victoria. Outside the structure, two tall totem poles face the lagoon (as depicted in this park souvenir; fig. 11.2). After descending the stairs inside, one enters a spacious restaurant with walls of windows offering an underwater view of the animals that populate the lagoon. Along the ledge of these windows are labels with information about undersea creatures in Kwakwa̱ka̱'wakw mythology, such as Killer Whale, "warrior and messenger of Kumuge, the King of the World of the Undersea." A trail surrounding the lagoon is further punctuated by Kwakwa̱ka̱'wakw carvings of single figures.[5]

The story of how these works found their way to the Netherlands begins in 1996, when the Dolphinarium's managers asked the Canadian embassy to recommend a First Nations group who might bring some indigenous culture to the park. They wanted to include an educational component with their exhibits and thought information on a maritime people would be appropriate. At first they had hired a European designer to make derivative designs, and only when a complaint was lodged that this process should be undertaken legitimately did they contact the embassy. Directed to Alert Bay and the U'mista Cultural Society, the team began a collaboration with the community's carvers and advisors. Essential to this endeavor was *authenticity*—other parks had replicas, but the Dolphinarium had to have original, truly Native-made artwork (Smit 2003). Just as the park used real North Sea seawater for the lagoon, it needed carvings from a real Native group. The park wanted to focus on a group with strong connections to both water and nature; their preliminary visit to Vancouver Island clearly demonstrated the Kwakwa̲ka̲'wakw dependence on the sea. The designers were also delighted to discover the large number of Kwakwa̲ka̲'wakw stories and legends about animals of the watery realm; thus, they could use real stories rather than making up tales. And they realized that the damp, cloudy climate of the Northwest Coast greatly resembled their own, adding a further justification for the otherwise rather stretched association.

So a team of carvers in Alert Bay—Bruce Alfred, Stephen Bruce, Vincent Shaughnessy, and Joe Wilson—began their commission: seven figures, each approximately eight feet tall, from the legend of the undersea kingdom; a thirteen-foot carving of K̲umugwe, Chief of the Sea; two seven-foot sea lions; two multifigured totem poles, one thirty feet, the other thirty-five feet tall; and three full-scale house façades. In January of 1997, all of these pieces were shipped to Harderwijk, installed, and celebrated by a delegation of Kwakwa̲ka̲'wakw who performed dances for the public. That spring, the Dutch cast several of the figures from the undersea kingdom in fiberglass to be installed underwater where diners at the restaurant could see them while eating Native-themed food out of Northwest Coast–style bowls. Unfortunately, the water is so murky and the underwater pole so covered in algae that the image of K̲umugwe can barely be seen from the restaurant (fig. 11.3).[6]

11.3. Underwater fiberglass figure of K̲umugwe, king of the undersea world, Dolphinarium, Harderwijk, The Netherlands, 2003. Photograph by Aldona Jonaitis.

Knott's Berry Farm uses Native art to convey the message of family values. At the Dolphinarium, similar art communicates profound respect for the environment and delivers an ecological message. According to the guidebook, "Kwakwaka'wakw Indians are at home on the sea. . . . They get their food from the sea and they can cover enormous distances in their canoes. Dolphinarium Harderwijk has invited the Kwakwa̲ka̲'wakw to show us in their own unique way how special the sea is. *The legend of Kumuge, the lord of the Undersea World, illustrates the message that there must be harmony between human beings and nature, both above water and below it*" (Dolphinarium brochure, n.d. [italics ours]). Stories of K̲umugwe, like so many other Northwest Coast stories, typically involve an ancestor who goes into the undersea kingdom and, by so doing, acquires wealth, status, and the right to portray the undersea spirit. It is *not* a story with an environmentalist message.

Today, the principals who created the Dolphinarium have left, replaced by a new administration less focused on the carvings. That is not surprising, as the vast majority of the hundreds of thousands of visitors a year come not for Kwakwa̲ka̲'wakw art and culture but for the sea mammals. According to the park's education director, Ida Smit, it is a great challenge to interest the public in the carvings, for independent visitors almost always ignore the structures and poles. Only when visitors take a guided tour that includes information on this maritime culture do they become interested. Realizing this, the Dophinarium has accepted that they are unlikely to impart much cultural information to their visitors. A general sense of ecological conservation is deemed a sufficient message for these totem poles and house façades to convey, so far away from their site of origin (Smit 2003).

INFOTAINMENT AT THE CANADIAN MUSEUM OF CIVILIZATION

A historical focus on artifacts alone has left many museums losing in the competition with theme parks for visitation. Until recently, the highest priority for most museums has been education, which has sometimes been realized in an uninspiring fashion. For years, people wandered through galleries containing endless vitrines of mounted animals, displays of ethnography, and art works positioned one after another on white walls, all interpreted by dry information. This setting can stultify even the totem pole. Because of their size, poles usually stand where space allows. Monuments which once lined village shorelines, challenging rivals and impressing visitors, now stand here and there, fully decontexualized.

In 1989, George MacDonald, then director of the Canadian Museum of Civilization, wrote, "World's fairs have stimulated museum development, particularly in exhibition techniques and special events programming. . . . Expo '86 . . . stamped its own mark on the history of international expositions, partly for its widespread use of participatory theatre—indeed, some feel the fair seemed more of a performance than an exhibition" (MacDonald and Alsford 1989, 51–52). He suggested that one contemporary, permanent version of the world's fair, EPCOT Center in Orlando, Florida, could serve as a model for museums that should include environmental and sensory experiences, films, live performances, people movers, food vendors, marketplaces, and original artifacts (MacDonald and Alsford 1989, 53). Although MacDonald comments, "Museums need neither embrace nor outrightly reject the Disney formula for success," he suggests that they can, however, "analyze it, learn from it, and borrow what seems best or most applicable to museums" (MacDonald and Alsford 1989, 55).

MacDonald decided to challenge the traditional museum exhibit of totem poles by employing concepts derived from theme parks. In Gatineau/Hull (the French Canadian city on the Quebec side of the Ottawa River, opposite the Canadian capital of Ottawa), he imagined this museum integrating the presentation of historic poles with a theme-park-inspired setting of replicated historical scenes and interactive, media-intensive displays. MacDonald had been greatly influenced by his teacher, Marshall McLuhan, who believed that new technologies had power to shape human relations and understanding. Assuming that museums were visited less frequently than theme parks because people want entertainment more then education, MacDonald designed an engaging multisensory experience unfettered by distractions such as extensive label copy. The result was the new Canadian Museum of Civilization, which opened in 1989.

The centerpiece of this museum of national culture is the Grand Hall, a row of six new Northwest Coast house façades associated with ten new or restored poles (fig. 11.4). When MacDonald, engaged in preliminary plans for the new building, asked curators which objects in the museum's collections qualified as "world class," the undisputed answer was totem poles. Instead of using the decontextualized artifacts characteristic of most totem pole displays, MacDonald decided to erect the CMC's collection in a reconstructed village with houses dating from between 1880 and 1920. The museum's interpretive plan explained this decision: "It is from this period that the CMC collections come; it is about this period that most of the ethnographies were written; it was in this period that the dilemmas posed by the meeting of the Pacific Coast people and Europeans became acute. . . . To the visitor who brings the twentieth century with him, this village is yesterday" (quoted in Ostrowitz 1999, 51). The buildings in the Grand Hall replicate nineteenth-century Coast Salish, Nuu-chah-nulth, Kwakwa̱ka̱'wakw, Nuxalk, Haida, and Tsimshian houses, most known today only through photographs. The designers wanted the structures to be embedded in a setting that conveyed the special nature of the Northwest Coast environment: "The curved lines of the Grand Hall simulate the shape of sheltered bays and rivers along the Pacific Coast of British Columbia, where traditional Native villages were located. Villages were often built on narrow coastal plains only a few steps from the sea" (Ruddell 1995, 2). To reinforce the sense of place, the hall includes models of a tidal pool and an estuary, polished sections of floor that look wet with seawater, replicas of berry bushes, and piped-in sounds of ravens crying and waves lapping. Behind the village is an enormous scrim upon which is projected a dark, moody forest scene.

11.4. "Grand Hall" poster. Image by Harry Foster, 2004. Photograph © Canadian Museum of Civilization, Gatineau, Quebec, T2004-003.

The Grand Hall collapses time and conflates ethnicity. Each house represents one of six coastal cultures, and the houses merge seamlessly with the older poles from the museum's collections. Carvers and painters from each represented nation had considerable say in selecting the designs and creating the houses, several of which have façade paintings that provide an art historical survey of two-dimensional style—from the spare line drawings of the Salish and the more dynamic and fluid Nuu-chah-nulth images to the increasingly elegant formlines of the Kwakwa̱ka̱'wakw and Tsimshian (Laforet 1992). Tall, thin poles flank the Salish structure. Old poles stand before and next to these houses, as does a new pole by Tim Paul positioned to the side of the Nuu-chah-nulth house. Attached to the façade of the newly built Haida house is a monumental entrance pole purchased by Charles Newcombe in 1901. Nearby are two more poles, one of which stood before Chief Wiah's house in Massett, the other a house post. Three poles, one a simple shaft surmounted by a box and a bird, the others fully carved monuments, stand near the Tsimshian house. A pole from Alert Bay is attached to the Kwakwa̱ka̱'wakw structure based on the Wakas house. On the opposite side of the great room, standing before immense windows looking out onto the Ottawa River and the nation's capital beyond, are still more poles from the CMC's considerable collection.

Some poles stand before replicas of the structures with which they were originally associated, while others have only a generic relationship with the house they accompany. For example, the Haida frontal pole serves as entrance to a six-beam house (one of two types on the Queen Charlottes) that does not represent the particular structure to which the pole was originally attached. The other Haida poles around that same house were not originally found together. This, and other combinations that reconstruct history imaginatively, can be considered problematic. While each house and its associated poles are meant to "stand for" the creations of the entire tribe, each also serves as a unique artwork.[7] As Ostrowitz comments, "The resulting combination of impressive houses in the Grand

Hall village, although derived from an unprecedented blend of Native traditions, has the effect of a plausible if fantastic street scene. Reminders of nature, evocative sound effects, and the ambitious scale of the entire undertaking create a complex environment that functions as a weighty teaching tool" (1999, 79).

The Grand Hall of the CMC has been a great success, having been visited by hundreds of thousands of visitors.[8] In addition to its entertainment and educational functions, this hall represents perhaps the ultimate use of totem poles in the (re)creation of a place that never actually existed. The Grand Hall's message also extends beyond the realm of Northwest Coast ethnology. In French Canadian Gatineau, across the river from English Ottawa, this exhibit joins six entirely different ethnic groups into one unified presentation. Like Knott's Berry Farm—but to very different political ends—the CMC imports the picturesque totem-pole cultures of the Northwest Coast into the heart of the national capital, as the dramatic centerpiece of the national museum. The houses, although of varying architectural styles, have harmonious proportions and work together in the way a housing development of several different yet related homes might work. The message of cultures different yet equal, together creating an integrated entity, extends into the ideology and policy of multicultural Canada. It is indeed fitting that the national museum of human history features an "imagined community" of various Native nations to buttress the equally imagined community of English, French, and other ethnic groups which together constitute Canada.

CONTEMPORARY CULTURAL TOURISM AND ECOTOURISM

One of the fastest-growing sectors of the international tourism market is ecotourism, which focuses primarily on the environment but also often includes some structured experiences with indigenous people. Tour operators often embrace the stereotype of the "ecological Indian," based on the popular assumption that indigenous people are intrinsically both components and custodians of nature. The Campbell River–based and Native-owned and -operated Aboriginal Journeys offers guided ecotours into surrounding Kwakwa̱ka̱'wakw territory and villages, and have a local First Nations dance group that provides customers with a live performance to supplement their wildlife-viewing excursions. Many First Nations–owned tourism operations offer live song and dance presentations or storytelling sessions. Such performances, in the age of multiculturalism and state policies supporting pluralism, are now a critical component of animating ethnic "art" through the demonstration of cultural knowledge, and of authenticating Native people in the public eye. These performances further distinguish Native-run outfits from their non-Native competitors. Moreover, cultural difference is made safe, nonthreatening, and physically comfortable (a hallmark of tourism), as Aboriginal Journeys invites guests to "sit back, relax and enjoy" an indigenous ceremony. This is certainly not what a witness to a potlatch or spirit dancing would be invited to do; instead, obligations would be placed on their attention and memory.

Native business owners, acknowledging the strength of this assumption, often choose to capitalize upon rather than dispel it. For example, Kwakwa̱ka̱'wakw Tom Sewid, on his Aboriginal Orca and Grizzly Bear Adventures with Village Island Tours Web site, reassured his prospective customers that his connection to an environmentally sensitive tradition made him the best possible guide: "Now, I can look and see the many that come to our regions and call themselves guides. Yes, they are guides, but they will never have what we First Nations have. We have a culture and heritage that is directly tied into our surroundings. Food harvest of land and sea ensures our bond with the environment."

Sewid offered a variety of different tours to see wildlife, all of which include learning extensive information about Kwakwa̱ka̱'wakw culture. One could supplement an orca adventure with visiting some Native sites, including Village Island, Sewid's "ancestral home where ancient carved poles and big house structures can still be seen." Sewid's Web site made frequent mention of his knowledge of his culture

11.5. Tourists at Ninstints, Haida Gwaii, 2004. Photograph by Aldona Jonaitis.

and its traditions, as well as of the land and its animals. However, a careful reading of the text made it clear that the tours centered on nature—in particular on the experience of seeing whales, seals, orcas, and grizzlies close up. Indeed, the home page of the Web site had one photograph of Sewid, one of cabins with façades painted with Northwest Coast designs, one of the boat, and five shots of animals. Sewid appeared to recognize that, as attractive as tourists might find traveling with an aboriginal guide, the demand for environmental tourism exceeds that for cultural tourism.[9]

One arena in which cultural and ecological tourisms merge well is on Haida Gwaii, where for years the Haida have managed their historical sites. As Ninstints and other remote villages began to attract increasing numbers of tourists, the Haida assumed responsibility for their care and protection by forming the Haida Watchman Program in 1981. The name and symbol of this program derive from the three human figures (often seen wearing tall hats and perched atop Haida poles) that are said to warn of approaching enemies. At first, volunteers used their own boats to travel to villages such as Skedans, Tanu, and Ninstints, where they camped for the summer, telling visitors of Haida culture and history. Now the program is formal, and two to four watchmen spend their summers (May through September) greeting visitors and explaining Haida traditions, while protecting Tanu, Skedans, Windy Bay, Hot Spring Island, and Ninstints (fig. 11.5).

All of the Haida sites have resident watchmen who supervise visitors, but few Haida actually own the tourist businesses on Haida Gwaii. There was one operation, Gwaii Ecotours and Lodging, that stated on its home page, "Proud to be a 100% owned and operated Aboriginal Business!" But the owners were not Haida; the man is Métis, his wife an adopted daughter of Chief Skedans. Gwaii Ecotours offered "vacation retreat packages for personal, professional, and spiritual growth."[10] These kinds of specialized travel opportunities have become increasingly common along the entire coast as traditional resource industries such as fishing and logging have withered. The operation's multiday camping and paddling adventures, described as spiritual journeys to old Haida village sites and various natural locales, promised that you, the traveler, would: "Reconnect to the earth. . . . Rediscover your relationship with the environment. . . . Reflect on your personal experiences and accomplishments. . . . Renew and move forward." Although there were no special packages for totem pole excursions, the site did provide good images of old villages and mention the poles available for current viewing.

Ninstints today, with its old (read: "authentic") totem poles, is one of the most attractive—and certainly one of the most difficult to reach—tourist destinations on Haida Gwaii. In fact, its remoteness and relative inaccessibility do much to enhance its value as a destination for serious cultural tourists or ecotourists hoping to stray from the beaten path. Archeologist and museum director George MacDonald, in a booklet on the site, refers to Ninstints as one of the three "holiest" experiences in Canada (the other two being the stone *inuksuit* at Eskimo Point, in the Northwest Territories, and Bill Reid's sculpture *Raven and the First Man* at MOA). In MacDonald's view, Canadian religiosity rests solely on the indigenous inhabitants and their material culture. He waxes poetic about Ninstints:

> The struggle between man's fragile efforts to create cultural monuments and nature's inevitable reclamation of those monuments is fascinating to behold. There are but a few places in the world where this struggle between nature and culture is locked in a suspended state, where it is hard to say whether man or nature predominates. Most are in remote jungles and have such magical names as Ankor Wat or Ankor Thom in Cambodia, and Palenque or Chichen Itza, Mayan cities. . . . Ninstints is just this kind of site, although its jungle is of the high-latitude variety (MacDonald 1983a, 1).[11]

MacDonald celebrates Native achievements, comparing Haida work with some of the greatest archeological sites of the world. The intrepid traveler has several options for visiting Ninstints: a sailboat trip, a chartered floatplane or helicopter, or a group kayaking expedition. The Haida make it clear to the companies that arrange the tours as well as to the clients that *they* give permission to visit *their* cultural treasures.

Despite the efforts of First Nations to assert their territorial and cultural sovereignty, the increasing popularity of ecologically oriented tours, some catering to the New Age seeker of spiritual knowledge or communion with nature, perpetuates the stereotypical depictions long typical of the tourist industry. Butterfly Tours is a non-Native-owned operation that brings kayakers to Haida Gwaii.[12] On their Web site, photographs of poles as well as a video draw the prospective tourist to this remote locale. In the video, a paddler floats by a rocky promontory to see a curved beach upon which stand tilted, ancient carvings; the camera pans the scene, then zooms in on the best-preserved pole, lingering on its fine imagery. The slide show has a series of photographs, with captions reading "first view of the totem poles of Sgang Gwaii (Ninstints)," "the ancient Haida village," and, beneath a detail of a pole, "carved over a century ago." Thus the mystique of antiquity and sun-bleached ruins, a vague sense of spirituality, and a presumed oneness with nature—as depicted in florid words and vivid paint by turn-of-the-last-century visitors—is perpetuated today in virtual reality.

ETHNOKITSCH

Another aspect of travel that has not changed—and does not promise to—is the fact that tourists to the coast appreciate returning home with memories of their journey. Sometimes these are photographs, sometimes they are souvenirs—the favorite for Alaska travelers naturally being model totem poles (fig. 11.6). Some of these are handmade by Northwest carvers and have verification of their origin; these can be considered descendants of the early twentieth-century tourist totem poles. But others are made by non-Native people, and many are mass-produced, often overseas. In the early 1900s, Lily Lockwood (1906, 337) complained that Joseph Standley, of Ye Olde Curiosity Shop in Seattle, ordered some of his model poles from Japan.[13] Today, almost any tourist-oriented store in Washington, British

11.6. Alaska totem pole magnet souvenirs, Ketchikan, 2007. Photograph by Aldona Jonaitis.

Columbia, or Alaska confronts the visitor with shelves of totem poles ranging in size from a few inches to over a foot tall, either multicolor or pseudo-argillite black (fig. 11.7). One Alaskan variety is made from a particular local clay that produces a brown and white piebald surface. Some totems wear the often dubious label "native made"; others are manufactured in China and Indonesia. Most share uniformly poor quality in their carving, in their depiction of formline style, and in their proffered interpretations. Some stores offer items with visual fidelity to Northwest Coast motifs, even if in innovative forms or of novel materials. For instance, in Vancouver, a confectionary named Chocolate Arts has created die-cast chocolate totem poles for their window displays and has licensed designs from Robert Davidson for chocolate medallions with Northwest Coast motifs (see Townsend-Gault 1997).

In addition to these models, the totem pole-as-icon appears on a vast array of objects purchased by the souvenir-happy tourist: T-shirts, refrigerator magnets, bumper stickers, toothpick holders, nail clippers, shot glasses, snow globes, beer bottle openers, Christmas tree ornaments, pewter jewelry, and backscratchers. Children can put together totem pole models from cardboard, foam, or plastic. Lego Wild West and Playmobil sets contain totem poles that can be placed by tipis and marauding Indians on horses, thereby blurring the cultural and regional distinctions between Native Americans. In the slightly more pricey category are salt and pepper shakers; cut glass or ceramic liquor decanters; or a teapot, creamer, and sugar bowl set stacked one on top of the other, each bearing a "totem" face. A few years ago it was possible to find small packets of cedar cones marketed as "totem pole seeds" so that one could grow one's own totem pole—no carving required! (see following photo essay).

Amusing as these examples of "ethnokitsch" may be, they raise several relevant issues. The overseas manufacture of Native-looking articles has become a serious global issue, hardly limited to totem pole copies. In virtually every case, this deprives Native artists and communities of an important source of revenue. For example, today replications of Alaska Eskimo ivory carvings are being made in Indonesia and sold alongside the foreign-made wooden totem pole models in tourist stores. These copies sell for far less than the pieces of indigenous manufacture, leading to a reduction in demand for local creations and an increase in imported fakes. This is one of many negative aspects of globalization, one that affects indigenous minorities in economically prosperous lands. Increasingly, indigenous people worldwide have been turning to intellectual and cultural property legislation to help limit the uncontrolled commodification and circulation of their cultural patrimony. It is not always that they are unwilling for such images and objects to travel; it is simply that they insist on having more direct control over and benefit from that process.

What of the items actually made by Native carvers, such as the "made by Alaska Native" poles? Or those designs that the original artist has authorized manufacturers to replicate, in effect legitimizing affordable "kitsch" items as ethnic expressions? For example, Garfinkel Publications, based in Vancouver, licenses designs from practicing artists and applies them to all kinds of inexpensive items—clothing, note cards, mouse pads, travel mugs, temporary tattoos—that are always accompanied by the artist's name and tribal affiliation and, often, information about the image. In such cases, the circulation of an image is in part controlled by a Native person, contributing (if in a

CONTEMPORARY TOTEM POLE KITSCH

Barcelona store window. Photograph by Aaron Glass.

Totem pole model kit. Aaron Glass collection.
Photograph by Aaron Glass.

Totem pole models. Aldona Jonaitis collection.
Photograph by Aaron Glass.

Totem pole Frisbee. Aldona Jonaitis collection.
Photograph by Aldona Jonaitis.

Totem pole salt and pepper shakers made in Japan. Aldona Jonaitis collection. Photograph by Aldona Jonaitis.

Totem pole magnet kit. Aaron Glass collection. Photograph by Aaron Glass.

Totem pole teapot, teacup, and tea. Aldona Jonaitis collection. Photograph by Aldona Jonaitis.

Totem pole model kit. Aldona Jonaitis collection. Photograph by Aldona Jonaitis.

Totem pole 3-D puzzle. Aaron Glass collection. Photograph by Aaron Glass.

11.7. Tourist art display, Ketchikan, Alaska, 2007. Photograph by Aldona Jonaitis.

minor or subtle fashion) to his or her artistic representation. Indeed, some of these seemingly trivializing depictions—like earlier Native-made tourist art—might be interpreted as signifiers of Native culture that deny public access to indigenous knowledge. In other words, the message by the creator of such kitsch might be: "These visual representations embody aspects of our complex and deep history, but, because of the debased medium for this message, you—ignorant outsider and non-Native tourist—believe it to be meaningless." It is in a sense this foreclosure on cultural communication that facilitates the mass distribution of images otherwise related to restricted privileges.

One might consider the production of such kitsch items as being somewhat liberating for the indigenous artist, who is otherwise bound by local, community protocol or by art world standards regarding visual representation; there is no pressure to "authenticate" a Northwest Coast mouse pad design by presenting it in a ceremony (and thus validating its cultural importance within the group) so that it will fetch a higher market value. By strategically withholding a measure of detailed cultural content while insisting on a significant degree of control over manufacturing, Native artists and communities can better regulate the spread of their visual culture. Thus, despite their maligned appearance by fine arts standards, some of these tourist souvenirs might retain a kind of political and semiotic potential to complicate the simple binary oppositions of authentic/fake, appropriate/appropriated, meaningful/commodified, Native/non-Native, traditional/modern. With their overtly commercial status, often-ephemeral material condition, and ambiguous aesthetic value, such ethnokitsch retains a certain power to mediate intercultural relations by remaining resistant to academic, art world, and government appropriations.[14]

TOURISM AS EXPERIENCE AND IDEOLOGY

Anthropologist Johannes Fabian astutely commented that "the Other is never simply given, never just found or encountered, but made" (1983, 208). The totem pole as an indicator of indigenous social standing is constructed by Native people, but the same monument, as the subject of a touristic gaze, is also fabricated—by guidebooks, travel narratives, and advertisements. From the early days of Northwest Coast travel, it was believed that interaction with Native people could offer an experience of life as it was led in earlier, easier times. While early tourists found living Native people hopelessly acculturated and dismissed them as uninteresting, they often remained fascinated by totem poles, which became signifiers of ancient tradition, embodiments of authentic Nativeness, and compelling presentations of the mythic world that could render invisible the often dismal circumstances of their creators. Scidmore, for example, construed Howkan as a magical locale based on the presence of its poles, not its people. For well over a century, tourist literature has been replete with expressions of the totem pole's antiquity and connection to nature; the more romanticizing passages project onto the pole an aura that transforms it from the ordinary into the extraordinary.[15]

It would be wrong to think of any kind of tourism, however sensitive or Native-controlled, as providing unmediated experiences with First Nations people and their totem poles (MacCannell 1992, 1). In every case, the belief system implicit in guidebooks and advertisements and expressed by tour leaders frames the visitor experience, highlighting certain features and omitting others. Touristic framing of coastal Native culture was evident at the end of the nineteenth century, as it is today. Steamship line brochures concentrated on the positive—even "cultured"—aspects of Native life, such as art and dance. For example, Alaska Native residents in the Pacific Coast Steamship Company's 1891 publication *All about Alaska* were said to be of higher quality than other North American Indians, and "naturally bright and intelligent people" (Pacific Coast Steamship Co. 1891). Today, tourist information on Native people is presented more sensitively. An index of this major transition, *Traveler's Guide to Aboriginal B.C.* not only emphasizes First Nations tours, galleries, events, and cultural centers but also offers "A protocol for visiting First Nations territories and communities" (Coull 1996, 5). This guidebook provides information on the specific rules of behavior within different First Nations groups so that intercultural encounters can be better informed and more mutually rewarding.

The August 1997 edition of *Alaska Airlines Magazine* carried the article "Out of the Woods," which provided a balanced, intelligent, and informative overview of poles in both British Columbia and Alaska, highlighting not just historic poles but contemporary totem pole carvers as well (Schuesser 1997). The essay explains the different styles of pole carving; identifies several common images; discusses their social meaning; addresses

11.8. Thunderbird Park, Victoria, 2003. Photograph by Aldona Jonaitis.

the nineteenth-century events—epidemics, missionization, and colonization—which affected pole carving; describes the efforts to collect, preserve, and replicate poles; and identifies the locations where one can see poles. It ends optimistically:

> Newly carved and freshly painted, totem poles around Alaska and the Pacific Northwest now share the spotlight with their predecessors, monoliths that have been standing for more than 60 years. They represent a juxtaposition of past and present—a history steeped in tradition yet complemented by new styles, stories and inspirations. And, like any art, totem pole carving will continue to evolve in the hands of a new generation. Says UBC's [Marjorie] Halpin, "This art is still very much alive" (Schuesser 1997, 63).

The people too are still very much alive. How different from the earlier laments of visitors to the Northwest Coast.

12

FAMILY TREES AND TRIBAL TREATIES

ON THE POLITICS OF POLES

The old totem pole stood at the old Kitlope village site of Misk'usa. This place has great significance to the Haisla people as it is at the very entrance to the Kitlope Valley—the world's largest unlogged coastal temperate rainforest ecosystem and ancestral homeland of the Xenaksiala. . . . While the protection of the Kitlope's 800,000 acres of wild forest lands, rivers, mountains and lakes is secure, the Haisla believe the Kitlope will never be truly protected until the missing pole is returned. . . . It is the desire [of the Haisla Nation] to provide . . . leadership with the repatriation of one of the most important cultural artifacts to be taken from the Northwest Coast last century. This will be much more than the return of a totem pole. It will be a cultural and educational exchange of extraordinary value, something that could set new standards for how museums deal with repatriation issues, and be yet another step toward the rebuilding of Northwest Coast cultures and communities in British Columbia. (Haisla Culture Web site)

Totem poles have always expressed political relations. When they stand before the houses of the elite, they articulate a local politics of prestige. Memorial or mortuary poles celebrate the power of the dead and facilitate the transmission of that power to their heirs. New poles mark marriage unions and the transference of crests and ceremonial prerogatives. Some Alaskan poles, discussed earlier, have depicted Europeans in a negotiation of dynamic and shifting colonial relations. The poles the Kwakwa̱ka̱'wakw erected during the first decade of the twentieth century served as declarations of chiefly power as well as collective expressions of resistance to the potlatch prohibition.

During the twentieth century, numerous poles were raised to convey multidimensional and intercultural political statements. One of the first was the Thunderbird Dynasty Pole, carved by Squamish Chief Mathias Joe (also known as Mathias Joe Capilano, after the reserve on which he lived) and raised in 1936 at Prospect Point in Stanley Park (fig. 12.1; see Green 1939 and Hawker 2003, 100). Unlike the other three poles raised during Vancouver's Golden Jubilee (see chapter 5), Capilano's pole—as it has been known—had not been transported south from a community where it had served social and political functions, but instead was carved in Vancouver expressly to stand in Stanley Park. Prior to that time, many Salish people had carved interior house posts in their characteristic minimalist style, but they had erected no tall, multifigured "totem poles" such as the Prospect Point carving. While the images on this carving depicted beings in a Salish creation story—Thunderbird, with his wife, son, and daughter, and a sea monster—Joe's model was a Kwakwa̱ka̱'wakw-style pole with assertively carved and vividly painted images surmounted by an open-winged Thunderbird (not unlike the Charlie James house posts). Purportedly, this pole commemorates the Squamish's first encounter with Captain George Vancouver on June 13, 1792. S.W.A. Gunn, author of a 1965 booklet on the poles of Stanley Park, comments that this pole, created by local Indians, "appropriately constitutes one of the most memorable landmarks of the City of Vancouver" and, with its

Thunderbird imagery communicating a story of the Creation, "commemorates the meeting of the Indians and the White man [which] opened up an entirely new world for both" (Gunn 1965, 22–23).

In reality, Capilano's pole represents the first recorded large-scale Salish totem pole and one of the first urban poles to embody an explicitly political statement, for what appears to be a celebration of a historic event was a subtle assertion of Squamish rights to their territory. The Squamish had been exceptionally active in their attempts to obtain sovereignty over their land; in 1906, a delegation of Salish chiefs had made an unsuccessful trip to London to request that King Edward II accept their sovereignty. In 1912, the Coast Salish, along with the Nisga'a, Haida, and Interior Salish, joined together to form the Allied Tribes of British Columbia to contest the McKenna-McBride commission findings, delaying its ratification for several years. Squamish chief Andrew Paul, along with Haida Peter Kelly, labored especially diligently toward this end, but ultimately to no avail. In 1927, the Allied Tribes disbanded, in part due to their failure to achieve their goals, and in part due to a new section of the Indian Act making it illegal to solicit funds to pursue land claims (Kew 1990, 166). In the context of these continual rebuffs to Native land claims, the 1936 Capilano pole served as a quiet, legal mechanism to proclaim Squamish rights to the Vancouver region using a recognizable northern-style marker. This political statement likely went over the heads of most observers, who were content with the pole's stated purpose as a monument to colonial contact.[1]

Fast-forward fifty years. In 1987, the Kitsumkalum Band commissioned Frieda Diesing, a 'Ksan alumna, to carve a pole for a Native roadside gift shop.[2] Instead of designing just one pole, Diesing decided to design three: two for the Native community, and one for the nearby predominantly non-Native town of Terrace. For Kitsumkalum, Diesing, assisted by a team of women carvers (Dorothy Horner, Myrtle Laidlaw, and Sandra Westley) as well as two younger men (Norman Horner and Norman Guno), made one pole as a replica of a monument lost a century earlier in a flood and another

12.1. Chief Mathias Joe Capilano (Salish) pole, Stanley Park, 1936. City of Vancouver Archives, P192.1N103.1.

pole that depicted crests of the village's families. These poles, one symbolizing the past and the other the community's future, were the first to be erected in this Tsimshian community in 150 years. The third pole, which Diesing carved with assistance from both Horners and Guno, depicts the personal crests of the carvers and was donated to the city to celebrate Terrace's Diamond Jubilee. Diesing hoped that this pole would help forge a spirit of goodwill, friendship, and mutual respect between the sometimes antagonistic Natives and non-Natives of the region (Diesing 1989).

Ceremonies associated with these pole raisings addressed two distinct but intimately interconnected issues: the resurgence of cultural pride based in part on awareness of Native traditions, and the recognition of and respect for what historian Cole Harris terms the "politics of difference . . . policies that respect and support Native distinctiveness" (2002, 301).[3] The Tsimshian pole-raising ceremony, called *Su-Sit' Aatk*, meaning "a new beginning," was a community-wide potlatch feast attended by over two thousand Native and non-Native people, by far the community's largest ceremony in recent history.[4] At the raising, Victor Reese declared that a recognition of "another culture, our culture" be made, and he had the band play "O Canada," thus acknowledging the multiple national affiliations that often characterize Native peoples living in settler societies (McDonald 1990).

Like many Native communities, Kitsumkalum has a Web site that covers a variety of topics, including the tribe's history, natural resources, social programs, and treaty information. Along with other communities, the band is negotiating with the federal and provincial government for land, resources, political autonomy, and cultural preservation and enhancement. The Kitsumkalum home page integrates the totem pole raisings in 1987 with the efforts to finally resolve the conflicts that have plagued colonial relationships in British Columbia since the mid-nineteenth century:

> Since the Su-sit' Aatk ceremonies, Kitsumkalum is in the process of the eventual revival of its Tsimshian culture practices. Kitsumkalum plans to make advancements toward the resolution of the treaty for Kitsumkalum and the Tsimshian Nation for future generations. Kitsumkalum is also seeking out an official form of self-government in the near future. Indian reservations really restrict First Nations from growing to the potential that we have in our own ways, not the European assimilation way. . . . And someday, the Governments of British Columbia and Canada will completely restore the property and human rights to the Tsimshian and to all of the First Nations people of North America (Kitsumkalum, n.d.).

This quote even implies that the current movement was somehow or in part initiated by the pole raising itself.

After the 1960s, Northwest Coast Native peoples started to vociferously and successfully reclaim their culture and reappropriate their heritage. Northwest Coast art was flourishing, the result of reinvigorated interest in Native American culture, the enhanced value of Native art, the systematization of the northern Northwest Coast canon, and growing demonstrations of First Nations pride. In 1969, Robert Davidson and his brother, Reg Davidson, erected the first pole in almost 100 years on Haida Gwaii in their community of Old Massett (fig. 12.2). Totem poles began once again to "stand for" things of great importance to Northwest Coast Native people, both as individual family privileges and as more general tribal markers (see appendix G). Poles today mediate political relations at a variety of levels—locally (between family and community members), regionally (as territorial markers and tourist attractions), interculturally (especially between indigenous people and the nation or state), and, sometimes, internationally (as poles are both gifted to nations and repatriated from them).

In the Introduction, we noted that the opening gambit of the 1997 Asia Pacific Economic Community meeting in Vancouver was set in the Museum of Anthropology before a backdrop of totem poles. A few years earlier, U.S. president Bill Clinton and Russian leader Boris Yeltsin had conducted one of their summits in the same location (fig. 12.3). These deployments of the totem pole in the context of international politics

12.2. Robert and Reg Davidson (Haida) totem pole, Old Massett, raised in 1969. Photograph by Aldona Jonaitis, 2002. Courtesy of Robert Davidson.

12.3. Boris Yeltsin and Bill Clinton at the Museum of Anthropology, 1993. Courtesy of Museum of Anthropology.

rest largely on the ideas of neoliberalism, globalization, and a kind of naturalized multiculturalism. Against many of these values, in recent years aboriginal people worldwide have been reasserting local and regional sovereignty over their lands and insisting on more voice in government, education, economic development, and the arts. Australian Aborigines, New Zealand Maoris, Pacific Islanders, Scandinavian Sami, Canadian Inuit, and Latin American indigenous peoples have all become significant forces within their countries and as part of international coalitions. Concomitant with these actions of empowerment, First Nations communities such as Kitsumkalum have used their artistic traditions to express identity, celebrate heritage, forge viable economic futures, and, at times, make direct political statements. On the Northwest Coast, the totem pole has assumed new meanings as Native Americans and Canadians join these global struggles for indigenous sovereignty.

TOTEM POLES AND THE LAND: ALASKA

Land rights remained a major political issue in both Alaska and British Columbia throughout the twentieth century and continues to be so today. Alaska Native people had great difficulties with the federal government over land rights, as only Metlakatla had reservation status; ownership of all other territories was uncertain. In 1935, Congress passed a law allowing Native people to sue the federal government for lands taken by the United States, but when the Tlingit claimed land that had been appropriated for the Tongass National Forest, they were denied. In an effort to resolve some of these challenges, in 1946 the Commissioner of Indian Affairs assigned anthropologist Walter Goldschmidt; Theodore Haas, counsel for the U.S. Office of Indian Affairs; and Joseph Kahklen, Tlingit Alaska Native service teacher, to study and then write a report on who owned Tlingit and Haida lands and waters in southeast Alaska, and under what kinds of aboriginal laws. The resultant report (reproduced in mimeographed form), "The Possessory Rights of the Natives of Southeastern Alaska," made a strong case that historical evidence supported Native land claims in the region, and it eventually helped resolve these claims.[5] Within the section entitled "Customary Land Use and Rights of the Tlingit and Haida" is the statement that "title to land and other property was frequently recorded in totem poles, the most dramatic and widely publicized art form of the Tlingit." This is supported by anthropologist Viola Garfield's words, "Very often records of the properties owned by house groups are carved on totem or grave poles, though the reference is not always easy to ascertain" (Goldschmidt and Haas 1998, 16). Totem poles in nineteenth-century villages communicated the history and privileges of the extended families that owned them; this proprietary facet of totem poles became marshaled for larger political claims to land title itself.

In 1959, when Alaska finally became a state, discussion continued on the question of land claims, for while the statehood act recognized Native people's rights to some Alaska land, specific territories were not designated as Native. These problems remained unsettled until 1971, when, somewhat ironically, an event quite unrelated to Native issues ultimately led to a solution: the discovery of oil on the North Slope. In the Prudhoe Bay area of the Arctic Ocean was an oil field of approximately ten billion barrels—by far the largest in the United States. The problem of getting that oil to market could be solved by building a pipeline from Prudhoe Bay to the ice-free port of Valdez on the Gulf of Alaska.

Some Native groups claimed parts of the land through which the pipeline would run, and litigation about these land claims could have prevented the flow of oil. If that happened, the United States would have been denied its oil and Alaska would have suffered economically. So in 1971 President Nixon signed into law the Alaska Native Claims Settlement Act (ANCSA), which gave Native peoples title to forty-four million acres—10 percent of the land—and $962.5 million in compensation. Regional and village corporations were formed to administer the land and invest the funds. Under ANCSA, the Tlingit (along with the smaller number of Haida who live in southeast Alaska) formed the Sealaska Regional Corporation, which received title to 200,000 acres of land. Ten smaller village corporations acquired surface rights to 23,000 additional acres. The resolution of these land claims opened the way for regional and village corporations to promote not only economic development but cultural programs as well.

After years of organizing highly successful Tlingit language programs, the Sealaska Heritage Institute, the not-for-profit affiliate of Sealaska Corporation, has recently initiated a program to support young Native men and women to make traditional art, including totem poles.[6] These poles have come to represent the general claims on the land and new corporate levels of social affiliation, as well as more abstract concepts of personal and cultural healing (Dauenhauer and Dauenhauer 2004, 270–71).

TOTEM POLES AND THE LAND: BRITISH COLUMBIA

In 1951, the Canadian government dropped the anti-potlatch section of the Indian Act. However, until 1982, Canadian Native peoples were subject to the laws of the 1867 British North American Act and the 1876 Indian Act that denied First Nations their sovereignty and defined them as wards of the state. In keeping with national and international aboriginal rights movements, British Columbia First Nations, along with other Native Canadians, struggled to win back their independence as semiautonomous units with self-determining political, social, and economic sovereignty. The realization of these goals has been slow, as only in 1982 did First Nations appear as a category of citizens in the Canadian constitution. Article 35 explicitly states, "The existing aboriginal and treaty rights of the aboriginal peoples of Canada are hereby recognized and confirmed. . . . In this Act, 'aboriginal peoples of Canada' include the Indian, Inuit and Metis peoples of Canada." But because most B.C. First Nations never signed treaties with the federal or provincial governments, land rights and control of resources remain to this day highly contentious issues. Recognizing the need to address these issues in order to come to some mutually acceptable agreements, in 1991 a task force on land claims, consisting of representatives of the federal and provincial governments, as well as First Nations, was established. This group recommended the establishment of the British Columbia Treaty Commission, which began operation in 1993 and soon received statements of intent to negotiate from numerous British Columbia groups. As of this writing, the treaty process is ongoing. The Nisga'a, who had commenced discussions before this time, negotiated a comprehensive treaty that was ultimately ratified at the provincial and federal levels and put into effect in 2000.[7]

Poles can serve as particularly strong signifiers of autonomy and authority over Native land, especially in the highly politicized terrain of Canadian First Nations. Recall that in the 1950s, the people at Kitwancool tied their participation in the Royal British Columbia Museum's (RBCM) totem pole restoration program to the publicization of their claims over land title. In the decade leading up to the historic 1997 Delgamuukw court decision establishing aboriginal title based on oral history testimony, the Gitk'san raised a series of totem poles as part of larger political strategies for claiming territorial sovereignty (Demetzer, Muldon, and Derrick 2005). All over the coast, new totem poles are being erected in front of band council offices and community-run schools, serving as emphatic statements of cultural as well as political sovereignty.

REPATRIATION

In addition to raising new poles, some communities have been active for many years in attempting to repatriate old ones. One of the most well-known recent cases goes back to 1929, when a Swedish consul stationed in Prince Rupert worked through the local Indian agent to acquire a Haisla pole from the Kitlope Valley. Although it received considerable attention on its arrival into Stockholm, the pole remained in storage for fifty years until a new building for the Etnografiska Museet, Stockholm, opened in 1980 with a space designed especially for it. For years the Haisla had sought the return of this particular pole, which is considered to be one of their most significant cultural treasures, and, starting in 1991, worked to have it repatriated. In the epigraph for this chapter, the Haisla expressed the meaning this project has had to their own sense of history and identity on their band Web site. Elsewhere on that same Web site, the Haisla reassert their ownership of the land and reiterate the fact that they never alienated its title.

The Haisla insisted that this object-return not be one-way. As part of their agreement with the Swedish institution, the Haisla arranged for carvers Henry Robertson, Derek Wilson, Barry Wilson, and apprentice Patricia Robertson to carve a new pole for the Etnografiska Museet. They began the work in Kitamaat Village and finished it in Stockholm in 2000 (fig. 12.4). In addition to Haisla representatives and Swedes, some Sami were involved with the ceremonies at the pole's raising, bringing together two geographically distant yet similarly marginalized indigenous minorities. That same year, a similar replica was carved and erected in the pole's original site in the Kitlope Valley (fig. 12.5). In British Columbia, a spectacular site marked by a new pole now replaces the old one. In 2006, the original pole was finally returned to the Haisla, where it will be installed in a cultural center.[8]

Each of these monuments has meanings compounding their signification of clan or family heritage; all play a role in the globalized world of aboriginal land rights, ecological preservation, the timber industry, and the international museum community. As Glass (2004a) and J. Kramer (2006) have suggested, the process of articulating repatriation claims—regardless of their material result—frequently mobilizes indigenous communities to assert historical grievances, demand political redress, and negotiate the terms of contemporary membership and cultural identity.

PRÄRIEN

(opposite)
12.4. Haisla pole, original (upright) and copy (horizontal), at the Museum of Ethnography, Stockholm, Sweden, 2006. Photograph by Tony Sandin. Museum of Ethnography.

12.5. Haisla pole, copy, in Kitimaat, British Columbia, 2000. Ecotrust Canada, 2007.0090941575.

THE HARRIMAN EXPEDITION REPATRIATION

In 1899, two separate excursions to southeast Alaska sailed home with full-size poles taken from Native villages. One was removed from a southern Tlingit village and erected in Pioneer Square in Seattle with much fanfare and poetry recitation (see page 146). Several more were taken by a ship from an expedition led by the railroad magnate Edward H. Harriman. Harriman organized this voyage to accomplish several objectives: to enjoy a family holiday hunting Kodiak bears; to conduct an investigation into the feasibility of a trans–Bering Sea railway line; and to orchestrate a major scientific study of a relatively unknown region. He chartered the *George W. Elder* and, in addition to fourteen family members and servants, brought along a twenty-five-member "scientific party" that included some of the country's most distinguished scientists, environmentalists, and artists: preservationist John Muir; ornithologist John Burroughs; paleontologist William Healey Dall; director of the Missouri Botanical Garden William Trelease; artists Fred Dellenbaugh and Louis Agassiz Fuertes; and photographer Edward S. Curtis. This distinguished group traveled up the Inside Passage, traversed the Gulf of Alaska to the Alaska Peninsula and Kodiak Island, navigated the Bering Sea as far north as the Seward Peninsula and Chucotka, then retraced its route south (Goetzman and Sloan 1982). Both Curtis and biologist C. Hart Merriam took photographs of Native villages featuring totem poles and Alaskan Natives.

One of the most notorious activities of the Harriman Expedition was its shameless removal of six totem poles from the southern Tlingit village of Gash on Cape Fox. On July 25, the ship anchored near this presumably abandoned village (fig. 12.6). On the beach stood nine-

12.6. Harriman expedition members on beach at Cape Fox, 1899. Photograph by Edward S. Curtis. University of Washington Libraries, Special Collections, NA2130.

teen totem poles. According to John Burroughs's notes, "there was a rumor that the Indians had nearly all died of smallpox a few years before and that the few survivors had left under a superstitious fear, never to return. It was evident that the village had not been occupied in seven or eight years. Why not, therefore, secure some of these totem poles for the museums of the various colleges represented by members of the expedition?" (Burroughs 1986, 116–17). That agreed upon, the crew took down six of "the more striking poles" and floated them to the ship, an action which John Muir, by that point thoroughly disenchanted with his colleagues, reacted to with repugnance and labeled a "robbery."[9]

In that era, travelers often composed poems about their adventures. For example, J. Stanley-Brown, a Harriman Expedition team member, cast the totem pole theft in cheerful carefree verse. After describing the beginning of the project ("Who'll go ashore today with me/ And gather some totems—say two or three?") and the difficulty of lowering the poles ("We pulled and strained till the light grew shy/ Till our hands were blistered and our tongues were dry/ But those figures still grinned at the stars in the sky"), Stanley-Brown concluded his poem:

The "boss" knew nothing of Indian lore;
Happily, my friends, yo ho!
He got very wet and mildly swore,
As in raiment scant he paced the shore
"I'll have 'em yet, my friends, yo ho!
Just let 'pure science' have its fling,

And I'll show them how to do this thing!"
And he sent for the crew who came with a swing
Cheerily, my friends, yo ho!
Mockingly, my friends, yo ho!
With a long, long pull and a strong, strong pull
The trophies came down with a din
But we'll tell later on to our friends in town
How WE gathered those totems in (Goetzman and Sloan 1982, 167).

To the Tlingit way of thinking, the Cape Fox village had not been abandoned. The residents had moved from their traditional houses to live closer to employment opportunities in the Native town of Saxman, near Ketchikan. While some had indeed succumbed to epidemics, the community was by no means wiped out. As a Native who lived in Alaska at that time could have verified, the families, wherever they lived, still owned their traditional village lands and treasured clan property such as totem poles. Thus the Harriman Expedition literally stole property from the shores of Cape Fox Village.

During the 1980s, Native Americans began seriously petitioning for the return of their ancestors' burial remains as well as objects that had been improperly alienated from their villages. In response, the U.S. Congress passed the 1990 Native American Grave Protection and Repatriation Act (NAGPRA) that provided for the return of human remains and certain types of objects. The first phase of this act was for museums to inventory their collections and send tribes information on the materials from their communities. Descendants of Cape Fox Village thus learned the locations of their totem poles and petitioned the Smithsonian Institution, the Field Museum, the Peabody Museum of Archaeology and Ethnology at Harvard, the Johnson Museum of Art at Cornell University, and the Burke Museum at the University of Washington for the return of their pilfered monuments. Even prior to NAGPRA, some museums had returned items that their owners had proved to have been stolen; this was certainly one such case, and these poles would be returned as stolen items.

These requests led to generally friendly and highly productive dialogues between those museums and the Tlingit people. As a result, in 2001 some of these poles returned to southeast Alaska—during, of all things, a reenactment of the original Harriman Expedition on the small cruise ship *Clipper Odyssey*. It was a festive occasion when that ship pulled into Ketchikan harbor and was greeted by large numbers of regalia-clad Tlingit. Some of the poles had already been shipped to Ketchikan but remained in crates. The Burke Museum pole was trucked to Prince Rupert and put on the boat there. Then, still in its box, it was lifted by a crane onto the dock, where it was ceremonially greeted. A celebratory parade accompanied the treasures to the civic hall, where they were all uncrated and displayed (figs. 12.7 and 12.8).

During this emotional repatriation a Tlingit village elder insisted that totem poles are a part of the community itself:

> First you've got to realize that it's not art. You have to look at it as something different. . . . [Totem poles] help define who we are. Let me use an example from Western culture: when you get up in the morning, you put on your makeup, comb your hair really nice, put on the outfit you're going to wear—you're putting on your face, you're putting on the image you want to project. And that's what these poles do, they project the identity of the owner. They are not trying to show wealth like Western people think of wealth. And they are not trying to tell history in the same context as Western history. . . . These artifacts, they have a life of their own. These are not artifacts to me, and they are not art—they are part of us, an integral part of us. That's not a pole that was taken from us. It was part of us that was taken away (Caughran 2003, 76).[10]

The empowered Tlingit had requested their treasures back, and the museums had obliged. The result was a bittersweet victory that could not overlook a troubled history or forget what had been lost. Like the writers of the early twentieth century, the Tlingit themselves mourn aspects of their vanished past. Yet assuaging this pain is part of their own vitality as a community

12.7. Lowering crated pole from ship at repatriation of Cape Fox poles, Ketchikan, 2001. Photograph by Robin Wright.

12.8. Opening crate with carvings at repatriation of Cape Fox poles, Ketchikan, 2001. Photograph by Robin Wright.

12.9. Nathan Jackson (Tlingit), with Dorica Jackson, Grizzly Bear house post, Burke Museum, 2005. Photograph by Doug McTavish.

still capable of celebrating a splendid repatriation with displays of cultural heritage. The cultural richness of twenty-first-century Tlingits differs considerably from that of their nineteenth-century ancestors, but nevertheless remains resilient, vibrant, and enduring.

The stories of these poles did not end with their celebratory return to Ketchikan. To express their appreciation to the museums that returned its poles, the Cape Fox community gave each one a fine cedar log for a replica.[11] Since the Burke Museum had returned two house posts that depicted the bear mother, it received two logs; it then commissioned Nathan Jackson and his son, Stephen Jackson, to carve two new poles (figs. 12.9, 12.10, and 12.11.). The difference between the two poles is striking, for the father's carving adheres to classic Tlingit style, while the son's

CAPE FOX POLE

BY STEPHEN JACKSON, TLINGIT ARTIST

A "house post" but too fragile to bear weight.

The rot of nature or the mark of the collector?

Bentwood boxes in "The Transforming Image." Why are we offered items already so abstract that we can't tell what they represent? Are we really supposed to believe they represented a specific animal in the first place?

Why a clean white background? Instead, a dirty, sprayed, whitewashed graffiti over aluminum, on cedar.

Why clean? When there was [occasional?] intention in painted irregularities.

12.10. Stephen Jackson (Tlingit), Grizzly Bear house post nearing completion, Burke Museum, 2005. Photograph by Anna Hoover. Courtesy of Stephen Jackson.

(far right)
12.11. Detail of Jackson's Grizzly Bear house post. Photograph by Ray Troll. Courtesy of Stephen Jackson.

Exaggeration of what was already there. Embody the flow. Exaggerate nonconcentricity but avoid containment. Reserved Indian. Give and take. Repatriate.

Why containment of the ovoid? Idealistic. Polemic without making what you want? Or have to show the opposite. Warhol? Both? Why the war photographer? Preventive? Watch for the glamour of violence, fascination of the flesh.

Grow conceptually without an accompanying visual/stylistic growth and you could be piddling with the same imagery. Potential in that too, but . . .

Can I approach without relying on a dissection of my project identity? Without fighting for a group identity?

Starting from the subject matter. The story? The commission? The act of anyone making an object for a museum. Giving back. What can I give back? Just taking what's already there.

The story. Decollation, death. An abstraction made visceral, reflecting an abstract quality of the gap between human and animal that still eludes us?

Later, fill in the gaps.

draws on the formline tradition but represents an innovative departure from convention.

CONSERVATION

The Haisla repatriation project has been entangled in larger discourses of conservation. One major issue for coastal Native people is the environment—for the stream, lake, and ocean waters upon which so many still depend for subsistence and livelihood have been depleted by rapacious fishing and logging. Some recent totem poles have focused almost completely on the dominant society's misuse of natural resources.

12.12. Joe David (Nuu-chah-nulth), Cedar Man during protest against logging on Meares Island, 1984. Victoria, British Columbia. Photograph by Bob Soderland. Courtesy of Ha-Shilth-Sa.

Nuu-chah-nulth artist Tim Paul sometimes creates large-scale carvings that depict not crest images but environmental narratives such as salmon habitat destruction. On one pole, stenciled salmon appear in addition to images of the moon, Killer Whale, and Eagle. As Paul explains, "The silhouettes are negative images of salmon. They are confused—having no parent stream to return to. They do not address *your* question, 'What's happening to the migratory salmon?' They pose *mine*, 'Where are the parent streams?'" (in Macnair 2000, 372). In 1984, another Nuu-chah-nulth artist, Joe David, carved a twenty-one-foot welcome figure, Haa-hoo-ilth-quin (Cedar Man), which was erected before the British Columbia Parliament building in Victoria as part of a large demonstration of Native people and environmentalists protesting the logging of Meares Island by commercial enterprises (figs. 12.12 and 12.13). Many logging and pulp companies have an ambivalent relationship with Native communities. While they are often at odds with First Nations over land claims and have resisted demands for financial compensation to Native bands for profits made off traditional lands, the lumber industry has long supported many aspects of the Northwest Coast art world. The two core Northwest Coast collections at the UBC Museum of Anthropology, the MacMillan and Koerner collections, came from the private collections of the heads of timber companies. The forest industry also provided the poles for many of the restoration and centennial projects in British Columbia, as they do today for many publicly commissioned works. By doing so, they benefit from the positive public relations, which diffuse attention from compelling and competing environmental and economic interests. But those interests remain problematic.

For David this statue was not a statement about Meares Island alone but a plea for preserving all the natural resources of the Nuu-chah-nulth people (Gerber and Katz-Lahaigue 1989, 77). It is important to note that this figure was raised at the protest with its arms down, signifying that the loggers were not welcome on this land; today, David's figure stands before the University of British Columbia Museum of Anthropology with arms extended in a welcoming gesture to museum visi-

HAA-HOO-ILTH-QUIN (CEDAR MAN)

BY JOE DAVID, NUU-CHAH-NULTH ARTIST

In 1984 I was asked by my very good friends, Steve and Suzanne Lawson, of Wicaninish Island, to help do something for Meares Island in Clayoquot Sound, as it was on the verge of being clear-cut by Mac/Blo [MacMillan Bloedel Ltd., a lumber company]. I responded by saying I needed four days to think about exactly what it was I'd be doing. Four days later I told them I would be carving a large cedar man. I carved a miniature and set out for the coast with my friend Loren White. During a visit with my uncle, Dan David, I mentioned I'd thought I'd heard somewhere that there had been an old such figure on Meares Island and he said that there had been and that it belonged to our family, and then told me the story about the figure. Two hundred years ago, when white people first started coming to the West Coast, our ancestor was a chief among the Mowachaht. And the ten high chiefs of the village got together to discuss these new peoples and events. Our ancestor, Chief Chowi-doa, was the only one of the ten who warned that these new people would invade in more and more numbers and in fact would be responsible for the destruction of our people's known world, the land, sea, and air. Our lands, sea, and air and all creatures of it were ancient and powerful and had powerful names in history, songs, and dances. And the other chiefs couldn't believe the warning. So Chowi-doa asked his family to carve a cedar figure and invite relatives from other villages to a gathering where it would be told who and what the new standing cedar figure represented. This is a very short and almost meaningless version of a very important and powerful piece of my people's history and the history of Canada. My uncle's version was very long and very eloquent and full of power.

12.13. Joe David (Nuu-chah-nulth), Cedar Man on grounds of University of British Columbia Museum of Anthropology, 2004. Photograph by Aldona Jonaitis.

tors, as similar nineteenth-century figures would have welcomed visitors coming by canoe to a village.

CULTURAL PRIDE AND SOVEREIGNTY

Joe David has described the sense of responsibility to community that defines his role as a Native artist today: "If I had to say what was my contribution as an artist, I'd want to say that I understood my heritage, and I understood my position—that I took responsibility for my tribe, for my people, and for our heritage. I want to be remembered as trying to make a reasonable contribution" (quoted in Duffek 2000, 361). Other artists of his generation, such as Tony Hunt and Robert Davidson, have voiced similar concerns since the 1970s and have made efforts to integrate their commercial careers with ceremonial obligations. Like the more overt messages in the poles just described, there is a political dimension to artistic statements of cultural pride, community participation, and tribal sovereignty.

The Kwakwa̲ka̲'wakw, always innovative in their declarations of cultural autonomy and resistance, had Mungo Martin to thank for Wa'waditla, the first bighouse built after the elimination of the potlatch ban. But this structure stands in Victoria, miles from Kwakwa̲ka̲'wakw territory. In 1965, during the lead up to the British Columbia centennial, Alert Bay built its own ceremonial bighouse. Considerable financial support from centennial funds and the Massey Report mandates had become available for capital projects, including the new Royal British Columbia Museum and the Vancouver Museum. Chief engineer James Sewid—the chief councilor at Alert Bay in 1963—along with chief carvers Charles George of Blunden Harbour and Henry Speck of Turnour Island, were major proponents of the bighouse project. They originally intended it as a place to manufacture and sell Kwakwa̲ka̲'wakw carvings. Sewid commented that "many of our people are poorly educated and we are attempting to interest them in the basic Indian crafts as a means of livelihood . . . [and to] give our young people the chance to keep alive the culture of their people" (quoted in *U'mista News* 1995, 13). Forest companies donated logs, members of the public contributed funds, the Department of Indian Affairs sponsored work programs. The house was completed in 1965, officially opening the following year. Numerous totem poles still stood in Alert Bay, and the new bighouse contributed to the town's presentation of itself as a center of a vital and resurgent Kwakwa̲ka̲'wakw culture.[12]

It is of interest that Sewid publicly promoted a concept that complemented the other centennial projects in parks and museums in that he envisioned the bighouse as a significant tourist attraction and as a place to provide Native people with a source of income. But soon the building became a place for celebrating the ongoing potlatch tradition. In 1965, Mr. and Mrs. James Knox hosted the first potlatch in the house, which would be followed over the years by scores of others.[13] As S.W.A. Gunn writes in his booklet on the bighouse, "Into this physical construction is woven the dream of the Kwakiutl Nation: to have a tribal rallying point, as well as a point from where radiates the spirit of ancestral tradition" (Gunn 1967a, 11).

This structure, initially justified as an economic initiative, also became a statement of Native identity and nation-building. The *U'mista Cultural Society Newsletter*, in its history of the bighouse, stated "We owe a thank you to the elders . . . for their perseverance and caring enough in the culture to re-establish such an important part of our culture to continue to relive and create our history. . . . The people [who constructed the bighouse] shared their knowledge unselfishly to ensure that we as a nation will continue to grow with strength, pride and identify as aboriginal First Nation Natives" (*U'mista News* 1995, 14). Thus, as it turned out, the residents of Alert Bay obtained funds from the provincial and national centennial committees and used them for a nonpublic construction that enhanced their sense of Native community and aided their efforts at revitalization. In 1997, an arsonist burned down this bighouse, which the community soon rebuilt; they decided to replicate the poles and paintings of the earlier structure in honor of the importance the original had had for the Alert Bay community and all Kwakwa̲ka̲'wakw people. This new house's rededication ceremony proved a moment to once again articulate claims to the land, to political and cultural survival, and to sovereignty.

Politics has influenced totem pole–related activities beyond the Northwest Coast, and in at least one case has challenged the cultural homogenization deeply entrenched in white consciousness. As a gift to the new Canadian Museum of Civilization, the RBCM commissioned Nuu-chah-nulth carver Tim Paul to carve a pole for the Great Hall (see the carved pole, second from the right, on the side of the house in fig. 11.4). When the Hesquiaht band of Nuu-chah-nulth arrived in Ottawa for the museum opening and pole dedication ceremonies, they were asked by the museum administration to canoe up the Ottawa River in a fiberglass Haida canoe and perform dances on a platform in front of the Kwakwa̲ka̲'wakw house. This would certainly have been entertaining and nonproblematic for the non-Native audience, and it resonates with past First Nation–conflating practices. But the Nuu-chah-nulth firmly turned down both requests, asserting their independence from both their northern and eastern neighbors. Instead, they arrived at the Grand Hall on foot, and danced not on the elevated platform that was designed for this kind of ceremony but on the floor right in front of the Nuu-chah-nulth house (Macnair 2000, 367). No longer would First Nations carvers allow their poles to be forced into homogenized slots of generalized Northwest Coast Indians; they would instead claim and assert what was rightfully theirs—their unique ethnic identities.

In addition to erecting new poles at museums as symbols of contemporary cultural sovereignty, some First Nations carvers have chosen to replicate—and in the process resignify—existing poles. Recall the Thunderbird Pole that Ellen Neel carved for UBC in 1948, the year that William Scow officially gifted the right to use the crest figure as a school mascot. In the wake of repeated defacement and environmental exposure, the "Victory through Honour" Pole was removed from campus display in the late 1990s (and its remnants were returned to Alert Bay). A few years later, a committee—made up of academics as well as Neel and

12.14. Calvin Hunt (Kwakwa̲ka̲'wakw) with Mervin Child (Kwakwa̲ka̲'wakw) and John Livingston, "Victory through Honour" Pole, University of British Columbia campus, Vancouver, British Columbia, 2004. Photograph by Aaron Glass, 2007.

Scow family members and local Musqueam representatives—was formed to investigate the pole's history, and UBC commissioned Calvin Hunt to carve a replica (he was assisted by John Livingston and Mervin Child). The new "Victory through Honour" Pole was dedicated in 2004 at a multitribal ceremony that integrated Kwakwa̲ka̲'wakw, Musqueam, and university protocols (fig. 12.14). This time around, the Musqueam were formally asked permission to have the pole raised in their territory, a statement—in the words of Musqueam leader Larry Grant—of the newfound peace between his people and their former enemies, the Kwakwa̲ka̲'wakw, as well as their guest, the university. Friendship and partnership were the major themes of the event, as many speakers recalled Neel's initial words about and intentions for her 1948 gift: "To the Native people of the whole province we can give our assurance that your children will be accepted at this school by the staff and student council, eager to smooth their paths with kindness and understanding." In exchange for the selectively authorized right to use the Thunderbird, UBC was to ensure that the university become a space friendly to First Nations students; this new pole-raising ceremony itself was held up as a partial satisfaction of that promise. Edwin Newman, a nephew of Ellen Neel, stated that his ancestors "didn't carve a pole just for art work—when they carved a pole, it told a story and a history of the people," and he emphasized that scholars and institutions had to recognize Native title to the land and to their own cultural narratives. Frank Nelson sang songs and recounted a lengthy narrative relating to the Kwikwasut'inuxw origins of the pole and its figures. As if to both seal the ceremonial seriousness of the event and, perhaps, gently mock the non-Native reverence toward First Nations artists, cedar chips from the pole were given as gifts to audience members (called "witnesses" in the parlance of the potlatch). This pole replication project and rededication ceremony offered the opportunity to clarify the terms of the original 1948 "gift" and to emphasize the reciprocal social and political obligations that gifts on the Northwest Coast engender.[14]

POLES ON NATIVE LAND

After 1953, Mungo Martin began carving and raising totem poles in Native communities as well as in civic centers. In 1969, the young Robert Davidson made a strong statement about cultural endurance and pride when he raised his pole on Haida Gwaii (see fig. 12.2). Since the early 1970s, new poles have been regularly going up in Native villages all along the coast (see appendix G). In 1982, David Boxley carved the first new pole for his home town of Metlakatla. Earlier in this chapter we stated that the 1987 Kitsumkalum poles were the first to be raised in that village in 150 years. Many Kwakwaka'wakw villages have recent poles, which range from those in front of private residences, band offices, schools, and bighouses, to those among the impressive stand of memorial poles in the 'Namgis burial ground, one of the largest assemblages of unrelocated poles on the coast (fig.12.15). In the mid 1990s, the Alert Bay Kwakwaka'wakw won a local political victory

12.15. 'Namgis (Kwakwaka'wakw) burial ground, Alert Bay, 2000. Photograph by Aaron Glass.

when they persuaded the city council to push back the main road about fifteen feet, resulting in the need for new concrete railing at the tide line, because the road had been built over the edge of this burial ground. Today's tourists are allowed to photograph these poles, but they are asked not to trespass into the grassy area itself.

Nine years after Robert Davidson raised his pole in Massett, his mentor, Bill Reid, assisted by Gary Edenshaw, Joe David, Gerry Marks, and Davidson, created Reid's only large, uncommissioned work—a fifty-two-foot pole for his ancestral village of Skidegate (Wyman 1986). Unlike Davidson, who had been raised on Haida Gwaii and had an intimate connection with Massett, Reid had never lived in Skidegate. Nevertheless, he wanted to repay some of the debt he owned to his Haida ancestry, and felt this village should not be without a pole (Shadbolt 1986, 56). The community apparently exhibited little interest in the actual carving of the pole, but came through on the raising day by helping produce a feast for 1,500 people. Reid later said, "The totem pole I carved for Skidegate may have put the village back in time" (Shadbolt 1986, 175). Reid may have meant by this that the pole helped take people's thoughts back in time to the old days, or that it helped re-introduce the people to the march of Haida cultural time, out of which they had fallen.

The images on Reid's pole—Bear of the Bear Mother story, Raven, Killer Whale, and Dogfish—represent the two Haida moieties (fig. 12.16). Reid went further in universalizing his pole, for the animals also symbolize the elements of land, sea, and air. Doris Shadbolt suggests how Davidson's and Reid's poles diverged from earlier Haida carvings; "Perhaps these are the first poles in Native villages not concerned with family status, but which instead, as the work of socially and historically aware contemporary artists, aspire to a broader relevance. The irony, as Reid points out, is that the old ranking customs and modes of thought have retreated so far into the past that probably few if any villagers recognize the animals in his pole, or wonder what their meaning might be" (Shadbolt 1986, 131–33). This last comment was typical of Reid's attitude toward his Haida contemporaries, which fluctuated between condescension for their lack of knowledge and disdain for those who invent new ceremonialism. For example, Reid once claimed, "Hopping around with your face painted is not dancing. Scratching on a piece of silver is not art. Invented ritual is church basement entertainment. . . . [My pole] was a memorial to the Haida of the past, not a drive to turn the clock back" (Shadbolt 1986, 172). The last comment was inspired by his disappointment over the revived—or, by his view, contrived—ceremonialism that accompanied his Skidegate pole raising.[15] Regardless of Reid's own views on the subject, his totem pole on the beach in Skidegate remains a key historical marker for local Haida as well as a major attraction for visitors anxious to see a "real" totem pole on "real" Native ground.

Today over 850 residents representing fourteen

12.16. Bill Reid (Haida) totem pole, Skidegate, British Columbia, 1978. Photograph by Aldona Jonaitis, 2004.

12.17. Kay'llnagaay Heritage Centre (Haida), Skidegate, British Columbia, 2007. Photograph by Robin Wright.

Haida clans live in Skidegate. Wanting to celebrate their distinctive artistic heritage as well as benefit from opportunities in cultural tourism, the Skidegate band decided to embark on an ambitious venture: to build the Kay'llnagaay (Sea Lion) Heritage Centre in Skidegate as the center of Haida cultural education. Knowing they could not realize this dream alone, in 1998 representatives of the Skidegate band, the University of Northern British Columbia, Simon Fraser University, Northwest Community College, the Emily Carr Institute of Art and Design, School District 50, the Canada Council for the Arts, Haida Gwaii/QCI Community Skills Centre, Indian and Northern Affairs Canada (INAC), and Parks Canada all joined together to form a partnership to create the $25,000,000 project that will include a 68,000-square-foot complex featuring the Haida Gwaii Museum, the Bill Reid Arts Centre, a lodge, and a restaurant—all built to look like a row of Haida longhouses facing the water (fig. 12.17). The goal of this complex is to provide information on the Haida, to train young artists, and to develop tourism in this attractive yet somewhat remote part of the Northwest Coast. It is also intended to help Haida unemployment, promote language skills and cultural knowledge, and ultimately repatriate artifacts from around the world.

The first phase of this costly project was to commission and then raise a line of poles that face the sea. Major issues had to be addressed, issues by no means unique to this project. These included the expectation that clan chiefs would pay for poles that memorialized their ancestors, and the inappropriateness of the elite accepting government funds for such clan-related activities. Another problem had to do with the unsuitability of clan signifiers standing before the public, communal assemblage of buildings envisioned for the Kay'llnagaay Heritage Centre. The decision was then made to modify the tradition of poles referring to clans and instead to raise poles that would represent the principal Haida villages. Each pole was to include all the crests of that particular village, which might be affiliated with more than one clan.

Because the poles would not be clan-centered, chiefs would not be selecting carvers, as had traditionally been the practice. Instead, as in most contemporary commissions, carvers would submit proposals to be selected by the board of the Kay'llnagaay Heritage Centre, the Haida Gwaii Museum, the Skidegate Band Council, the local community, and Parks Canada. The call for proposals in the form of drawings went out to all known Haida pole carvers. Robert Davidson was invited to consult on the proposals, and he offered a two-day workshop for the carvers and their assistants. The winners could not request to carve a pole for a particular village, for their assignments were made by selecting straws.

The six Haida teams commissioned to carve poles representing the major historic southern Haida towns—Skidegate, T'aanuu, Nan Sdins (Ninstints), Ts'aahl (Chaatl), K'uuna (Skedans), and Cumshewa—were led by Garner Moody, Jim Hart, Tim Boyko, Giitsxaa, Norman Price, and Guujaaw. Each carver had apprentices, and all worked to depict the crests appropriate to the village that their pole represented, sometimes researching old photographs for inspiration and information. Because the poles had not been commissioned in the traditional clan-related fashion, the carvers had somewhat more freedom to determine their actual graphic outcome.

From June 4 through 9, 2001, Skidegate hosted a lavish celebration for the raising of these six poles. Assistant band manager Babs Stevens told a reporter, "We haven't raised many poles in Skidegate since the beginning of the last century. Our culture never died, but it's a big venture, to carve and raise a totem pole. It used to be an individual thing, but now it's a community thing." Band manager Willard Wilson added, "This will really help to revitalize our community, which is so very important . . . we need to raise poles to keep the culture alive" (Mahonen 2001, 3). The sense of pride was palpable during the days of pole raising. The poles embodied a clear political message. As Guujaaw, president of the Council of the Haida Nation and master carver who oversaw the Cumshewa pole, asserted, "The poles are the crests of the people. It's about our relationship to the land. This is why when we see our forests being deliberately ripped apart and our seas being depleted, we stand up and say no!" On the sixth day, deputy prime minister Herb Gray attended the raising of the HlGaagilda'llnagaay (Skidegate) pole carved by seventy-year-old Norman Price and his team. The pole's theme is the strength of the Haida. Price prayed, "Many hands working together. We have weathered the storm; we are still here; and for that we thank you." Reverend John Williams added, "May this pole remind us of what has been and what can be again." And Chief Skidegate, quoting his grandfather, asserted, "People are like trees . . . trees intertwine their roots so strongly it is impossible for the strongest wind. . . . to uproot the forest" (Collingridge 2001).

These days were opportunities for extraordinary cultural displays. Men and women wore finely woven spruce root hats, Chilkat robes, and button blankets. They carried carved staffs. Chief and artist Jim Hart arrived in a fifty-foot Haida canoe, surrounded by attendants waving painted paddles. Men and women danced, drummed, and prayed while masked beings participated in the ceremonies. Every day, all feasted. On the last day, 1,500 people attended the potlatch that repaid those many people who had helped with this ambitious and historic multiple pole-raising ceremony.

Today, the poles and houses of Kay'llnagaay Heritage Centre line a curving beach, a simulacrum of a nineteenth-century Native village. But of course, it is much more than that, for the poles standing at Skidegate now communicate not only Haida art and architectural history but also cultural pride, renewed interest in monumental sculpture, and direct political statements. The Haida are fully aware of the power of poles in the non-Native imagination and have reappropriated them as the most visible expression of their modern culture and contemporary agency. Poles state emphatically that the Haida are alive and well. But they also support Haida land claims, a significant part of which concern forests and Haida demands to alter logging practices. In order to maintain their culture and have the materials for poles and canoes, 600-year-old trees need to remain standing for the needs of future generations. This concern for preservation becomes an element in indigenous arguments that the Natives never

MY GRANDFATHER'S MEMORIAL

BY DAVID BOXLEY, TSIMSHIAN ARTIST

In 1990 I asked my grandfather, Albert Bolton, if I could put on a potlatch for his one-hundredth birthday in 1994. He smiled. I guess he knew more about what I was getting into than I did, but he said, "If that's what you want to do, David."

My grandparents, Albert and Dora, both full-blood Tsimshians, were born and raised in our village of Metlakatla, Alaska. Their parents were among the Tsimshian pioneers who left their ancestral home in British Columbia, Canada, in 1887 to follow an Anglican missionary named William Duncan to find a new home in Alaska. That in itself is a story.

I was raised by these truly wonderful and amazing Tsimshians. The best days of my life were spent with them, fishing, hunting, gathering food on the beaches and in the woods near the village and out on nearby islands. They were my teachers, my protectors, my dearest friends and a solid link with our heritage. From them I learned not only subsistence skills but *shimalgyak* (the Tsimshian language) and the pride and strength that being Tsimshian brings.

My grandmother died in 1980. She was the sweetest woman—all of 4'8", maker of the best homemade bread, smoked salmon, and cedar baskets. I miss her. She never got to see the change in careers that took me from teaching school and coaching sports to making my living as a Native artist and being deeply involved in our culture, writing songs and creating dances to teach our own people as well as to show the world that Tsimshian culture was still alive and well.

My grandfather was my hero. I've never met a better man. He was a man of his time, the transition time between the old ways and the modern world. He was born in 1884,

12.18. David Boxley (Tsimshian), grandfather's memorial pole, 1994. Photograph © Lawrence Migdale / www.migdale.com.

so long ago, in a time when our people still had a grip on tradition, language, and survival skills on this sometimes unforgiving coast. He was an expert fisherman, hunter, boat builder, and carpenter, and he was also one of the few Natives who belonged to a union (AFL-CIO) as a "fireman" cannery boiler operator who supplied the steam power for our cannery to operate. I loved my "YaYa." The things I learned following him through the woods or out on his boat are still with me today. When I began to carve, he made my first adze for me, then proceeded to make himself a set of knives and started carving model canoes; that was how I learned that his father was a full-size canoe maker. From the beginning, YaYa was there as I struggled with the art, guiding and advising me from the importance of quality in flat design to just how to take the tree down for a totem pole.

When my grandfather died on Christmas Day in 1991, I lost my mentor, my example, my friend. His birthday potlatch, however, became so much more in 1994. The whole community, all four clans, made it unforgettable. So much happene; we fed 1,000 people a night for four nights, dedicated over fifty new button robes, and raised three totem poles, including the one shown here (fig. 12.19). A memorial raised to my grandfather, the figure at the top holding a rainbow, remembers those who have gone before us.

There isn't a day that my grandparents are not with me as I still try to make them proud. *Wai aam.*

gave up title to the land. In their current lawsuit, the Haida insist that they control the resources on Crown land in Haida Gwaii but are willing to work with the Crown to develop them properly. Thus, the poles that stand today in the Kay'llnagaay Heritage Centre, and those that will join them in the future, embody goals related to economic development, cultural education, and the unceasing efforts on the part of the Haida to correct past wrongs.

Although we have been focusing on totem poles raised on First Nations reserves, many poles erected in urban spaces lay claim to those metropolitan zones as Native-used (if not Native-owned) land. A precedent in Vancouver was established when Native residents of the Collingwood neighborhood carved and raised a pole at a new housing co-op in the mid-1980s; since then, many similar monuments have been erected.[16] More recently, in 2005, three new poles were raised at the Ketchikan Indian Community Tribal Health Clinic to honor the main Native groups served by the organization: the Tlingit (represented by a pole by Israel Shotridge), the Tsimshian (pole by David Boxley), and the Haida (pole by Donald Varnell; fig. 12.19). Although such poles often blur in the minds of many viewers, with the myriad displays of urban carvings seen on the Northwest Coast, the poles at the sites of First Nations habitation are clearly distinct in meaning. Rather than simply representing the entire province or city as "totem pole territory" (which in the case of Vancouver, Victoria, or Seattle is geohistorically inaccurate), they clearly mark *particular places* as being indigenous space, much like poles in front of houses function to advertise family or clan possession and presence.

At the University of British Columbia, First Nations students sought a place for themselves that would contain palpable reference to their heritage, so in 1985 the off-campus Native Education Centre asked Norman Tait to carve a pole named "The Place Where People Gather." Although it was requested that this pole's imagery represent all British Columbia Indians, Tait instead selected a Nisga'a story of the origin of Man, given him by Tsimshian elder Hattie Ferguson. On his pole, the first human, Bear (representing land), Blackfish or Killer Whale (water), and Raven (sky) depict images from that origin story, to which Tait added some more personal characters—a wolf cub (for his son) and a moon face (from his favorite story of Raven stealing the sun). At the base, his assistants, Chip Tait, Isaac Tait, Wayne Young, and Hammy Martin, each carved one of four small faces. A unique book, *Where the People Gather: Carving a Totem Pole* (1992) by photographer Vickie Jensen, documents the creation and raising of this pole. Jensen describes in her introduction how, in contrast to most totem pole

12.19. Ketchikan Indian Community Tribal Health Clinic, Ketchikan, Alaska. Poles by Israel Shotridge (Tlingit), David Boxley (Tsimshian), and Donald Varnell (Haida), 2005. Photograph by Aldona Jonaitis.

images taken after the poles were erected, she wished to illustrate the creation of a pole from log to finished product. Tait was delighted when Jensen's book was done; as he wrote in the foreword, "As an experienced Nisga'a carver, anything I do inspires young carvers. . . . I think the book will continue that inspiration and even help other carvers who might not have tackled a major project yet. . . . This book . . . is the printed experience of a totem pole coming to life" (Jensen 1992, viii). The fundamental message of the book—that the totem pole is a living art, important for the past but vital for the future—marks a significant shift from earlier representations. How very different from the lament in de Menil and Reid's *Out of the Silence*.

THE COMING OF AGE OF COAST SALISH ART

The Salish on occasion have used monumental art to support their claims of sovereignty, such as Chief Mathias Joe's 1936 Stanley Park pole. In 1988, the Sechelt Salish band raised two poles to mark recognition of their own municipality by the provincial and federal governments. These and other Salish monuments, which stand in some of the most heavily populated parts of British Columbia, borrow the stylistic tenets of Kwakwa̱ka̱'wakw art. Indeed, all of the Kwakwa̱ka̱'wakw-style poles in southern British Columbia and northern Washington could lead the unsuspecting visitor to assume that the First Nations of that region made vividly colored totem poles with multiple stacked figures surmounted by open-winged birds. The challenge to contemporary Salish artists is to rediscover their own unique art style, not co-opt that of the more flamboyant and better-known northern groups.[17] Susan Point, member of the Musqueam band of the Halkomelem Salish, has successfully met that challenge.

In 1981, Point studied northern-style art at Vancouver Community College. Because of the absence of courses on Salish art, she visited museums in preparation for making prints based upon traditional Salish images and for sculpting Salish-style works in various

INTERACTION

BY SUSAN POINT, MUSQUEAM (COAST SALISH) ARTIST

Although each of the house posts that I've carved over the years means a lot to me, I have selected the two house posts I call *Interaction* that are connected with a crossbeam. In creating these two posts, I tried to portray the celebration of water and wildlife that enriches the lives of everyone.

The one post depicts a woman with her arms and hands extended upward, coupled with the paws of a mountain lion emerging from a cave. The paws and hands symbolize the recognition and tolerance that animal and human have for each other. Between the woman and the mountain lion is a copper dome, which mirrors their shared environment. The human and animal relationship is a metaphor for the respect we must have for the world and for our environment if we are to continue to survive. The second house post is representative of the ocean. On the top is a killer whale with its tail curled up at the base. Two salmon arc below the killer whale's mouth and, at the same time, are balanced atop a circular disk that represents the sun. The sun is life, and the salmon egg within it is new life. Two herring are carved on the outer ring of the sun, and the two bars inlaid with copper disks extending downward represent two containers of valuables carried by the sun. The imagery within the whale's curled tail at the base is that of a shark's head, and, at the same time, this base is designed as a seat. It was my intention that whoever sits here completes the sculpture by connecting to the life cycle. Joining these two house posts is a connecting beam, the beam that would carry the rafters for the roof planks in a traditional longhouse. On the very top of the beam are circular motifs representing celestial images—the stars and the moon. On one side of the beam is Xels, a supernatural being from the past who could fly and transform into any creature or object it wished. The other side of the beam consists of two eagles with a silver dome incorporated within that represents the full moon.

Initially, these posts were done for my solo show in November 2000 at the Spirit Wrestler Gallery in Vancouver, British Columbia. Unfortunately, they did not sell during the show, but during the summer of 2001, Lee Brooks (who owns Arctic Raven Gallery in Friday Harbor, Washington),

12.20. Susan Point (Musqueam, Coast Salish), *Interaction*, 2004. Friday Harbor, Washington. Photograph by Aldona Jonaitis 2006. Courtesy of Susan Point.

along with his assistant, Barbara Marritt, brought two of his clients (Karen Westrell and Bill Rosser) to my studio in Vancouver. This couple had purchased one of my pieces at Spirit Wrestler Gallery and wanted to meet me. I showed them all around my studios, and it was at this time that they all saw my *Interaction* house posts. They were so intrigued with the house posts, and because there was a major renovation about to begin at the Port of Friday Harbor, they felt that these posts would fit in perfectly with the new plans for the island's ferry terminal.

These people were determined in acquiring these house posts for Friday Harbor, and over the next few months there was much discussion and thought put into this whole process of purchasing the house posts. A volunteer group was immediately put in place to raise funds in order to bring *Interaction* to San Juan Island, a venture (of raising funds for public art) totally new to the volunteer group. On their own time and money—and unwavering perseverance—information packages and a visual proposal were put together for potential donors, signatures on petitions were acquired supporting this overall project, fairs were held, and so on; the fundraising aspect was endless. For the next two and a half years, Barbara Marritt and Lee Brooks, along with many other people in Friday Harbor, worked very hard to come up with the funds to purchase the *Interaction* house posts. They dedicated so much energy, despite many obstacles. Throughout this whole time, articles on this fundraising project appeared in various papers and magazines. As Barbara Marritt and her crew once stated to me, "The magic of the house posts seem to have taken on a life of its own."

In the summer of 2002, the Port of Friday Harbor commissioners approved the installation of the posts on port property along the waterfront, provided all costs were funded through donations. The volunteer group and supporting community strongly felt that public art, in any sense, reflected community pride; and, in this particular case, purchasing the *Interaction* house posts would be a major cultural contribution and an exceptional focal point in Friday Harbor. Finally, after all the community's hard work, their dream became a reality: they raised the funds to purchase the *Interaction* house posts, and on May 22, 2004, the house posts were unveiled. I was there, along with my two younger children, Thom and Kelly—a historic experience we will never forget! After all these years, the original inhabitants of Friday Harbor, the Mitchell Island Tribe, have finally reinstated the footprint of our Salish peoples upon their lands by allowing me to erect my house posts at the Port of Friday Harbor.

media. Prior to this time, Cicero August and Simon Charlie had made Salish-style works, as had Point's contemporaries Ron Modeste and Stan Green. With her serigraphs, Point joined numerous other Northwest Coast artists who had been making prints since the 1970s. She began working in wood and in 1991 became one of the few female carvers of monumental sculpture when she carved a twelve-foot house post for the First Nations House of Learning on the UBC campus. Depicting a raven standing atop a spindle whorl with southern relief patterns, this was the first contemporary Salish-style totem pole in Vancouver, a city on Salish land, where so many poles of other British Columbia nations have been erected for almost a century.

Point integrates her Salish artistic heritage into a statement of Musqueam sovereignty over the very first place many visitors to Vancouver pass through: the international terminal of the Vancouver International Airport. At the top of the escalator that arriving international passengers take on their way to customs—that official space where the government regulates what visitors bring in and take away with them—is a monumental sixteen-foot-diameter spindle whorl of red cedar suspended over a waterfall symbolizing Salish rivers (this was completed in 1994 with the assistance of John Livingston and Jeff Cannell). Two large, flying eagles envelop in their wings images of the Coast Salish people, and within those human figures are salmon. Two welcome figures carved in 1996, the male and female ancestors of the Musqueam, stand facing the spindle whorl and cascade (fig. 12.21). This pair greets arriving passengers as they descend the escalator. Behind these figures are two panels called *Flight* that depict eagles made of glass and humans with upraised arms. These poles are certainly meant to function as emblems for Vancouver, British Columbia, and Canada, as have others for decades. But they also emphatically assert Musqueam sovereignty over the specific land in Vancouver and the increasing Salish presence in the contemporary Northwest Coast art world.

Point's images are meant to convey several ideas to new visitors to the province. A diplomatic gesture, they welcome guests to Musqueam traditional land. The eagle, a motif found in earlier Salish art, straddles the ancient and the modern by alluding to natural and man-made flight. The salmon and water signify not only the traditional economic basis of the Salish but the contemporary struggles for fishing rights. The airport Web site absorbs these art works into a message focusing more on nature: "The interior design of the International Terminal was inspired by British Columbia's great outdoors and the art of the Northwest Coast that depicts British Columbia's wildlife, mountains, rivers, forests, and aboriginal heritage. Travelers from around the world will form a first and lasting impression of B.C."[18] Once again Native art enhances the touristic experience and is folded into depictions of the environment. Yet it now also speaks loudly in the first person, in the voice of its First Nations creators.[19]

12.21. Susan Point (Musqueam, Coast Salish), male and female ancestor welcome figures, Vancouver International Airport International Arrivals Building, 1996. Photograph by David Jensen. Courtesy of Susan Point.

With Point's Vancouver International Airport carvings, Northwest Coast artwork, cultural traditions, the world of international travel, references to a subsistence economy, and the declaration of Native land ownership have become inseparably intertwined in the contemporary totem pole. Neither Point's ancestors nor the Hudson's Bay Company traders nor Franz Boas could have possibly imagined this present, optimistic, politically charged chapter in the history of the totem pole. Poles have been transported and transformed according to non-Native agendas since the advent of Europeans on the Northwest Coast. Today they once again stand at home on reserves and in nearby urban spaces as emphatic statements of indigenous cultural survival, social strength, and political sovereignty. It turns out that in the early twenty-first century, "the totem pole"—as a category of popular cultural imagination built up over a century from widely diffused (often confused) depictions and (mis)representations—has been reclaimed by the indigenous people of the coast, where actual totem poles again rise to announce aboriginal pride of place in their characteristically monumental tones.

TOTEM POLES AND THE MEDIATION OF COLONIAL ENCOUNTER

The National Railway speeds through the mountain walled valleys of British Columbia toward the land of the Tsimshian, where totem poles and costumed Indians recall the glories of a vanished past.

—VOICEOVER IN FILM *THE TSIMSHIAN INDIANS OF THE SKEENA RIVER OF BRITISH COLUMBIA*, 1927

My boy died in 1991 of a cocaine overdose. This was a very hard thing for me to accept. A friend said, "Stan, why don't you make a totem pole?" At that time I didn't feel like making a totem pole. It was about a year later that I started. A lot of times I wondered why I started the Healing Heart Project. After a while, everything was so positive—the way people accepted and helped with the pole. They knew what it stood for. Now, this has reached farther than I really expected and people are beautiful working together.

—STAN MARSDEN IN THE FILM *CARVED FROM THE HEART*, 2000

Throughout this book, we have seen how totem poles have consistently been found at the crossroads of colonial encounter and exchange, dialogue and diatribe, conflict and collaboration. A surprising breadth of intercultural relations over the past 250 years has been expressed through representation of, alteration to, or projection onto the material form of the carved column. Totem poles have proved to be a quite flexible technology for mediating cultural contact and communication across shifting historical and political fields. Both Natives and non-Natives have mobilized poles for projects ranging widely from nationalist appropriation to ethno-national resistance, from aesthetic celebration to racist condemnation, from cheap commodification to international diplomacy. We have paid particular attention to the transformation and circulation of the "totem pole"—as an idea, icon, stereotype, and condensation of intercultural dynamics—as it has been represented in various media, such as photography, illustration, advertisement, literature, and souvenir craft. Perhaps no contemporary medium has held a firmer grip on the popular imagination than motion pictures, especially when it comes to representing Native North Americans. Thus it is fitting that we conclude this chapter of the biography of the totem pole not with actual carvings but instead with films in which the poles have played various roles. The history of the filmic depiction of totem poles mirrors and encapsulates many of the themes developed in the preceding chapters, expressing the shifting intercultural relations—of ambivalence and ambiguity, appropriation and appreciation—that continue to characterize the (not-yet-post)colonial encounter on the Northwest Coast.

CELLULOID SA(L)VAGES: A CENTURY OF TOTEM POLES IN FILM

Like so many other representations of totem poles, filmic depictions have conveyed multiple stories and different messages ever since Edward S. Curtis first captured them on celluloid in a 1914 silent melodrama *In the Land of the Headhunters*. Later movies, mostly anthropologically oriented documentaries, approached their subject matter more seriously, while reflecting various changing stereotypes and shifting historical and political paradigms. And then, of course, there is the ubiquitous totem pole in Hollywood westerns, with their often-fanciful conflation of indigenous material culture. Not surprisingly, cinematic totem poles have been variously portrayed as everything from romantic monuments of a vanished race to symbols of contemporary Native strength and endurance. These differences resonate with the multiple representations of poles during the colonial and current eras, and highlight the disjuncture between the cultures of those who make totem poles and those who receive them. Descriptions of Native cultures in general—like those of totem poles specifically—tend to reflect more about the values and beliefs of the describers than they express some "truth" about Native people.[1]

For many people today, the standard photographic image of the American Indian is that constructed by Edward S. Curtis and widely disseminated in the past twenty years via popular coffee-table books, documentary films, and museum exhibits. Curtis earned a reputation as the photographer who best captured the "vanishing American Indian" and who performed salvage photography (as Boas and others had practiced salvage ethnology) by photographing hundreds of people from the Plains, the Southwest, the Arctic, and the Northwest Coast, usually in traditional (pre- or early contact) dress. If old-style clothing was not available, it was reconstructed for Curtis's pictures. Curtis also dressed many of his subjects in wigs to contribute to the illusion.[2] Curtis spent considerable time in British Columbia and published photographs of the Nuu-chah-nulth, Haida, Tsimshian, Salish, and Kwakwa̱ka̱'wakw in his twenty-volume book series about Native Americans; many of these remain popular as contemporary postcards.[3]

In order to finance his publishing efforts, Curtis produced a feature-length motion picture for commercial consumption entitled *In the Land of the Head Hunters* in 1914. This historic landmark of cinematography, produced eight years before Robert Flaherty's *Nanook of the North*, was a romanticized and fictionalized look at the supposed precontact culture of the Kwakwa̱ka̱'wakw. Along with extensive footage of canoe paddling and ceremonial dancing, it also included the first appearance of totem poles in a film. Although the film was well received by critics, it was a commercial failure and remained mostly unseen for decades. In the mid-1920s, Curtis sold the rights to the film to the American Museum of Natural History, but they did little with it. It was not until the late 1960s that anthropologist George Quimby found an old and damaged print of the film in the Field Museum's archives and worked with Bill Holm at the Burke Museum to restore and reedit it. They also recorded a soundtrack (the original film had, of course, been silent), with dialogue, sound effects, and music from the Kwakwa̱ka̱'wakw of northern Vancouver Island. Since the designation of these people as headhunters became impolitic in the 1970s, Quimby and Holm changed the movie's name to *In the Land of the War Canoes* (Holm and Quimby 1980).

Curtis wanted this melodramatic, "boy gets girl, boy loses girl, boy gets girl again" story to take place among the Kwakwa̱ka̱'wakw just prior to contact, and his movie was carefully staged to appear authentic and unacculturated, as per Curtis's standard modus operandi. The village in which the story took place, the clothing the Kwakwa̱ka̱'wakw actors wore, and the masks and ritual regalia they used all needed to seem "traditional." Neither Alert Bay nor Fort Rupert appeared sufficiently ancient for Curtis, both having buildings made of milled lumber. So Curtis shot some scenes at remote Blunden Harbour and hired Native artists (coordinated by George Hunt, Boas's main collaborator) to create a set on an island near Fort Rupert, replete with elaborate painted façades, scaled-down totem poles, and house posts. George Hunt himself carved a tall frontal pole with an open mouth serving as entrance (now in the UBC Museum of Anthropology collection). The Wakas pole in Alert Bay was replicated and, after the filming was over,

13.1. Yaklus' warriors in Edward S. Curtis film *In the Land of the Head Hunters*, (1914). Photograph by Edmund August Schwinke. Courtesy of the Burke Museum of Natural History and Culture.

left to decay in situ (fig. 13.1); according to Holm and Quimby (1980, 47), it was better carved than the original. Another house frontal pole was actually a flat board with painted images of a whale; next to it stood a shorter carved entry pole with a Thunderbird and whale. The last exterior pole was a plain shaft with some simple beings attached. The crew also wove cedar bark and raffia into costumes, carved cedar masks and canoes, and crafted old-style fishing and hunting equipment, all to ensure the verisimilitude of this production.[4]

Within the three-walled house set were two large house posts by Charlie James depicting the bear and the Thunderbird, much like the Alert Bay poles (fig. 13.2). In order to reuse the poles to represent the interior of a different house, Curtis had the wings removed and additional heads and bodies added. One pole ultimately made its way to Stanley Park in Vancouver, where it stood for almost three quarters of a century until it deteriorated and was removed; a replica was then carved by Tony Hunt (see pages 79, 82, and 106). Visitors who have had their photographs taken in front of this winged pole in the urban park would probably never imagine its complicated biography: it emerged from the workshop of a distinguished artist to satisfy a Kwakwa̱ka̱'wakw chief's crest display; it was rented by a brilliant yet failed cinematographer and played two different roles in his films; it was purchased and erected at one of the world's most famous totem parks; it was replicated by a contemporary master carver; and it was rendered in salt by a direct descendant of its creator. Furthermore, it has been subject to innumerable reproductions in the form of tourist souvenirs meant to signify Vancouver, British Columbia, Canada, and even Alaska.

Curtis saw his mission as recording elements of disappearing cultures, and concern for dying traditions motivated his photographic and filmic activities. Nevertheless, *In the Land of the Head Hunters*—and, even more so, *In the Land of the War Canoes*, with its

13.2. Edward S. Curtis and George Hunt filming a Kwakwa̲ka̲'wakw wedding scene. Charlie James (Kwakwa̲ka̲'wakw), bear and thunderbird house posts from a stage set on an island near Fort Rupert, British Columbia, for Edward S. Curtis film *In the Land of the Head Hunters* (1914). Photograph by Edmund August Schwinke. Courtesy of the Burke Museum of Natural History and Culture.

soundtrack of actual Native voices—challenges some premises of the colonial lament. The Kwakwa̲ka̲'wakw community was aware that Curtis, who depended heavily upon the consultation of George Hunt for accuracy, had respect for their indigenous traditions. But it does not appear that the Kwakwa̲ka̲'wakw themselves felt as if they were "disappearing"—they profited from the film, making good money as artists and actors. For some time, many outsiders, such as museum collectors, had admired and purchased Kwakwa̲ka̲'wakw artwork, and the community enjoyed the opportunity to create new carvings and to dance without fear of trouble from the Indian agent (the potlatch was, of course, still against the law at this time). Moreover, by all accounts the Kwakwa̲ka̲'wakw had a good time during the filming (see Makepeace 2000 and 2001). Certainly their culture had changed considerably since the time they wore clothing of shredded cedar bark, but they still adhered to their hierarchies, still potlatched, and still maintained a very strong identity as Kwakwa̲ka̲'wakw people. What was meant by Curtis to be a record of a vanishing race instead functions today as a filmic record of Kwakwa̲ka̲'wakw cultural persistence during the colonial era.[5]

For decades numerous anthropologists set out to salvage the last vestiges of indigenous culture. Marius Barbeau starred in *Saving the Sagas* in 1927, which traced his efforts to document the vanishing Nisga'a culture, while Boas shot footage of Kwakwa̲kwa̲'wakw games and dances in the 1930s.[6] The film Harlan Smith produced, *The Tsimshian Indians of the Skeena River of British Columbia* (1927), blends ethnography with tourism and celebrates the role of government officials and the Canadian National Railway as saviors of a dying tradition. Among scenes of the landscape and local wildlife and Native subsistence, transportation, woodworking, and ceremonialism, the film features frequent totem poles. The camera pans up to their tops, reveals broken poles on the verge of decay, and gives close-ups of exquisitely carved figures. Toward the end, the film shows an overgrown graveyard, where "tombstones and grave-houses replace the older totem poles," but it points out that opportunities to see the older poles still exist, for tourists travel from great distances to see and photograph totem poles in these communities. That the Dominion government was assisting the restoration of these poles was made clear by the shot of a fallen pole with a caption assuring the viewer that it too was soon be "reerected with the others and reproduced on a ten-cent post stamp." The final view, of a row of standing poles, makes it clear that poles might otherwise have rotted away, were it not for the foresight and energies of the railway and the Canadian government, who saw to it that these monuments were restored and reerected (R. Morris 1994, 66–68).

These two films were made by and for a largely scientific audience. In subsequent decades, however, a number of Hollywood films circulated ridiculous depictions of totem poles, a clear index of their growing cultural popularity and emblematic status. As mentioned in chapter 1 above, scenes from both the 1936 and 1954 versions of *Rose Marie* feature Alert Bay–style winged poles in a Plains setting, as does the 1950 film *The Cariboo Trail*. Disney's 1953 animated classic *Peter Pan* placed numerous poles at the center of Neverland's Indian village. As Hollywood Indians were increasingly depicted as generic cinematic foils to cowboys, settlers, and cavalry (not to mention cartoon pirates), the totem pole was marshaled as a typical and recognizable sign of Indianness.

Once museums began showing Native carvings and paintings in exhibits such as the 1927 Canadian West Coast Art: Native and Modern and the 1941 Indian Art of the United States, there emerged a gradual acceptance of the aesthetic qualities of Northwest Coast art. This attitude was apparent in *Totems: Indians of British Columbia*, made in 1943 by Laura Bolton and the National Film Board of Canada, with Marius Barbeau as a consultant. The film declares that the totem pole represents "the most sophisticated art form of all North American Indians." It takes the viewer to Ninstints, Yan, and the Gitk'san region; introduces the Tsimshian and Haida; and poetically describes "their carving, [which] like their music, was abstract and rhythmic," high praise during a period when abstraction in painting had growing popularity. Even more admiring is the narrator's observation that "poles were in keeping with natural surroundings. Spectacular and subtle, naturalistic and symbolic, these carvings have the balance and repose of all great art." Two films about the Ninstints project—Canadian Broadcasting Company's (CBC) *Totem* (1959), narrated by Bill Reid, and Bernard Atkins's *The Silent Ones* (1961)—express this attitude as well, blending ecological romanticism with aesthetic modernism. Like the earlier Associated Screen News production of *Totem Land* (1927), a short film intended to preface commercial screenings, these films were meant to bring academic, salvage-based, and aesthetic perspectives to a more general audience.

Yet this aesthetic approach was slow to replace—or even supplement— ethnographic efforts to document the technological craft of totem carving. As mentioned earlier, Audrey Hawthorn and Ben Hill-Tout filmed Mungo Martin at the University of British Columbia for *Carving a Totem Pole* (1951). Barely any mention is made of beauty in this film or in the anthropologically oriented *The Totem Pole*, a 1963 film about the Kwakwa̲ka̲'wakw sponsored by the American Indian Film Project at the University of California and directed by anthropologist Samuel Barrett. Barrett was fascinated by the Northwest Coast as a "wood culture" and wanted the film to concentrate on totem poles and other carvings. In a letter he sent to Audrey Hawthorn of the Museum of Anthropology (MOA), Barrett reveals his inclination: "I have remarked on various occasions when someone asked me here, where we go to get Indian pictures is any place where anyone can show me an Indian doing anything authentic and interesting" (quoted in Jacknis 2000, 119). With the assistance of Wilson Duff, Barrett and filmmaker William Heick traveled to British Columbia, filming Henry Hunt and Mungo Martin carving at the British Columbia Provincial Museum (BCPM), Stanley Park, MOA,

Kingcome Inlet, Gilford Island, and Alert Bay. The film presents straightforward ethnographic information on Northwest Coast cultures and varieties of poles, and covers the creation of a pole from choosing a tree to raising the finished work. Near the end, the film praises the museum replication efforts to salvage those few remaining poles that, without such help, would rot into the ground.

Barrett had a specific goal for *The Totem Pole* and his other films. Like Curtis, he wanted to portray "old-style" ways: "We are not interested in the modern things that are being turned out but rather in the old type of object in every case" (quoted in Jacknis 2000, 132). He was also dismissive of the new anthropological interest in acculturation: "The modern training that ethnologists get is too often slanted very decidedly toward culture change and all that sort of thing without regard to the ancient cultures, which is our particular province and our particular concern" (quote in Jacknis 2000, 132–33). So, despite metal tools having been used for generations, Barrett insisted that the totem pole be carved—or appear to be carved—with stone implements. Thus a sequence shows Mungo Martin and Henry Hunt felling a tree with only wedges and stone hammers, and the absence of any use of a power saw. The film also describes traditional natural paints, never referring to the commercial pigments that had been in use for decades. Instead of revealing what was actually being done with totem poles—power tools and all—Barrett's film stages pastness, with the anthropologist determining what era would be best to portray. In keeping with the paradigm of salvage ethnology, the anthropologist controls the representation and chooses the "authenticity" of antiquity rather than the intercultural reality of the present.

Neither anthropologists nor First Nations have much control over the depictions of totem poles that seep ever outward into popular culture. Even a brief and cursory survey of mainstream movies and television shows reveal the extent to which totem poles are being recontextualized wildly: *Starman* (1984), in which poles hold up an "Indian Country" gift-shop sign in Arizona; *The Crush* (1993) and *Intersection* (1994), both featuring formal receptions filmed in MOA's Great Hall but set in cities other than Vancouver; *Addams Family Values* (1993), which depicts numerous totem poles in a New York summer camp; *White Fang 2* (1994), set among the Haida of the Queen Charlotte Islands, who, absurdly, are starving from a lack of caribou; *Cobb* (1994), about the legendary baseball player, who gambles in a Midwestern casino decorated with cowboy motifs and totem poles; the television show *Bachelorettes in Alaska* (2002), in which desperate contestants vie for the available hunks under a glacier peak with a wooden canopy supported by totem poles; and *The Simpsons Movie* (2007), in which Homer consults a shaman in Alaska (who lives in a Siberian-style yurt decorated with Northwest Coast-esque masks and practices something like Inuit/Eskimo throat singing) and receives a spiritual epiphany under the watchful eyes of towering totems. Representations of a different, more ethnographically informed sort can be found in one 1993 television episode of *Northern Exposure* (with its Alaskan-set Tlingit village filmed in Washington State), in which the Native politics of a local pole raising are explored, and in the 1995 Jim Jarmusch film *Dead Man*, in which the eponymous hero dies in a (reconstructed) nineteenth-century Makah village on Puget Sound, complete with a replica of the Wakas pole from Alert Bay and its snapping beak-door. What all of these filmic stereotypes share is a marked lack of cultural or regional specificity regarding totem poles—a hallmark of any denatured visual icon.

TOTEM POLES AND SOCIAL ISSUES

Recent films have documented repatriation cases and have provided a format for disseminating indigenous stories of colonial violence and contemporary redress. *Full Circle* (2002) is a short film about the return of the Peabody Museum pole—taken during the Harriman Expedition reenactment—to the Tlingit community of Cape Fox. *Totem: The Return of the G'psgolox Pole* (2003) takes the viewer through the moving experiences of the Haisla discovering the G'psgolox pole in the Etnografiska Museet, Stockholm, and their efforts to repatriate it. The film focuses on the complex interactions between the museum and the Haisla of Kitamaat (and backgrounds the land-related issues that formed the social context of the repatriation claim). At the end of the film, we learn that the pole has not yet returned to Kitamaat, to the apparent dismay of the filmmaker, Gil Cardinal, who criticizes both the Swedes and the Canadian government for not helping the Haisla build their cultural center in order to regain possession of the invaluable pole (the pole has since been returned). In Cardinal's mind, at least, the behavior of non-Natives dictating the correct treatment of a Native cultural treasure demonstrates that some have not yet shed colonial attitudes.

Other recent documentary films, sensitive to the real lives of actual First Nations people, represent cultural endurance, but frequently through the lens of contemporary hardship, poverty, and discrimination. A few address social problems within Native communities by portraying totem poles as instruments of salvation. In *The Washing of Tears* (1994), filmmaker Hugh Brody brings the viewer into the Mowachaht/Muchalaht community of Gold River on Vancouver Island, where alcohol, sexual abuse, and health problems all contribute to what seems to be a hopelessly disabled community. The film reveals how a revitalized connection with their heritage in the form of dancing, singing, and revisiting an ancient shrine used for whaling (now at the American Museum of Natural History) have inspired within the group a culture of healing, thus encouraging a positive outlook on the future (Jonaitis 1999). At the film's end, a group of Mowachaht and Muchalaht erect a newly carved totem pole in their old, now-defunct church in a gesture of optimism tied to their aboriginal culture. The visual image of the raising of the pole—a group of men straining to place it correctly—hauntingly suggests an elevation of the cross, reinforced by the setting of this event. The filmic suggestion of salvation results from a subtle blending of Native practices and Euroamerican symbols.

The association between poles and healing is made explicit in *Carved from the Heart* (2000), filmed by Ellen Frankenstein and Tlingit Louise Brady, about the pole Stan Marsden made in conjunction with the town of Craig, Alaska, on Prince of Wales Island. When Marsden, a Tsimshian, tragically lost his son to cocaine, he decided to invite the entire community, both Natives and non-Natives, to help him carve the Healing Heart Totem Pole (see chapter epigraph). The video examines not only drug abuse but other social ills, including suicide, family violence, and lingering problems experienced by Vietnam War veterans. It demonstrates how a ceremonial activity and community project can assist the emotionally wounded and provide support for the grieving. The pole has become a redeeming factor in a contemporary tragedy.

For the past century, films have been used to document the history of the totem pole as presented in this book. Curtis staged the precontact past; mainstream movies paired the totem pole with Plains Indian stereotypes; Marius Barbeau and Harlan Smith promoted government-sponsored restoration efforts while contemporaneous filmmakers encouraged tourism to the coast; Samuel Barrett and Wilson Duff continued efforts to salvage ancestral remnants while Bill Reid and Audrey and Harry Hawthorn promoted museum-based preservation projects; Hollywood unreflectively litters modern films with decontextualized totem pole images; and current documentary filmmakers have focused on the totem pole to tell stories of colonial oppression and current struggles for self-determination and cultural healing. Because of popular assumptions that film is essentially an archival and documentary mode of representation (even when fictional), it is no surprise that it has been used to create, recreate, and capture images of totem poles as documents of one of humanity's greatest and most dramatic—if most misunderstood—cultural and artistic icons.

CONCLUSION: AUTHENTICITY AND THE POLITICS OF THE PAST

During the last decades of the twentieth century, an unprecedented number of new museums—from small local historical societies to Native cultural centers to vast national institutions—were created. As opposed to

CARVING THROUGH THE BORDERS OF RACE, MULTICULTURALISM, AND INDIGENEITY: THE JOMAR LANOT MEMORIAL TOTEM POLE

BY ALICE CAMPBELL, ANTHROPOLOGIST

You might consider Sir Charles Tupper Secondary School—an inner-city high school in Vancouver, British Columbia, that raised a new totem pole in 2007—a school in crisis. The school has been reeling and recovering from the 2003 murder of one of its Filipino ESL students, seventeen-year-old Jomar Lanot, who had immigrated to Vancouver only a year earlier. One autumn evening, Lanot was beaten to death on school grounds by a group of South Asian teenagers seeking retribution for damage to their vehicle—an act Lanot and his friends were unconnected to.

Although the school board's official position is that Lanot's murder was a random act of youth violence, unconnected to race, Lanot's death has nevertheless compelled some at Tupper to reflect on the nature of systemic racism fostered in the educational system, including that directed toward Aboriginal students. Like most other high schools in Vancouver, Tupper has an Aboriginal youth worker, and as part of its healing strategy from Lanot's death, the school hosted a storytelling evening led by members of the local Musqueam First Nation. Following the success of this event, the school decided to raise a memorial pole for Jomar Lanot, carved by Martin Sparrow (Musqueam) and Joe Bolton (Tsimshian). Several teachers at the school integrated the pole carving into their curriculum to learn about Aboriginal cultural forms in the context of the systemic racism Aboriginal people in British Columbia endure.

13.3. Martin Sparrow (Musqueam Coast Salish) and Joe Bolton (Tsimshian), Jomar Lanot Memorial Totem Pole, Vancouver, 2007. Photograph by Alice Campbell.

When viewed through the twinned histories of civic bodies in settler colonial societies appropriating Aboriginal cultural forms to legitimize national interests, and the legacy of non-Aboriginal peoples viewing Aboriginal cultures as "magical" or "spiritual," it is tempting to see the school's decision to commission and raise a totem pole in Lanot's memory as an appropriative act—yet another scripted use of Aboriginal cultural materials to assuage or heal that which troubles non-Aboriginal, and usually White, people. In the case of the Jomar Lanot totem pole, racial tensions become superseded by a commitment to affirming cultural diversity. However, what makes the Jomar Lanot pole particularly compelling is that the decision to name the pole in Lanot's memory was made by the school's Aboriginal youth worker, Native carvers undertook the production, and the log for the pole was a gift from the nearby Kwantlen First Nation.

The Jomar Lanot Memorial Totem Pole is only one recent instance of how a discourse of "healing" becomes a strategy for promoting humanism and reckoning with race, through the collaborative production of totem poles led by Aboriginal people. In the summer of 2007, the Spirits Rising Memorial Society began a program—welcoming "all people, men and women, from all races and religions"—to collaboratively produce a totem pole in commemoration of sixty-nine impoverished women (many of whom are Aboriginal and sex trade workers) who have gone missing from Vancouver's downtown eastside neighborhood. One carver, who has also led collaborative Aboriginal art projects as a form of healing in youth detention centers, proudly calls his work "multicultural."

Such collaborative projects open up crucial questions about the relationship of multiculturalism and indigeneity. Can the power relations that structure race be transcended by humanistic concerns—particularly when these emerge from Aboriginal people? And why are those Aboriginal people who sincerely believe in multiculturalism as grounds for community building often absent from the accounts of those scholars who vigorously critique how multiculturalism romanticizes "diversity" and therefore insidiously perpetuates Aboriginal people's ongoing subjugation?

Perhaps it is the case that wrestling with the sincerity and political aims of Aboriginal multiculturalism entails tarrying with humanism. In the study of non-Western cultural forms, humanism can become dangerous territory indeed, as it can too easily be associated with a mid-twentieth-century universalistic mode of inquiry—one that aimed to sweep from view the relations of power that structure social differences along axes of race, gender, and class.

The production of the Jomar Lanot Memorial Totem Pole and other such healing poles trouble such hard distinctions between humanism and difference. They challenge us to closely examine how racial and other forms of difference are produced and subsequently mediated by popular forms of material culture.

the cult of progress that characterized early twentieth-century modernity, Andreas Huyssen situates this expansion of places dedicated to representing the past within what he considers the emergence of a culture of memory in recent years: "Since the 1980s, it seems, the focus has shifted from present futures to present pasts" (2001, 57). The dramatic increase in museums, the redevelopment of urban centers, the popularity of things "retro," and the increase in television shows devoted to historical events indicate that "memory has become a cultural obsession of monumental proportions across the globe" (Huyssen 2001, 63). Such attention to the past may offer traditional forms of identity to people in an increasingly deterritorialized world. Huyssen warns, however, that the pressure to continually and innovatively represent (and romanticize) the past paradoxically isolates us even further from it, threatening to dislodge its anchoring potential. More to the point, most Native people define their rootedness to the land—their very indigeneity, their (ab)originality—in opposition to this kind of trend toward deterritorialization. Their temporal and geopolitical *priority* is what defines current indigenous claims to land, to sovereignty, and to self-determination. This is one reason why totem poles remain important to the people of the Northwest Coast, as poles literally and symbolically anchor them to the earth, to specific places, to their ancestors.

So deeply ingrained is the totem pole as an essential (if not ancient) element of Northwest Coast heritage in the self-definition of contemporary First Nations people, that scholarly reconstructions of its history (like those offered in chapters 2 and 3) are sometimes questioned. Tim Paul, for example, once asserted, "An anthropologist from UBC told someone Nuu-chah-nulth poles were new. How does he know? He's never been to the West Coast, to our villages. He's never sat with our elders. It all comes from Boas. It's the Bible for anthropologists. We had names, we had places, we had images. Who's to say we had no poles. . . . We lost a lot. We could have lost our old poles" (T. Paul 1996). Paul resists the concept that the totem pole has the kind of history presented here, or, perhaps more accurately, that the intercultural history is the *most important* one to tell. To his mind, depriving the Nuu-chah-nulth of ancient totem poles deprives them of their heritage and of a central element of what it is to be a Northwest Coast Native person today. As we have demonstrated in this book, there is no single linear history of the totem pole; its national and international popularity results in part from the mythologizing that resulted from colonial despair, government appropriations, artistic (mis)representations, scholarly mistakes and myopia, Native promotional strategies, and efforts of the tourism industry. Like so many other Native people who articulate cultural history in the contemporary climate of land claims, Paul expresses an essentialist notion of the singular totem pole. However, his essentialism has a different political focus and discursive force from those offered by colonial agents or evolutionary scientists or modernist artists or postmodernist academics.

In his analysis of contemporary aboriginal art, Nicholas Thomas (1999, 198) identifies two hierarchies of value: the primitivist's archaizing preference for tradition, and the contemporary critic's deconstruction of the essentialism underlying that primitivism. The latter critique challenges the romance of the past and the insistence that accommodation to the contemporary world renders culture inauthentic. "The significance and effects of indigenous art can only be misunderstood if we insist on celebrating *either* the so-called 'traditionalist' expressions or the 'contemporary' ones, instead of acknowledging both" (Thomas 1999, 199). The totem poles of the late twentieth century have become interesting articulations of the "authentically primitive" and the commoditized, contemporary world of art; while some consumers may fantasize that their contemporary poles are genuinely "traditional," these artworks are the products of two centuries of intercultural exchange. They are very obviously a living tradition that refuses to stay fossilized in an archaic—and possibly imagined—Golden Age. Nonetheless, many contemporary totem poles are greeted by both Native and non-Native peoples with, in the words of Thomas (1994, 188), a "fetishization of an unacculturated authenticity." This is because such a notion of authenticity retains a very strong set of values—an aesthetic value for consumers of indigenous art, a scientific value for salvage-oriented anthropologists, and a political value for negotiators of indigenous land claims and treaties.

One relatively minor but insightful arena in which such tensions play out is in the debate over the use of power tools. Some people who see a Native person cutting the main shapes of a pole with a chain saw bemoan the loss of tradition and departure from authenticity. This is sometimes felt by Native people themselves. In 1984, Sealaska Corporation purchased a lot in Wrangell for the creation of a totem park dedicated to the people of the community. Several poles that had stood in different places in Wrangell were brought together: the Kiks.adi pole that once stood in the park site, having been raised there in 1895; the Raven pole that was originally near the Baptist church; the Keetkeet pole that had stood near the downtown harbor; and the One-Legged Fisherman pole that had been raised in the Indian cemetery. Tlingit Wayne Price and non-Native Steve Brown, who replicated the Kiks.adi pole in Wrangell, were charged by the descendants of the original carvers not to use power tools. As Brown said, the original carver of the Kiks.adi pole, the son of William Ukas, "was also a carver of totem poles and did not think chainsaws and other power tools appropriate to totem pole art" (H. Stewart 1993, 172). Moreover, Ukas wanted the replica to be as close in spirit to the original as possible.

Other carvers have a very different perspective. Tsimshian Chip Tait insists that his ancestors always used what they had available: "My father used [a chainsaw] when he had the chance. My grandfather never used a chainsaw because he didn't have one. That's not tradition, that's availability. . . . Using a chainsaw is not a guideline—it's a luxury. In my village, nobody gives me a ride to work, so I have to walk every morning. Here I can take the bus—it's a luxury. The way I see it, the chainsaw is just a technical shortcut." Tait goes on to insist that it is not the tool that makes a pole traditional, it is "how you go about finding out what you're going to do on a pole" (Jensen 1992, 57). According to Bill Holm (2003), "There are a number of jokes regarding chain saws: 'Chain saws are called Haida saws, because you have to hide 'em when the tourists come."' Robert Davidson, roughing out a carving with a chain saw at Massett, was once admonished by a tourist who said, "I bet your grandfather never used a chain saw." Robert looked at him and said, "Did you come here in a covered wagon?" (Davidson 2003). Here is one venue in which Native people internally debate the relative merits of cultural transformation, invoking a familiar academic language of "tradition" and "culture."

The primary focus of this book has been to untangle and analyze the complex transformations that have occurred and continue to occur to this inherently multivocal and co-constructed icon in the shifting spaces of global intercultural encounters. In contemporary settler society, Native people are in a continuing colonial bind. To revitalize their cultures, to regain a sense of pride, to compete in a global market for indigenous arts and tourism, and to legitimize their societies to dominant national governments, they need to demonstrate unbroken ties to some kind of past deemed "traditional," to practices deemed "authentic" (often according to dominant legal, official, or scholarly criteria). At the same time, and for all the same reasons, they need to participate fully in modernity, with all of its political, technological, legal, economic, and cultural implications. Their maintenance of some of these practices—such as speaking Native languages, perpetuating spiritual beliefs and rituals, wearing traditional regalia, or carving totem poles—can act as political statements of their alterity, survival, and sovereignty. The point is that such decisions have long been monitored and adjudicated by colonial authorities. The global political advancements of recent decades have increasingly placed the onus of negotiating the past and present, tradition and modernity, upon the indigenous people who rightfully deserve the freedom to decide their own fates. It is no wonder that totem poles—those pillars from the past and of the future—have been and remain so central to this cultural dynamic.

Totem poles abound in the contemporary world in various forms. Both historic nineteenth-century poles as well as their contemporary descendants are culturally esteemed Native creations, but when transformed by processes of representation, they have also come to signify much more than their originary functions. In some cases totem poles express issues of importance to their creators: family and clan affiliation, cultural pride, resistance to colonial authority, a means of subsistence, and claims to the land. In other contexts, their meanings are overdetermined by non-Native attitudes toward indigenous people: they become transportable icons of a generalized Indianness, visual embodiments of an archaic Golden Age when man and nature were in harmony, signifiers of national or regional identities, artifacts that help prove some anthropological theory or other, examples of fine art infused with aesthetic sophistication and/or Native spirituality. Totem pole models, photographs, paintings, postcards, films, Web sites and kitschy souvenirs—even scholarly histories—can appear relatively neutral, unproblematic, and objective; yet they can also be either dismissive or openly romanticizing, reflecting emotions ranging from disdain or suspicion to spiritual yearning or aesthetic appreciation. Through such widely circulating, intercultural representations, totem poles have proved amenable to nearly infinite recontextualization and resignification.

Despite—or perhaps because of—this semantic and material flexibility, such diverse depictions have also contributed significantly to the development of a popular notion of "the totem pole," one filled with as many misconceptions as accuracies. It is in the wake of a legacy of (mis)representation that Native peoples today insist on the right to self-representation, self-definition, and self-government, to assert their lasting presence and cultural vitality. Northwest Coast Native artists have carved more poles between 1970 and 2000 than their ancestors did between 1870 and 1900. This fact indicates that they and their communities are gaining more authority in the ongoing negotiations with those who share their territories, and thus are wresting from non-Native people control over the ongoing transformations to the ever-changing yet ever-enduring totem pole.

APPENDIX A

A SELECTED AND ANNOTATED LIST OF BOOKS ON TOTEM POLES

A good number of books provide accurate information on poles. Marjorie Halpin's *Totem Poles: An Illustrated Guide* (1981), focusing on the collection at the University of British Columbia Museum of Anthropology, provides an excellent introduction to poles. Edward Keithahn's *Monuments in Cedar* (1963) and Edward Malin's *Totem Poles of the Northwest Coast* (1986) are useful for their broad scope, abundant examples, and mostly accurate information. Marius Barbeau's *Totem Poles of the Gitk'san* (1929) is an early and informative source on one specific group, and Robin Wright's *Northern Haida Master Carvers* (2001) is a more recent comprehensive account of some of the most highly regarded totem poles from the coast. Hillary Stewart's *Looking at Totem Poles* (1993) guides the reader/traveler to pole locations from the Washington–British Columbia border north to Juneau, Alaska. Helpful guides to totem parks are Viola Garfield and Linn Forrest's *The Wolf and the Raven: Totem Poles of Southeastern Alaska* (1948; revised 1961), and Vickie Jensen's *The Totem Poles of Stanley Park* (2004).

More personal accounts of poles and pole makers include Adelaide de Menil and Bill Reid's *Out of the Silence* (1971), a poetic photographic essay on the decaying monuments at Ninstints and other Northwest Coast sites; Phil Nuytten's *The Totem Pole Carvers* (1982), a unique account of three important Kwakwa̲ka̲'wakw artists; and Vickie Jensen's *Where the People Gather: Carving a Totem Pole* (1992), a photographic document of the creation and raising of a pole in Vancouver by Nisga'a artist Norman Tait and his crew.

Other books, although readily available, are less useful. Marius Barbeau's two-volume *Totem Poles* (1950, reprinted in 1990) represents an in-depth survey of hundreds of poles along the coast but despite its comprehensive scope remains seriously flawed by factual errors and misleading illustrations (which collage poles from various sites into single images). Pat Kramer's tourist-oriented *Totem Poles* (1995) also suffers from errors of fact and omits the identities of many photographed individuals and locations.

Unfortunately, many book searches for "totem pole" return items such as *How to Carve and Paint Totem Poles* (1977) by Paul Luvera Sr., a remarkable effort on the part of an untrained amateur to teach anyone to make these objects. Because no commercial publisher would accept Luvera's book, he published it on his own and sent *Chicago Daily News* columnist Mike Royko a copy. Royko's September 27, 1977, column, "Want to own a totem pole? Just carve one yourself," describes the book and notes that carving a pole oneself saves thousands of dollars (the going rate for a pole then was $6,000). Royko also describes the origin of the pole as inspired by South Sea prototypes which made their way to the Northwest Coast, where "an Indian saw one, and said, in effect, 'Hey, honey, that would look great in front of the tepee.'" One must contend with such entries when surveying the vast literature on totem poles.

The same holds true when searching the term "totem poles" on the Internet. There exist today numerous sites that contain information on these monuments, some from legitimate scholarly sources such as museums and universities, others being commercially oriented advertisements for stores, attractions, and individual artists. There are also numerous sites that contain fanciful, stereotypical, and even completely erroneous information. As is so often today the case with the Internet, one must be constantly vigilant about such illegitimate sources of poor information.

APPENDIX B

PRIMARY EIGHTEENTH- AND NINETEENTH-CENTURY REPORTS OF MONUMENTAL CARVINGS ON THE NORTHWEST COAST (1778–1900)

Abbreviations

EG	Gunther 1972
EK	Keithahn 1963
EM	Malin 1986
JH	Henry 1984
JJ	Jacobsen 1977
MB	Barbeau 1950
PD	Drucker 1948
RW	Wright 2001
WD	Duff 1964b
WDP	Wilson Duff Papers, n.d.
WN	Newcombe 1931
WS	Suttles 1987

YEAR	REPORTER	SITE	TYPE	REFERENCE
1778	Webber (Cook)	Yuquot	House posts (drawing)	MB (801)
1785	Walker	Yuquot	House posts	Walker (1982, 47)
1786	Woodcock	Near Sitka	Funerary monuments	JH (88)
1787	Haswell	Clayoquot	House posts/portal pole	MB (803); Howay (1941, 69)
1788	Meares	Clayoquot	Portal pole	MB (803); EM
	Meares	Langara	Exterior pole	EK (38)
1789	Douglas	Dadens	Wooden image	WN (238); WDP (6–9)
1790	Ingraham	Cloak Bay	Two posts/40' high carvings	MB (806); EM
	Quimper	Nootka (?)	House posts/portal pole	MB (805)
	Hoskins	Haida Gwaii	Exterior/frontal poles	MB (806)
	Bacstrom	(Tlingit)	Double mortuary posts (drawing)	Holm and Vaughan (1982, 212)
1791	Hoskins	Haida Gwaii	Frontal poles	WD (91)
	Marchand	Dadens/Langara	Painted frontal poles	MB (803); EG (130); RW (55)

YEAR	REPORTER	SITE	TYPE	REFERENCE
	Bartlett	Dadens/Langara	Frontal pole (drawing)	MB (803); JH (191); RW (50)
	Cardero (Malaspina)	Yakutat	Funerary monuments (drawing)	MB (807, 820); JH (162); EK (39)
1792	Moziño	Yuquot	House posts (drawing)	Moziño (1970, 18)
	Boit	Clayoquot	Frontal poles	EG (74)
	Ingraham	Tanu	House posts	WDP (6–18)
1792/93	Puget (Vancouver)	Puget Sound	Funerary monuments	Puget (1939, 215)
	Vancouver	Haida Gwaii	Double mortuary, house posts	EK (41); EM
	Vancouver	Yuquot	House posts	MB (808)
	Vancouver	Roscoe Inlet (Heiltsuk)	(Unidentified)	WN (241)
1793	Vancouver	52° 17" north	Detached poles (same as above?)	EK (42)
	MacKenzie	Bella Coola	House posts	EK (41)
1794	Haswell	Clayoquot	House façade/frontal pole	PD (391)
	Howay/Magee	Kiusta	Pole raised by Capt. Roberts (drawing)	MB (815); WD (90); ED (39); RW (70)
1795	Bishop	Skedans	Memorial poles	WD (91)
1795	Lisiansky	Sitka	Funerary monuments (he destroyed)	EM (19)
1799	Boit/Haswell	Clayoquot	Frontal/portal poles	EM
	Burling	Kiusta	Pole raised by Capt. Roberts (drawing)	RW (84)
	Ship *Eliza*	Langara Island	Mortuary poles	EM
1805	Lisiansky	Sitka	Carved crest on house roof	EK (42)
1808	Fraser	Kwantlen (?)	Portal pole with carvings above	WS (114); Lamb (1960, 103)
	Fraser	Yale	Carved mortuary boxes	WS (127)
	Fraser	Spuzzum	Funerary monuments	Lamb (1960, 98)
1818	de Roquefeuil	Massett & Nootka	House posts/portal poles	MB (809)/RW (95)
1824	Péron	Cape Flattery (Kwakwa̱ka̱'wakw)	No poles/carvings mentioned	MB (810)
1829	Green	Skidegate	Freestanding/painted ship masts	MB (820); EK (42, 110)
1833	Tolmie	Milbanke Sound	House posts	WN (239)
1837	Belcher	(Tlingit)	Mortuary box (drawing)	MB (808)
	Belcher	Sitka	No mortuary poles; European pillar	EK (42)
1841	Simpson	Sitka	Mortuary boxes	MB (821); EK (42)
1845	Kane	Victoria	Mortuary figures; portal poles; house posts (drawing)	MB (811)
1847	Kane	Clallam	Human mortuary figure (drawing)	WS (127)
1854	Alden	Victoria	Grave posts (drawing)	WS (127)
1858	Wilson	Fraser River	Decorated houses	WS (114,125)
1860s	Deans	(Haida)	Many carved columns	MB (814–16)
	?	Comox (Salish)	Freestanding poles (photo)	WN (240)
1862	Deans	Fort Simpson	Tall columns	MB (810)

YEAR	REPORTER	SITE	TYPE	REFERENCE
1867	Davidson	Port Simpson	Many freestanding poles	WN (241)
	Porcher	Fort Simpson	Many freestanding poles	Porcher (2000, 53, 6)
	Emmons	Old Wrangell	Many poles	WN (240)
1872	Deans *(in 1889 Deans reports that locals had shot the penis off after becoming Christians)*	(Haida)	Post of a man with large penis	MB (812)
1873	Powell	Knights Inlet	Freestanding poles (photo)	Holm (1983, 38)
1874	Swan	(Haida; Tsimshian)	Freestanding poles	MB (813)
1876	Dufferin	Skidegate	A "forest of poles" (painting)	Hall (1986, 4, 50)
		Fort Simpson	Bare pole with bird on top	Hall (1986, 4, 50)
		Alert Bay	Bighouse with painted façade (photo)	Hall (1986, 4, 50)
1878	Dawson	Skedans	New memorial pole raised	WDP (6–16)
1879	Muir	Old Wrangell	Post with a bear figure (drawing)	EK (38)
1881	Jacobsen	(Kwakwa̱ka̱'wakw)	Many tall freestanding poles	JJ (7)
	Jacobsen	(Tsimshian)	Model multifigured poles	JJ (15)
	Jacobsen	Port Simpson	No poles left/European houses	JJ (27)
	Jacobsen	(Haida)	Painted poles/selling poles	JJ (18, 25)
	Dossetter	Knights Inlet	Fully carved poles (photo)	Dossetter 1881
	Dossetter	Newitti	Fully carved pole (photo)	Dossetter 1881
1881/82	Krause	Wrangell	Many high poles	EK (135)
1883	Swan	Tanu	New house built	WDP (6–18)
1884	Chittenden	Tanu/Ninstints	25 carved posts	WDP (6–18)
1885	Dawson	(Kwakwa̱ka̱'wakw)	Few detached/interior poles	G. Dawson (1888)
	Niblack	Kasaan (Haida)	Mortuary poles (drawing)	Niblack (1888, plates 2 and 3)
	Niblack	(Northern Tlingit)	Poles gone already (only stumps)	Niblack (1888, 329)
	Krause	Haida	No new poles raised anymore	Krause (1956, 208)
1889	?	Tongass	Many poles (photo)	EK (40)
1890s	Barbeau	Wrangell; Ketchikan	Occasional new poles	MB (819)
	Keithahn	Wrangell; Kake; Ketchikan	New poles	EK (47–8)
1894	Boas	Fort Rupert	Many simple poles	Holm (1983, 38)
1895	Barbeau *(by 1905, Barbeau reports that Kake stopped carving due to missionary influence)*	Kake	Still carving memorials	MB (819)
1899	Harriman Exp.	Alaska	Poles at (abandoned?) villages	Harriman 1899

APPENDIX C

A SELECTION OF EARLY ILLUSTRATIONS OF TOTEM POLES AND MAJOR PHOTOGRAPHIC EXPEDITIONS (1778–1900)

Record-keeping visual depictions were made on eighteenth- and nineteenth-century voyages of exploration, when artists drew and painted the sights they saw. The majority of these images were intended as records, and thus differ from the self-conscious artistic depictions by twentieth-century painters of totem poles. Many of the following depictions have been published numerous times (see appendix B for some specific references; see also Cole 1976 and 1980; Holm and Vaughan 1982; Keithahn 1963; and Barbeau 1950).

1778	Webber	Drawing of Yuquot house posts (fig. 2.1)
1790	Bacstrom	Drawing of Tlingit double mortuary posts
1791	Bartlett	Drawing of Dadens portal pole (fig. 2.3)
1791	Cardero	Drawing of Yakutat grave monument
1792	Moziño	Drawing of Maquinna's house posts
1794	Howay	Drawing of Kaigani pole raised by the white Captain Roberts
1837	Belcher	Drawing of Tlingit pole and graves
1839	Alfred Agate and Titian Peale (Wilkes Expedition)	Various
1845	Kane	Drawings of Salish mortuary figures, house posts, portal pole
1870s	Frederick Whymper (with Western Union Telegraph Co.)	Various
1876	Lord Dufferin	Watercolors of Skidegate
1879	Muir	Drawing of Old Wrangell bear mortuary monument
1885	Niblack	Drawing of Kasaan mortuary poles
1885	Vincent Colyer (first U.S. Indian commissioner)	Various

Anthropologists found photography useful as data for reconstructing culture; soon after the more portable cameras were introduced in the 1870s, photographs became valued sources of cultural survey information. Like artifacts, they were documents to be archived by the thousands (see Blackman 1981; Webber 1985; Francis 1996; and Macnair and Stewart 1999).

In 1873 and 1874, Israel Wood Powell, commissioner of Indian Affairs for British Columbia, was accompanied on survey trips by Richard Maynard, who learned photography from his wife, Hannah Maynard, after they moved from the East to Victoria. Other photographers accompanied Powell on later tours, including O. C. Hastings in 1879 and Edward Dossetter in 1881; both men were Americans who lived in Victoria, BC. The American Museum of Natural History commissioned Edward Dossetter to take photographs for their archives during his 1881 tour with Powell; these have become some of the most compelling images of Northwest Coast architecture. Hastings later accompanied Franz Boas on his historic trip to Fort Rupert in 1894, where he produced what appear to be fog-enshrouded images of the village, as well as an elaborate sequence of photographs of the winter ceremonies. George Dawson took photographs in 1879 and 1884 for the Canadian Geological Survey. The Field Museum of Natural History in Chicago hired Edward P. Allen to accompany collector George Dorsey to the Queen Charlottes and the Skeena River in 1897. The American Museum of Natural History's Jesup North Pacific Expedition (1897–1902) resulted in hundreds of survey photographs. Charles Newcombe, the English physician occasionally employed by the Victoria museum, took photographs in southeast Alaska between 1900 and 1902. Both Edward Curtis and C. Hart Merriam took photographs of Alaskan villages on the 1899 Harriman Expedition; Curtis then included many images of totem poles in the Northwest Coast volumes of his monumental *The North American Indian* book series. In 1915, a team of well-known and highly respected photographers of Alaska Native life and culture, Lloyd Winter and Percy Pond, published a small pamphlet, *The Totems of Alaska*, illustrated by photographs they took in 1895 and 1896. In addition, Herbert Horace Draper and William Howard Case took many images of Alaskan Native life at the turn of the twentieth century.

APPENDIX D

A SELECTIVE LIST OF POLES COLLECTED OR COMMISSIONED FOR DESTINATIONS ABROAD (1880–1970)

1882 A Haida pole is sent from Massett by Bertram Buxton to Fox Warren, near Weybridge, England (to the residence of Mrs. Charles Buxton, his mother; Barbeau 1950, 567; Tylor 1898a). This pole was repatriated to the National Museum of Canada (now the Canadian Museum of Civilization) around 1978 (see Neary 1986; Laforet 1992, 44).

1884 Johan Adrian Jacobsen ("in company with the Nihilist Count S") collects a large Haida (Kayung) pole for Berlin's Royal Museum of Ethnology, one of the first in a European collection (Cole 1985, 64; Jacobsen n.d. and 1977).

1885 Jacobsen brings nine Nuxalk to Germany, where (in Leipzig, at least) they build a bighouse with frontal poles (illustration in Cole 1985, 69).

1887 R. H. Hall of the Hudson's Bay Company in Port Simpson, with the help of James Innes (superintendent of Government Dockyard, Esquimalt Harbour), sends two Haida house posts to Pitt Rivers Museum, Oxford (Barbeau 1950, 538; Tylor 1898b).

1897 Charles Newcombe collects a Tanu pole for BC premier J. H. Turner (who gives it as a gift to the Royal Botanical Gardens at Kew) and a Skidegate pole for Dr. Hugo Schauinsland (destined for the Bremen Museum; Barbeau 1950, 538; Cole 1985, 179–81).

1900 Lord Bossom collects a Howkan (Kaigani) pole, lashes it to the deck of his ship, and sails it around Cape Horn to England. It was returned to Canada (and the CMC) in 1969 (Canadian Museum of Civilization 1995, 35).

1900 R. H. Hall of the Hudson's Bay Company sends a Fort Simpson Tsimshian pole to the Pitt Rivers Museum in Oxford (Cole 1985, 232).

1902 Newcombe collects a thirty-eight-foot Haida pole, along with its legend, at Yan, and sends it to Charles Read at the British Museum (Cole 1985, 196; Joyce 1903). It turned out to be the pole from which a model had been made and sent to the museum by Reverend Keen in 1898 (Cole 1985, 293).

1902 Pitt Rivers Museum, Oxford, acquires a pole from Massett, which joins the two house posts gathered from there in 1887 (Tylor 1902; Barbeau 1950, 567).

1911 Newcombe, requested by George Dorsey, buys a Skidegate pole for Baldwin Spencer at the Melbourne Museum (Cole 1985, 231).

1929 Barbeau purchases a Nass River pole for Sir Henry Thomson, who presents it as a gift to the French government. It was apparently gaudily repainted by railway workers before shipping (P. Kramer 1995, 29).

1929 Mr. Olaf Hanson (Swedish consul at Prince Rupert) collects a "Kwakiutl" (actually Haisla) pole from Kitlope and sends it to the Ethnographical Museum in Stockholm (Lindblom 1936). In 1994 the museum transferred ownership to the Haisla and began negotiations to move it to Kitimaat, which has now finally occurred (see pages 229 and 255) on this repatriation process and its documentation).

1930 Barbeau and the Canadian National Railway give a Nisga'a pole (carved by Oyay) to the Trocadero in Paris (Kerr 1931; Barbeau 1950, 11–12).

1931 The Royal Scottish Museum, Edinburgh, receives a pole from the Nisga'a village of Angyada, collected by Barbeau for sale to the museum. The pole is named Hlkwaroet ("small hat") or Masrayait ("white bullhead"). It was originally owned by Neestsaw, a memorial to Tsawit (next in line for chief), and was carved by Oyay and Gwanes (Kerr 1931).

late 1930s The Capilano family carves copies of the "Squamish/Capilano Totem" of Chief Mathias Joe (see pages 224–25) and sends them to London and Germany (Green 1939).

1939 A heraldic pole was unveiled at the entrance of the Musée de l'Homme, Paris, on January 20, 1939. It was reported in an article by the French surrealist poet Benjamin Péret, appearing in *Paris-Soir* (January 21, 1939) under the sensational title "Krikiett, the Tallest Totem Pole in Europe." The sixteen-meter-high pole, once standing on the ridge of Bulkley Canyon in the Wet'suwet'en village of Hagwilget, was acquired in September 1938 by the Swiss surrealist painter Kurt Seligmann (see Mauzé sidebar, page 139).

1950 Ellen Neel (Kwakwaka'wakw) carves a model pole/talking stick for the Vancouver mayor Charles Thompson to present as a gift to Australia (Nuytten 1982, 48).

c.1950 Ellen Neel is commissioned by a director of social services in Quebec to carve a model pole as a gift for a monk in France whose monastery had a good art collection (Nuytten 1982, 51).

1950s Ellen Neel gives a "Totemland" pole as a gift to Maria Tallchief, the star of the Ballet Russe de Monte Carlo (Nuytten 1982, 59, 64).

1951 Ellen Neel carves a small pole as a wedding present from some Vancouver friends to Lord and Lady Selkirk in London (Nuytten 1982, 54).

1953 Ellen Neel carves an eleven-foot pole for a museum in Copenhagen, Denmark. The pole has a thunderbird with spread wings, sea bear, killer whale, and sculpin, and is influenced by Charlie James in style (Nuytten 1982, 55).

1954 Ellen Neel is commissioned by Senator W. Rupert Davies to carve a thunderbird pole for the Boy Scouts in Welshpool, Wales (Nuytten 1982, 57).

1958 "The Royal Pole." Mungo Martin (Kwakwaka'wakw) is commissioned by the B.C. provincial government to carve a pole for Queen Elizabeth II as part of B.C. centennial celebrations (a duplicate still stands in front of the Vancouver Maritime Museum). He worked with assistants Henry Hunt and David Martin, and Governor F. M. Ross made the first cut during a special ceremony. The pole has ten crests of the various Kwakwaka'wakw bands. It was raised in Windsor Great Park, London, and repainted in 1985 by Richard Hunt and Tim Paul (Nuytten 1982, 104; B.C. Indian Arts Society 1982, 21; H. Stewart 1993, 68).

1959 Martin carves a twenty-five-foot pole for H.M.S. Excellent, the Royal Navy's gunnery school at Whale Island, near Portsmouth, England, in recognition of the long association with the Royal Canadian Navy. The first cut was made by Capt. E.T.G. Madgwick, chief of staff to the flag officer, Pacific Coast. The pole features thunderbird (for "the roar of guns"), killer whale (for Whale Island), and a speaker figure (for the gunnery instructors; B.C. Indian Arts Society 1982, 27).

1961 Martin carves a thirty-seven-foot pole as a goodwill gift to Mexico City, commissioned by the Canadian government. His last pole, it had a thunderbird and Sisiutl in honor of similar beasts in Mexican indigenous art (B.C. Indian Arts Society 1982, 27).

1963 After "Ambassador Richard P. Bower decided a totem pole would be a suitable symbol of Canada," a sixty-five-foot pole is commissioned from Henry Hunt (Kwakwaka'wakw) for the Canadian Embassy in Argentina, to stand in Plaza Canada, Buenos Aires (Keithahn 1963, 120).

c.1964 Bill Reid (Haida) is commissioned to do a pole for the Shell Centre in London, England.

1969 Mayor Koro Sasaki of Nikko, Japan, conceives of a totem park there to symbolize cultural and economic links to Alaska and to attract tourists and educate the young. Yoshio Katsuyama, director of Alaska's cultural office in Japan, researches poles and creates a file of photographs from which fifty art students from the University of Arts, Tokyo, copy thirty-eight Alaska and twelve BC poles. The official opening is blessed by Shinto priests and attended by Japanese, Canadian, and American officials (Patty 1969).

1969 Canadian Forces donate a totem pole by Doug Cranmer (Kwakwaka'wakw) to the city of Zweibrücken, Germany. This was the first of many contemporary (especially Kwakwa̱ka̱'wakw) totem poles carved in or acquired by Germany.

1970 William Jeffrey, chief of the Gitwilgyet, carves a fifteen-foot pole for Adelaide, South Australia, in honor of their Timber Week celebrations (*North Vancouver Citizen*, 1970).

1970 Robert Davidson (Haida) carves a ten-foot raven pole for the World Council of Craftsmen in Dublin, Ireland. It was then given to the city of Dublin, and stands now in a pavilion at the Dublin Zoo (Steltzer and Davidson 1994, 25–26). (This is only one of many poles in global zoos.)

APPENDIX E

A SELECTION OF TOTEM POLES AT REGIONAL, NATIONAL, AND INTERNATIONAL EXPOSITIONS (1876–1994)

1876 **Philadelphia, Pennsylvania: United States Centennial International Exposition**

▸ The first large display of Northwest Coast art in North America, organized by Otis Mason and including many pieces collected by James Swan (for Spencer Baird at the Smithsonian). Among the highlights: a Haida pole commissioned at Kasaan (in the Smithsonian Building); a Tsimshian pole collected from Fort Simpson, and a Kwakwa̱ka̱'wakw pole from Alert Bay (in the U.S. Government Building). Plans for a Native village were not realized (see Cole 1985, 29).

1884 **New Orleans, Louisiana: Cotton Centennial Exposition**

▸ Ten totem poles and house posts (eight Heiltsuk, two Nuxalk), collected by Swan for Baird at the Smithsonian, are displayed in the U.S. Government exhibit (Cole 1985, 45).

1893 **Chicago, Illinois: World's Columbian Exposition**

▸ *Anthropology Building:* Featured an exhibit organized by Frederick Putnam (of the Peabody Museum at Harvard), assisted by Franz Boas and Harlan Smith, intended to show human evolutionary progress through a visual record of material works. The building included Kwakwa̱ka̱'wakw material (collected by George Hunt); Tlingit objects (assembled by Sheldon Jackson and Edward Ayer); Haida material (collected by Newton Chittenden) and a scale model of Skidegate with miniature houses and totem poles (collected by James Deans); Gitk'san objects and a pole (collected by a Tsimshian woman, O. Morison); and Nuxulk material and a pole (collected by Johan and Fillip Jacobsen). (Most of this material is now in the Field Museum in Chicago.) Outside the building were a Haida house (from Skidegate, obtained by Deans) and a Kwakwa̱ka̱'wakw house (from Newitti, collected by Hunt and Deans), as well as totem poles and posts from the Haida, Tsimshian, Nuxalk, Salish, and Tlingit. In addition, a group of around fifteen Kwakwa̱ka̱'wakw, organized by Boas and Hunt, lived and performed at the fair in and around the two houses (Cole 1985, 125–33).

▸ *U.S. Government Building:* Featured an exhibit arranged by the U.S. National Museum, the Bureau of American Ethnology, and the Smithsonian Institution, and organized largely by Otis Mason. This display set the standard for "culture-area" classifications based on John Wesley Powell's linguistic work. Northwest Coast life groups were planned for by William H. Holmes, but not realized. The building also included displays of the Interior Department showing natural and human resources of Alaska, including George Emmons's Tlingit collection (now in the American Museum of Natural History, New York).

▸ *Washington State Building*: Featured an exhibit of material collected by James Swan and Reverend Myron Eells (now in the Burke Museum, Seattle).

▸ *Canadian Pavilion*: Featured objects from British Columbia collected by Indian commissioner A. W. Vowell (now in the Canadian Museum of Civilization, Gatineau/Hull).

▸ *Commercial displays on Midway*: Included a private collection of Northwest Coast material owned by Carl Hagenbeck and collected by the Jacobsen brothers (now in the Field Museum).

Additional Native American villages here featured no Northwest Coast content.

▸ *Women's Building*: Featured an ethnographic display with comparative examples of typical women's manufacturing (e.g., weaving and basketry), including some Northwest Coast items.

1901 **Buffalo, New York: Pan-American Exposition**

▸ Dedicated to the growing trade interest with the East and the expansion of American territories, the fair included a display of Alaskan Indians (featuring the Tlingit and Eskimo), but focused primarily on the Philippines.

1904 **St. Louis, Missouri: Louisiana Purchase Centennial International Exposition**

▸ *Anthropology exhibit grounds:* In a comparative, evolutionary assembly of Native American "types" organized by W. J. McGee, the Northwest Coast was chosen to represent "light-skinned fishermen" and their unique house design. Two Kwakwa̲ka̲'wakw (Charlie Nowell and Bob Harris) and five Clayoquot (Dr. Atlieu and his family, and Jack Curley) were brought to the fair by Charles Newcombe, where they lived in a Nuu-chah-nulth house (collected by Newcombe), danced for the public, and carved and sold model totem poles. In addition, one full-size pole was set up, donated by the Smithsonian (Cole 1985, 200–208).

▸ *Alaska State Building:* Collected by Governor John Brady in 1903, around fourteen totem poles and two houses, all Tlingit and Kaigani Haida from Alaska, were set up around the Alaska State Building (the first building of its kind at a world's fair).

▸ *U.S. Model Indian School*: Outside the building containing the school was a large Haida pole loaned by the Smithsonian.

▸ *"Eskimo Village" concession on the Pike:* Contained one of the Brady poles, damaged in transit and subsequently adorned with electric lights.

1905 **Portland, Oregon: Lewis and Clark Centennial Exposition**

▸ The Brady totem poles (Haida and Tlingit poles from Prince of Wales Island) were exhibited in Portland, after being shipped from St. Louis following its fair (Lockwood 1906; see also District of Alaska 1905, 57). Brady also brought Tlingits Louis and Florence Shotridge from Alaska to demonstrate Chilkat weaving and dyeing.

▸ Additional posts were displayed in the Alaska Exhibit, Department of the Interior, behind a marker revealing the price paid for the state.

▸ One post was also installed near the stairway of an unidentified building.

1909 **Seattle, Washington: Alaska-Yukon-Pacific Exposition**

▸ The fair's south entrance was decorated with plaster totem poles, and totem pole souvenirs—most featuring the "Seattle Pole" in Pioneer Square—were common.

▸ A Northwest Coast display organized by the Smithsonian included Tlingit material and objects collected by Boas and Swan, but featured mostly Eskimo and Pacific peoples. Emmons's collection was displayed in the Alaska State Building, along with paintings by Theodore Richardson, who won a "Grand Prize." For the fair, a 17.4-meter canoe was carved at Massett by Alfred Davidson and Robert Davidson Sr. and painted by Charles Edenshaw.

1915 **San Francisco, California: Panama-Pacific International Exposition; and San Diego, California: Panama-California International Exposition**

▸ Minimal if any Northwest Coast exhibits, as these fairs were again focused on the Pacific and Philippines. Theodore Richardson displayed some of his Alaska paintings.

1939 **New York, New York: World's Fair**

▸ Two winged Kwak'wa̲ka̲'wakw poles, most likely by Mungo Martin, stood outside the Canadian Pavilion in Flushing Meadow Park, Queens. After the fair, they were sent to a Boy Scout camp on Staten Island.

1939 **San Francisco, California: Golden Gate International Exposition**

▸ Two Alaskan Haidas (John Wallace and his son Fred) carved poles at the fair, which were then erected in a courtyard between the Indian and Government buildings as part of a Bureau of Indian Affairs display (in 1941, one of these poles went to the MoMA exhibit in New York City).

▸ Many totem poles were displayed in a large room as part of the Native American art exhibit organized by René d'Harnoncourt, general manager of the Indian Arts and Crafts Board.

▸ Jock Macdonald's painting *Indian Burial, Nootka* was displayed in the Canadian Pavilion.

1948 **Vancouver, British Columbia: Pacific National Exhibition**

▸ At this year's version of the annual agricultural and commercial fair, Ellen Neel (Kwakwaka'wakw) had a display at which she and her family carved a large totem pole, which won the sculpture award and brought her many commissions. The family also carved and sold model poles, and Neel gave out autographs on cedar chips (Nuytten 1982, 51).

1960 **Stratford, Ontario: Stratford Summer Shakespearean Festival**

▸ Ellen Neel carved a twenty-two-foot pole to complement an exhibit of Northwest Coast art from the National Museum of Man and Emily Carr paintings from the Vancouver Art Gallery. The pole was commissioned by a collector in Michigan (Nuytten 1982, 67).

1964 **New York, New York: World's Fair**

▸ Three poles from the Sitka National Historic Park were erected at the Alaska State Building (at least two of these were then replicated back in Sitka over the next decade or so).

▸ A copy of the Abraham Lincoln pole was displayed at the Illinois Pavilion.

1967 **Montreal, Quebec: Expo '67**

▸ Wilson Duff helped coordinate the Indian Pavilion, which included the carving and raising of poles by Kwakwaka'wakws Henry and Tony Hunt (Abbott 1981, 43).

1969–1970 **Montreal, Quebec: "Man and His World"**

▸ Following the Expo, Montreal reinstalled the fairgrounds and gave two pavilions to the UBC Museum of Anthropology to publicly exhibit their extensive Northwest Coast collection for the first time (Hawthorn 1993).

▸ In the summer of 1970, Robert Davidson (sponsored by MOA) carved a ten-foot Haida pole at the fair, which was later given to the City of Montreal (Thom 1993, 72).

1970 **Osaka, Japan: Expo '70**

▸ The British Columbia provincial government commissioned Kwakwaka'wakw Sam Henderson to carve a pole for the Expo, after which it was sent to the Kwagiulth Museum in Cape Mudge, where it still stands at the entrance (see H. Stewart 1993, 139).

▸ The Gitk'san lent a pole to the fair with the proviso that it be returned afterward.

▸ The Peabody Museum at Harvard lent its Cape Fox Tlingit pole to an exhibit of American folk art.

▸ One of the "world's tallest totem poles," carved by Carl Heinmiller and his Alaska Indian Arts Inc., was displayed and then returned to Kake, Alaska.

1971 **Seattle, Washington: Sealaska Travel and Trade Fair**

▸ Held at the Seattle Center, the fair included "Talkalot," a walking, talking totem pole (a person in a plush totem suit, á la Disneyland's roving cartoon mascots).

1974 **Spokane, Washington: World's Fair**

▸ Bill Reid's "Eagle Crest/Bear Mother" mortuary pole and double Haida mortuary pole (carved with Doug Cranmer) were displayed. These are now in front of MOA's Haida house display (H. Stewart 1993, 57, 60).

1986 **Vancouver, British Columbia: Expo '86**

▸ Joe David (Nuu-chah-nulth) carved two welcome figures that flanked the entrance to the British Columbia Pavilion (now lent by the Vancouver Museum to the Vancouver International Airport; H. Stewart 1993, 70).

▸ Earl and Brian Muldoe (Gitk'san) were commissioned by the Koerner Family Foundation to carve a pole (now at the entrance to Van Dusen Botanical Gardens; H. Stewart 1993, 72).

▸ Earl Muldoe and Walter Harris (Gitk'san) carved three Gitk'san poles for the Plaza of Nations (now installed at the international terminal at Vancouver Airport; H. Stewart 1993, 75–77).

▸ Earl Muldoe also carved three replica poles at the Royal British Columbia Museum, one Nuxalk, one Haida, and one from Kitwancool, which were lent to the British Columbia Enterprise Pavilion at Expo '86 (*Khatou News* 1988a, 10).

- Doug Cranmer and other Kwakwaka'wakw carvers created house posts and a bighouse-like set for the General Motors Pavilion and its Spirit Lodge theatrical attraction.
- At Skidegate, Bill Reid carved a 15.2-meter canoe, which was launched in False Creek at the opening ceremonies of Expo (now at MOA).

1988 **Brisbane, Australia: Expo '88**

- Richard Hunt (Kwakwaka'wakw) and Terry Starr (Tsimshian) carved a nine-meter pole for the Canadian Pavilion (*Khatou News* 1988b, 7).

1989 **Auckland, New Zealand: Commonwealth Games**

- A thirty-six-foot pole was raised in front of the Maori Cultural Centre at the closing ceremonies (in 1990) to welcome people to Victoria for the Commonwealth Games of 1994. The Nuu-chah-nulth pole was carved by Tim Paul (then working with the RBCM), with Pat Amos, Art Thompson, and Kevin Cranmer (Kwakwaka'wakw). It was named Hakis'piqa, "Standing on the Rock," and tells an origin story of the Hesquiaht band. Nuu-chah-nulth and Salish danced at the raising.
- A second pole, carved by Cicero August (Coast Salish), was raised in Victoria simultaneously, linked by satellite television (*Khatou News* 1989, 14–15).

1990 **Seattle, Washington: Goodwill Games**

- Lee Wallace (Tlingit) of Saxman carved a talking stick to replace the "Olympic" torch as it was passed across the country before the start of the games. David Boxley (Tsimshian) carved a different stick for ceremonial use; inside hollow chambers in the American Eagle and Russian bear figures were placed letters by George Bush and Mikhail Gorbachev, respectively (Watson 1990, A1).

1990 **San Francisco, California: Festival 2000**

- Haidas Jim Hart and Reg Davidson were present to carve poles, sponsored by Capp Street Project, Headlands Center for the Arts, and Society for Arts Publications of America (Moser 1990, 24).

1992 **Seville, Spain: Expo '92**

- Cousins Stan Bevan and Ken McNeil (Tahltan, Tlingit, and Tsimshian/Nisga'a) carved a totem pole for the Canada Pavilion.

1994 **Victoria, British Columbia: Commonwealth Games**

- The (then) "world's tallest totem pole," carved by a team representing various First Nations communities, was raised in Victoria's Inner Harbour.
- The "Queen's Baton," a silver ceremonial baton, was designed by a trio of Northwest Coast artists from the Coast Salish (Charles Elliot), Nuu-chah-nulth (Art Thompson), and Kwakwaka'wakw (Richard Hunt).

APPENDIX F

A SELECTION OF TOTEM POLES AT BRITISH COLUMBIAN AND CANADIAN CELEBRATIONS (1936–1986)

1936 **Vancouver Golden Jubilee**

- Salish and Kwakwaka’wakw-esque poles are set up in Stanley Park’s “Indian village.”
- One Haida and two Kwakwaka’wakw poles are collected and added to Stanley Park’s display at Lumberman’s Arch.
- Mathias Joe’s (Squamish) Thunderbird Dynasty pole is raised at Prospect Point.
- Souvenir pillowcases with Stanley Park’s Thunderbird totems are sold by the local Scenery Shop curio store.

1946 **Vancouver Diamond Jubilee**

- Mungo Martin carves a pole for the governor general of Canada and gives him the name “Nakapankim.” Martin and other Kwakwaka’wakw dance for the public in Kitsilano Park.

1958 **B.C. Centennial** (mainland colony of British Columbia is founded)

- “Klow-ha-ya (Welcome) from Totemland” postcards are produced featuring poles from provincial museum collections.
- Mungo Martin carves two identical poles for Queen Elizabeth II (sent to London) and for the Maritime Museum (in Vancouver).

1966/67 **B.C./Canadian Centenary** (mainland and island colonies unite into one single B.C. province; creation of the Dominion of Canada)

- The “Route of the Totems” is established at transit points throughout British Columbia, with poles carved by / located at:

Henry Hunt (Kwakwaka’wakw) / Victoria (a replica of a Tanu Pole collected by RBCM in 1954); Swartz Bay; Kelsey Bay

Tony Hunt (Kwakwaka’wakw) / Sidney; Horseshoe Bay

Simon Charlie (Cowichan) / Qualicum; Duncan

Stan Modeste (Cowichan) / Malahat

Jimmy John (Nuu-chah-nulth) / Nanaimo; Ladysmith

Sam Henderson (Kwakwaka’wakw) / Campbell River; Tsawwassen

Mathias Joe (Squamish) / Shannon Falls

Kwakwala Arts and Crafts Group (Kwakwaka’wakw), including James Sewid, Charley George Jr. and Henry Speck / Courtenay; Parksville; Departure Bay

Charlie Walkus (Kwakwaka’wakw) / Port Hardy

Jack James (Kwakwaka’wakw) / Nimpkish River

William Jeffrey (Tsimshian) / Prince Rupert

Charlie Dudoward (Tsimshian) / Port Simpson

1971 **B.C. Centennial** (entry of British Columbia into Dominion)

- Poles were given to each Canadian province as a gift from British Columbia. Pole carvers / locations included:

Alfred Joseph (Hagwilget /Carrier) / Province House and Confederation Centre, Charlottetown, Prince Edward Island

Lloyd Wadhams (Kwakwaka’wakw) / legislative building grounds, Regina, Saskatchewan

James Dick (Kwakwaka’wakw) / Victoria, British Columbia

Oscar Matilpi (Kwakwaka’wakw) / legislative grounds, Edmonton, Alberta

Daniel Matilpi (Kwakwaka’wakw) / Ontario Place, near waterfront on Lake Ontario, Toronto

Henry Hunt (Kwakwa̱ka̱'wakw) / south of the National Arts Centre, in Confederation Park, Ottawa, Ontario; legislative building grounds, Winnipeg, Manitoba
Stan Modeste (Cowichan) / a "conspicuous spot" in Fredericton, New Brunswick
Jimmy John (Nuu-chah-nulth) / St. John, Newfoundland
Frank Knighton (Nitinaht) / legislative building, Yellowknife, Northwest Territories
Simon Charlie (Cowichan) / Quebec City, Quebec
William Jeffrey (Tsimshian) / entrance to the Yukon Regional Library, Whitehorse, Yukon
Paterson McKay (Greenville Indian Band / Prince Rupert) / Port Hastings, Halifax, Nova Scotia
Victor Mowatt (Hazelton)
Sam Henderson (Kwakwa̱ka̱'wakw)
(Tony Hunt, Bill Reid, Robert Davidson, and Doug Cranmer showed initial interest then declined to participate)

1986 **Vancouver Centennial** (see Expo '86 in appendix E)

APPENDIX G

A SELECTION OF POLES RAISED IN OR FOR NATIVE COMMUNITIES (1957–1988)

NOTE: Poles are listed chronologically by language-group, from north to south. We include some poles that stand in urban centers but were intended for their Native residents. A few are discussed further in the text. This list is highly selective and provisional; we include it as such to indicate some of the various contexts and timelines that different communities used to revitalize noncommercial totem pole carving. We encourage readers to compile additional information on totem poles carved by and for indigenous communities on the Northwest Coast within this period and to inform the authors for inclusion in subsequent editions of this book.

Tlingit

1970 Nathan Jackson replicates the Nexadi Halibut Pole in Ketchikan.

1972 Edward Kunz, William Smith, Tom Jimmy, and Edward Kunz Jr. carve two poles honoring Raven and Eagle clans for the Auk Tribe building in Juneau. The Raven Pole was based on an original pole from Wrangell by Willaim Ukas.

1980 Before carving two poles celebrating Juneau's centennial in 1980, Nathan Jackson consulted elders from Auk and Angoon, the two nearest Tlingit communities, as to the most appropriate subject matter. Following their recommendation, he created one pole that tells the story of the Wooshkeetaan people of Angoon and Juneau, which includes the image of Uncle Sam as a reminder of the navy's shameful attack on Angoon in 1882. The other pole depicts crests of the Raven Clan from Auk (H. Stewart 1993, 181–83).

1983 Interior Tlingit Dempsey Bob is commissioned by the Tongass Historical Museum to carve a pole depicting Raven Stealing the Sun, which honors the Tongass people (H. Stewart 1993, 170).

1984 Steve Brown and Wayne Price replicate old poles at Wrangell for Kiks.adi Totem Park (H. Stewart 1993, 175–78).

Haida

1969 Robert Davidson carves a pole for his ancestral community of Massett, the first in over half a century raised on Haida Gwaii. After consulting Barbeau texts for a suitable model, he chose Raven and Eagle crests to better represent the entire Massett (and Haida) community. Audrey Hawthorn from MOA collected a $3,000 Cultural Fund grant to help support him. When the pole was raised in front of the local Anglican church, Davidson says he witnessed his first Haida ceremony, his first "real cultural event" (Davidson 1997; see also Blackman and Hall 1982, 32; Steltzer and Davidson 1994, 21–25).

1978 Davidson carves four house posts for the Charles Edenshaw Memorial Longhouse in Massett (partly commissioned by the National Museum of Man, partly funded under a Manpower Canada project). He carved two posts with Raven crests and two with Eagle, in addition to model poles of all as a guiding tool for his assistants, including Jim Hart (Steltzer and Davidson 1994, 29; Thom 1993, 24, 63, 88).

1978 Bill Reid carves a pole for his ancestral village of Skidegate, the first raised there in almost a century. On this pole—Reid's only large uncommissioned work—he was assisted by Gary Edenshaw,

Joe David, Gerry Marks, and Robert Davidson. It was raised in front of the Skidegate Band Council office (see Wyman 1986, 51; Shadbolt 1986).

1986 Reg Davidson carves and raises a pole for his father, Claude Davidson, in front of his house. It was Reg Davidson's first solo pole, although he had assisted Robert in 1969 when he was only fourteen (H. Stewart 1993, 152).

Tsimshian

1982 David Boxley carves a pole for his ancestral community of Metlakatla, Alaska.

1987 Frieda Diesing (with Dorothy Horner, Myrtle Laidlaw, and Sandra Westly) is commissioned by the Kitsumkalum Band to carve two poles, which are raised at a roadside Native gift shop. One shows crests from the families of the village, the other is a replica of an old pole lost to a flood over a century ago (and copied from an old photo). These are the first poles raised here in 150 years (H. Stewart 1993, 156–57).

Nisga'a

1973 Norman Tait and his father, Josiah Tate, raise a thirty-seven-foot, four-crest "Tribal Unification Pole"—his first totem pole—at Port Edward to commemorate the town's incorporation. It was the first Nisga'a pole raised in over fifty years. The Taits put many animals on it to represent the diverse Native population of the town. Tait was given his first formal Nisga'a name at the pole's raising (L. Fisher 1985, 78–82; Jensen 1992, 9–10).

1975 Norman Tait carves an eighteen-foot pole for the first Native-run cannery in Port Simpson. It tells the story of "the beginning of man" (a version of the same narrative as that on his pole at the Native Education Centre in Vancouver).

Gitk'san

1970 The opening of K'san Village is accompanied by the carving of many new poles, most with local crests or versions of old narratives. One unusual pole is carved by Duane Pasco (with other K'san carvers) specifically for raising at the opening ceremony. It has a white man on top, representing the British Columbia government, with dogwood tree leaves (the official floral emblem of British Columbia). These are stacked on three village crests: eagle, wolf, and mosquito/human (a Fireweed Clan crest) (H. Stewart 1993, 159–62).

1971 Walter Harris carves and raises a pole in Kispiox.

1972 Walter Harris replicates a pole from the early 1900s. Following tradition, he appoints his uncle from another clan to "stand over" and guide the carving. It was raised with great ceremony (H. Stewart 1993, 167).

1973 Walter Harris (with Earl Muldoe and Victor Mowatt) carves a pole at Kispiox showing a mountain goat crest with other supernatural or mythological figures (H. Stewart 1993, 166).

1976 Earl Muldoe combines the crests from two old poles—the 1845 White Owl Memorial Pole and the c. 1880 Grizzly Bear of the Sun Pole (both carved for two chiefs of the same name, Gitludahl)—into one new pole. It is carved from an inverted tree, so that it is wider at the top, as was one of the original poles (H. Stewart 1993, 168).

1978 Walter Harris raises two poles at the Kispiox Band office (H. Stewart 1993, 164–65).

Kwakwaka'wakw

1957 Mungo Martin carves a Thunderbird pole for Courtenay, British Columbia. Andy Frank, chief of the local Comox Band, oversees the raising ceremony (McKenzie 1957, 48).

1960 Mungo Martin carves a memorial pole for his son, David (who died the year before in a boating accident), which was raised at Courtenay by the Comox Band then moved to the Comox reserve in 1974 (H. Stewart 1993, 124–25).

1970 Henry and Tony Hunt carve a memorial pole for Mungo Martin (who died in 1962). It is carved in Thunderbird Park in Victoria and raised in the Alert Bay burial ground. As he was the first chief to openly host a potlatch after the ban was lifted, it is appropriate that Martin's was the first pole raised in Alert Bay in over twenty years (H. Stewart 1993, 140–41).

1976 A memorial pole for Jonathan Hunt, carved by Tony and Calvin Hunt, Peter Knox, and John

Livingston, is raised in Alert Bay. Jonathan Hunt had attended Martin's pole raising in 1970 and asked his family to do one for him when he passed away (H. Stewart 1993, 142–43).

1978 Doug Cranmer carves a memorial pole for his father, Daniel Cranmer. It is modeled after an early Alert Bay pole and raised in that village (H. Stewart 1993, 144).

1978 Sam Henderson carves a memorial pole for his wife, May, which displays her family crests and is raised in the We-Wai-Kum Band cemetery in Campbell River (H. Stewart 1993, 136).

1983 Bill and Ernie Henderson carve and raise a memorial pole for their father Sam in the We-Wai-Kum Band cemetery in Campbell River (H. Stewart 1993, 135).

1986 Bill Henderson (with Sam Henderson Jr. and Patrick Hunt) carves a memorial pole for Chief Bill Roberts of Campbell River. It is carved forty-two-feet high because Roberts always cut his trolling poles to that dimension. It stands in front of the We-Wai-Kum community hall (H. Stewart 1993, 134).

Nuu-chah-nulth / Makah

1977 Art Thompson, Joe David, and Ron Hamilton carve a pole at Nitinaht, the first new pole in the carvers' lifetimes.

1977 Art Thompson carves a pole for the village at Nitinaht.

1980 Steve Brown carves a pole for Neah Bay.

Coast Salish

1988 The Sechelt Band raises two poles to mark recognition of Sechelt by the provincial and federal governments as its own municipality. One pole is carved by Jamie Jeffries (with Dwayne Martin, Howard Paul, Martin Baptiste) in a loosely Kwakwa̱ka̱'wakw style. A plaque at its base reads, "In celebration of practicality, good will and reasonableness, showing what can be achieved when governments work together," reinforcing the Sechelt's claim to self-governance (H. Stewart 1993, 93).

NOTES

PROLOGUE

1 This dress came out when Jonaitis was at the American Museum of Natural History; because of connections within the museum, she was given the opportunity to wear this dress at the gala that celebrated the exhibit Chiefly Feasts: The Enduring Kwakiutl Potlatch. She visited the Mizrahi studio and tried on the dress, which, not surprisingly, did not fit.

2 See Engeman (1990) for an in-depth discussion of this comic opera, its relationship to the blatant self-promotion of Seattle, the commercial ties between Alaska and Seattle, and the then-forthcoming Alaska-Yukon-Pacific Exposition of 1909.

3 This (mis)conception has even made it into a book title. In his introduction to Harry Allen Smith's 1941 *Low Man on a Totem Pole*, Fred Allen jokingly writes, "If Smith were an Indian he would be low man on any totem pole" (H. A. Smith 1941, xiii).

4 We are especially indebted to Zena Pearlstone for so faithfully clipping images of poles in various publications and sending them to us.

5 A note on terminology employed in this book: As the most general descriptor, we use the term "Native" to refer to the inhabitants of the American continent at the time of European conquest, as well as to their descendants. General synonyms for "Native" include the increasingly popular—and more politicized—terms "indigenous" and (in Commonwealth countries such as Canada and Australia, at least) "aboriginal." In the United States, the term "Native American" is generally preferred (although "American Indian" is maintained in certain contexts), while Canada officially employs three basic terms: "First Nations," "Inuit," and "Metis." In the United States, many Native people live on "reservations" governed by "tribal councils," while in Canada, they live on "reserves" managed by "band councils." In both countries, many Native cultural and political bodies increasingly refer to themselves as unique nations (e.g., Haida Nation, Navajo Nation) within their respective nation-states.

CHAPTER 1

1 British Columbia Natives often point out that the "North" in the term "Northwest Coast" is somewhat America-centric; in Canada, the Pacific region and its inhabitants are known simply as "West Coast," and Vancouver and Victoria are securely in the southwest of that region.

2 One quite imaginative description of poles as expressions of spirituality is offered by Louis Effler, in *My Flight to Totem Land* (1943, 40): "It is an integral part of their religious concepts—a belief in the supernatural, which they have found difficult to express—and have mixed up therefore, with grotesquerie, fanaticism, mysticism in a web of legend and traditions! This is as near as any White man may come to evaluating the true meaning of the totem pole to a Northwest Coast Indian."

3 Indigenous terms for carved poles are too numerous to list here, as there is an enormous linguistic diversity on the coast (a number of mutually unintelligible languages), and as terms often differed for the various types of columns within each language and subdialect.

4 There is an age-old debate in the human sciences over whether many indigenous societies had concepts or words for "art" prior to contact and exchange with Europeans. While a worthy ethnographic and philosophical question

in itself, we do not take it up here. Rather, we focus on the different uses of, contexts for, and attitudes toward the totem pole among both Natives and non-Natives. As we discuss, "art" is simply one of the many lenses through which poles have been viewed by diverse colonial communities.

5 The most important contribution to this movement was the 1984 Museum of Modern Art exhibition and its catalogue, *"Primitivism" in 20th Century Art: Affinities of the Tribal and the Modern* (Rubin 1984), which juxtaposed and drew formal parallels (as well as lines of more direct influence) between indigenous and modern art. This gave rise to a critical discourse on the aesthetic and conceptual role of the "primitive" in both modern art and modernity, aspects of which we address in subsequent chapters here; see, for example, Clifford (1988), Price (1989), Hiller (1991), Connelly (1995), Rushing (1996), and Jessup (2001).

6 These "new art historians" wrote in the last several decades of the twentieth century. See, for example, Clark (1973), Belting (1987), and Pollock (1988).

7 In 1986, Igor Kopytoff articulated this concept of the "cultural biography of things." He suggested that the unique and shifting values of objects can be best appreciated by investigating the sociological aspects of a work (where it came from, who used it throughout its life and in what contexts) and by asking in particular, "How does the thing's use change with its age, and what happens when it reaches the end of its usefulness?" (Kopytoff 1986, 66–67).

8 Guy Debord (1994) proposes that the increasing focus on the visual has come about in part from the transformation of contemporary Western culture into a "society of the spectacle" in which the visual assumes a central place in the construction of capitalist culture. A significant aspect of the field of visual culture is the recognition of the global dimensions of the subject of study, as well as the roles that imperialism and postcolonialism have played in the creation of modern, global culture. See Mirzoeff (2002), and W.J.T. Mitchell (1994) for insights into the study of visual culture.

9 That attitude still exists among those people who judge accommodations on the part of Native people to the modern world as "inauthentic." Examples of this include the denunciation of Alaskan Eskimos who hunt whales with motorized harpoons, and contemporary totem pole carvers who block out their carvings with chain saws.

10 See R. Phillips (1998) for extensive analysis of this phenomenon in the Eastern Woodlands region of North America. For other critical and influential essays on more recent anthropological approaches to art, visual culture, and shifting contexts of value, see Graburn (1976), Appadurai (1986), Marcus and Myers (1995), Phillips and Steiner (1999), and Myers (2001). Following Gell's (1998) influential argument about the agency—the ability to directly act on the world and affect social relations—latent in art objects themselves, a number of scholars (see Pinney and Thomas 2001, and Miller 2005) explore how the specific and sensual materiality of objects contributes to their aesthetic, economic, cultural, and political efficacy.

11 See Hawker (2003) and Dawn (2007) for such analyses of British Columbian and Canadian engagement with Northwest Coast art. Nicholas Thomas (1999, 2001) and Fred Myers (2002) offer examples of this colonial cultural dynamic from nineteenth- and twentieth-century Australia and New Zealand.

12 For the Northwest Coast, see Codere (1950) on the changing Kwakwa̱ka̱'wakw potlatch; Blackman (1976) on transformations of Haida visual culture; and Harkin (1997) for a discussion of such phenomena among the Heiltsuk.

13 Nicholas Thomas (1994) takes issue with the essentialization of colonialism and argues that the culture of colonialism undergoes numerous transformations unique to the specific example at hand, responding to various political, economic, cultural, and historical influences. Thomas takes especially to task the concept of colonialism's "fatal impact," which sometimes exaggerates the colonizers' powers and underestimates the Native people's creative accommodations and resistances. He also disputes the good vs. evil discourse on colonialism, where all whites are bad and all Native people good, insisting that the accurate story is naturally far more complicated.

14 These two notions, "transculturation" and "contact zones," have been productively explored further by James Clifford (1997) as they relate to colonial contacts, the production of ethnography, and the collection and promotion of art.

15 Nicholas Mirzoeff stresses the connection between colonialism and material objects (such as totem poles) in his assertion that "collectively, the visual culture of colonialism had a significant role to play in explaining, defining and justifying the colonial order" (Mirzoeff 2002, 474); how the visual culture is represented becomes

part of that explanation, definition, and justification. Art historian Terry Smith (2002) identifies three primary modes of colonial representation: calibration, obliteration, and aestheticization. Likewise, David Spurr (1993), in his analysis of colonial discourse, identifies twelve different ways of writing about Native people—including debasement and idealization— several of which resonate with Smith's three tropes. For Spurr, these representations function within the establishment, maintenance, and dissolution of a colonial authority that rests on simultaneous recognition of sameness and difference.

16 hese terms are borrowed from the field of literary criticism and refer to the distributed authorship of most "texts." Rather than assume the absolute referential meaning of any given piece of writing, the term "intertextual" implies that fragments of text are meaningful only in relation to all other occurrences (references, citations, allusions, quotations, borrowings) of similar statements. Likewise, rather than assume the absolute creative authority of writers, the term "multivocal" recognizes that texts become fully meaningful only through the collaboration of various voices (authors, characters, readers, critics, etc).

17 For an intriguing analysis of other aspects of Northwest Coast culture, some of which are touched upon in this book, see Raibmon (2005).

18 For a discussion about the vitality of objects in the context of Kwakwa̱ka̱'wakw food culture, see Jonaitis (2006).

CHAPTER 2

Quoted in Wright (2001, 95).

1 These travelers rarely explained how they learned anything, so Moziño's comments are particularly unusual. Typically, early accounts are silent on the use of translators or gestures to communicate, and on whether anyone on the ships learned Native languages. Without such documentation on sources and methods of information gathering, these accounts offer valuable, yet incomplete portrayals of late-eighteenth-century Northwest Coast people.

2 See appendix C for a list of early images of poles as well as major photographic expeditions.

3 From a conversation with Ḳi-ḳe-in; transcribed by Aaron Glass and edited by Glass & Ḳi-ḳe-in.

4 According to Steve Brown (personal communication, 2003), very early Tlingit poles existed prior to the settlement by Haida in southern Alaska, such as one old pole in Kasaan, the last village to become "Haidaized." Recent research (Strankman 2003) reveals that the Kadjisduaztc poles in Old Kasaan were in fact commissioned by the Haida residents after they moved into the village (Wright, personal communication, 2006).

5 The Tlingit often used spruce, along with hemlock, for house posts and planks.

6 Albert Niblack, in his report "The Indians of the Northwest Coast" (1888, 329) interprets the nonexistence of totem poles among the northern Tlingit as their having *lost* the tradition as a result of missionary activity. He claims that Tongass, Kasaan, and Skidegate represent the most "primitive" villages, thus explaining the presence of poles there. This is simply one indication that by the 1880s totem poles had become the iconic image of Northwest Coast cultures, used as a sort of litmus test for their traditionality or authenticity.

7 In his "The Southern Extent of Totem Pole Carving," Barnett (1942) details the appearance of numerous pole-like carvings among the Salish, definitively placing the southern limits of family crest poles at the Comox and Pentlatch; "By contrast, the emblems used over the rest of the area lacked both the distinctive variety and the sanction of antiquity which made them definitely family (as opposed to individual) privileges in the north" (Barnett 1942, 388).

8 In *Marvelous Possessions* (1992), Stephen Greenblatt describes the prevalent use of familiar categories, such as "ex voto," in attempting to describe the highly unfamiliar when Europeans encountered new cultures full of elements apparently unique to them.

9 See, for example N. Thomas (1999). These debates are further reminiscent of the great sixteenth- and seventeenth-century dialogues over whether the newly "discovered" American Indians had fully developed souls like the Europeans or were inferior and thus natural-born slaves (see Pagden 1982). The fundamental distinction between seeing indigenous people as "like" or "not like" Europeans is also intrinsic to the more contemporary philosophical and epistemological tension between a modernism based upon the universality of humanism and the postcolonial/postmodern politics of radical alterity.

10 The original drawings done in the field were as accurate as possible, considering the unfamiliarity artists had with

formlines. Many of the shipboard artists were trained naturalists capable of great realism and veridicality in their images. But when their drawings were transformed into prints for publication in Europe, they were at times made more sensational to reinforce the European notion of indigenous barbarism. For example, features might be exaggerated or skulls added to the base of poles.

11 In *The Middle Ground* (1991), historian Richard White analyzes the early encounters between Native people and Europeans in the Great Lakes as profitable and reciprocally influential for both.

CHAPTER 3

Quoted in Hinckley (1996, 385).

1 For literature on this colonial history, see Duff (1964a), R. Fisher (1977), Titley (1986), Tennant (1990), Galois (1994), and C. Harris (2002).

2 Coppers are often emblazoned with individual or family crests. They are the most valuable form of symbolic, material wealth on the coast, and are passed within and sometimes between families for generations, accruing value through each transaction

3 We are indebted to Steve Brown (personal communication, 2003) for this information. A similar borrowing occurred among the Nuxalk, when Chief Clellamin added a Bavarian-style peaked roof line to his bighouse following a Nuxalk visit to Germany in the 1880s; though clearly influenced by European architecture, the peaks themselves referred to a unique privilege mentioned in a clan legend (Laforet 1992, 36–37). This house thus represented both ancestral and intercultural encounters.

4 The Haida clans, like other Northwest Coast people, were organized into opposing moieties, social groupings that performed ritual and cultural services for one another. Margaret Blackman, in her important 1973 article, "Totems to Tombstones: Culture Change as Viewed through the Haida Mortuary Complex," was among the first to analyze this transformatory aspect of Haida culture. Such indications of cultural endurance have by and large been overlooked. In the romanticizing modernist tradition we have described, the disappearance of the great totem poles overshadows such a hybrid indication of cultural adaptation.

5 The concept that photographs defy time and history is a central tenet of many analyses of photographs, especially of ethnographic subjects. In her book on photography, Elizabeth Edwards (2001, 236) suggests a more complex process in which a kind of history is revealed through these images. "In photographs there meet for a moment histories of the colonial, of the colonialised, and of anthropology as a discipline represented through its instruments of fieldwork, the archive and the museum."

6 For biographical treatments of Boas, see Cole (1999) and Rohner (1969); for an assessment of Boas's influence on North American anthropology, see Darnell (2001) and Stocking (1974).

7 Boas's dismissal of what he judged acculturated groups was unfortunate for subsequent generations of scholars, for very valuable information could have been assembled on these groups that revealed their varied and often ingenious responses to colonization. What might have appeared on the surface as complete acquiescence to white authority often concealed elements of resistance and adherence to tradition.

8 The first was Edward Sapir, one of Boas's star students, who became the director of the nascent Ethnological Survey of Canada in 1910. Sapir's presence guaranteed the influence that Boasian perspectives would have on early Canadian anthropology. (See Freedman 1976, Darnell 2001, and references therein).

9 Barbeau had some fairly outlandish notions, such as his proposal that Hawaiian Natives traveling on late-eighteenth-century trading ships stimulated the creation of Northwest Coast poles and that the Northwest Coast crest system was borrowed wholesale from whites, with the eagle and Thunderbird inspired by Russian shields, and the beaver by the Hudson's Bay Company emblem (Barbeau 1950).

10 The rejection of this concept is fundamental to many contemporary anthropological studies. Arjun Appadurai (1991), for example, argues that cultural models need to move beyond the boundary-specific and holistic, to acknowledge the constantly changing social, temporal, and historical relations of groups, while James Clifford (1997) confronts classic notions of ethnic localization, arguing that contact and movement are central to the formation and maintenance of ethnic identities. In the realm of Northwest Coast studies, Wayne Suttles (1997) argues that the denigration of Salish culture as "inferior" to that of the groups farther north was a result of imposition of an essentialist model on the region's cultures

that appraised the Salish as an "imitative" people lacking the sophisticated elements of groups farther north.

CHAPTER 4

1 This trope was still common in the mid-twentieth century, as is evident in the popular book *Out of the Silence* by Adelaide de Menil and Bill Reid (1971), which combines compelling black-and-white photographs of decaying totem poles in situ, with a poetic text mourning their fate.
2 As Erve Chambers (2000, 74) points out in his analysis of modern tourism, a brief wilderness encounter highlights man's tenuous relationship with nature while stimulating a kind of nostalgia for the urban tourist's distance from that nature.
3 Dean MacCannell (1992, 17–18) uses the term "neo-totemism" to describe the contemporary fascination with "the primitive." See Bruner and Kirshenblatt-Gimblett (1994) for a study of such responses to the Maasai of East Africa.
4 David Spurr (1993, 7) describes the "colonial paradox" as colonizers wanting their subjects to be radically different from themselves as a way of legitimizing their authority, but wanting them to also be fundamentally similar, as only such sameness can guarantee prospects for civilization. See Karp and Krantz (2000) for an essay on how this ambivalence often works itself out in museum exhibitions.
5 Modernity, the prevailing ideology of America from the late nineteenth century to, arguably, the present, represents the modern as superior to the premodern or primitive. However, modernity comes at a cost and sometimes inspires nostalgia for the past, for the simple, and for the primitive. In *The Tourist* (1989), first published in 1976, Dean MacCannell noted that modernity has come at the price of alienation and inauthenticity. This, in turn, inspires the craving for a truly authentic experience that often impels tourism.
6 Barbara Kirshenblatt-Gimblett, in her book *Destination Culture* (1998), describes how tourism and the practices it entails help turn neutral spaces into meaningful places, marked by certain traveler expectations, represented by particular images and icons, and memorialized by specific souvenirs.
7 Jane Desmond's *Staging Tourism* (1999) approaches the hula and other expressions of the exotic in Hawaii from an intercultural perspective similar to that of this chapter.
8 These two crests belong to opposite moieties and thus cannot appear together on a pole.
9 In her section on the Queen Charlottes, Scidmore (1897, 38) speculates on the possible origin of the totem pole. Noting similarity with some Polynesian sculpture, she suggests a possible influence from the New Zealand "tiki." Her other hypothesis, evidently influenced by Franz Boas's early theories, is that the "imitative and adaptive rather than originative" Haida, inspired by the Kwakiutl's simpler and earlier version, "carried [the totem pole] to its finest development."
10 In a recent book about Carr, Gerta Moray (2006) offers a more sympathetic and nuanced reading on Carr's relationship with First Nations people.

CHAPTER 5

1 Some guidebooks do mention the origins of some poles, especially those in Ketchikan and Sitka, but concentrate more on the pole as an indicator of Native culture rather than an object that emerged from interactions between whites and Natives.
2 The British Columbia Native land claims are complicated. The federal and provincial governments differed on the size of allotments. Nationally, Canadian Indians received 160 acres or one square mile per family, while traditionally, coastal British Columbia Native bands, as corporate entities, controlled several small areas for their seasonal subsistence activities. The Dominion government, recognizing the difference in subsistence patterns between coastal and other Canadian Natives, proposed that each British Columbia Native family receive eighty acres. The province insisted twenty acres was sufficient. The disagreements continued until 1912, when Premier Richard McBride formed a special five-member Royal Commission on Indian Affairs, chaired by J.A.A. McKenna, to finally determine the appropriate size of British Columbia Native allotment on a case-by-case basis. In 1916, after three years of traveling and conducting extensive interviews, the commission produced a report, which was ratified by both Dominion and provincial governments as the McKenna-McBride Agreement in 1924. On the colonial history of British Columbia and the administration of Indian affairs, see Duff (1964a), R. Fisher (1977), Titley (1986), Tennant (1991), and C. Harris (2002).
3 For the history of the potlatch ban, see LaViolette (1961)

and Cole and Chaikin (1990). For an aboriginal perspective, see Sewid-Smith (1979) and the film *Potlatch: A Strict Law Bids Us Dance* (Wheeler 1976). For postcolonial perspectives on the potlatch—and resistance to it—as law, see Bracken (1997) and Loo (1992).

4 In 1961, that museum moved to a new building in Vanier Park, where it remains today.

5 The totem poles of Stanley Park are some of the most extensively written about in the world; see also Raley (1945), Gunn (1965), H. Stewart (1993), Hawker (2003), and Jensen (2004).

6 By the 1960s, most of the Stanley Park poles were seriously decaying and in need of restoration, and various artists contributed to recreating these poles. Kwak'wa̲ka̲'wakw carver Doug Cranmer restored the Nhe-is-bik, the Wakas, and the Sisa-kaulas poles; Ellen Neel, Charlie James's granddaughter, restored his Thunderbird house posts. The Haida mortuary post had been torn down in 1962, so the Vancouver Parks Board commissioned Bill Reid to carve the replica. In 1963, all of these sculptures were moved to Brocton Point, where they stand today. In 1976, Kwak'wa̲ka̲'wakw carver Ellen Neel's son restored a pole his mother had carved in 1955 for Woodward's Department store in Edmonton, which was then erected in Stanley Park. Because the Thunderbird house posts were evidently beyond repair, in 1988 Tony Hunt replicated one, using photographs to retrieve the original designs. Over the years, several original poles joined the others: a Tsimshian pole by Norman Tait (1987), a Nuu-chah-nulth pole by Art Thompson and Tim Paul (1988), and an unusual carving by Kwak'wa̲ka̲'wakw Beau Dick (1991) that contains both Kwak'wa̲ka̲'wakw and eastern Canadian Native motifs.

7 In his analysis of material culture, Nicholas Thomas points out that objects are subjected to transforming forces that emerge from their particular cultural biographies. "Objects are not what they were made to be but what they have become. . . . Insistence on the fact that objects pass through social transformations effects a deconstruction of the essentialist notion that the identity of material things is fixed in their structure and form. Hence, although certain influential theorists of material culture have stressed the objectivity of the artifact, I can only recognize the reverse, the mutability of things in recontextualization" (N. Thomas 1991, 4, 28).

8 According to an undated manuscript in the Ketchikan Library entitled "1903 Totem Pole Donors from Prince of Wales Island, Alaska," Gov. Brady secured the following poles from these owners and villages: at Klinkwan, the Frog Raven Pole from Edward Scott; at Quilas /Kionglas, the Golden Hill Pole and Wolf Pole from L. Yealtatsee; at Klawock, the Wasgo Pole from Kooneit; at Sukkwan, the Trader Legend Pole from Douglas Suk-qua, the Mosquito Legend Pole from Hattie Wallace, and the Lakich'inei Pole from John Kanow/Jones; at Old Kasaan, the Yaadass Crest Pole and two corner poles from John Baronovich; at Tuxekan, the Raven Shark Pole from Chief Taki'et, the Gaanax.adi Raven Crest Pole from Chief Gunyah, the Cormorant Mortuary Pole from George Stanley, the Raven Memorial Pole from Thomas Snuck, and the Diving Raven Pole from Yunnaii.

9 This sale took place the year after Indian agent William Halliday arrested Kwak'wa̲ka̲'wakw potlatch participants and confiscated their regalia. When Ottawa officials learned that he had sold some of the items to George Gustav Heye, an American collector, they chided him for allowing the material to leave Canada.

10 As an indication of this project's "success," Smith describes how some Gitk'san opened their houses to tourists to show off their regalia (H. Smith 1928, 82). Where the visitors may have presumed this to be some prelude to commercial transaction, the Gitk'san were just as likely asserting their status through displays of their hereditary possessions.

11 This represents one of many examples of Native people using white law to achieve their cultural ends. During the potlatch ban, they frequently hired lawyers to defend their interests and sent signed petitions to the various levels of government. In Alaska, the Kiks.adi Clan even once sued a rival clan in court for "copyright infringement," requesting an injunction against their rivals' use of a contested frog crest. They won the case (Alaska State Historical Library, 1899).

12 We are indebted to Steve Brown (personal communication, 2003) for providing this information.

CHAPTER 6

1 As Molly Lee (1991, 28) points out, sometimes the tourist would go so far as to remove pieces of actual poles and bring them home to display. While merely fragmentary,

these chunks directly index the authenticity of their source.

2 The souvenir, Stewart argues, "contracts the world to expand the personal" (S. Stewart 1984, xii) and "reduces the public, the monumental, the three-dimensional into the miniature, that which can be enveloped by the body, or into the two-dimensional representation, that which can be appropriated within the privatized view of the individual subject" (137–38). The souvenir, as a miniature, becomes the "interiorization of an exterior" (144), an object of nostalgia that refers to the past, to the preindustrial. See also R. Phillips (1998, 72ff) for a compelling discussion of the miniature and the souvenir among Eastern Woodlands Native people.

3 For example, some Kwak'wa̱ka̱'wakw chiefs have ceremonial names indicating the great height of their stockpiles of blankets.

4 Just as photographs are more complex representations than they at first appear, so are objects such as souvenirs. Arjun Appadurai notes that an object can often experience a phase in its biography when it becomes a commodity and when its relevant feature is "exchangeability (past, present or future) for some other thing" (Appadurai 1986, 13). A fruitful field for investigation is the transformation of objects from unique, inalienable items used in their originating culture into commodities that can be sold and bought by others outside that culture. Objects become recontextualized as they move from the state of inalienability within a prestige economy (such as the Northwest Coast, where images were "owned" by chiefly families) to the status of commodity that results from processes of collection, exhibition, and transnational circulation (N. Thomas 1991). The involvement in this process of institutions ranging from museums and the academy to the tourist industry cannot be underestimated, but indigenous producers, brokers, and consumers participate as well.

5 This phenomenon is hardly unique to Alaska; rail (and later auto) tourism to the American Southwest at the time was integrally connected with trade in Native art, which was consolidated in that region by the Fred Harvey Company.

6 Leslie Drew and Douglas Wilson, in *Argillite: Art of the Haida* (1980), suggest that prior to contact, shamans smoked tobacco in argillite pipes. Peter Macnair and Alan Hoover, in *The Magic Leaves: A History of Haida Argillite Carving* (1984), disagree, contending that the earliest pipes were made circa 1820 for ceremonial use within communities and that later carvers then began crafting works specifically designed for foreigners.

7 It is important to note that not all Haida miniatures were fine carvings; as the market increased, people who were not trained began to produce works that they could sell. This was common among other coastal groups as well.

8 This disreputable tradition continues today, with shops selling carvings of fossilized mammoth ivory made in Indonesia but carefully labeled "made from Alaska material."

9 Edited from correspondence Suttles sent to Jonaitis before his death (Suttles 2003).

10 Decades ago, anthropologist Nelson Graburn (1976) began to investigate such commodities as valid artistic products of the intercultural encounter.

11 Daniel Miller (1987) suggests that we actually define ourselves by that which we consume, in the process transforming those consumables into things invested with meaning and personal significance. The model totem pole is not just a "thing" separate from its owner but a part of the owner's experience, very much owned (claimed, incorporated) by the consumer and not simply possessed. Recontextualized commodities, like our tourist's model pole, assume new, profound meanings to their new owners in a process of objectification: "Objectification describes the inevitable process by which all expression, conscious or unconscious, social or individual, takes specific form" (Miller 1987, 81). Consumption of the material item, then, becomes a process of subjectification whereby the individual social subject constitutes himself or herself in part through the object's subsequent ownership.

12 In her study of filmic representations of Northwest Coast Native peoples, Rosalind Morris (1994, 89) applies this concept of the fetishization of the object to totem poles: "In this light, the supremacy of the totem pole, as image and artifact in museums and film making, assumes new significance. In an important regard, it is the doubled sign of ethnographic process: the pole itself becomes the totem that ethnographers assign to Northwest Coast culture in general. And in . . . museum halls . . . the history of coastal cultures is surreptitiously reduced to these towering sculptures and the relations between them." This entire

process facilitates decontextualization, circulation, and resignification, for scholars and museum collectors as well as for tourists.

13 *Better Homes and Gardens* (1948).

14 As Nicholas Thomas (1994, 30) suggests, even to this day, "primitive" art "in the bourgeois living room . . . offers a spiritual palliative to our overheated, overconsuming, unnatural, postindustrial world."

15 Decades later, a generic Alaskan bird-topped pole appeared on the cover of the May 16, 1993, *New York Times Magazine*'s special edition of "The Sophisticated Traveler," where a line of diverse Americans carry objects that have become "classic" icons of America and its tourist destinations: a small African American boy pulls a cart with a bald eagle; a woman carries a Thanksgiving turkey; Martha Washington carries a model of Mount Vernon; a California mission monk carries a candle; a grass-clad Hawaiian woman carries a palm tree; and a bearded lumberjack carries an iconic totem pole. It is of considerable interest that it is not a Native American carrying that pole, but a logger from the industry that has created considerable environmental and political stress in the Northwest Coast region.

16 The two sets of poles may represent a common lineage prerogative, despite the stylistic variation. The Alert Bay poles have a thicker diameter and different painted designs. The top figure on the Alert Bay poles is a Thunderbird (with curved horns), while the Stanley Park poles feature an eagle; the hands of the bear on the Alert Bay poles cover a human head, under which is the body of a copper, while the Stanley Park bears hold the humans around the torso.

17 Many poles in Alert Bay feature a Thunderbird as the mythical creature that helped the legendary ancestors of the local 'N̲amgis to raise the house beams of their first bighouse.

18 At the other end of the size spectrum, perhaps the world's smallest totem pole, measuring only 4.4 centimeters, was carved by Oweekeno artist Roy Hanuse in 1972 and is in the University of British Columbia Museum of Anthropology (Webb 2000, 11).

19 Since it was made, several other taller poles have been raised; the Web site acknowledges this, but assures readers that "Ed's probably continues to be the world's largest concrete totem pole" (Roadside America, n.d.).

CHAPTER 7

Quoted in Cole (1985, 30).

Quoted in Barrett (1940, 8).

1 James Clifford (1997) designates the appearance of cultural phenomena outside their "traditional" geographic locales as "traveling cultures." He discusses how these displaced and replaced objects become focal points for the negotiation of values and social relations between originating peoples and the communities and institutions through which objects pass.

2 The most thorough general surveys of world's fairs are Rydell (1984) and Greenhalgh (1988).

3 Historian Douglas Cole, in his masterful history of Northwest Coast artifact collecting (1985), describes this as the "scramble for Northwest Coast artifacts."

4 See Jonaitis (1988).

5 Some of these museums purchased poles from dealers, while others, like the American Museum of Natural History, funded their own collectors.

6 Most social evolutionary theories of the Victorian era—influenced primarily by Lewis Henry Morgan, Edward Tylor, and James Frazer—posited three (sometimes four) stages of universal human development: savagery, barbarism, and civilization. Each was characterized by particular technologies, social and economic structures, and religious and cultural expressions.

7 In his important study of world's fairs, historian Robert Rydell (1984) argues that displays of "ethnic types" at many American fairs marked the replacement of class consciousness with race consciousness.

8 National Museum of Natural History, catalogue number 54298.

9 Denver Art Museum, catalogue number 1946.251.

10 The Smithsonian's ethnologist in charge of the Philadelphia exhibit, Charles Rau, embraced the notion that representations of "primitives" served whites well; in an address in New York, Rau stated that "the extreme lowness of our remote ancestors cannot be a source of humiliation; on the contrary, we should glory in our having advanced so far above them, and recognize the great truth that progress is the law that governs the development of mankind" (quoted in Rydell 1984, 24). Fairgoers embraced such attitudes. In a novel about the fair, James Dale described the wax Indian figure "with his small, cruel black eyes, his coarse, unkempt locks, and the

chains of his wide cheekbones, and large animal mouth" (quoted in Rydell 1984, 26). William Dean Howells, in the *Atlantic Monthly*, wrote the following about Philadelphia's Native exhibits: "The red man, as he appears in effigy and in photograph in this collection, is a hideous demon, whose malign traits can hardly inspire any emotion softer than abhorrence." Such evaluations recall the attempts made by early explorers to describe totem poles themselves. For Howells, the only solution to the "Indian problem" was their final extinction—a fate many people felt was in the future of such inferior beings (quoted in Rydell 1984, 26).

11 The reference to poles with "huge noses projecting like pump-handles" and faces with lidless eyes could allude to more than just the Native carvings under observation and may reveal the racism so prevalent at the time among Anglo-Saxon Americans; Asians could be dismissed as having similarly "lidless brows," while Jews were often mocked for their "huge noses."

12 As we pointed out in chapter 3, Boas later modified his position on the centrality of the Kwak'wa̲ka̲'wakw in Northwest Coast history.

13 The Kwak'wa̲ka̲'wakw at the Chicago fair have been subject to extensive research. See in particular Jacknis (1991). Raibmon (2000) offers an intriguing analysis of their performances as expressions of resistance to colonialism, although Glass (2006) qualifies some of her conclusions. See N. Harris et al. (1993) and Hinsley (1991) for analyses of Native people at the fair.

14 This means he was a very wealthy high-status man who hosted a great potlatch.

15 For a children's book on the biography of the Indianapolis pole, see Feldman (2003).

16 This exhibition trope—of simulating firelight in the gallery context to dramatically illuminate masks and totem poles—was likely originated by Samuel Barrett, of the Milwaukee Public Museum, in his 1940 reinstallation of Northwest Coast material on the grounds of the recently ended fair in San Francisco. It has since come to be common in displays of Northwest Coast art.

17 Ethnonym appearing as "Hwitsowitenne" in Jenness (1943, 475).

18 Kaiget is a crest to both the Gilhersu and the Laksilyu clans (Mills 1994, 86). See legend of Kaiget in Barbeau (1929b), Jenness (1934), and Chapman (1965).

19 Myers draws on insights outlined by James Clifford (1997), who described how conflicting and often contradictory values are inscribed onto objects from non-Western cultures as they circulate through global economies and institutions. See also Kirshenblatt-Gimblett (1998); N. Thomas (1991); Price (1989); and Errington (1998).

CHAPTER 8

Quoted in Hill (1995, 192).

1 Greater Vancouver hosted similar events, such as the Tyee Potlatch of June 25–July 5, 1924, held to welcome the visiting British fleet. Such a use of the term "potlatch" suggests a regional variation on the widespread use of "powwow" to refer to any gathering of leaders. Both terms were clearly misunderstood, as were the indigenous ceremonies to which they purportedly refer.

2 For a thorough analysis of Canadian identity formation through visual arts on the Northwest Coast, see Dawn (2006).

3 In the 1910s and 1920s, Ottawa-based ethnographers Harlan Smith (1917, 1923), Edward Sapir, and Marius Barbeau all suggested using indigenous images in mainstream design and manufacturing to help support a distinctively Canadian commercial aesthetic (as did the Reverend George Raley in British Columbia in the 1930s); see also Sapir to Scott, 20 December 1917 and 18 May 1818, Correspondence files, box 633, file 15, CMC. A similar and contemporaneous movement was occurring in America: the American Museum of Natural History in New York mounted a 1919 show encouraging the use of American Indian motifs in modern design (Vaillant 1939, 2). Boas reported in 1922 to the British Columbia Natural History Society that Tiffany's in New York was collecting Indian art to develop their designs (Reel 1763, vol. 43, Folder 39, NFP); see also Coster (1916) and Jacknis (2002, 118–19).

4 A similar relationship of direct influence—loosely extended into the realm of more spiritual "affinities"—was later explored in MoMA's famous 1984 exhibit, Primitivism in 20th Century Art: Affinities of the Tribal and the Modern (Rubin 1984; see chapter 1, note 15).

5 After the fair, Audrey Hawthorn installed almost all of the University of British Columbia Museum of Anthropology's Northwest Coast collection in buildings on the former fairgrounds as part of the two-year Man and His World exhibition, where Robert Davidson could be seen carving a totem pole for the city of Montreal.

6 As was the case in the 1958 centennial, some totem pole depictions had little to do with First Nations populations. For example, the 1966 trophy for the thirty-first tournament of the National Association of Left-Handed Golfers, held for the first time outside the United States, includes a totem pole "hand-carved by Indian carver Raymond Williams [of Nitinaht] considered one of the finest Indian craftsmen in the Pacific Northwest" (*B.C. Centennial Spokesman,* February 1966, 2).

7 Information on the 1971 totem project is located in the Provincial Archives of British Columbia, Victoria, GR 1450, box 28 P-T-4.

8 Totem poles were also deployed in 1971 in less monumental—though no less symbolic—ways. For instance, a play entitled *In the Blood* was commissioned from England-born writer Reg Watts by the North Vancouver Arts Council. According to the synopsis, the play "captures the cultural heritage of Canada's Native people and the strength and spirit of the early pioneers. . . . The story reaches a climax when [the young white protagonists] are shipwrecked on Totem Island and a struggle for their lives is fought between the Lulaks (spirits of the dead) and the magic totem poles." The script, complete with a Foreword by Chief Dan George, was published in 1974 by R.J. Watts & Associates Ltd., Vancouver.

9 See H. Stewart (1993) for profiles of many of the individual poles in Duncan and along the Route of the Totems.

CHAPTER 9

Duff (1957, 22).

Duff (1967, n.p.).

1 Quote from the 1955 film *Making a Totem Pole* by Audrey Hawthorn and B. Hill-Tout (Vancouver: University of British Columbia).

2 This museum was renamed the Royal British Columbia Museum (RBCM) in 1987.

3 The actions of the joint Native/non-Native projects to restore, replicate, and celebrate Northwest Coast totem poles represent examples of what Nicholas Thomas (1994) calls "colonialism's culture." Such public endeavors hope to negate the discrete socioeconomic boundaries between dominant and subservient groups by forming localized means of negotiating between the desires and drives to appropriate lands and resources, and the genuine values of civility and humanitarianism. The results transform both the colonizers and the colonized, often in unexpected ways.

4 According to Jacknis (2002, 147), Hawthorn approached Neel after he heard her talk at the 1948 conference on Native issues at UBC.

5 See Nuytten (1982) and K. Phillips (2000). This privileging of a particular idea of "traditional" authenticity represents an example of the imposition of what Nelson Graburn (Ostrowitz 1999, vii) terms the "pastness" that still characterizes so many approaches to Native art.

6 On September 27 and 28, 2003, Chief Peter Knox, Martin's only grandson, rededicated the house on its fiftieth anniversary. The house front and pole were repainted by David Mungo Knox, Peter's son, and two evenings of dances honored the original event for the public and invited guests.

7 Although most of the published information on Martin stresses the contributions he made to both the MOA and the RBCM, the attention he brought to Kwakwa̱ka̱'wakw culture, and his outstanding corpus of poles and other carvings, he himself benefited significantly from his relationships with those museums. As Glass (2006a) has demonstrated, Martin took strategic advantage of these commissions to benefit himself and his family. He achieved considerable fame, hosted a grand potlatch in a very public setting, and displayed numerous privileges. Thus, in a cosmopolitan and distinctly Kwakwa̱ka̱'wakw way, Martin enhanced his own status, not by hosting a potlatch in his home village but instead by negotiating opportunities offered by the museum staff and mobilizing the fame he garnered in the big city as a result.

8 During negotiations, a mistake in protocol occurred, for the highly significant and meaningful Ha-ne-lal-gag Pole of Chief Gamlakuyelt, who had signed the agreement, was not included in the document. As Gamlakuyelt outranked the other chiefs, to replicate their poles before his constituted an insult. As a result, his pole was removed and replicated as well (Duff 1958).

9 Information on this project is primarily located in Duff, Wallen, and Clark (1969).

10 Between 1940 and 1969, paint was often used in the efforts to preserve the Alaska poles. According to Steve Brown (personal communication, 2003), those who did the repainting—who were rarely Native—did not understand the carvings as well as the CCC carvers had, and thereby

obscured the original craftsmanship.

11 Lecture notes in Duff (1971).

12 Duff (1952), Dawn (1981), and Anderson and Halpin (2000) include accounts of Gitk'san potlatches, feasts, and totem pole raisings during the mid- to late 1940s.

13 "Ethnology" is not something one exhibits; it is an anthropological mode of studying cultural forms in order to posit social scientific rules. Ethnology and art are two different modes of presenting and evaluating objects from any culture; Northwest Coast objects had until then simply been received primarily through the frame of ethnology and had been presented in museums of ethnology. See Clifford (1988), Price (1989), and Errington (1998).

14 The following interpretation is heavily influenced by Benedict Anderson's *Imagined Communities* (1983), in which he analyses how colonial governments in Southeast Asia took control over various major historic monuments for their own purposes.

15 The result of this symposium was the 1982 publication *Indian Art Traditions of the Northwest Coast*, edited by Roy Carlson.

16 See Abbott (1981, 307–14) for a selection of Duff's poems. This volume was produced as a memorial to Wilson Duff several years after his death. More recently, E. N. Anderson (1996) edited a volume of Duff's previously unpublished writings, notes, and poems. They reveal his late obsession with art (Northwest Coast art especially) from a very abstract, metaphysical perspective.

CHAPTER 10

George Dorsey (1898, 167).

Jackson (2003).

1 Recent scholars have argued that the connotations implied by the term "renaissance" give a misleading impression of the social and cultural activity of First Nations in the twentieth century (see Duffek 1983; Duffek and Townsend-Gault 2004; Crosby 1991; Jonaitis 1993; Glass (forthcoming). Specifically, they address the primary role of non-Native patrons in the process, the inaccuracy of the analogy with the European Renaissance, and, most importantly, the reality of cultural continuity for many Native communities. If we deny the truth of absolute cultural death, then colloquial "rebirth" is a poor model of artistic revitalization.

2 On the notion of art worlds, see Danto (1964), Becker (1982), Alsop (1982), and Bourdieu (1993). For the history of the Northwest Coast art world, see Duffek (1983), Ames (1992), Hawker (2003), and Glass (2002).

3 Mungo Martin exerted a great personal, scholarly, and stylistic influence on Bill Holm as well.

4 Holm has always denied the extent of influence often credited to him. This denial likely stems from three sources: his characteristic humbleness and generosity; his personal experience with Native communities during a time that later scholars have oversimplified; and, no doubt, his wish to avoid undue entanglement in what became in the 1980s a contentious front in the politics of representation.

5 For a variety of views on Reid's art and life, see *Bill Reid and Beyond* (2004), a collection of essays from a 1999 conference on Reid's legacy, edited by Karen Duffek and Charlotte Townsend-Gault. In that publication, Glass (2004b) investigates the question of Reid's association with his heritage by identifying his involvement with the two different histories implicated in the Northwest Coast renaissance, that of "making, performing and living" the art and culture, the other the growth of awareness and appreciation of the art. For a highly critical analysis of Reid's life, see Tippett (2004).

6 That is to say, "primitive art," even when highly valued, was typically placed in the realm opposite from modern art, via a series of binary criteria (tradition-bound vs. innovative; communal/anonymous creation vs. individual genius; utilitarian vs. art-for-art's-sake; culture-bound vs. universal; artifact vs. art; natural history museum vs. art gallery/museum). See, for example, the work of Price (1989) and Errington (1998).

7 This was true of the movements of African Americans and Hispanic Americans as well.

8 First Nations people had an additional appeal for some who saw resonances between their own mystical leanings and experimentation with psychotropic drugs. Hippies were delighted by the supposed parallels between their experiences of altered states with what they understood shamans to experience. Thus, around this period, the stereotype of Indian as shaman developed. And, as environmental concerns became increasingly pressing, the noble savage was resurrected as the first environmentalist (Jonaitis 1981 and Krech 1999).

9 The years around 1950 proved a synchronous turning point in the Northwest Coast art world: Inverarity published

his book, MOA opened and soon hired Mungo Martin, the Massey Commission mandated federal support for "Canadian" art, and the potlatch ban was lifted. Although the effects of this final act took years to manifest, lifting the ban opened a space for a return to the ceremonial context for raising new totem poles.

10 Sargent 1964 (located in the Royal British Columbia Museum library). Among the Gitk'san, it was critical that a family paid for the pole-raising ceremony in order to validate the pole publicly. STPRS needed to find some way to defray the ceremonial costs to the families of repairing and reerecting their poles while maintaining proper protocol. Sargent came up with an ingenious idea to avoid the expense of feasting and ceremonies: by restoring an entire village at one time rather than repairing individual poles.

11 This represents one of the historic reversals in which the government now helped pay for the "restoration" of cultural practices, but as part of its own nationalizing efforts; multiple agendas were thus being served, some of which were in political tension. Another example from the same time was the use of centennial funds to help support the building of the Alert Bay bighouse, which simultaneously was used to promote tourism and revitalize the potlatch (see page 238).

12 'Ksan (n.d.)

13 Despite occasional controversy in the carving shed, press, or classroom, there has been little sustained scholarly attention to the issue of non-Native production of Northwest Coast–style art; however, see Campbell (2004).

14 Over time, the art market—often influenced by Native pressure—responded with some practical solutions, including careful listing of Native artists' tribal affiliations or narratives of their cultural experiences and knowledge, or using the term "Northwest Coast style" to refer to the work of non-Native artists. These tactics help manage but do not solve the political or ethical issues involved in this particular appropriative dynamic.

15 Alaska Indian Art (n.d.)

16 The prices of these carvings ranged from Beasley's three-foot *Rain Man Trail Marker* ($5,500) to Calvin Hunt and Livingston's seven-foot, nine-inch *Tlingit House Post* ($22,500).

17 Thanks to Charlotte Townsend-Gault for comments on MacDonald's sculpture.

CHAPTER 11

Dolphinarium (1998).

1 Government of Canada (n.d.); British Columbia Archives (n.d.); Black (n.d.); Wright (n.d.); University of Washington Libraries (n.d.); Library of Congress (n.d.).

2 Although most observers believe the promotional material that claims that elaborate holographic technology had been used to create these illusions, Bill Holm convincingly demonstrates that Spirit Lodge used old-fashioned mirrors and reflections (2003).

3 The Knott family was and is famously religious; there is even an active chapel on the park's grounds, located in the vicinity of the Spanish mission models, so that visitors can stop and pray between rides on the Montezuma's Revenge roller coaster.

4 In his comparison of contemporary productions and performances of Native culture with world's fair presentations, Nick Stanley (1998) argues that today it is not as clear as it once was who is representing what for whom. Aboriginal people perform with a keener sense of the benefits to them of tourism and economic awards. Audiences appreciate the exoticism of an unusual performance but find its site of presentation—a theme park designed for pleasure—comfortable and reassuring.

5 This was not the first time that totem poles appeared at an aquarium attraction. At some point in the 1980s or early '90s, SeaWorld (in San Diego, California) temporarily decorated the JumboTron screen behind their orca pool/theater with schematic winged totem poles and panels with generic Northwest Coast-esque motifs (see photograph in Rugoff 1995, 8). There is no indication that the Dolphinarium was aware of this, but it is possible.

6 Totem-themed restaurants have also been found at Disneyworld in Orlando, Florida, at the Milwaukee Public Museum, and at the old Musée de l'Homme in Paris.

7 The Grand Hall can even be understood as a materialization of the misleading collaged photographs in Marius Barbeau's "Totem Pole" volumes, which visually juxtapose poles from separate locations, giving the illusion of proximity.

8 Not everyone favors this popular approach to museology, which is so heavily influenced by theme parks, and some criticize the contemporary museum for being too welcoming to the masses, too accessible to the public, and insufficiently serious. For example, cultural historian

Andreas Huyssen criticizes how "the museum itself has been sucked into the maelstrom of modernization" commercialized and spectacularized for profit and fame (Huyssen 1995, 21).

9 This site was accessed in 2002. The business is no longer operating.

10 This site was accessed in 2002. The business is no longer operating.

11 One imagines that these names are not "magical" for Native speakers of the local languages. Like the touristic framing of totem poles mentioned above, "magic" here seems to be used as a synonym for the lure of the "untranslated" or even the "unknowable."

12 See Butterfly Tours (n.d.)

13 The relationship between totem poles and Japan is complicated. Not only have souvenir poles been manufactured there for decades, one of the "world's largest totem poles" was exhibited in Osaka at the 1970 Expo, along with a pole by Kwakwa̱ka̱'wakw Sam Henderson and a pole lent by the Gitk'san. As Robin Wright points out (e-mail to Aldona Jonaitis 2006), there have been some interactions between Northwest Coast artists and Ainu carvers—there are even Ainu poles in Vancouver near Simon Fraser University.

14 We are grateful to Charlotte Townsend-Gault for suggestions toward such a reading. (See Townsend-Gault 1997, 2004).

15 Andreas Huyssen (1995, 33), drawing on Walter Benjamin, comments that there is a modern need for *auratic* objects (objects with an aura): "Longing for the authentic is a form of fetishism."

CHAPTER 12

Haisla totem (n.d.).

1 Today, the semantic neutralization of this tacit political message is further achieved by the reproduction of the Capilano pole as a small foam puzzle-model sold in Vancouver toy and souvenir shops; the puzzle box pictures the silhouette of the Capilano Suspension Bridge, another contemporary tourist icon of the city, which shares the name but not the location of the totem pole (see page 221).

2 Diesing was of Haida origin, but studied at 'Ksan and lived at Terrace in Tsimshian territory.

3 Postmodern or post-structuralist theories critique the univeralistic aspects of a humanist modernism by embracing an often radical politics of difference. This is not the kind of alterity imposed on Native people by evolutionary categories or colonial discourse of savagery, but one often espoused by Native people to assert their indigeneity (their priority, their (ab)originality on the land). In addition, the national discourse of multiculturalism in Canada, born from the Québécois issue as much if not more than the Native or immigrant presence, provides for a history and model of diversity different from the "melting pot" metaphor of the United States. This has ramifications for differences in national Native policy.

4 On October 26, 2001, the replica of the older pole fell in a windstorm. It was left where it fell, in respect for tradition. One might read the decision not to restore or replicate it (again) as part of this larger return to more "traditional" social protocol. Kitsumkalum First Nation (n.d.).

5 This report, along with previously unpublished testimony from eighty-eight witnesses and additional appendices, was published in 1998 as *Haa Aani—Our Land: Tlingit and Haida Land Rights and Use* (Goldschmidt and Haas 1998).

6 Sealaska and the village corporations became involved with logging, fishing, and tourism. See D. Mitchell (2001) and McClanahan (2006).

7 See Pointing (2006); Rose (2000); and Molloy and Ward (2006).

8 Similar agreements to supply museums with replicas (and often on-site pole-carving demonstrations) in exchange for repatriation have been worked out by Harvard's Peabody Museum and the Burke Museum at the University of Washington.

9 Ultimately these poles were distributed to the California Academy of Sciences, the Chicago Field Museum, Michigan State Museum, the Washington State Museum, Cornell University, the Museum of the American Indian Heye Foundation (later National Museum of the American Indian), and the Peabody Museum at Harvard (Cole 1985, 309).

10 Glass (2004a) discusses how claims for repatriation often couch the objects in question in terms of kinship relations, as members of the extended family, or as specific parts of the (social) body.

11 See Caughran (2003) for a detailed biography of the pole that made its way to the Peabody Museum. A short documentary film, entitled *Full Circle* (Qin 2002), recounts the social biography of this particular totem.

12 See Duff (1953) for a detailed description of all the poles in Alert Bay as of August 2, 1953. See also Spradley (1969) for James Sewid's account of the creation of the bighouse.

13 James Knox adopted Mungo Martin's grandson Peter after the latter's father, David Martin, died. Peter was initiated by Knox at this 1965 potlatch and today is the recognized "owner" of Wa'waditla, Martin's house in Thunderbird Park.

14 We would like to thank Charlotte Townsend-Gault, instigator of the "Victory through Honour" Pole Committee, for bringing this event to our attention and sharing with us her videotape of the event. See also Lewis (2004), UBC Alma Mater Society (2004).

15 See Tippett (2004) and Duffek et al. (2004) on Reid and his complicated relationship to his own Haida ethnicity.

16 In Vancouver alone, totem poles adorn the Aboriginal Friendship Center, low income housing, and the Native Education Center, all found on the city's east side, where the majority of nonreserve Native people live. On the campus of UBC, the First Nations House of Learning, the administrative center of aboriginal curricula, was designed with indigenous architectural principles in mind and contains a hall supported by totem poles representing five different coastal language groups. These poles supplement the many other urban totems scattered throughout the city—in parks, museums, malls, and in front of civic buildings, such as the downtown Canadian Broadcasting Centre.

17 In their publications, Bill Holm (1990) and Steve Brown (1998, 2000) have made significant contributions to the reassessment of Salish art. See also Ostrowitz (1999) for interesting insights into the process of replicating the past.

18 See Vancouver International Airport (n.d.).

19 These "simulacra" spaces in the airport—the "natural scenes"—are replete with actual wave pools and recorded bird songs among the simulated rocky landscape, out of which "emerge" Native carvings. Nonetheless, these artworks are labeled with culturally sensitive and accurate discursive panels, presenting First Nations voices and perspectives. So stereotype can coexist with active voice, appropriation with agency.

CHAPTER 13

H. Smith (1927).

Frankenstein and Brady (2000).

1 See Robert Berkhofer's groundbreaking book, *The White Man's Indian* (1978), for a detailed history of literature on Native people since contact from this perspective.

2 For an early and important discussion of Curtis's photographic methods, see Lyman (1982).

3 Cultural historian James Clifford (1997, 127) reacted with some surprise when, at the Kwagiulth Museum in Cape Mudge, British Columbia, he saw Curtis's postcards for sale. He initially felt disappointed, and asked, "Have I traveled all the way to Quadra Island to encounter these well-known, even stereotypical, faces?" He soon realized, however, that the cards' captions identified the actual individuals—specific information that has meaning for community members. "What the image communicates here may be quite different from the exoticism and pathos registered by an audience of strangers," Clifford cogently concluded.

4 Many of the props from the film are now in the Burke Museum collection at the University of Washington in Seattle.

5 Clifford writes, "[Curtis's] interest in a 'vanishing' culture seems to have overlapped productively with their own interest in a way of life which some knew through their parents and grandparents and with which they felt a strong continuity through changing times" (1997, 127). (See http://www.curtisfilm.rutgers.edu).

6 On both of these films, see R. Morris (1994, 45–66).

Boas never edited or released his film footage. Bill Holm annotated and released Boas's footage in 1973 under the title *The Kwakiutl of British Columbia* (Seattle: University of Washington Press).

REFERENCES

Abbott, Don, ed. 1981. *The World Is as Sharp as a Knife: An Anthology in Honour of Wilson Duff*. Victoria: Royal British Columbia Museum.

Aboriginal Journeys. N.d. Wildlife and Adventure Tours. http://www.aboriginaljourneys.com. Accessed August 18, 2008.

Aboriginal Orca Adventure. N.d. North Island Kayak Rentals and Tours. http://www.kayakbc.ca/Guided%20Kayak%20Tours/Expedition%20Tours/Aboriginal%20Orca%20Adventure.htm. Accessed September 7, 2008.

Acheson, Steve. 1980. Ninstints Village. *Datum* 5 (2): 13–17.

Alaska Indian Arts. N.d. Alaska Indian Arts: Commissioning a Totem. http://www.alaskaindianarts.com/2pic.html. Accessed August 18, 2008.

Alaska State Historical Library. 1899. Kiks.adi Clan case. August 8. 1988.0001 vertical file.

American Baptist Home Mission Society. 1911. *Alaska: Totem Poles, Polygamy, Slavery, Ingenuity, Thrift & Pride of Office*. Chicago: American Baptist Home Mission Society.

Ames, Michael. 1992. *Cannibal Tours and Glass Boxes: The Anthropology of Museums*. Vancouver: University of British Columbia Press.

Anderson, Benedict. 1983. *Imagined Communities*. New York: Verso.

Anderson, E. N., ed. 1996. *Bird of Paradox: The Unpublished Writings of Wilson Duff*. Surrey, B.C.: Hancock House Publishers.

Anderson, Margaret, and Marjorie Halpin. 2000. *Potlatch at Gitsegukla*. Vancouver: University of British Columbia Press.

Anderson, Ross. 2003. Still Standing: From Fine Art to the Trinket Trade, a Native Tradition Survives. *Seattle Times*, March 2, Pacific Northwest section.

Appadurai, Arjun, ed. 1986. *The Social Life of Things: Commodities in Cultural Perspective*. Cambridge, UK: Cambridge University.

———. 1991. Global Ethnoscapes: Notes and Queries for a Transnational Anthropology. In *Recapturing Anthropology*, edited by R. Fox, 191–210. Santa Fe: School of American Research Press.

———. 1997. *Modernity at Large: Cultural Dimensions of Globalization*. Minneapolis: University of Minnesota Press.

Arima, Eugene. 1983. *The Westcoast (Nootka) People*. Victoria: Royal British Columbia Museum.

Atkins, Bernard. 1961. *The Silent Ones*. Victoria: British Columbia Department of Recreation and Conservation.

Augaitis, Daina. 2005. *Brian Jungen*. Vancouver: Vancouver Art Gallery.

Ayre, Robert. 1933. Canadian Group of Painters. *Canadian Forum* 14: 98, 100.

Badger, Reid. 1979. *The Great American Fair: The World's Columbian Exposition and American Culture*. Chicago: Nelson Hall.

Baird, Jill. 1995. Kla-how-ya Hello from Totem Pole Land, or, A Bit of the Other to Enhance the Blank Landscape of Whiteness. Paper submitted to John O'Brien Fine Arts 443, University of British Columbia.

Bannister, C. N.d. *The Story of Our Totem Poles*. Vancouver: C. Bannister.

Banta, Melissa, and Curtis Hinsley. 1986. *From Site to Sight: Anthropology, Photography, and the Power of Images*. Cambridge, MA: Peabody Museum Press.

Barbeau, Marius. 1928. *The Downfall of Temlaham*. Toronto: Macmillan.

———. 1929a. Ancient Culture Vignettes Past. *CNR Magazine* 15 (7): 33.

———. 1929b. *Totem Poles of the Gitksan*. Ottawa: National Museums of Canada.

———. 1930. Totem Poles: A Recent Native Art of the Northwest Coast of America. *The Geographical Review* 20: 258–72.

———. 1931. Our Indians—Their Disappearance. *Queen's Quarterly* 38 (Autumn): 691–707.

———. 1938. The Modern Growth of the Totem Pole on the Northwest Coast. *Journal of the Washington Academy of Sciences* 28 (9): 387–91.

———. 1950. *Totem Poles*. Ottawa: National Museums of Canada.

Barnett, Homer. 1942. The Southern Extent of Totem Pole Carving. *Pacific Northwest Quarterly* 33, no. 4 (October): 379–89.

———. 1955. *The Coast Salish of British Columbia*. Eugene: University of Oregon Press.

Barrett, S. A. 1940. The Peoples of North America. In *Aboriginal Cultures of the Western Hemisphere: Golden Gate International Exposition, 1940, Treasure Island, San Francisco*, U.S. Golden Gate International Exposition Commission, 8–12. San Francisco: Pisani Printing and Publishing.

Barrett, Samuel. 1963. *The Totem Pole*. The American Indian Film Project. Berkeley: University of California.

Baudrillard, Jean. 2001. *Jean Baudrillard: Selected Writings*. 2nd ed. Palo Alto: Stanford University Press.

B.C. Centennial Spokesman. 1966. Special Trophies for Southpaws Hand Made by Indian Carver. February 2.

B.C. Indian Arts Society. 1982. *Mungo Martin: Man of Two Cultures*. Sidney, B.C.: Gray's Publishing.

Beaglehole, J. C., ed. 1967. *The Journals of Captain Cook*, vol. 3. Cambridge, UK: Cambridge University Press.

Belting, Hans. 1987. *End of the History of Art?* Chicago: University of Chicago Press.

Berkhofer, Robert. 1978. *The White Man's Indian*. New York: Alfred A. Knopf.

Bernstein, Bruce. 1999. Contexts for the Growth and Development of the Indian Art World in the 1960s and 1970s. In *Native American Art in the Twentieth Century*, edited by W. Jackson Rushing III, 57–74. New York: Routledge.

Better Homes and Gardens. 1948. Clipping from May issue. Ye Olde Curiosity Shop Archives. Courtesy of Kate Duncan.

Bhaba, Homi. 1994. *The Location of Culture*. London: Routledge.

Bird, S. Elizabeth. 1996. *Dressing in Feathers: The Construction of the Amerindian in American Popular Culture*. Boulder, CO: Westview Press.

Black, Martha. 1997. *Bella Bella: A Season of Heiltsuk Art*. Toronto: Royal Ontario Museum.

———. 1999. *HuupuKanum Tupaat, Out of the Mists: Treasures of the Nuu-chah-nulth Chiefs*. Victoria: Royal British Columbia Museum.

———. N.d. Totem Poles in the Royal BC Museum. http://www.royalbcmuseum.bc.ca/Content_Files/Files/TotemPoles.pdf. Accessed August 21, 2008.

Blackman, Margaret. 1973. Totems to Tombstones: Culture Change as Viewed through the Haida Mortuary Complex. *Ethnology* 12: 47–56.

———. 1976. Creativity in Acculturation: Art, Architecture and Ceremony from the Northwest Coast. *Ethnohistory* 23 (4): 387–413.

———. 1981. Window on the Past: The Photographic Ethnohistory of the Northern and Kaigani Haida. *National Museum of Man Ethnology Service Papers* 74.

———. 1982. *During My Time: Florence Edenshaw Davidson, a Haida Woman*. Seattle: University of Washington Press.

Blackman, Margaret, and Edwin S. Hall, Jr. 1982. The Afterimage & Image After: Visual Documents and the Renaissance in Northwest Coast Art. *American Indian Art Magazine* 7, no. 2 (Spring): 30–39.

Boas, Franz. 1887. Museums of Ethnology and Their Classification. *Science* 9: 587–89.

———. 1888. The Development of the Culture of Northwest America. *Science* 12: 194–96.

———. 1893. Ethnology at the Exposition. *Cosmopolitan* 15 (5): 607–9.

———. 1897. The Social Organization and the Secret Societies of the Kwakiutl Indians. *Report for the U.S. National Museum for 1895*. Washington, D.C.: Smithsonian Institution.

———. 1922. Reel 1763, vol. 43, folder 39, MSS. 1077. Charles Newcombe Family Papers. British Columbia Provincial Archives.

———. 1955. *Primitive Art*. New York: Dover Press. (Orig. pub. 1927.)

Bohrer, Frederick. 2003. *Orientalism and Visual Culture: Imagining Mesopotamia in Nineteenth-Century Europe*. Cambridge, UK: Cambridge University Press.

Bolton, Laura. 1943. *Totems: Indians of British Columbia*. Ottawa: National Film Board of Canada.

Boltz, Peter, and Hans-Ulrich Sanner. 1999. *Native American Art: The Collections of the Ethnological Museum Berlin*. Seattle: University of Washington Press.

Boswell, Sharon, and Lorraine McConaghy. 1996. "Seattle Spirit" Soars on Hype. http://seattletimes.nwsource.com/special/centennial/march/golden_potlatch.html. Accessed August 16, 2008.

Bourdieu, Pierre. 1993. *The Field of Cultural Production*. New York: Columbia University Press.

Boyd, Richard. 2000. L'Exposition universelle de Chicago, à la fin du XIX siècle. *Cahiers de Sociologie économique et culturelle: Ethnopsychologue* 33: 55–83.

Boyd, Robert. 1999. *The Coming of the Spirit of Pestilence: Introduced Infectious Diseases and Population Decline among Northwest Coast Indians, 1774–1874*. Seattle: University of Washington Press; Vancouver: University of British Columbia Press.

Bracken, Christopher. 1997. *The Potlatch Papers: A Colonial Case History*. Chicago: University of Chicago Press.

Bridgewater, Alan, and Gill Bridgewater. 1991 *Carving Totem Poles and Masks*. New York, NY: Sterling Publishing Company.

British Columbia Provincial Museum. 1958. An Agreement Between the People of Kitwancool and the Provincial Museum of British Columbia Concerning Certain Totem Poles of Kitwancool. Wilson Duff Papers. Reel B6045, file 61 T51-W-0024.

———. N.d. British Columbia Archives. http://search.bcarchives.gov.bc.ca/sn-49FC2AA/search. Accessed August 21, 2008.

Brody, Hugh. 1994. *The Washing of Tears*. Vancouver: Nootka Sound and Picture.

Bronner, Simon. 1989. *Consuming Visions: Accumulation and Display of Goods in America, 1880–1920*. New York: W. W. Norton & Co.

Brown, Julie. 1994. *Contesting Images: Photography and the World's Columbian Exposition*. Tucson: University of Arizona Press.

Brown, Steve. 1987. From Taquan to Klukwan. In Corey 1987, 157–76.

———. 1995. *The Spirit Within: Northwest Coast Native Art from the John H. Hauberg Collection*. Seattle: Seattle Art Museum.

———. 1998. *Native Visions: Evolution in Northwest Coast Art from the Eighteenth through the Twentieth Century*. Seattle: University of Washington Press; Vancouver: Douglas and McIntyre Press; Seattle Art Museum.

———. 2000. *Spirits of the Water: Native Art Collected on Expeditions to Alaska and British Columbia, 1774–1910*. Seattle: University of Washington Press.

Bruner, Edward, and Barbara Kirshenblatt-Gimblett. 1994. Maasai on the Lawn: Tourist Realism in East Africa. *Cultural Anthropology* 9: 435–70.

Burroughs, John, and John Muir, eds. 1986. *Alaska: The Harriman Expedition, 1899*. New York: Dover Publications.

Butterfly Tours. N.d. Sea Kayak Haida Gwaii. http://www.butterflytours.bc.ca. Accessed August 21, 2008.

Campbell, Alice. 2004. About Humanity, Not Ethnicity? Transculturalism, Materiality and the Politics of Performing Aboriginality on the Northwest Coast. Master's thesis, University of British Columbia.

Campbell-Johnston, Ronald. 1924. *The Story of the Totem*. Vancouver: J. T. Pyott.

Canadian Broadcast Company. 1959. *Totem*. Narrated by Bill Reid.

Canadian Museum of Civilization. 1995. *Raven's Village: The Myths, Arts, and Traditions of the Native People of the Pacific Northwest Coast*. Hull: Canadian Museum of Civilization.

———. 1997. "Totem Poles: Myths, Magic and Monumental Art on the Pacific Northwest Coast." CD-ROM. Burnaby: VR Didatech.

Canadian National Railways. N.d. Totems of Kitwanga and Northern Central British Columbia. Pamphlet.

Cardinal, Gil. 2003. *Totem: The Return of the G'psgolox Pole*. Ottawa: National Film Board of Canda.

Carlson, Roy, ed. 1982. *Indian Art Traditions of the Northwest Coast*. Burnaby, B.C.: Archaeology Press, Simon Fraser University.

Carr, Emily. 1927. Newcombe Papers, British Columbia Archives and Record Service, Victoria. Add. Mss. 1077.

———. 1941. *Klee Wyck*. Toronto: Clark, Irwin and Company.

———. 1966. *Hundreds and Thousands: The Journals of Emily Carr*. Toronto: Clarke, Irwin and Company.

———. 1971. *Growing Pains: The Autobiography of Emily Carr*. Toronto: Clarke, Irwin and Company.

———. 1993. *The Emily Carr Omnibus*. Vancouver: Douglas & McIntyre.

Cathedral Grove. N.d. Cathedral Grove: Totem Pole Web sites. You Don't Know What You've Got . . . 'Til It's Gone. http://catherdralgrove.se. Accessed August 28, 2008.

Catton, Theodore. 1997. *Inhabited Wilderness: Indians, Eskimos, and National Parks in Alaska*. Albuquerque: University of New Mexico Press.

Caughran, Jack. 2003. Coming out of the Cave: The Biography of a Totem Pole. Bachelor's thesis, Harvard University.

Chambers, Erve. 2000. *Native Tours: The Anthropology of Travel and Tourism*. Long Grove, IL: Waveland Press.

Chandonnet, Ann. 2003. *A History of Alaskan Totem Poles*. Anchorage: Arctic Circle Enterprises.

Chapman, Anne. 1965. Mâts totémiques. Amérique du Nord, Côte nord-ouest. *Catalogues du Musée de l'Homme*, Série H. Paris: Musée de l'Homme.

Chittenden, Newton. 1884. *Hyda Land and People: Official Report of the Exploration of the Queen Charlotte Islands for the Government of British Columbia*. Victoria: Government of British Columbia.

Clark, T. J. 1973. *Image of the People: Gustav Courbet and the 1848 Revolution*. New York: Thames and Hudson.

Clifford, James. 1988. *The Predicament of Culture*. Cambridge, MA: Harvard University Press.

———. 1997. *Routes: Travel and Translation in the Late Twentieth Century*. Cambridge, MA: Harvard University Press.

Codere, Helen. 1950. *Fighting with Property: A Study of Kwakiutl Potlatching and Warfare, 1792–1930*. Monographs of the American Ethnological Society, vol. 18. New York: J. J. Augustin Publisher.

Coe, Ralph. 1977. *Sacred Circles: Two Thousand Years of North American Indian Art*. Kansas City: Nelson-Atkins Museum of Art.

Cole, Douglas. 1976. Cook at Nootka: The Engraved Record. *Canadian Collector* 11 (3): 27–29.

———. 1980. Sigismund Bacstrom's Northwest Coast Drawings and an Account of His Curious Career. *B.C. Studies* 46.

———. 1985. *Captured Heritage: The Scramble for Northwest Coast Artifacts*. Seattle: University of Washington Press; Vancouver: Douglas and McIntyre Press.

———. 1999. *Franz Boas: The Early Years, 1858–1906*. Seattle: University of Washington Press; Vancouver: Douglas and McIntyre Press.

Cole, Douglas, and Ira Chaiken. 1990. *An Iron Hand upon the People: The Law against the Potlatch on the Northwest Coast*. Vancouver: University of British Columbia Press.

Collingridge, Shirley. 2001. Raising Hope, Raising Poles. http://www.shirleycollingridge.com/Haida.htm. Accessed August 21, 2008.

Collis, Septima M. 1890. *A Woman's Trip to Alaska: Being an Account of a Voyage through the Inland Seas of the Sitkan Archipelago in 1890*. New York: Cassell Publishing.

Connelly, Frances. 1995. *The Sleep of Reason: Primitivism in Modern European Art and Aesthetics, 1725–1907*. University Park: Pennsylvania State University Press.

Connoly, Jay. 1990. *Duncan: City of Totems*. Pamphlet. City of Duncan, British Columbia.

Cook, Captain James. 1784. *A Voyage to the Pacific Ocean: Undertaken by the Command of His Majesty, for Making Discoveries in the Northern Hemisphere*. 3 vols. London: Printed by W. and A. Strahan for G. Nicol and T. Cadell.

Coombes, Annie. 1991. Ethnography and the Formation of National and Cultural Identities. In Hiller 1991, 189–214.

Cordova Times. 1940. Sitka National Monument. March 24.

Corey, Peter, ed. 1987. *Faces, Voices, and Dreams: A Celebration of the Centennial of the Sheldon Jackson Museum*. Sitka: Sheldon Jackson Museum.

Corser, H. P. 1932. *Totem Lore of the Alaska Indians and the Land of the Totem*. Juneau: Nugget Shop.

Coster, Esther. 1916. Decorative Value of American Indian Art. *The American Museum Journal* 16: 301–7.

Coull, Cheryl. 1996. *A Traveler's Guide to Aboriginal B.C.* Vancouver: Whitecap Books.

Cranmer, Douglas. 1995. Interview with Aaron Glass, Alert Bay, August.

Crosby, Marcia. 1991. Construction of the Imaginary Indian. In *Vancouver Anthology: The Institutional Politics of Art*, edited by Stan Douglas, 267–91. Vancouver: Talonbooks.

Curtis, Edward. 1914. *In the Land of the Head Hunters*. Chicago: Field Museum of Natural History.

———. 1973. *In the Land of the War Canoes*. Seattle: Burke Museum and University of Washington Press. (Released by Milestone Films.)

Dall, William. 1895. Alaska as It Was and Is. *Philosophical Society of Washington Bulletin* 8.

Daly, Richard. 2005. *Our Box Was Full: An Ethnography for the Delgamuukw Plaintiffs*. Vancouver: University of British Columbia Press.

Danto, Arthur. 1964. The Artworld. *Journal of Philosophy* 61: 571–84.

Darling, David, and Douglas Cole. 1980. Totem Pole Restoration on the Skeena, 1925–30: An Exercise in Heritage Conservation. *BC Studies* 47: 29–48.

Darnell, Regna. 2001. *Invisible Genealogies: A History of Americanist Anthropology*. Lincoln: University of Nebraska Press.

Dauenhauer, Nora Marks, and Richard Dauenhauer, eds. 1994. *Haa Kusteeyi: Our Culture*. Seattle: University of Washington Press.

———. 2004. Evolving Concepts of Tlingit Identity and Clan. In *Coming to Shore: Northwest Coast Ethnology, Traditions, and Visions*, edited by Marie Mauze, Michael Harkin, and Sergei Kan, 253–78. Lincoln: University of Nebraska Press.

Davidson, Robert. 1997. Talk given at Emily Carr Institute of Art and Design, Vancouver. January 16.

———. 2003. Telephone conversation with Aldona Jonaitis.

Davidson, Robert, and Ulli Seltzer. 1994. *Eagle Transforming: The Art of Robert Davidson*. Seattle: University of Washington Press; Vancouver: Douglas and McIntyre Press.

Dawn, Leslie. 1981. Ksan: Artistic, Museum and Cultural Activity among the Gitksan Indians of the Upper Skeena River, 1920–1973. Master's thesis, University of Victoria.

———. 2001. How Canada Stole the Idea of Native Art: The Group of Seven and Images of the Indian in the 1920s. PhD thesis, University of British Columbia.

———. 2006. *National Vision, National Blindness: Canadian Art and Identities in the 1920s*. Vancouver: University of British Columbia Press.

Dawson, George. 1880. Report on the Queen Charlotte Islands, 1878. Montreal: Dawson Bros.

———. 1888. Notes and Observations on the Kwakiool People and the Adjacent Coasts. *Proceedings and Transactions of the Royal Society of Canada for the Year 1887*. Montreal: Dawson Brothers.

Dawson, Michael. 2004. *Selling British Columbia: Tourism and Consumer Culture, 1890–1970*. Vancouver: University of British Columbia Press.

Deans, James. 1893. Totem Posts at the World's Fair. *American Antiquarian* 15 (5): 281–86.

———. 1899. *Tales from the Totems of the Hidery*. Chicago: Archives of the International Folk-Lore Association.

Debord, Guy. 1994. *Society of the Spectacle*. Translated by Donald Nicholson-Smith. New York: Zone Books. (Orig. pub. 1967.)

de Laguna, Frederica. 1972. *Under Mount Saint Elias: The History and Culture of the Yakutat Tlingit*. Washington, D.C.: Smithsonian Institution.

———. ed. 1991. *The Tlingit Indians*. By G. T. Emmons. Seattle: University of Washington Press.

de Menil, Adelaide, and Bill Reid. 1971. *Out of the Silence*. Toronto: New Press.

Demetzer, Harold, Earl Muldon, and Elmer Derrick. 2005. *The Tradition Continues: Monumental Sculpture in the Gitanyow and Gitxsan Territories, 1986–1996*. Thunder Bay, Ont.: H. Demetzer Publishing.

Demmert, Dennis. 1973. Alaskan Indian Culture. *Historic Preservation* (January-March): 31–34.

Dennison, Merrill. 1929. The Complete Hotel. *CNR Magazine* 15: 1, 3, 42.

Desmond, Jane. 1999. *Staging Tourism: Bodies on Display from Waikiki to Sea World*. Chicago: University of Chicago Press.

de Wit, Wim. 1993. Building an Illusion: The Design of the World's Columbian Exposition. In Harris, de Wit, Gilbert, and Rydell 1993, 41–98.

d'Harnoncourt, René. 1939. North American Indian Arts. *Magazine of Art* 32 (3): 164–67.

Diamond, Stanley. 1982. *Totems*. New York: Open Book/ Station Hill.

Diesing, Freda. 1989. Notes from interview by Janet Berlo, Vancouver, August 22–24.

District of Alaska. 1905. *The Exhibition of the District of Alaska at the Lewis and Clark Centennial Exposition*. Portland, OR: District of Alaska.

Dixon, George, ed. 1789. *A Voyage around the World; But More Particularly the North-West Coast of America, Performed in 1785, 1786, 1787, and 1788*. London: George Goulding. Reprint, New York: De Capo Press, 1968.

Dolphinarium. 1998. *Houden van Dolfinjnen*. Harderwijk: Dolphinarium Harderwijk.

Dombrowski, Kirk. 1995a. *Against Culture: Development, Politics and Religion in Indian Alaska*. Lincoln: University of Nebraska Press.

———. 1995b. Totem Poles and Tricycle Races: The Certainties and Uncertainties of Native Village Life, Coastal Alaska, 1878–1930. *Journal of Historical Sociology* 8 (2): 136–57.

Donovan, Carrie. 1991. The Magnificent Eight. *New York Times Magazine*, June 2, 48–52.

Dorsey, George A. 1898. A Cruise among Haida and Tlingit Villages about Dixon's Entrance. *Popular Science Monthly* 53: 160–74.

Dossetter, Edward. 1881. Edward Dossetter Fonds. British Columbia Archives, 98604–12.

Douglas, Frederic, and René d'Harnoncourt. 1941. *Indian Art of the United States*. New York: Museum of Modern Art.

Downey, Dennis. 2002. *A Season of Renewal: The Columbian Exposition and Victorian America*. Westport, CN: Praeger.

Drew, Leslie. 1964. Forest of Totems. *The Beaver* 12: 49–55.

Drew, Leslie, and Douglas Wilson. 1980. *Argillite: Art of the Haida*. Vancouver: Hancock House.

Drucker, Phillip. 1948. The Antiquity of the Northwest Coast Totem Pole. *Journal of the Washington Academy of Sciences* 38: 389–97.

——. 1951. The Northern and Central Nootkan Tribes. *Bureau of American Ethnology Bulletin* 144.

——. 1958. The Native Brotherhoods: Modern Intertribal Organization on the Northwest Coast. *Bureau of American Ethnology Bulletin* 168.

Drucker, Phillip, and Robert Heizer. 1967. *To Make My Name Good: A Reexamination of the Southern Kwakiutl Potlatch*. Berkeley: University of California Press.

Duff, Wilson. 1952. *Gitksan Totem Poles: 1952*. Victoria: British Columbia Provincial Museum.

——. 1953. Wilson Duff Papers. British Columbia Provincial Archives and Records Services, Victoria. Reel bg6043, file 4HAI-w-003.

——. 1954a. A Heritage in Decay: The Totem Art of the Haidas. *Canadian Art* 11: 56–59.

——. 1954b. Preserving the Talking Sticks. *Powell River Digester* 30 (6): 10–12.

——. 1957. Totem Poles Recall Vanished Seafarers. *The Crowsnest* 9: 22–25.

——. 1958. The Project. Wilson Duff Papers, British Columbia Provincial Archives and Records Services, Victoria. GR 2809 or microfilm B 6046, file 112e.

——. 1959. *Histories, Territories and Laws of the Kitwancool*. Victoria: Royal British Columbia Museum.

——. 1963. *Thunderbird Park*. Revised edition. Victoria: B.C. Government Travel Bureau.

——. 1964a. *The Indian History of British Columbia*. Vol. 1, *The Impact of the White Man. Anthropology in British Columbia*, memoir 5. Victoria, B.C.: British Columbia Provincial Museum. Reprint, Seattle: University of Washington Press, 1997.

——. 1964b. Contributions of Marius Barbeau to West Coast Ethnology. *Anthropologica* 6: 63–96.

——. 1965. Materials on "Route of the Haidas." British Columbia Provincial Archives and Records Services, Victoria, B.C., Provincial Secretary, GR 1598, box 1, file 4.

——. 1969. MOA Duff Papers, box 3, file 11.

——. 1971. Lecture notes. MOA Duff Papers, box 9, file 21.

——. 1975. *Images, Stone, B.C.: Thirty Centuries of Northwest Coast Indian Sculpture: An Exhibition Originating at the Art Gallery of Greater Victoria*. Seattle: University of Washington Press.

——. 1976. Mute Relics of Haida Tribe's Ghost Villages. *Smithsonian* 7 (6): 84–91.

——. 1981a. Mungo Martin: Carver of the Century. In Abbott 1981, 37–40.

——. 1981b. The World Is as Sharp as a Knife. In Abbott 1981, 209–24.

——. 1996. *Bird of Paradox: The Unpublished Writings of Wilson Duff*. Edited by E. N. Anderson. Surrey: Hancock House.

——. N.d. *Thunderbird Park*. Victoria: British Columbia Provincial Museum.

——. N.d. MOA Duff papers, box 6, file 16, 18.

Duff, Wilson, Bill Holm, and Bill Reid. 1967. *Arts of the Raven*. Vancouver: University of British Columbia Press.

Duff, Wilson, and Michael Kew. 1957. *Anthony Island: A Home of the Haidas*. Victoria: British Columbia Provincial Museum.

Duff, Wilson, Jane Wallen, and Joe Clark. 1969. Totem Pole Survey of Southeast Alaska: Report of Field Work and Follow-Up Activities, June-October 1969. Manuscript. Alaska State Museum Archives.

Duffek, Karen. 1983. *A Guide to Buying Contemporary Northwest Coast Indian Arts*. Vancouver: University of British Columbia Museum of Anthropology.

——. 1986. *Bill Reid: Beyond the Essential Form*. Vancouver: University of British Columbia Museum of Anthropology.

——. 2000. Tla-kish-wha-to-ah Stands with His Chiefs: From a Conversation with Joe David. In Hoover 2000, 352–62.

Duffek, Karen, and Charlotte Townsend-Gault, eds. 2004. *Bill Reid and Beyond: Expanding on Modern Native Art*. Vancouver: Douglas and McIntyre Press.

Duncan, Kate. 2000. *1001 Curious Things: Ye Olde Curiosity Shop and Native American Art*. Seattle: University of Washington Press.

Durkheim, Emile. 1912. *Elementary Forms of the Religious Life*. New York: Free Press.

Edwards, Elizabeth. 2001. *Raw Histories: Photographs, Anthropology and Museums*. London: Berg.

Effler, Louis. 1943. *My Flight to Totem Land*. Press of Buettner and Breska.

Eifert, Virginia. 1947. Lincoln on a Totem Pole. *Natural History* (February): 64–66.

Emmons, George Thornton. 1991. *The Tlingit Indians*. Edited and annotated by Frederica de Laguna. Seattle: University of Washington Press.

Engeman, Richard. 1990. The "Seattle Spirit" Meets *The Alaskan*. *Pacific Northwest Quarterly* 81 (2): 54–66.

Ernst, Alice. 1952. *The Wolf Ritual of the Northwest Coast*. Eugene: University of Oregon Press.

Errington, Shelly. 1998. *The Death of Authentic Primitive Art and Other Tales of Progress*. Berkeley: University of California Press.

Ettawageshik, Frank. 1999. My Father's Business. In Phillips and Steiner 1999, 20–29.

Evans-Pritchard, Diedre. 1989. How "They" See "Us": Native American Images of Tourists. *Annals of Tourism Research* 16: 898–1005.

Everett, Marshall. 1904. *The Book of the Fair*. St. Louis: St. Louis Exposition.

Fabian, Johannes. 1983. *Time and the Other: How Anthropology Makes Its Object*. New York: Columbia University Press.

Falk, Randolph. 1976. *Lelooska*. Milbrae, CA: Celestial Arts.

Feder, Norman. *1972. Two Hundred Years of American Indian Art*. New York: The Whitney Museum.

Feldman, Richard. 2003. *Home before the Raven Caws: The Mystery of the Totem Pole*. Cincinnati: Guild Press/Emmis Books.

Feldman, Richard, and Judith Scherer. 1994. Reaching Across a Continent: The Story of the Golden Hill Totem Pole. *Traces* 6 (4): 40–47.

Field Museum of Natural History. 1982. Big Beaver Comes to Chicago. *Field Museum of Natural History Bulletin* 53 (6): 3–8.

Fisher, Lizanne. 1985. Big Beaver: The Celebration of a Contemporary Totem Pole by Norma Tait, Nishga. Master's thesis, University of British Columbia.

Fisher, Robin. 1977. *Contact and Conflict: Indian-European Relations in British Columbia, 1774–1890*. Vancouver: University of British Columbia Press.

Florian, Mary-Lou, and Richard Hebda. 1981. The Totem Poles and the Vegetation at Ninstints Village, Anthony Island. *Datum* 6 (3): 10–16.

Flurieu, Charles Pierre Claret de. 1801. *A Voyage around the World Performed during the Years 1790, 1791, and 1792, by Etienne Marchand*. 2 vols. London: T. N. Longmans and O. Rees. Reprint, New York: De Capo Press, 1970.

Forrest, Linn. 1947. *Tourist Development Possibilities in Alaska: A Survey of Potential Resort Sites*. Juneau: Alaska Development Board.

———. 1971. Transcript of interview with anonymous interviewer. Juneau: Tongass Historical Museum.

Foster, Mary, and Steve Henrikson. 1991. Symbols of Russian America: Imperial Crests and Possession Plates in North America. *Alaska State Museums Concepts*. Technical paper number 5.

Francis, Daniel. 1992. *The Imaginary Indian: The Image of the Indian in Canadian Culture*. Vancouver: Arsenal Pulp.

———. 1996. *Copying People: Photographing British Columbia First Nations, 1860–1940*. Saskatoon: Fifth House Publishers.

Frankenstein, Ellen, and Louise Brady. 2000. *Carved from the Heart*. Boston: Fanlight Productions.

Frazer, Sir James. 1935. *The Golden Bough: A Study in Magic and Religion*. New York: Macmillan Company. (Orig. pub. 1890.)

———. 1937. *Totemica; A Supplement to Totemism and Exogamy*. New York: Macmillan Company. (Orig. pub. 1887.)

Freedberg, David. 1991. *The Power of Images: Studies in the History and Theory of Response*. Chicago: University of Chicago Press.

Freedman, Jim, ed. 1976. *The History of Canadian Anthropology*. Proceedings 3. Ottawa: Canadian Ethnology Society.

Freud, Sigmund. 1950. *Totem and Taboo: Some Points of Agreement between the Mental Lives of Savages and Neurotics*. New York: W. W. Norton & Company. (Orig. pub. 1918.)

Friday, Chris. 2003. *Lelooska: The Life of a Northwest Coast Artist*. Seattle: University of Washington Press.

Frohman Trading Company. N.d. *Alaska, California and Northern Indian Baskets and Curios*. Portland, OR: Frohman Trading Company.

Fulford, Robert. 1993. The Trouble with Emily. *Canadian Art* (Winter): 32–39.

Fullerton, Aubry. 1924. The Last of the Totem Poles. *The Mentor* 12 (2): 41–42.

Galanin, Nicholas. 2006. Interview with Aldona Jonaitis, May 3.

Galois, Robert. 1994. *Kwak'waka'wakw Settlements, 1775–1920: A Geographical Analysis and Gazetteer*. Vancouver: University of British Columbia Press; Seattle: University of Washington Press.

Garfield, Viola. 1939. Tsimshian Clan and Society. *University of Washington Publications in Anthropology* 7:167–340.

———. 1941. Manuscript. UW Libraries, Special Collections, box 10, notebook I, Hydaburg, Klawock.

———. 1996. *Seattle's Totem Poles*. Bellevue: Thistle Press.

(Orig. pub. as *The Seattle Totem Pole*, Seattle: University of Washington Press, 1940.)

Garfield, Viola, and Linn Forrest. 1948. *The Wolf and the Raven: Totem Poles of Southeastern Alaska*. Seattle: University of Washington Press.

Garfield, Viola, and Paul Wingert. 1966. *The Tsimshian: Their Arts and Music*. Seattle: University of Washington Press. (Orig. pub. 1951.)

Gell, Alfred. 1998. *Art and Agency: An Anthropological Theory*. Oxford: Oxford University Press.

Gerber, Peter, and Vanina Katz-Lahaigue. 1989. *Indianische Kunstler der Westkuste Kanadas*. Zurich: Volkerkundemuseum der Universitat Zurich.

Gessler, Trisha. 1980. Emily Carr on the Queen Charlotte Islands. *The Queen Charlotte Islands Museum Society* 5: 30–40.

Glass, Aaron. 1994. Field notes, trip to Wyoming.

——. 2002. (Cultural) Objects of (Cultural) Value: Commodification and the Development of a Northwest Coast Artworld. In *On Aboriginal Representation in the Art Gallery*, edited by Lynda Jessup and Shannon Bagg, 93–114. Hull: Canadian Museum of Civilization.

——. 2004a. Return to Sender: Repatriation, Restitution, and the Politics of Cultural Property. *Journal of Material Culture* 9 (2): 115–39.

——. 2004b. Was Bill Reid the Fixer of a Broken Culture or a Culture Broker? In *Bill Reid and Beyond: Expanding on Modern Native Art*, edited by Karen Duffek and Charlotte Townsend-Gault, 190–206. Vancouver: Douglas & McIntyre.

——. 2006a. From Cultural Salvage to Brokerage: The Mythologization of Mungo Martin and the Emergence of Northwest Coast Art. *Museum Anthropology* 29 (1): 20–43.

——. 2006b. Conspicuous Consumption: An Intercultural History of the Kwak'w̲ak̲a'wakw Hamat'sa. PhD diss., New York University.

——. Forthcoming. History and Critique of the "Renaissance" Discourse. In Townsend-Gault, Kramer, and Hamilton.

Gleach, Frederic W. 1995. From Cape Fox, Alaska, to Cornell University: The Changing Meanings of a Totem Pole. Paper presented at the American Society for Ethnohistory annual meeting. www.gleach.com. Accessed February 15, 2009.

Goetzman, William, and Kay Sloan. 1982. *Looking Far North: The Expedition to Alaska, 1899*. New York: Viking Press.

Golden Gate International Exposition. 1940. *Official Guide Book: 1940*. San Francisco: Golden Gate International Exposition.

Goldschmidt, Walter, and Theodore Haas. 1998. *Haa Aani–Our Land: Tlingit and Haida Land Rights and Use*. Seattle: University of Washington Press.

Goodfellow, John C. N.d. *The Totem Poles in Stanley Park, Vancouver*. Vancouver: Art, Historical and Scientific Association of Vancouver.

Gormly, Mary. 1977. Early Culture on the Northwest Coast, 1774–1795: Analysis of Spanish Source Material. *Northwest Anthropological Research Notes* 11: 1–80.

Gosden, Chris, and Chantal Knowles. 2001. *Collecting Colonialism: Material Culture and Colonial Change*. Oxford: Berg.

Gottdeiner, Mark. 1997. *The Theming of America: Dreams, Visions and Commercial Spaces*. Boulder, CO: Westview Press.

Government of Canada. N.d. Canada's Digital Collections. http://collections.ic.gc.ca. Accessed August 21, 2008.

Graburn, Nelson. 1976. *Ethnic and Tourist Arts: Cultural Expressions from the Fourth World*. Berkeley: University of California Press.

Green, Edward. 1939. The Squamish Totems. *The Beaver* 19 (1): 36–37.

Green, Stanley. 1984. *The World of Musical Comedy*. Cambridge, MA: Da Capo Press.

Greenblatt, Stephen. 1991. *Marvelous Possessions: The Wonder of the New World*. Chicago: University of Chicago Press.

Greenhalgh, Paul. 1988. *Ephemeral Vistas: The Expositions Universelles, Great Expositions, and World's Fairs, 1851–1939*. Manchester, UK: Manchester University Press.

Grinnell, George Bird. 1986. Natives of the Alaska Coast Region. In Burroughs and Muir 1986, 137–83.

Groves, Naomi Jackson. 1968. *A. Y.'s Canada*. Toronto: Clarke, Irwin & Company.

Guédon, Marie-Françoise. 1984. An Introduction to Tsimshian Worldview and Its Practitioners. In Seguin 1984, 137–59.

Gunn, S.W.A. Gunn. 1965. *Totem Poles of British Columbia*. Series 1, *Stanley Park*. Vancouver: Whiterock Publications.

——. 1966. *Totem Poles of British Columbia*. Series 2, *Kwakiutl House and Totem Poles*. Vancouver: Whiterock Publications.

——. 1967a. *Kwakiutl House and Totem Poles*. Vancouver: Whiterock Publications.

——. 1967b. *Haida Totems in Wood and Argillite*. Vancouver: Whiterock Publications.

Gunther, Erna. 1966. *Art in the Life of the Northwest Coast Indians*. Portland, OR: Portland Art Museum.

——. 1967. Notes on November 17th meeting in Juneau. *Conference on Southeast Alaska Native Artifacts and Monuments, Juneau, Alaska*. Duff Papers, MOA, box 3, file 11.

——. 1972. *Indian Life on the Northwest Coast of North America, As Seen by the Early Explorers and Fur Traders During the Last Decades of the Eighteenth Century*. Chicago: University of Chicago Press.

Haisla Culture. 2002. *Haisla Totem Pole Repatriation Project* www.haislatotem.org/culture/index.html. (This Web site is no longer active, since the pole has been returned. For recent information, see www.haisla.ca.)

Hall, Judy. 1986. A Forest of Poles. *The Beaver* (June/July): 4–14.

Halliday, Jan, and Gail Chehak. 1996. *Native Peoples of the Northwest*. Seattle: Sasquatch Books.

Halpin, Marjorie. 1981. *Totem Poles: An Illustrated Guide*. Vancouver: University of British Columbia Press.

——. 1984. "Seeing" in Stone: Tsimshian Masking and the Twin Stone Masks. In Seguin 1984, 281–307.

——. 1986. *Jack Shadbolt and the Coast Indian Image*. Vancouver: University of British Columbia Press.

Harkin, Michael. 1997. *The Heiltsuks: Dialogues of Culture and History on the Northwest Coast*. Lincoln: University of Nebraska Press.

Harriman Alaska Expedition of 1899. Album. University of Washington Libraries. Special Collections, PH Coll 333.

Harris, Cole. 2002. *Making Native Space*. Vancouver: University of British Columbia Press.

Harris, Neil, Wim de Wit, James Gilbert, and Robert Rydell. 1993. *Grand Illusions: Chicago's Worlds' Fair of 1893*. Chicago: Chicago Historical Society.

Hart, E. J. 1983. *The Selling of Canada The CPR and the Beginnings of Canadian Tourism*. Banff, B.C.: Altitude Publishing.

Hauser, Stephan E. 1997. *Kurt Seligmann, 1900–1962. Leben und Werk*. Basel: Schwabe & Company.

Hawker, Ronald. 1991. Frederick Landsberg: A Pioneer Indian Art Dealer in Victoria, Canada. *Western Sates Jewish History* 23 (2): 128–39.

——. 2003. *Tales of Ghosts: First Nations Art in British Columbia, 1922–61*. Vancouver: University of British Columbia Press.

Hawthorn, Audrey. 1965. A Living Haida Craft: Some Traditional Carvings for Our Times. *The Beaver* 13: 4–11.

——. 1967. *Kwakiutl Art*. Vancouver: University of British Columbia Press; Seattle: University of Washington Press.

——. 1971. Totem Park: An Introduction. *Davidsonia* 2 (2): 10–21.

——. 1993. *A Labour of Love: The Making of the Museum of Anthropology UBC: The First Three Decades, 1947–1976*. Vancouver: University of British Columbia Museum of Anthropology.

Hawthorn, Audrey, and Ben Hill-Tout. 1951. *Carving a Totem Pole*. Vancouver: University of British Columbia Press.

Hay, Jonathan. 1999. Toward a Theory of the Intercultural. *Res* 35 (Spring): 5–9.

Hazen, Donald. 1969. Alaska First Stop for Tallest Totem. *Ketchikan Daily News*, July 29, 7.

Henrickson, Steven. 2001. Letter to Aldona Jonaitis, September 27.

Henry, John F. 1984. *Early Maritime Artists of the Pacific Northwest Coast, 1741–1841*. Seattle: University of Washington Press; Vancouver: Douglas and McIntyre Press.

Higginson, Ella. 1908. *Alaska: The Great Country*. New York: Macmillan Company.

Hill, Charles. 1995. *The Group of Seven: Art for a Nation*. Ottawa: National Gallery of Canada.

Hiller, Susan, ed. 1991. *The Myth of Primitivism: Perspectives on Art*. London: Routledge.

Hinckley, Ted. 1964. Sheldon Jackson as Preserver of Native Culture. *Pacific Historical Review* 33: 411–24.

——. 1965. The Inside Passage: A Popular Gilded Age Tour. *Pacific Northwest Quarterly* 56 (2): 67–74.

——. 1996. *The Canoe Rocks: Alaska's Tlingit and the Euromerican Frontier, 1800–1912*. Lanham, MD: University Press of America.

Hinsley, Curtis. 1991. The World as Marketplace: Commodification of the Exotic at the World's Columbian Exposition, Chicago, 1893. In *Exhibiting Cultures: The Poetics and Politics of Museum Display*, edited by I. Karp and S. Levine, 344–65. Washington, D.C.: Smithsonian Institution Press.

Hoagland, Alison. 1997. Totem Poles and Plank Houses: Reconstructing Native Culture in Southeast Alaska. In *Shaping Communities: Perspectives in Vernacular Architecture*, edited by Carter Hudgins and Elizabeth Collins Cromley, 174–85. Knoxville: University of Tennessee Press.

Holder, Glenn. 1973. *Talking Totem Poles* New York: Dodd, Mead & Company.

Holm, Bill. 1965. *Northwest Coast Art: An Analysis of Form.* Seattle: University of Washington Press.

——. 1983. *Smokey-Top: The Art and Times of Willie Seaweed.* Seattle: University of Washington Press.

——. 1987. *Spirit and Ancestor: A Century of Northwest Coast Art at the Burke Museum.* Seattle: University of Washington Press.

——. 1990. Art. In *Handbook of North American Indians.* Vol. 7, *The Northwest Coast.* Edited by Wayne Suttles, 602–32. Washington, D.C.: Smithsonian Institution Press.

——. 1998. Conversation with Aldona Jonaitis, May.

——. 2003. Letter to Aldona Jonaitis, May 16. Comments on the manuscript for this book.

Holm, Bill, and George I. Quimby. 1980. *Edward S. Curtis in the Land of the War Canoes: A Pioneer Cinematographer in the Pacific Northwest.* Seattle: University of Washington Press.

Holm, Bill, and Thomas Vaughan. 1982. *Soft Gold: The Fur Trade and Cultural Exchange on the Northwest Coast of America.* Portland: Oregon Historical Society.

Hoover, Alan, ed. 2000. *Nuu-chah-nulth Voices, Histories, Objects and Journeys.* Victoria: Royal British Columbia Museum.

Howard, Kathleen, and Diana Pardue. 1996. *Inventing the Southwest: The Fred Harvey Company and Native American Art.* Flagstaff, AZ: Northland.

Howay, F. W. 1990. *Voyages of the "Columbia" to the Northwest Coast, 1787–1790 and 1790–1793.* Portland: Oregon Historical Society.

Hrobsky, Arthur. 1985. A Friend of the Park Goes Home. *Friends of the Parks Newletter* (Fall): 1, 6.

Huhndorf, Shari. 2001. *Going Native: Indians in the American Cultural Imagination.* Ithaca: Cornell University Press.

Huyssen, Andreas. 1995. *Twilight Memories: Marking Time in a Culture of Amnesia.* New York: Routledge.

——. 2001. Present Pasts: Media, Politics, Amnesia. In *Globalization*, edited by A. Appadurai, 57–76. Durham, NC: Duke University Press.

Inverarity, Robert. 1950. *Art of the Northwest Coast Indians.* Berkeley: University of California Press.

Jacknis, Ira. 1985. Franz Boas and Exhibits: On the Limitations of the Museum Method of Anthropology. In Stocking 1985, 75–111.

——. 1990. Authenticity and the Mungo Martin House, Victoria, B.C.: Visual and Verbal Sources. *Arctic Anthropology* 27 (2): 1–12.

——. 1991. Northwest Coast Indian Culture and the World's Columbian Exposition. In *Columbian Consequences*, vol. 3, edited by D. H. Thomas, 91–118. Washington, D.C.: Smithsonian Institution Press.

——. 1996. The Ethnographic Object and the Object of Ethnology in the Early Career of Franz Boas. In *Volksgeist as Method and Ethic: Essays on Boasian Ethnography and the German Anthropological Tradition*, edited by George Stocking, 185–214. Madison: University of Wisconsin Press.

——. 2000. Visualizing Kwakwaka'wakw Tradition: The Films of William Heick, 1951–1963. *BC Studies* 125/126: 99–146.

——. 2002. *The Storage Box of Tradition: Kwakiutl Art, Anthropologists, and Museums, 1881–1981.* Washington, D.C.: Smithsonian Institution Press.

Jackson, A. Y. 1927. Rescuing Our Tottering Totems. *McLean's Magazine* (December 15): 23.

Jackson, Nathan. 2003. Conversation with Aldona Jonaitis, Ketchikan, Alaska.

Jacobsen, Johan Adrian. 1977. *Alaskan Voyage, 1881–1883: An Expedition to the Northwest Coast of America.* Translated by Erna Gunther. Chicago: University of Chicago Press.

——. N.d. Reise. In Newcombe papers. Original German and translation. Vol. 42, folder 52, BCPARS.

Jenkins, David. 1993. The Visual Domination of the American Indian: Photography, Anthropology, and Popular Culture in the Late Nineteenth Century. *Museum Anthropology* 17 (1): 9–21.

Jenness, Diamond. 1934. Myths of the Carrier Indians of British Columbia. *Journal of American Folklore* 47: 184–85.

——. 1943. The Carrier Indians of the Bulkley River. Their Social and Religious Life. *Bureau of American Ethnology Bulletin* 133, Anthropological Papers 25.

Jensen, Vickie. 1992. *Where the People Gather: Carving a Totem Pole.* Seattle: University of Washington Press.

——. 2004. *The Totem Poles of Stanley Park.* Vancouver, B.C.: Subway Books.

Jessup, Lynda, ed. 2001. *Antimodernism and Artistic Experience: Policing the Boundaries of Modernity.* Toronto: University of Toronto Press.

——. 2002. *On Aboriginal Representation in the Gallery.* Hull: Canadian Museum of Civilization.

Johnson, Katie N., and Tamara Underiner. 2001. Command

Performances: Staging Native Americans at Tillicum Village. In Meyer and Royer 2001, 44–61.

Johnson, Rossiter. 1897. *A History of the World's Columbian Exposition Held in Chicago in 1893*. New York: D. Appelton and Company.

Jonaitis, Aldona. 1981. The White Man's Perceptions of Northwest Coast Indian Art from the 1930s to the Present. *American Indian Culture and Research Journal* 5: 1–45.

——. 1986. *Art of the Northern Tlingit*. Seattle: University of Washington Press.

——. 1988. *From the Land of the Totem Poles: The Northwest Coast Art Collection at the American Museum of Natural History*. Seattle: University of Washington Press.

——. 1991. *Chiefly Feasts: The Enduring Kwakiutl Potlatch*. Seattle: University of Washington Press.

——. 1993. Traders of Tradition: Haida Art from Argillite Masters to Robert Davidson. In Thom 1993, 3–24.

——. 1995. *A Wealth of Thought: Franz Boas on Native American Art*. Seattle: University of Washington Press.

——. 1999a. *The Yuquot Whalers' Shrine*. Seattle: University of Washington Press.

——. 1999b. Northwest Coast Totem Poles. In Phillips and Steiner 1999, 104–21.

——. 2006. Smoked Fish and Fermented Oil: Taste and Smell Among the Kwak'wa̲ka̲'wakw. In *Sensible Objects: Colonialism, Museums and Material Culture*, edited by Elizabeth Edwards, Chris Gosden, and Ruth Phillips, 141–67. New York: Berg.

——. 2008. A Generation of Innovators in Southeast Alaska: Nicholas Galanin, Stephen Jackson, Da-ka-heen Mehner and Donald Varnell. *American Indian Art* 33 (4): 56–67.

Jonaitis, Aldona, and Aaron Glass. 2004. Totem Poles and Contemporary Tourism. In *The Challenges of Native American Studies: Essays in Celebration of the Twenty-Fifth American Indian Workshop*, edited by B. Saunders and Lea Zuyderhoudt, 67–82. Leuven: Leuven University Press.

Joyce, T. A. 1903. A Totem Pole in the British Museum. *Journal of the Royal Anthropological Institute of Great Britain and Ireland* 33: 90–95.

Kan, Sergei. 1989. *Symbolic Immortality: The Tlingit Potlatch of the 19th Century*. Washington, D.C.: Smithsonian Institution Press.

——. 1999. *Memory Eternal: Tlingit Culture and Russian Orthodox Christianity through Two Centuries*. Seattle: University of Washington Press.

Kaplan, Susan, and Kristin Barsness. 1986. *Raven's Journey*. Philadelphia: University of Pennsylvania Museum Publications.

Karp, Ivan, and Corinne Kranz. 2000. Reflections on the Fate of Tippoo's Tiger: Defining Cultures Through Public Display. In *Cultural Encounters: Representing "Otherness,"* edited by E. Hallam and Brian Street, 194–227. New York: Routledge.

Katou News. 1986. Three Haida Totems Destined for New York. 4 (8).

——. 1988a. Urban Totems. Pt. 2: A Legacy of Expo '86. 6 (2).

——. 1988b. Totem Goes Down Under. 6 (3).

——. 1989. Totem Pole Bound for Commonwealth Games. 7 (24).

——. 1990. Replication of Totem Poles Creates Jobs. 8 (3).

——. 1991. Totem Park's Newest Pole: An Achievement of Unity and Pride. 9 (8).

——. 1993. World's Largest Totem Pole to Be Erected. 2 (8).

——. 1996. Sechelt Nation Celebrates 10 Years of Self-Government: With the Unveiling of a Totem Pole and the Grand Opening of the Shashishalhem Longhouse to Mark the Occasion. 5 (11).

K̲ay'llnagaay Heritage Centre. 2001. *The Pole Raising at Qay'llnagaay*. Pamphlet. Skidegate.

Keithahn, Edward. 1963. *Monuments in Cedar*. Seattle: Superior Publishing Company.

Kennedy, Michael S. 1973. Theodore J. Richardson. *The Alaska Journal* 3 (1): 31–40.

Kerr, R. 1931. A Totem-pole from the Nass River, British Columbia. *Man* (February): 20–21.

Ketchikan Chronicle. 1939a. Totems to Be Seen at S.F. Fair. January 17.

——. 1939b. Totem Poles for S.F. Fair Brought Here. January 21.

Ketchikan Daily News. 1970. Old Mattresses Needed to Wrap Totem Poles. July 29.

Kew, Michael. 1980. Sculpture and Engraving of the Central Coast Salish Indians. *Museum Note No. 9 UBC Museum of Anthropology*. Vancouver: Museum of Anthropology.

——. 1990. History of Coastal British Columbia since 1849. In *Handbook of North American Indians*, vol. 7, *The Northwest Coast*, edited by Wayne Suttles, 159–68. Washington, D.C.: Smithsonian Institution Press.

Kihn, W. Langdon. 1926. The Gitksan on the Skeena. *Scribner's Magazine* 79: 170–76.

King, J.C.H. 1981. *Artificial Curiosities from the Northwest Coast of America: Native American Artefacts in the British Museum Collected on the Third Voyage of Captain James*

Cook and Acquired Through Sir Joseph Banks. London: British Museum Publications.

Kirk, Ruth. 1986. *Wisdom of the Elders: Native Traditions on the Northwest Coast*. Vancouver: Douglas & McIntyre.

Kirmse, H. D. N.d. H. D. Kirmse: Pioneer Jeweler and Curio Dealer. Brochure. Skagway: H. D. Kirmse.

Kirshenblatt-Gimblett, Barbara. 1998. *Destination Culture: Tourism, Museums, and Heritage*. Berkeley: University of California Press.

Kitsumkalum First Nation. N.d. Kisumkalum: People of the Robin. http://www.kitsumkalum.bc.ca. Accessed August 21, 2008.

Kizzia, Tom. 1997. One Totem, Many Stories: Lincoln Pole Symbolizes the Clash of Visions, Emotions at the Heart of Indian Country. *Anchorage Daily News*, July 5, 1997, 28.

Kollin, Susan. 2000. The Wild, Wild North: Nature Writing, Nationalist Ecologies, and Alaska. *American Literary History* 12 (62): 41–78.

——. 2001. *Nature's State: Imagining Alaska as the Last Frontier*. Chapel Hill: University of North Carolina Press.

Kopytoff, Igor. 1986. The Cultural Biography of Things: Commoditization as Process. In *The Social Life of Things: Commodities in Cultural Perspective*, edited by A. Appadurai, 64–91. Cambridge, UK: Cambridge University Press.

Kraft. September 1953; September 1973; November 1985; November 1986. Newsletters and press releases. Glenview, IL: Kraft.

Kramer, Jennifer. 2006. *Switchbacks: Art, Ownership and Nuxalk National Identity*. Vancouver: University of British Columbia Press.

Kramer, Pat. 1995. *Totem Poles*. Vancouver: Altitude Publishing Canada

Krause, Aurel. 1956. *The Tlingit Indians*. Seattle: University of Washington Press.

Krech, Shepard. 1999. *The Ecological Indian: Myth and History.* New York: W. W. Norton.

Krieger, Herbert. 1928. Indian Villages of Southeast Alaska. *Annual Report of the Board of Regents of the Smithsonian Institution for the year 1927*, 467–508.

'Ksan. 1972. *Ksan: Breath of Our Grandfathers*. Hazelton, B.C.: 'Ksan Association.

——. N.d. 'Ksan Historical Village: "The People of the River of the Mist." http://www.ksan.org. Accessed August 18, 2008.

Kuh, Katherine. 1966. Alaska's Vanishing Art. *Saturday Review* (October 22): 25–31.

Laforet, Andrea. 1986. The Wakas Pole: Its History and Context. In *Symposium 86: The Care and Preservation of Ethnological Materials Proceedings*. Canadian Conservation Institute, 147–55.

——. 1992. *The Book of the Grand Hall*. Hull: Canadian Museum of Civilization.

Lamb, W. Kaye, ed. 1960. *The Letters and Journals of Simon Fraser, 1806–1808*. Toronto: Macmillan of Canada.

LaViolette, Forrest. 1961. *The Struggle for Survival: Indian Cultures and the Protestant Ethic in British Columbia.* Toronto: University of Toronto Press.

Lawrence, Erma. 1975. *Xaadas Gutilaa Gyaahlangaay: Haida Stories and History.* Ketchikan: Society for the Preservation of Haida Language and Literature.

Lee, Molly. 1991. Appropriating the Primitive: Turn-of-the-Century Collection and Display of Native Alaskan Art. *Arctic Anthropology* 28 (1): 6–15.

Legacy Gallery. 1996. Press release for exhibit Monuments in Cedar: Totem Poles of the Northwest Coast.

Leslie, Virginia. 1982. Probing the Roots of the Lincoln Park Totem Pole. *Field Museum of Natural History Bulletin* 53 (6): 18–21.

Lewis, Shauna. 2004. Victory through Honour: The Ellen Neel Kwakwa̱ka̱'wakw Pole Returns to Its Home at the University of British Columbia. First Nations Drum. http://www.firstnationsdrum.com/Winter%202004/CulTotem.htm. Accessed August 21, 2008.

Library of Congress N.d. American Memory. http://memory.loc.gov/ (search "totem poles"). Accessed February 15, 2009.

Light, Lois. 1966. Tallest Totem in the World. *B.C. Motorist* 5 (2): 22–23.

Lindblom, Gerhard. 1936. A Kwakiutl [Haisla] Totem Pole in Stockholm. *Ethnos* 1 (6): 137–41.

Linsley, Robert. 1991. Painting and the Social History of British Columbia. *Vancouver Anthology: The Institutional Politics of Art*, edited by Stan Douglas, 225–45. Vancouver: Talonbooks.

Lipps, Oscar. 1937. *The Indian Tribes of Southeast Alaska: Tlingit, Tsimpshian, Haida: A Report on Their Location, Village Organization and Their Social and Economic Conditions*. Study for Commissioner of Indian Affairs.

Litt, P. 1992. *The Museum, the Masses and the Massey Commission*. Toronto: University of Toronto Press.

Litwen, Thomas, ed. 2005. *The Harriman Alaska Expedition Retraced*. New Brunswick: Rutgers University Press.

Llwyd, Rev. J.P.D. 1909. *The Message of an Indian Relic*. Seattle: Lowman & Hanford.

Lockwood, Lillie Le Grand. 1906. Good Bye, Totem. *Sunset Magazine* 16 (4): 336–41.

Loo, Tina. 1992. Dan Cranmer's Potlatch: Law as Coercion, Symbol, and Rhetoric in British Columbia, 1884–1951. *Canadian Historical Review* 73 (2): 125–65.

Lordon, Ian. 2000. Drawing Connections. *SpruceRoots Magazine* (September/October). http://www.spruceroots.org/SeptOct.00/Qay.html. Accessed August 21, 2008.

Lowe, D. 1925. Preserving Historic Totem Poles of British Columbia Indians. *Vancouver Province*.

Lowe, Jeannette. 1941. Lo, the Rich Indian: Art of the American Aboriginals. *Art News* 39: 7–8, 20.

Lowenstein, Tom, and Pat Partnow. N.d. *Totem Poles Tell Stories*. Alaska Multimedia Education Program, Juneau: Alaska State Museum.

Luvera, Paul, Sr. 1977. *How to Carve and Paint Totem Poles*. Seattle: Blackmore Graphic Design.

Lyman, Christopher. 1982. *The Vanishing Race and Other Illusions: Photographs of Indians by Edward S. Curtis*. Washington, D.C.: Smithsonian Institution Press.

MacCannell, Dean. 1989. *The Tourist: A New Theory of the Leisure Class*. New York: Schocken Books.

——. 1992. *Empty Meeting Grounds: The Tourist Papers*. New York: Routledge.

MacDonald, George. 1983a. *Haida Monumental Art: Villages of the Queen Charlotte Islands*. Vancouver: University of British Columbia Press.

——. 1983b. *Ninstints: Haida World Heritage Site*. Vancouver: University of British Columbia Press.

——. 1988. Epcot Centre in Museological Perspective. *Muse* 6: 27–37.

MacDonald, George, and Stephen Alsford. 1989. *A Museum for the Global Village*. Hull: Canadian Museum of Civilization.

MacDowell, Lloyd. 1906. *Totem Poles of Alaska and Indian Mythology*. Seattle: Alaska Steamship Company.

MacKenzie, Alexander. 1801. *Voyages from Montreal, on the River St. Lawrence, Through the Continent of North America, to the Frozen and Pacific Oceans; in the Years 1789 and 1793*. London: Printed for T. Caddell, Dr.

Macnair, Peter. 2000. Tim Paul: The Homeward Journey. In Hoover 2000, 363–74.

Macnair, Peter, and Alan Hoover. 1984. *The Magic Leaves: A History of Argillite Carving*. Victoria: British Columbia Provincial Museum.

Macnair, Peter, Alan Hoover, and Kevin Neary. 1980. *The Legacy: Continuing Traditions in Northwest Coast Indian Art*. Victoria: Royal British Columbia Museum.

Macnair, Peter, Robert Joseph, and Bruce Grenville. 1998. *Down from the Shimmering Sky: Masks of the Northwest Coast*. Seattle: University of Washington Press.

Macnair, Peter, and Jay Stewart. 1999. To the Totem Forests: Emily Carr and Contemporaries Interpret Coastal Villages. http://www.emilycarr.org. Accessed August 16, 2008.

Mahonen, Suvi. N.d. Qay'llagaay: Building a Heritage on Haida Gwaii. http://www.northword.ca/connections/Past_Issue/fall_01/qa'llnagaay.html. Accessed August 21, 2008.

Makepeace, Anne. 2000. *Coming to Light: Edward S. Curtis and the North American Indians*. American Masters television series; first aired January 28.

——. 2001. *Edward S. Curtis: Coming to Light*. Washington, D.C.: National Geographic Society.

Malin, Edward. 1986. *Totem Poles of the Northwest Coast*. Portland, OR: Timber Press.

Malloy, Mary. 2000. *Souvenirs of the Fur Trade: Northwest Coast Indian Art and Artifacts Collected by American Mariners, 1788–1844*. Cambridge, MA: Peabody Museum Press.

Marcus, George E., and Fred Myers. 1995. *The Traffic in Culture: Refiguring Art and Anthropology*. Berkeley: University of California Press.

Marshall, Yvonne. 1993. A Political History of the Nuu-chah-nulth People: A Case Study of the Mowachaht and Muchalaht Tribes. PhD thesis, Simon Fraser University.

——. 2000. The Changing Art and Architecture of Potlatch Houses at Yuquot. In Hoover 2000, 107–30.

Mauer, Evan. 1977. *The Native Americans Heritage: A Survey of North American Indian Art*. Chicago: Art Institute of Chicago.

McCabe, James. 1876. *The Illustrated History of the Centennial Exhibition*. Philadelphia: National Publishing Company.

McClanahan, Alexandra. 2006. *Alaska Native Corporations—Sakuuktugut, "We are working incredibly hard": The Land, the Money, the History of the Alaska Claims Settlement Act of 1971 and How Alaska Native People are Writing an Epic Story in Cultural and Economic Development*. Anchorage: CIRI Foundation.

McDonald, James. 1990. Poles, Potlatching and Public Affairs: The Use of Aboriginal Culture in Development. *Culture* 10 (2): 103–20.

McDougall, Anne. 1977. *Anne Savage: The Story of a Canadian Painter*. Montreal: Harvest House.

McIlwraith, T. F. 1948. *The Bella Coola Indians*. 2 vols. Toronto: University of Toronto Press.

McKenzie, C. V. 1957. The Totems Rise Again. *Family Herald* (October) 17: 48.

McLean, Isabel. 1977. Eliza Ruhamah Scidmore. *The Alaska Journal* 7 (4): 238–43.

McLennan, Bill, and Karen Duffek. 2000. *The Transforming Image: Painted Arts of the Northwest Coast First Nations*. Vancouver: University of British Columbia Press.

McMurty, Gerald. 1972. The Lincoln Totem—His First Monument. *Lincoln National Life Review* 5 (2): 6–7.

Meerriam, Dena. 1993. Duane Pasco: A Modern Vision in a Native American Art Form. *Sculpture Review* 42 (2): 6–11.

Meyer, Carter Jones, and Diana Royer, eds. 2001. *Selling the Indian: Commercializing and Appropriating American Indian Cultures*. Tucson: University of Arizona Press.

Miller, Daniel. 1987. *Material Culture and Mass Consumption*. Oxford: Blackwell.

———. 1998. Why Some Things Matter. In *Material Cultures: Why Some Things Matter*, edited by D. Miller, 3–21. Chicago: University of Chicago Press.

———, ed. 2005. *Materiality*. Durham, NC: Duke University Press.

Miller, Daniel, and Don Slater. 2000. *The Internet: An Ethnographic Approach*. New York: Berg.

Mills, Antonia. 1994. *Eagle Down Is Our Law: Witsuwit'en Law, Feasts, and Land Claims*. Vancouver: University of British Columbia Press.

Mirzoeff, Nicholas. 1999. *An Introduction to Visual Culture*. New York: Routledge.

———, ed. 2002. *The Visual Culture Reader*. 2nd ed. New York: Routledge.

Mitchell, Donald. 2001. *Take My Land, Take My Life: The Story of Congress's Historic Settlement of Alaska Native Land Claims, 1960–1971*. Fairbanks: University of Alaska Press.

Mitchell, Howard. 1925. Aboriginal Art Is Lost: Belated Efforts Being Made to Save Remaining Indian Totem Poles. *Vancouver Sun*, December 6.

Mitchell, W.J.T. 1994. *Picture Theory: Essays on Verbal and Visual Representation*. Chicago: University of Chicago Press.

———. 2002. Showing Seeing: A Critique of Visual Culture. In Mirzoeff 2002, 86–101.

———. 2005. *What Do Pictures Want? The Lives and Loves of Images*. Chicago: University of Chicago Press.

Molloy, Tom, and Donald Ward. 2006. *The World Is Our Witness: The Historic Journey of the Nisga'a into Canada*. Calgary: Fifth House Publishers.

Moray, Gerta. 2006. *Unsettling Encounters: First Nations Imagery in the Art of Emily Carr*. Seattle: University of Washington Press; Vancouver: University of British Columbia Press.

Morris, Bernadine. 1991. Reviews/Fashion. *New York Times*, April 13.

Morris, Rosalind. 1994. *New Worlds from Fragments: Film, Ethnography, and the Representation of Northwest Coast Cultures*. Boulder, CO: Westview Press.

Morrison, Ann Katherine. 1991. Canadian Art and Cultural Appropriation: Emily Carr and the 1927 Exhibition of Canadian West Coast Art—Native and Modern. Master's thesis, University of British Columbia.

Morrison, J. R. 1933. The Significance of Totems. *The Review* (January 2): 6–9.

Moser, Charlotte. 1990. Shifting Art Categories. *Artweek* 21, no. 37 (November 8).

Moziño, Jose Mariano. 1970. *Noticias de Nutka: An Account of Nootka Sound in 1792*. Edited by Iris Wilson. Seattle: University of Washington Press.

Muir, John. 1915. *Travels in Alaska*. Boston: Houghton Mifflin.

Museum of Anthropology and Virtual Museum of Canada. N.d. Respect to Bill Reid pole. http://www.virtualmuseum.ca/Exhibitions/Billreidpole. Accessed August 21, 2008.

Myers, Fred, ed. 2001. *The Empire of Things: Regimes of Value and Material Culture*. Santa Fe: School of American Research Press.

———. 2002. *Painting Culture: The Making of Aboriginal High Art*. Durham, NC: Duke University Press.

National Gallery of Canada. 2003. *Vernissage*. Cover photograph of Ellen Neel mask. Spring.

National Park Service. N.d. Iron Pergola and Totem Pole. http://www.nps.gov/history/nr/travel/seattle/s26.htm. Accessed August 16, 2008.

Neary, Alan. 1986. Arts of the Sacred Cedar: A Totem Pole for the Southwest Museum. *Masterkey* 59 (4): 3–10.

Nemiroff, Diane. 1992. Modernism, Nationalism and Beyond: A Critical History of Exhibitions of First Nations Art. In *Land Spirit Power: First Nations at the National Gallery of Canada*, edited by D. Nemiroff, 16–41. Ottawa: National Gallery of Canada.

Newcombe, W. A. 1931. Review of *Totem Poles of the Gitksan*, by Marius Barbeau. *American Anthropologist* 33: 238–43.

Neylan, Susan. 2003. *The Heavens Are Changing: Nineteenth-Century Protestant Missions and Tsimshian Christianity*. Montreal: McGill-Queen's University Press.

Niblack, Albert. 1888. Coast Indians of Southern Alaska and Northern British Columbia. In *Annual Report of the Board of Regents of the Smithsonian Institution for 1888: Report of the US National Museum*. Washington, D.C.: Government Printing Office.

North Vancouver Citizen. 1970. William Jeffrey, Chief of the Gitwilgyet, carves 15 foot pole for Adelaide, S. Australia, in Honour of Timber Week Celebrations. October 7.

Norton, Frank H., ed. 1877. *Frank Leslie's Historical Register of the United States Centennial Exposition, 1876*. New York: Frank Leslie's.

Nowry, Laurence. 1995. *Man of Mana: Marius Barbeau*. Toronto: NC Press.

Nuytten, Phil. 1982. *The Totem-Carvers: Charlie James, Ellen Neel, and Mungo Martin*. Vancouver: University of British Columbia Press.

——. 2003. Conversation with Aaron Glass and Aldona Jonaitis.

Omhid, Tom. 1953. Mungo Martin potlatch, December 13, 1953. Transcript. Ethnology Division, Royal British Columbia Museum, KWA-W-009.

Ostrowitz, Judith. 1999. *Privileging the Past: Reconstructing History in Northwest Coast Art*. Seattle: University of Washington Press.

Paalen, Wolfgang. 1943. Totem Art. *Dyn*, vols. 4–5.

Pacific Coast Steamship Co. 1891. *All about Alaska*. Seattle: Pacific Coast Steamship Company.

——. 1908. *Alaska Via Totem Pole Route: 1908 Summer Excursions*. San Francisco: Pacific Coast Steamship Company.

——. 1911. *Alaska via Totem Pole Route: Season 1911*. San Francisco: Pacific Coast Steamship Company.

Pagden, Anthony. 1982. *The Fall of Natural Man: The American Indian and the Origins of Comparative Ethnology*. Cambridge, MA: Cambridge University Press.

Patrick, Andrew. 2002. *The Most Striking of Objects: The Totem Poles of Sitka National Historical Park*. Anchorage: U.S. Department of the Interior.

Patty, Stanton. 1969. At Nikko: Japan Has Its Own Totem Park. *Seattle Times Magazine*, February 23, 14–15.

Paul, Tim. 1996. Conversation with Aaron Glass, Seattle, Washington. November 7.

Paul, William. 1971. The Real Story of the Lincoln Totem. *Alaska Journal* 2–16.

Paul, William Lewis. 1950. Letter to the *Saturday Evening Post*, February 10. Alaska Historical Library and Museum.

Pavilion of Spain, Vancouver World Exposition. 1986. *To the Totem Shore: The Spanish Presence on the Northwest Coast*. Madrid: Ediciones el Viso.

Pearlstone, Zena. 1995. Native American Images in Advertising. *American Indian Art Magazine* 20: 36–43.

Peet, Stephen. 1893. Commemorative Columns and Ancestor Worship. *The American Antiquarian* 15 (5): 261–86.

Peret, Benjamin. 1939. Krikiett, Tallest Totem Pole in Europe. *Paris-Soir*, January 21.

Phillips, Kimberly. 1999. Native Northwest Coast Images and the Construction of a Distinctive Provincial Identity in British Columbia. Graduate paper for Fine Arts 561, University of British Columbia.

——. 2000. Making Meaning in Totemland: Investigating a Vancouver Commission. Master's thesis, University of British Columbia.

Phillips, Ruth. 1998. *Trading Identities: The Souvenir in Native North American Art from the Northeast, 1700–1900*. Seattle: University of Washington Press; Montreal: McGill-Queen's University Press.

——. 2002. APEC at the Museum of Anthropology: The Politics of Site and the Poetics of Sight Bite. *Ethnos* 65: 172–94.

Phillips, Ruth, and Christopher Steiner, eds. 1999. *Unpacking Culture: Art and Commodity in Colonial and Postcolonial Worlds*. Berkeley: University of California Press.

Pinney, Christopher, and Nicholas Thomas. 2001. *Beyond Aesthetics*. London: Berg.

Pointing, Rick. 2006. *The Nisga'a Treaty: Polling Dynamics and Political Communication in Comparative Context*. Peterborough, Ontario: Broadview Press.

Pollock, Griselda. 1988. *Vision and Difference: Femininity, Feminism and the Histories of Art*. New York: Routledge.

Porcher, E. A. 2000. *A Tour of Duty in the Pacific Northwest*. Fairbanks: University of Alaska Press.

Porter, G. C. 1926. Famous Relics of British Columbia to Be Preserved. *Vancouver Sun*, January 15.

Powers, Mabel. 1950. How Old Abe Got on a Totem Pole. *Saturday Evening Post*, February 11.

Pratt, Mary Louise. 1992. *Imperial Eyes: Travel Writing and Transculturation*. London: Routledge.

Price, Sally. 1989. *Primitive Art in Civilized Places*. Chicago: University of Chicago Press.

Puget, Peter. 1939. The Vancouver Expedition: Peter Puget's Journal of the Exploration of Puget Sound, May 7–June 11, 1792. Edited by B. Anderson. *Pacific Northwest Quarterly* 30: 177–217.

Qin, Wen-jie. 2002. *Full Circle*. Watertown, MA: Documentary Educational Resources.

Raibmon, Paige. 2000. Theatres of Contact: The Kwakwa̲ka̲'wakw Meet Colonialism in British Columbia and at the Chicago World's Fair. *The Canadian Historical Review* 81 (2): 157–90.

———. 2005. *Authentic Indians: Episodes of Encounter from the Late Nineteenth-Century Northwest Coast*. Durham, NC: Duke University Press.

Raley, George. 1935. Canadian Indian Art and Industries: An Economic Problem of Today. *Journal of the Royal Society of Arts* 83.

———. 1937. *Our Totem Pole: A Souvenir of Vancouver*. Vancouver: Lumberman Print.

———. 1945. *A Monograph of the Totem Poles in Stanley Park, Vancouver, British Columbia*. Vancouver: Lumberman Print.

Reid, Dennis. 1976. *Edwin Holgate*. Ottawa: National Gallery of Canada.

Reid, William. 1974. *Bill Reid: A Retrospective Exhibition, the Vancouver Art Gallery, November 6 to December 8, 1974*. Vancouver: Vancouver Art Gallery.

Resources. 1926. Why Let Our Totem Poles Go to the U.S.? April 28–29.

Rhodes, E. M. N.d. *Indian Baskets and Curios*. Seattle: E. M. Rhodes & Company.

Richmond, Leonard. 1925. Canadian Pictures at the Whimbley. *Studio* 41: 244–47.

Riley, Linda, ed. 1988. *Marius Barbeau's Photographic Collection: The Nass River*. Canadian Ethnology Service, Mercury Series, paper 109.

Roadside America. N.d. Ed Galloway—World's Largest Totem Pole. http://www.roadsideamerica.com/story/9058. Accessed August 16, 2008.

Rohner, Ronald, ed. 1969. *The Ethnography of Franz Boas: Letters and Diaries of Franz Boas Written on the Northwest Coast from 1886 to 1931*. Chicago: University of Chicago Press.

Roquefeuil, Camile de. 1819. *Voyage autour du monde entre des annees 1816–1819*. Paris: Imprimére de Bethune et Plon.

Rosaldo, Renato. 1989. *Culture and Truth: The Remaking of Social Analysis*. Boston: Beacon Press.

Rose, Alex. 2000. *Spirit Dance at Meziadin: Chief Gosnell and the Nisga'a Treaty*. Madeira Park, B.C.: Harbour Publishing.

Rough, Stanley. 1964. They Fight to Save the Totems of the Upper Skeena. *BC Digest* 20 (93–94): 12, 51.

Roy, Susan. 2002. Performing Musqueam Culture and History at British Columbia's 1966 Centennial Celebrations. *BC Studies* 135: 55–100.

Rubin, William, ed. 1984. *"Primitivism" in 20th Century Art: Affinity of the Tribal and Modern*. New York: Museum of Modern Art.

Ruddell, Nancy. 1995. *Raven's Village: The Myths, Arts & Traditions of Native People from the Pacific Northwest Coast*. Hull, Quebec: Canadian Museum of Civilization.

Rugoff, Ralph. 1995. *Circus Americanus*. London: Verso.

Rushing, Jackson W. 1992. Marketing the Affinity of the Primitive and Modern: Rene d'Harnoncourt and "Indian Art of the United States." In *The Early Years of Native American Art History*, edited by Janet Berlo, 191–236. Seattle: University of Washington Press.

———. 1996. *Native American Art and the New York Avant-Garde: A History of Cultural Primitivism*. Austin: University of Texas Press.

Rydell, Robert. 1984. *All the World's a Fair: Visions of Empire at American International Expositions, 1876–1916*. Chicago: University of Chicago Press.

———. 1993. A Cultural Frankenstein? The Chicago World's Columbian Exposition of 1893. In Harris, de Wit, Gilbert, and Rydell 1993, 141–70.

Sanborn, Andrea. 1997. A Kwakwa̲ka̲'wakw Village in the Netherlands. *U'mista News* (Fall): 7–9.

Sapir, Edward. Letters, December 20, 1917, and May 18, 1918. Canadian Museum of Civilization, correspondence files, box 633, file 15.

Sargent, Polly. 1964. Letter to Wilson Duff, May 8. Royal British Columbia Museum Library, Totem Pole Restoration Society file.

Saturday Evening Post. 1957. Advertisement for Chevrolet, March 16.

Scheusser, Heidi. 1997. Out of the Woods. *Alaska Airlines Magazine* (August): 18–26, 59–63.

Schrader, Robert. 1983. *The Indian Arts & Crafts Board: An Aspect of New Deal Indian Policy*. Albuquerque: University of New Mexico Press.

Scidmore, Eliza Ruhamah. 1885. *Alaska: Its Southern Coast*

and the Sitkan Archipelago. Boston: D. Lothrop.

——. 1898. *Appleton's Guide-Book to Alaska and the Northwest Coast*. New York: D. Appleton.

Seattle Post-Intelligencer. 1899a. The Business Men's Excursion Departs: *Post-Intelligencer* Alaska Expedition on Voyage to the Famous Northland. August 18.

——. 1899b. Alaska Totem Pole Brought from Port Tongass by the *P.-I.* Excursion to Be Set Up in Pioneer Square. September 3.

——. 1899c. Totem Pole Stands at Last Unveiled. October 19.

Seguin, Margaret, ed. 1984. *The Tsimshian: Images of the Past, Views for the Present*. Vancouver: University of British Columbia Press.

Seligmann, Kurt. 1939. Le mât-totem de Gédem Skanish (Gyaedem Skanees). *Journal de la société des américanistes* 31: 121–28.

——. 1995. Entretien avec un Tsimshian. *Pleine Marge* 22: 93–96. Originally published in 1939.

Sewid-Smith, Daisy. 1979. *Prosecution or Persecution*. Cape Mudge, B.C.: Nu-yum-balees Society.

Shadbolt, Doris. 1986. *Bill Reid*. Seattle: University of Washington Press.

——. 1990. *Emily Carr*. Vancouver: Douglas & McIntyre.

Shearer, Cheryl. 2003. *Understanding Northwest Coast Art: A Guide to Crests, Beings, and Symbols*. Seattle: University of Washington Press.

Slate, Libby. 1992. Knott's Opens Doors to Indian Culture, Traditions, Theme Parks. *Los Angeles Times*, June 18.

Smit, Ida. 2003. Interview with Aldona Jonaitis, Dolphinarium, Harderwijk, The Netherlands, May 5.

Smith, Harlan. 1917. The Use of Prehistoric Canadian Art for Commercial Design. *Science* 46 (1177): 60–61.

——. 1923. *An Album of Prehistoric Canadian Art*. Bulletin no. 37. Ottawa: Canadian Department of Mines.

——. 1925. Letter to Chiefs. Reprinted in *Vancouver Province*, June 28, p.2.

——. 1927. *The Tsimshian Indians of the Skeena River of British Columbia*. Ottawa: National Museum of Canada.

——. 1928. Restoration of Totem-poles in British Columbia. *National Museum of Canada Bulletin* 50: 81–83.

Smith, Harry Allen. 1941. *Low Man on a Totem Pole*. New York: Doubleday.

Smith, Terry. 2002. Visual Regimes of Colonization: Aboriginal Seeing and European Vision in Australia. In *The Visual Culture Reader*, edited by Nicholas Mirzoeff, 483–94. New York: Routledge.

Smyly, John, and Carolyn Smyly. 1975. Haida Totems: A Salvage Operation. *The Beaver* (Spring): 55–59.

——. 1975. *The Totem Poles of Skedans*. Seattle: University of Washington Press.

——. 1976. Discovering Totem Poles. *Canadian Collector* 11 (3): 24–33.

——. 2008. *Saving the Silent Ones: The 1957 Totem Pole Salvage Expedition to Ninstints, World Heritage Site*. Victoria: Trafford Publishing.

Spradley, James. 1969. *Guests Never Leave Hungry: The Autobiography of James Sewid, a Kwakiutl Indian*. New Haven: Yale University Press.

Spurr, David. 1993. *The Rhetoric of Empire: Colonial Discourse in Journalism, Travel Writing, and Imperial Administration*. Durham, NC: Duke University Press.

Staff, Frank. 1966. *The Picture Postcard and Its Origins*. New York: Frederick A. Praeger.

Stanley, Nicholas. 1998. *Being Ourselves for You: The Global Display of Cultures*. Cambridge, UK: Middlesex University Press.

Starr, Frederick. 1893. Anthropology at the World's Fair. *The Popular Science Monthly* 43 (5): 610–21.

Steltzer, Ulli, and Robert Davidson. 1994. *Eagle Transforming: The Art of Robert Davidson*. Vancouver: Douglas & McIntyre Press.

Stewart, Hillary. 1993. *Looking at Totem Poles*. Seattle: University of Washington Press; Vancouver: Douglas & McIntyre Press.

——. 2003. *Looking at Indian Art of the Northwest Coast*. Seattle: University of Washington Press; Vancouver: Douglas & McIntyre Press.

Stewart, Susan. 1984. *On Longing: Narratives of the Miniature, the Gigantic, the Souvenir, the Collection*. Durham, NC: Duke University Press.

Stocking, George S. 1982. *Race, Culture, and Evolution: Essays in the History of Anthropology*. Chicago: University of Chicago Press.

——, ed. 1985. *Objects and Others: Essays on Museums and Material Culture*. Madison: University of Wisconsin Press.

Stoddard, Shari. 1996. Making the Art Experience Meaningful: Totem Poles Created by Pre-Service Teachers. *Art Education* 49 (3): 12–19.

Stott, Margaret. 1975. *Bella Coola Ceremony and Art*. Ottawa: National Museum of Canada.

Strankman, Anna. 2003. Recapturing a Legacy: In Search

of the Poles at Old Kasaan. Master's thesis, University of Washington.

Strickland, Rennard. 1997. *Tonto's Revenge: Reflections on American Indian Culture and Policy*. Albuquerque: University of New Mexico Press.

Suttles, Wayne. 1987. *Coast Salish Essays*. Seattle: University of Washington Press.

———. 1998. Essentialism and the Northwest Coast Indian. Talk given at Otsego Institute seminar on Northwest Coast art, Cooperstown, New York, August 7.

———. 2003. Letter to Aldona Jonaitis, February 5.

Swan, James. 1969. *The Northwest Coast: Or, Three Years' Residence in Washington Territory*. Seattle: University of Washington Press. (Orig. pub. 1857.)

Swanton, John. 1905. *Contributions to the Ethnography of the Haida*. Leiden: E. J. Brill.

———. 1908. Social Conditions, Beliefs, and Linguistic Relationships of the Tlingit Indians. *26th Annual Report of the Bureau of American Ethnology* 14.

Taussig, Michael. 1993. *Mimesis and Alterity*. London: Routledge.

Tennant, Paul. 1991. *Aboriginal Peoples and Politics: The Indian Land Question in British Columbia, 1849–1989*. Vancouver: University of British Columbia Press.

Thirkell, Fred, and Bob Scullion. 1996. *Postcards from the Past: Edwardian Images of Greater Vancouver and the Fraser Valley*. Surrey, B.C.: Heritage House.

Thom, Ian, ed. 1989. *The Prints of Edwin Holgate*. Toronto: Irwin Publishing.

———. 1993. *Robert Davidson: Eagle of the Dawn*. Vancouver: University of British Columbia Press.

Thomas, Alan. 1981–82. Photography of the Indian: Concept and Practice on the Northwest Coast. *BC Studies* 52: 61–85.

Thomas, Nicholas. 1991. *Entangled Objects: Exchange, Material Culture, and Colonialism in the Pacific*. Cambridge, MA: Harvard University Press.

———. 1994. *Colonialism's Culture: Anthropology, Travel, and Government*. Princeton: Princeton University Press.

———. 1999. *Possessions: Indigenous Art/Colonial Culture*. London: Thames and Hudson.

———. 2001. Appropriation/Appreciation: Settler Modernism in Australia and New Zealand. In Myers 2001, 139–63.

Tippett, Maria. 1979. *Emily Carr: A Biography*. Toronto: Oxford University Press.

———. 2004. *Bill Reid: The Making of an Indian*. Toronto: Random House.

Titley, Brian. 1986. *A Narrow Vision: Duncan Campbell Scott and the Administration of Indian Affairs in Canada*. Vancouver: University of British Columbia Press.

The Totem Pole. 1966. Two Years of Celebrations. 14 (1): 2–3.

Townsend-Gault, Charlotte. 1997. Art, Argument and Anger on the Northwest Coast. In *Contesting Art: Art, Politics and Identity in the Modern World*, edited by J. MacClancy, 131–63. Oxford: Berg.

Townsend-Gault, Charlotte, Jennifer Kramer, and Ki-ke-in (Ron Hamilton), eds. Forthcoming. *The Idea of Northwest Coast Native Art: An Anthology*. Vancouver: University of British Columbia Press.

Traubner, Richard. 2003. *Operetta: A Theatrical History*. New York: Routledge.

Trennert, Robert Jr. 1987. Selling Indian Education at World's Fairs and Expositions. *The American Indian Quarterly* 2: 203–20.

———. 1993. A Resurrection of Native Arts and Crafts: The St. Louis World's Fair, 1904. *Missouri Historical Review* 87: 274–92.

Tylor, E. B. 1898a. *Remarks on Totemism*. London: Harrison and Sons.

———. 1898b. On the Totem-Post from the Haida Village of Masset, Queen Charlotte Islands, Now Erected in the Grounds of Fox Warren, Near Weybridge. *Journal of the Royal Anthropological Institute of Great Britain and Ireland* 28: 133–35.

———. 1898c. On Two British Columbian House-Posts with Totemic Carvings, in the Pitt-Rivers Museum, Oxford. *Journal of the Royal Anthropological Institute of Great Britain and Ireland* 28: 136–37.

———. 1902. Totemism. *Man* 1 (2): 1–3.

U'mista Cultural Society. 1992. Pole Returns Home. *U'mista Cultural Centre Newsletter*, December 2.

U'Mista News. 1995. History of the Big House in Alert Bay. April 28, 12–14.

University of British Columbia Alma Mater Society. 2004. A Thunderbird for UBC. Pamphlet. Charlotte Townsend-Gault Collection.

University of Washington Libraries. N.d. Digital Collections. http://content.lib.washington.edu/cdm4/search.php. Accessed August 21, 2008.

Vaillant, George. 1939. *Indian Arts in North America*. New York: Harper & Brothers.

———. 1941. Indian Art of the United States. *Art Bulletin* 23: 167–69.

Vancouver, George. 1798. *A Voyage of Discovery to the North Pacific Ocean and around the World.* Vol. 1. London: G. G. and J. Robinson.

Vancouver International Airport. N.d. Vancouver International Airport Guide: Things to Do at Vancouver Airport. Art. http://www.yvr.ca/guide/todo/art/index.asp. Accessed August 21, 2008.

Vancouver Sun. 1925. Letter from Harlan Smith to Kitwanga Chiefs, June 28. Magazine section, p. 2.

Vaughan, James Daniel. 1985. Toward a New and Better Life: Two Hundred Years of Alaskan Haida Culture Change. PhD diss., University of Washington.

Victoria Times. 1971. Photograph of poles erected in front of British Columbia Provincial Museum, April 23.

Walker, Alexander. 1982. *An Account of a Voyage to the North West Coast of America in 1785 and 1786.* Edited by Robin Fisher and J. M. Bumsted. Vancouver: Douglas & McIntyre; Seattle: University of Washington Press.

Walker Art Center. 1972. *American Indian Art: Form and Tradition.* Minneapolis: Walker Art Center.

Wardwell, Allen. 1964. *Yakutat South: Indian Art of the Northwest Coast.* Chicago: Art Institute.

———. 1978. *Objects of Bright Pride: Northwest Coast Art from the American Museum of Natural History.* New York: American Museum of Natural History; Seattle: University of Washington Press.

Waterman, T. T. 1923. *Observations among the Ancient Indian Monuments of Southeastern Alaska.* Washington, D.C.: Smithsonian Institution.

Watson, Kerry. 1990. Wallace Carves Niche in Games. *Ketchikan Daily News,* June 14, A1.

Way, Walt. 1985. *Sculpturing Totem Poles.* Salt Lake City: Vestal Press.

Webb, Jennifer, ed. 2000. *Objects and Expressions: Celebrating the Collections of the Museum of Anthropology at the University of British Columbia.* Vancouver: University of British Columbia Museum of Anthropology.

Weber, Ronald. 1985. Photographs as Ethnographic Documents. *Arctic Anthropology* 22 (1): 67–78.

Wheeler, Dennis. 1976. *Potlatch: A Strict Law Bids Us Dance.* Alert Bay, B.C.: U'mista Cultural Society.

White, Richard. 1991. *The Middle Ground.* Cambridge, UK: Cambridge University Press.

Wickersham, James. 1924. The Oldest and Rarest Lincoln Statue. *Sunset Magazine* (February): 35.

Wingert, Paul. 1949. *American Indian Sculpture: A Study of the Northwest Coast.* New York: J. J. Augustin.

Winter, Lloyd, and Percy Pond. 1915. *The Totems of Alaska.* Juneau: Winter and Pond.

Woodyard, Chris. 1994. With Attendance Down, Knot's Berry Farm Hopes That Its Newest Attraction Will Get It Out of a Jam. *Los Angeles Times,* May 29.

World's Columbian Exposition. 1893. *Official Guide.* Chicago: World's Columbian Exposition.

Wright, Robin. 1991. *A Time of Gathering: Native American Heritage in Washington State.* Seattle: University of Washington Press.

———. 2001. *Northern Haida Master Carvers.* Seattle: University of Washington Press.

———. N.d. Totem Poles: Heraldic Columns of the Northwest Coast. University of Washington Digital Collections. http://content.lib.washington.edu/aipnw/wright.html. Accessed August 21, 2008.

Wyatt, Gary. 1994. *Spirit Faces: Contemporary Masks of the Northwest Coast.* Vancouver: Douglas and McIntyre Press; Seattle: University of Washington Press.

———. 1999. *Mythic Beings: Spirit Art of the Northwest Coast.* Vancouver: Douglas and McIntyre Press; Seattle: University of Washington Press.

———. 2000. *Susan Point: Coast Salish Artist.* Vancouver: Douglas and McIntyre Press; Seattle: University of Washington Press.

Wyatt, Victoria. 1986. A Unique Attraction: The Alaskan Totem Poles at St. Louis Exposition of 1904. *The Alaska Journal* 16:14–23.

———. 1989. *Images of the Inside Passage: An Alaskan Portrait by Winter and Pond.* Seattle: University of Washington Press.

Wyman, Max. 1986. New Dawn at Skidegate: Bill Reid and the Haida. *The Beaver* 66 (3): 48–55.

Young, Adah Sparhawk. 1902. The Indian Totems of Alaska. *The Christian Herald: An Illustrated Family Magazine,* October 29.

Zemans, Joyce. 1986. The Microcosmic/The Macrocosmic: Arthur Lismer and Lawren Harris. *Vanguard* 15: 12–17.

INDEX

Pages with illustrations are indicated by numbers in italics.

A

D

E

F

G

O

P

U

V

W

X

Y